meetings with
Morrissey

meetings with
Morrissey

Len Brown

OMNIBUS PRESS

London/New York/Los Angeles/Paris/Copenhagen/Madrid/Berlin/Sydney/Tokyo

Exclusive Distributors
Music Sales Limited,
14/15 Berners Street,
London, W1T 3LJ.

Music Sales Corporation,
257 Park Avenue South,
New York, NY 10010, USA.

Macmillan Distribution Services,
56 Parkwest Drive,
Derrimut, Vic 3030,
Australia.

Every effort has been made to trace the copyright holders of the photographs in
this book but one or two were unreachable. We would be grateful if the
photographers concerned would contact us.

Printed by Gutenberg Press Ltd, Malta.

A catalogue record for this book is available from the British Library.

Visit Omnibus Press on the web at www.omnibuspress.com

CONTENTS

"He's the best lyricist I've ever read . . . he's fucking revered man. His records will be listened to until George Bush blows the planet up."

— Noel Gallagher

"I think The Smiths totally spoke for now. The most realistic voices, musically and lyrically, of the Eighties. And it's not just self-bleatings. I think that's really, really true. I've never heard a group like The Smiths."

— Morrissey

"Whether he's gay or not, he is the gay Elvis. He is among the greatest entertainers of our time. The banter, the dancing, the stage-craft, it all conspires and you know exactly what Morrissey is. He is heroic. He is a total package, like Dean Martin or Prince."

— Rufus Wainwright

"I think I'm considered to be a British phenomenon . . . as well as a sex symbol."

— Morrissey

"He's an original of the species . . . I don't get the miserable thing at all. I find him very funny."

— Bono

"We were just doing what came naturally, with full-on passionate intensity . . . all bands that stand the test of time have a certain chemistry. Ours was peculiar and unique."

— Johnny Marr

"His work will last, and I have a very strong sense he knows that as well."

— J.K.Rowling

"Whether you like me or not, I remain an individual . . . individually nauseating or individually interesting. The key word in my vocabulary is individualism."

— Morrissey

For Bridget, Grace & Flora

INTRODUCTION

I FIRST approached Morrissey about a biography many years ago, some time between the death of The Smiths and the unwanted (as far as Morrissey was concerned) birth of Johnny Rogan's *The Severed Alliance*. After Morrissey had declared his famous fatwa on Rogan I went cold on the idea, despite several meetings with him. But in the summer of 2003, walking back along Deansgate in Manchester with Morrissey, after meeting him for a glass of Guinness in a pub near Granada's TV studios, he asked me if I owned the rights to my interviews with him. When I informed him I did, he seemed surprised I hadn't already cobbled them together into some sort of biographical collection. I'm slow, of course, but this set me thinking. After approaching him again about a book he was non-committal but, when he played Manchester Opera House on Sunday May 7, 2006, he announced from the stage: "As Len Brown *will* tell you I saw Mott The Hoople and Queen here in November 1973." (I'd caught the same Seventies tour with my brother Don, at Newcastle City Hall, a week earlier.)

Nevertheless I am a reluctant biographer. Firstly, as someone who has deliberately renounced music criticism and decided against a career rubbing shoulders or crossing swords with 'celebrity', perhaps I lack the arrogance and self-confidence to tell this story. Secondly, although I know my subject well as a journalist and music fan, I certainly cannot pretend to be an intimate or confidant, lover or close friend. Quite simply, on the occasions we've met and spoken at length, I've always liked Morrissey as a person and I still admire his art a great deal; his voice and his lyrics have played an important part in my life. As an interviewee, he always makes me laugh, he's provocative and thoughtful, and he's definitely one of the most interesting and original characters in popular culture. In fact, once you've met someone like Morrissey, 99 per cent of all other interviewees seem unintelligent, ordinary, safe, even bland.

This is not an authorised biography and I make no apology for, some-times, going over old ground. There have been several Morrissey biogra-phies before but most seem to have been written by cash-chasing

1

opportunists, stalking fanatics, gay cavaliers or scissors-and-paste Google merchants. Feel free to pigeonhole as you wish. Until now all the biographies have been written (or rather assembled) by individuals who've never interviewed the man. By and large, these books are not without merit. They tell the obvious stories in a third hand, journalistic jumble sale way but, apart from one notable exception, it's almost as if they've been rattled off in an afternoon to catch the latest Smiths or Morrissey bandwagon.

The exception, of course, is Johnny Rogan's *The Severed Alliance*. Even though Rogan did not meet Morrissey until 1996, he talked to the other Smiths and diligently tracked down the truth (or rather Rogan's version of the truth) about Morrissey's life. As with all Rogan's subjects – The Byrds, Neil Young, Van Morrison, The Kinks, John Lennon – the gumshoe detective work was impressive. Yet, for all his diligent research and scholarship, in my opinion *The Severed Alliance* failed to get to the heart and soul of its central character

This humble tome attempts to meet a need, perhaps fill a void. It is the first biography or memoir by someone who has had direct contact with Morrissey over a number of years. It is, inevitably, crammed with my own words and my impressions of Morrissey but I hope that, through my journalistic brushes with him – from first witnessing The Smiths live back in 1983 through to meeting up with him again on the 'Ringleader Of The Tormentors' tour in 2006 – a more rounded and fleshed-out portrait of the artist, his music and his sources of inspiration will emerge.

He is an extraordinary character. I have, through my work as a freelance journalist and as a television producer/director, had the good fortune to meet many famous recording artists; inspiring individuals such as Kate Bush, Youssou N'Dour, Noel Gallagher, Gil Scott-Heron and Peter Gabriel; likeable-but-awkward characters like Rod Stewart, Ringo Starr and Elton John; even brilliant-but-difficult talents including Ray Davies and Dusty Springfield. But Morrissey has always seemed special. Not just because of the quality of his poetry, the clever reference points and his brave willingness to tackle taboo subjects, but also because of the way in which he has achieved his goals by overcoming depressive tendencies and an almost criminal shyness.

Although clearly one of his great achievements has been the celebration – in lyrics, interviews, and through Smiths' cover art – of "outcast men", I'd also like to try and reclaim him from some of the minority groups who seem to think they own him. While he's rightly been embraced and championed by many members of the lesbian and gay community, and he's also become the darling of the animal rights and vegetarian lobbies, I also strongly feel it's important to take a much wider, less restricted view of his art. Quite simply, over the past 25 years he's tried to achieve, within the sphere of popular music, what his hero Oscar Wilde achieved dramatically exactly a century before him.

Arguing that art is by nature dissident, Wilde once said that "any attempt to extend the subject matter of art is extremely distasteful to the public; and yet the vitality and progress of art depend in a large measure on the continual extension of the subject matter". Morrissey has embraced this belief and risen to Wilde's challenge. Love him or hate him – there is no middle ground – he has clearly extended the subject matter of popular music. While most pop songs fail to deal with the real world or draw attention to its many faults – instead serving up a commercially attractive, radio-friendly, diet of love, money, 'conventional' sex, the pursuit of wealth and the desire for status symbols – Morrissey's lyrics have constantly questioned and challenged the status quo.

Inevitably, taking this path, riding these storms, resulted in controversy. As he said in 1992, "Within the exciting world of pop music, the reality is that we are restricted. Whether you choose to write about wheelchair-bound people, 'November Spawned A Monster', or the subject of racism, 'The National Front Disco', the context of the song is often overlooked. People look at the title and shudder and say, 'Whatever is in that song shouldn't exist because the subject to millions of people is so awful.'"

This is what makes Morrissey so different, so interesting and, importantly, so irritating to those who dislike him. Far from supporting the traditional, PR view of Great Britain – this arrogant, superior, we're-better-than-everyone-else England – Morrissey's art deliberately, un-flinchingly, holds up a mirror to modern British life, often reflecting on its victims and villains from the dark days of the past. Many of the gay icons he's quietly championed, for example, have been battered and beaten by the Establishment, from Oscar Wilde through to Joe Meek and Joe Orton. Clearly he believes we'll learn more from our casualties than our celebrities.

As a result, he's often accused of being negative, being deliberately miserable and of focusing on the downside of modern life: the racists, the child murderers, the corrupt coppers, the bullies, the homophobes, the football hooligans, the ganglords, the hypocrites . . . Strangely, others have targeted him equally for being nostalgic and addicted to some mythical Merry England. This misses the point entirely. As he once observed, "If I

3

praise something, a film or a record from the Sixties, I'm quite genuine about it, and it's not like I'm digging up some Viking Helmet and becoming very dreamlike about that. I think it was a very productive and interesting period. And art, in every respect, has diminished since the turn of the Seventies. The Seventies were horrible."

In this context, it's vitally important to understand the events that impressed and depressed and influenced him during the Sixties of his child-hood and the Seventies of his teenage years. It's not the unchallenging, uncritical, opiate-for-the-people raw material of mainstream Christian heterosexual popular culture, but the more challenging, tougher aspects of real life: the inter-racial sex and teenage pregnancy of *A Taste Of Honey*, the hard working class struggle of *Saturday Night And Sunday Morning*, the against-the-law (pre-'67) homosexual angst of films such as *Victim* and *The Leather Boys*, and the rise of Northern feminism as exemplified by Pat Phoenix as Elsie Tanner, who he once described as the first "angry young woman" of *Coronation Street*.

To my mind and ears, Morrissey looks back in a realistic rather than an idealistic way and – from the persecution of homosexuals (the "outcast men") to discrimination against disabled people (the in-*valids*), from the Government-inspired public hostility towards Irish people through to the rise of Right Wing political elements, from the gangland violence of the Krays, the Richardson and Manchester's own Quality Street Gang to the innocence-shattering Moors Murders – through his musical poetry he documents many of the extreme elements and events that shook and scarred him.

Michael Bracewell, in *The Observer* in 1995, compared Morrissey to Alan Bennett as a historian of vanishing Britishness while pointing out that "unlike Bennett, he has explored the presence of doomed and deluded nationalism – the nasty politics of East End no hopers." Not everyone has been so generous in their analysis. In the early to mid Nineties – exactly a century after Wilde's destruction – Morrissey was criticised, even vilified (particularly by the music press that had adored him in the Eighties) for even mentioning the taboo subject of right-wing extremism, even though it had played an aggressive, damaging part in the England of his, and our, youth.

With hindsight, it seems clear that Morrissey has refused to let us forget the problems we've faced as a nation and deliberately wanted to upset any "Cool Britannia" style PR parties that sought to project Britain as un-conditionally great. He's obviously someone that Margaret Thatcher's

Conservatives would have branded a "moaning Minnie", one of those irritating people who seem determined to drag into the light many of the swept-under-the-carpet, deliberately-forgotten aspects of this fine nation's history.

This, in my opinion, is what makes him a unique artist. True, many others have tackled difficult political and social subjects in other areas of the media, particularly film and television documentaries, but too few have attempted to discuss such complicated, controversial issues within the quick-fire medium of the three minute pop music.

Importantly, as a singer, a showman and a lyricist, he's established himself as a unique voice within pop culture. Like Michael Stipe, Bono, Kate Bush, James Brown, Bob Dylan, Youssou N'Dour, Al Green, Van Morrison, Stevie Wonder, Nina Simone, Brian Wilson, Michael Jackson, John Lennon (and I'd add Phil Ochs, Ismael Lo, Pete Docherty, Ron Sexsmith and Sandy Denny to be blatantly subjective), you instantly recognise Morrissey's voice when you hear it. Often imitated but never copied – no, not even by Bernard Manning when he memorably covered 'Girlfriend In A Coma' – he's rarely relied on controversy in his personal life to promote his product. His provocative interviews, his great body of work and his charismatic writhing body on stage have been enough to keep him in the limelight for 25 years. Why else, in 2007, would he have been voted Britain's second Greatest Living Icon behind Sir David Attenborough but ahead of Sir Paul McCartney?

Oscar Wilde once said, "I shall be an enigma to the world of Pleasure, but a mouthpiece for the world of Pain", and without doubt, Wilde's life, his philosophy, his way with words, has clearly been a blueprint for Morrissey's career as an agitator in British popular music. If Wilde declared that "the secret of life is art" then, unlike most other mortals, Morrissey seems to have sacrificed his life to this purpose. Perhaps on reading this book, many might come to the conclusion that Morrissey has aligned himself too closely with Wilde, and perhaps pilfered too many ideas or stolen too much of the eminent Victorian's style and wit and verve.

Morrissey has simply taken Wilde's manifesto and made it his own, with The Smiths and as a solo artist, making it more relevant and real to his late 20th, early 21st century audience. It goes beyond plagiarism, rises above grand larceny, and at times almost approaches reincarnation. Surely no one in the history of popular culture has modelled themselves so perfectly, so magnificently and so successfully on a legend of the past. Like John The Baptist in reverse, God only knows what would have become of Steven

Patrick Morrissey if his mother hadn't nurtured him on the Wildean Gospels.

I'd even go as far to say that, in the sphere of pop music, Morrissey's art continues to echo some of the fine truths expressed in Richard Ellmann's conclusion to his biography of Oscar Wilde: "We inherit his struggle to achieve supreme fictions in art, to associate art with social change, to bring together individual and social impulse, to save what is eccentric and singular from being sanitised and standardised, to replace a morality of severity by one of sympathy . . . He won admiration, and denigration. Legends sprang up about him, and unsavoury rumours too. He was accused of sins from effeminacy to plagiarism. That he was the kindest of men was not so widely known."

PREFACE

"For This Is The Cadogan Hotel"

IT begins and ends with Oscar Wilde.
When I first enter the foyer of the infamous Cadogan Hotel, just off London's Sloane Square, Morrissey sits alone, head lowered, looking nervous, back to the wall on a solitary leather chair. From behind the hotel desk, the middle-aged concierge stares at him suspiciously, as if seriously contemplating the eviction of this peculiar Mancunian from such a respectable establishment. Old habits die hard.

When Morrissey sees me he stands slowly, and quietly, shyly, says "hullo". Although I've heard him speak from stage and on the radio many times before, in person his voice seems deeper, warmer, more rounded and theatrical than expected; maybe I'd anticipated more falsetto. In the flesh he sounds less like Albert Finney, maybe closer to Ian McKellen. My *NME* colleague Paul Du Noyer once described it as a "softly cobblestoned Northern voice".

Nervously I push my hand towards Morrissey and, very reluctantly, he grasps at it, as if the action itself is foreign. There follows the strangest, most half-hearted shake. He watches our entwined hands rise and fall before recoiling, sliding his palm quickly away back into his jacket pocket. It feels like a criminal act.

We're saved by the hotel porter who loudly orders both of us, like an ill-suited married couple, to follow him to "your room". Once on board a clanking lift, we're forced to stand within each others' breathing space while the porter half-eyes us, up and down, as if examining suspects on an identity parade.

Morrissey's famous Billy Fury quiff has been trimmed into something less towering. He wears a brown corduroy jacket over a smart white shirt, and his designer jeans – resting on shiny buckled loafers – are no longer as baggy-arsed as back in the early days of The Smiths. Inevitably, I'm less remarkably dressed, clobbered in some ill-suited, ageing Indie-kid, *NME* 'uniform'; off-white promotional Smiths T-shirt under a vulgar red jumper.

Our introduction doesn't augur well for a positive interview. I can't look at Morrissey. As the lift rises I wonder what the hotel porter makes of us? Two young men, no luggage, room booked for the afternoon. This doesn't feel right. One of us should explain. Struggling to break the silence, I ask the porter, "Do many come here . . . you know, to visit it?"

"Visit what?"

"The room." (pause) "Where he was arrested."

"Arrested? I don't know anything about that, sir," he growls, more suspicious by the second. "I'm from Bristol."

"We have a warrant here, Mr. Wilde, for your arrest on a charge of committing indecent acts."

"Where shall I be taken?"

"To Bow Street."

Morrissey and I are sitting in the very room, number 118, where Oscar Wilde was apprehended by two plain clothes policemen on April 5, 1895.

"I'm almost quite speechless now," Morrissey declares, surveying the scene. "It's a very historic place and obviously it means a great deal to me . . . to be sitting here staring at Oscar's television and the very video that Oscar watched *The Leather Boys* on."

Why have you brought me here?

"I thought the aura of the room would create some interesting physical vibrations, and it does in a sense."

Following that Victorian Friday evening which wrecked Wilde's life – the beginning of a chain of events that would lead to his death aged only 46 – he would be sentenced to hard labour for two years, his plays and poetry were banned, and the management of the Cadogan Hotel would desperately cover up their role in the sordid affair. I suppose they were deeply embarrassed by their involvement in such a scandal.

"I'm sure they were."

Morrissey seems disappointed with the unspeakably comfortable, refurbished surroundings. Yet, regardless of the chintzy décor, this really is the room where Oscar Wilde was nicked? He was right here 103 years ago.

"Yes, he was dragged out into the street screaming and kicking . . ."

Really? I thought it was all very dignified?

"Yes, it was actually, very dignified. He was writing an opera at the time. A very moving end."

But why didn't Wilde leave the country before they arrested him? He knew they'd issued the warrant? He'd lost his libel action against the Marquis Of Queensberry (who'd branded him a 'somdomite', sic, over his relations with Queensberry's son Lord Alfred Douglas aka 'Bosie') and he knew that he'd be charged with the "grave offence" of being a homosexual. Why didn't he escape?

Morrissey speaks softly, sadly: "I don't think he really believed at the time that all his friends would turn against him. Or that the people whose lives he had built and brought to a degree of social prominence would instantly desert him. But they did. He obviously over-estimated his friends. Apart from really one friend, at a stretch two, in the last few years of his life he was completely deserted."

His wife deserted him too?

"Yes, she did desert him. And she wouldn't allow him to see his children. While he was in exile she had their surnames changed. When you consider this man had changed English literature and practically changed English language . . . a remarkably sad end to the most colourful life in literature.

"It would seem almost impossible, I think, at the height of his fame which was quite short, that he would end a few years later in such a bitter ruinous lonely state. And also have such a hideous death."

Did they stop performing his plays?

"I think for quite a few years in England at any rate he was practically banned, certainly censored in some way. But I think that from perhaps 1905 onwards he was revived. And to such a degree that in that period he is the most read writer. I think the reading public has been very loyal to him and has kept his name alive."

What's the great appeal for you?

"It was the diversity between the humour and the tragedy. There didn't seem to be any middle ground. The extremity of the words, the language, the simplicity! Until the time when I really began to discover and understand Oscar Wilde I did have the faint impression that, in order for a writer to be expressive, you had to be completely unreadable.

"I know they say that to be great is to be misunderstood. But Oscar Wilde is the first writer who used simplistic language so powerfully, so overwhelmingly, so amusingly. I'd never come across that before.

"Although he was the most intelligent, he simplified everything.

Therefore practically everybody could read Oscar Wilde and understand. He wasn't complicated. Yet he still left you lying on the bed . . . panting. It was so real and truthful."

Do you feel the same way about his poetry?

"Less so than other things. But also, and I think this is what really makes a truly absolute artist, his life and his personality were so captivating. Regardless of how he wrote, and how he lived in a public sense, his private life was just astounding. That's the final judgement of all artists. I don't think it's enough to switch on and switch off; to be there in the daytime but to be playing hockey at night time. It's not real to me."

Have you read everything?

"I've read practically everything. There's a few that I've never managed to find. But I have a vast collection of first editions. I've collected for years and years. I have a very impressive collection of books, one signed by Ellen Terry who was an old chick of Oscar's."

Morrissey has never made any secret of his love for Oscar Wilde. Throughout his time with The Smiths, Wilde stood head and shoulders above all other characters he'd embraced from history, pop culture and literature. Arguably more individually influential than the cast of *Corona-tion Street*, the camp inmates of the *Carry On* films, than the associates of Andy Warhol and the New York music scene (starring the New York Dolls and Patti Smith), than James Dean or Diana Dors, than the British female singers of the Sixties or the great pantheon of gay and feminist writers *all put together*, Wilde certainly seems to have been the omnipresent force in Morrissey's life as told to journalists.

As he once explained, "As I blundered through my late teens I was quite isolated. In a way, he (Wilde) became a companion, and as I get older, the adoration increases. I'm never without him. It's almost biblical, like carrying your rosary around with you." Even in 1997 he told the Los Angeles radio station KROQ: "Oscar Wilde was very special to me when I was younger because he was a great writer and his life was extraordinary really, probably the most prolific person in the history of literature. And, as time goes by, he becomes more interesting to people . . . He's the most quoted, perhaps even more so than Shakespeare really, because although people know Shakespeare quotes they don't really know what they mean."

I came to Oscar Wilde from a very different background to Morrissey. Like most children brought up as a Christian in the Sixties and Seventies, the general message from the pulpit seemed to be heterosexual equals good, homosexual equals bad. (Underneath the 21st century Anglican fence-sitting liberal flannel, the hymn remains the same.) Even though Wilde's plays were constantly performed in the theatre and on television during my youth, further schoolboy investigation into the artist's life or character would always be discouraged.

We'd study the lives of Shakespeare and Dickens, later even Hardy and Lawrence, but never ever Wilde. It begged the question 'Who was this man and why did teachers constantly refuse to talk about him?' It sounds hopelessly camp, I know (and not at all in keeping with the average macho blokist image I tend to project) but when I won a school reading prize aged 13 for my rendition of Wilde's *The Remarkable Rocket* I was firmly advised against buying a biography of the author with the book token I received. Naturally, this only increased my curiosity.

When I read the brief entry for Oscar Wilde in my parents' copy of *Chambers Biographical Dictionary* (published 1946) I began to think he must have been a truly appalling figure in British history. The account of his life ended with this sentence: "*The Ballad Of Reading Gaol* (1898) and *De Profundis* (1905) bear the impress of two years' hard labour for vicious practices." I guessed that Wilde must have been a mass murderer like Jack The Ripper or an evil poisoner like Dr Crippen.

When, finally, I got to read the full details of Oscar Wilde's fall, via a battered paperback account of his trials, I wasn't shocked or corrupted by the information, just intensely saddened. Even then, the moral of the story seemed to be much the same as Joe Orton's. Despite your creative talents, if you lived a 'bad' or sexually different life then that's what became of you; death or a fate worse than death. (As *Carry On* stalwart Charles Hawtrey once quipped, "Oh, pooh! I don't know about death, but I've tried the other thing and it's not nearly as bad as they make out.")

As a devoutly heterosexual teenager from a middle-class family in the north-east of England, it seemed unusual to me that – while I was nurtured and educated to be non-judgemental, non-racist and non-sexist – my parents and their peers nevertheless protected me, or shepherded me away, from anyone or anything they regarded as sexually unconventional.

At school it was compulsory to look normal, to act masculine, by isolating the kids who didn't look or act or dress in quite the same way as the rest of us. I didn't bully them or humiliate them, just sidelined them, kept my distance, as if they had some contagious disease. Perhaps, had I attended school with Steven Patrick Morrissey, I would have isolated him too.

In the real Seventies world, the black-and-white man's world of Newcastle's St James' Park on a Saturday afternoon, anti-black and anti-gay abuse were the order of the day, and assorted long-haired London footballers would be verbally abused for looking remotely different or simply stylish. The chorus of "What's it like to be a poof?" would be targeted at coiffeured players like Rodney Marsh and Mervyn Day. (Some might say it was all in jest but this is the same small-minded, homophobic Newcastle that Pet Shop Boy Neil Tennant fled from in 'Being Boring'.)

Strangely it seemed acceptable and permissible to laugh at or laugh along with non-masculine men, such as Stanley Baxter as Mother Goose at the Sunderland Empire, or John Inman in *Are You Being Served?*, or Dick Emery in drag, or Larry Grayson, or the feeble-but-very-funny figures of Hawtrey and Kenneth Williams in the *Carry On* films. Perhaps they weren't 'dangerous' when they were on stage or on television, camping it up, just as long as they didn't come too close.

Around the age of 17, when my mother was first made a magistrate, I remember being in the Windmill pub in Newcastle's Cowgate with school friends when a man we all knew from church approached and asked if he could have a quiet word with me. It seemed strange and got stranger. In private, he revealed that he'd been caught by the police in some public toilets near the Cathedral and that he was now worried that my Mum would have to deal with him in court. To my shame, I just walked away from him, angry, confused and disgusted, and never ever saw or heard from him again. All I know is that he was found guilty (although *not* by my mother), fined, pilloried in the local press and would never darken the doors of our church again.

In contrast to my 'conventional', homophobic youth, Morrissey seems to have been well aware of Oscar Wilde's life from an early age. As a result, he's intensely moved by Wilde's tragedy and his own take on life has clearly been affected deeply by the way Wilde was treated. Destroyed by Victorian society, tried and convicted by the Victorian legal system, Wilde fell victim to a Draconian change in the law against homosexuality which in the late 19th century increased the maximum sentence for those convicted to two years hard labour. (Wilde was the only well known figure victimised under this brief, cruel and unusual law change.)

Inevitably, Morrissey has always been fascinated by individuals who've tried to live their lives differently, even if it has meant being broken by the system. This obsession has inspired his own radical form of personal and sexual politics and, throughout his career, he's tried to celebrate artists who've lived and died as outcasts or outsiders.

To the Back To Basics conservatives of Victorian England (a philosophy revived in Thatcherite England of the Eighties), Wilde was the ultimate example of someone who'd threatened the status quo; a married man who'd deviated from common decencies of the day by committing acts of public outrage. For Morrissey, Wilde would always be the crucial influence. He stood for taste and courage and beauty and the will to challenge the Establishment; the will to be different and individual and strong while pursuing pleasure and art and truth.

Hated for loving – "the love that dare not speak its name" (the controversial line from *Two Loves* by his lover Lord Alfred Douglas) – Wilde served his two years hard labour in Pentonville, Wormwood Scrubs and finally Reading Gaol, where he wrote his famous ballad about the cruelty and injustice of Victorian prison life. After he'd served his sentence, Wilde spent the rest of his brief life, penniless and in broken health, begging on the streets of Paris, snubbed as a social pariah by the many friends who'd celebrated his brilliant wit and his great works but a few years earlier.

It's tea-time in Wilde's hotel bedroom in the Cadogan Hotel (which was also once the home of Oscar's friend and lover, the legendary actress Lillie Langtry). I'm on a fruit flan, Morrissey is wrestling with a cheese sandwich – "I'd never touch a gherkin," he proclaims – while across the English Channel in his Parisien boneyard, the great Irish wit and playwright must be resting peacefully in his grave.

Tell me more about Wilde's personality? What made him different, shocking even?

Morrissey replies warmly, passionately, as if enthusing about the love of his life: "He was a remarkably generous person, a remarkably accepting individual. Although he mocked in a very clever way, he mocked British society and British nobility etc. And that is ultimately why *they* were so pleased to finally net him and punish him. But he did it with great taste and great flair, also an astounding degree of sadness.

"I believe now that, for interesting reasons, in certain libraries they're trying to ban Oscar Wilde's books, because of the famous slant as it were. Things don't really change."

The "famous slant" – what Richard Ellmann in his biographical masterpiece *Oscar Wilde* referred to as his subject's challenge to "conventional maleness" – also graces many of Morrissey's lyrics; words which seek to ridicule social conventions and upset traditional roles; pop-poetry riddled with enticing, all-embracing, teasing sexual ambiguity.

As the early Morrissey once told *NME*, "I really like the idea of a male voice being quite vulnerable, of it being taken and slightly manipulated, rather than there always being this heavy machismo thing that just bores everybody . . . I just think it's time for a voice with a different slant to it."

In your own lyrics, you've often challenged the notion of "conventional maleness". Can you explain how Wilde did it?

"The power of language. This was part of his rebellion and also the reason why he became so feared, because people had never come across this before. It was too astounding to cope with."

Did someone like Joe Orton also face a similar reaction?

"I think it's fine if you're privately in your own home and not gaining any degree of popularity. And you're not really out on the street as it were. But once you become popular, and once you gain loyal listeners, it quite obviously becomes dangerous."

So you don't think society's changed that much since Oscar Wilde's day?

"I don't think it's changed at all in any way. It's entirely intolerant of individualistic performers. I think it's taken backward strides really. Not just in literature but quite obviously in pop music. No, it hasn't changed at all."

How do you feel about this room – where Oscar spent his last night of freedom just over 100 years ago?

Morrissey surveys the scene sadly: "I think they've painted over the energy. I'd be very surprised if there's anything left that was here when he was lounging about."

Some months later, one afternoon in my Brixton flat, I'm surprised to see an obscure film version of Oscar Wilde's life was being shown on television, starring the corpulent Robert Morley as Oscar opposite Ralph Richardson's Carson (the Irish school-friend of Wilde who later defeated him in court). Although it's understandably vague about the nature of Wilde's crimes – the film was made when homosexuality was still illegal in Britain – Gregory Ratoff's *Oscar Wilde* (1960) is nevertheless a moving and sympathetic take on the Irish playwright's tragic life.

Alongside John Neville portraying Lord Alfred Douglas, and Dennis Price as Wilde's intimate and loyal friend Robert Ross, close Morrissey observers should also note the presence of Tony Doonan as the 17-year-old rent boy and blackmailer Alfred Wood. Doonan's suicidal brother, Patric, would later be immortalised in one of Morrissey's finest solo tracks, 'Now My Heart Is Full' on *Vauxhall & I*.

As the end credits roll, the phone rings and Morrissey's soft, warmly camp voice starts talking about the film, as if our earlier Wilde conversation is still in full swing.

"It's a very rarely shown film made in the same year as *The Trials Of Oscar Wilde*, another film which starred Peter Finch as Wilde. Because *The Trials Of Oscar Wilde* was made in colour it really largely overshadowed the Morley version. Also *The Trials Of Oscar Wilde* was tremendous. And Robert Morley I couldn't really accept."

He wasn't a very attractive Wilde.

He laughs: "No, not to me anyway."

We discuss Richard Ellmann's celebrated life of Oscar Wilde. Ellmann had died the previous summer, having also written definitive studies of other great Irishmen, including Yeats and Joyce.

"Quite remarkably Ellmann's book is one of the biggest sellers of the year. It's such a great joy and such an excellent book. His actual writing is remarkable, regardless of the subject matter. The way he wrote the book is astounding. Did you see an Irish documentary on Wilde called *Spendthrift Of Genius*?" (With a screenplay by Ellmann, produced and directed by Sean O'Mordha, *Spendthrift* . . . was made for Irish television.) "It actually broadcasted for the first time what is believed to be an actual tape of Wilde's voice.

"To hear Wilde's voice is really quite moving. It makes him seem much more of a real person, so much more tangible. Interestingly, the voice sounded very much like John Hurt in *The Elephant Man*. Do you remember how he spoke? Very soft voice. I think it was modelled on theatre voices of the time because John Merrick was very interested in the theatre. And that's the way Wilde spoke."

(Sadly, there are doubts about the authenticity of this recording, of Wilde reading an extract from *The Ballad Of Reading Gaol*, supposedly made several months before his death while he was attending the International Exhibition in Paris in the summer of 1900. Like Morrissey, I want to believe the recording is genuine but many Wilde experts think otherwise.)

Morrissey continues, "Have you heard about another Oscar Wilde book? Called *Who Was That Man?* By Neil Bartlett. A name I'd never heard of. But it's a very, very different view of Wilde. Very London underground. 1888, it's really interesting."

A very different view, indeed. Bartlett's *Who Was That Man? A Present For Mr Oscar Wilde* was acclaimed by Edmund White as "a fantastic personal meditation on Wilde and the last hundred years of English homosexuality". The actor and writer Simon Callow also described it as "a valuable counterpart to Ellmann's perhaps excessively balanced biography".

In it Bartlett contrasts and compares gay life in the 1880s with the 1980s, detailing modern and Victorian sexual encounters, exploring Wilde's involvement with rent boys and "rough trade", as well as discussing the use of the 'polari/palare' secret slang among 'underground' men in Victorian England. This language would inspire Morrissey to call an album *Bona Drag*, partly also in tribute to the comedic and radical use of *palare* by Hugh Paddick and Kenneth Williams as Julian and Sandy in *Round The Horne* on BBC Radio between 1965 and 1968. Obviously it also encouraged Morrissey to write the single 'Piccadilly Palare' about male prostitution.

So does Wilde still remain the major influence on your life?

"Oh, totally, yes! And it gets stronger and stronger. But the *NME* repeatedly suggest that I've lived in his house, which is completely untrue."

The Tite Street house?

"Yes, it's flats apparently. One was for sale recently at £130,000."

Is that just a week's wages to you?

"Yes, royalties from an extra track on a CD. If only . . ."

It first began to strike me, there and then, that this one single, extraordinary figure from history had so greatly influenced, inspired, even dominated Morrissey's own life and his art. "Everything's linked, everything's traceable," he would tell me many years later. If this is true, then most things Morrissey, maybe everything, perhaps leads in some way back to . . . Oscar Fingal O'Flahertie Wills Wilde.

We talked further about Wilde in relation to an *NME* mission I'd made to Paris to interview the rebel South African musician Johnny Clegg. After meeting Clegg I decided to pay a visit to Oscar Wilde's last resting place in the nearby Pere Lachaise graveyard.

By now I knew in some detail of the importance of Wilde's influence on Morrissey's formative years. Not just from digesting the early interviews or my encounter with him at the Cadogan Hotel, but also from other obvious reference points: Smiths' tracks such as 'Oscillate Wildly' and 'Paint A Vulgar Picture'; the sample "everyone's clever nowadays"

16

(from John Gielgud in *The Importance Of Being Earnest*) at the end of
'Rubber Ring'; the Sarony portrait of Oscar plastered on the red-bricked
walls of Salford in the promotional film for 'Stop Me If You've Heard This
One Before', the Wildean run-out grooves such as "Talent Borrows
Genius Steals" on *The Queen Is Dead*, the celebration of Wilde in the
mis-spelt 'Cemetry Gates' . . .*

It was a grey day for visitors to Pere-Lachaise cemetery; last resting place
for important dead French people like Piaf, Proust, Moliere, Modigliani
and the headless Danton. But the real attractions were the eternal tourists
in this beautiful boneyard – international megastars such as Chopin,
Gertrude Stein, Jim Morrison and Oscar Wilde.

Doors' addicts would already be familiar with the grim condition of the
Lizard King's grave. The presence of Morrison's leathery bones had long
been a source of irritation and embarrassment to cemetery officials; they'd
even erased his name from graveyard maps to reduce the number of hippy
pilgrims.

Rumour had it that when his lease was up, they'd try and get Jim's
troublesome bones moved elsewhere. But still they came, to sit moist-
eyed on surrounding slabs, to lay wreaths, to replace the roses in a relevant
bottle of tequila. Jim's bust had been stolen, the unmarked stone lay face
down in the mud, and some cornball had scribbled "This is the end,
beautiful friend"! A sad, shabby scene.

Then we moved on towards Wilde's massive memorial, sculpted by
acclaimed artist Jacob Epstein. No one, I assured myself, would have dared
desecrate Oscar's grave.

But what was this scratched loud and clear: 'There Is A Light That Will
Never Go Out'!?!

What was the world coming to? You wouldn't get Chopin groupies
writing, in pianist envy, "You were top of the chops, Freddie"! Or Edith
Piaf fans scratching, "Unregrettable, that's what you are"!

How could any self-disrespecting Smiths' fan do such a thing? Surely
Morrissey could not approve?

Morrissey: "The graffiti?"

Have you seen it?

"No, but my mother went to the grave earlier this year and she jumped

* On *Coronation Street* in Spring 1974, the Amateur Dramatic Society's production of *The
Importance Of Being Earnest* starred Annie Walker as Lady Bracknell. In one episode, Ernie
Bishop gives Emily a copy of the works of Wilde.

back in horror and pride at what's happened. Though I must admit it wasn't completely blemish free before."

Aren't you shocked?

"Naturally I'm very very pleased. I don't mind the fact that it's been desecrated and so forth because it isn't a particularly attractive grave. It's just a big slab really."

But it's an Epstein!

"Yeeees . . . what exactly's been written on it?"

Well, for a start, "There is a light that never goes out" . . .

"Really, that's lovely."

And someone's also written "I love Morrissey" and "Manchester Forever".

"Oh you shouldn't have done that, Len."

But you wouldn't want to see Wilde's grave disintegrate the way Jim Morrison's has?

"No, but it won't. I remember seeing pictures of Patti Smith on Jim Morrison's grave, but it never really meant anything to me, the Morrison/ Doors story. Definitely a different man from Oscar."

So no rapped knuckles from the Mozzer for all you desecraters out there, but what would the serious 'art world' make of the scribbling on Epstein's masterpiece?

"Are you saying that someone's actually been inscribing Smiths' lyrics on the tomb?" exclaimed leading Wilde and Epstein authority Simon Wilson of the Tate Gallery. "The tomb is an important work of art and I think, on the whole, one should deplore any graffiti being put on the thing. On the other hand I quite like the idea of someone seriously linking up the world of serious rock music with Wilde. I'd agree with Morrissey that Wilde might have been interested."

Wilson, who owned two of Epstein's original preliminary sketches for the monument, also pointed out that Wilde's tomb – rather like its internee – has had a controversial and chequered life.

"The cemetery authorities insisted on a fig leaf being put on it not long after it was put there in 1909. That was later removed. But it was vandalised again in the 'Fifties when most of the genitals got knocked off. There are various theories about who did it and we did attempt to trace the broken bits. Apparently they were initially preserved by the supervisor of the cemetery as a paperweight. Yes . . . he used Oscar's balls as a paperweight!"

Balls or no balls, Oscar didn't get much rest when he turned his toes up on November 30, 1900. He was originally interred at Bagneux and only uprooted to Pere-Lachaise and buried beneath Epstein's controversial tomb in 1909. Since then he's been fuelling controversy with every play and every repeated pronouncement, and he continues to attract hordes of visitors to his posthumous pad in Paris.

And on his tomb, from *The Ballad Of Reading Gaol*, the words: "For his mourners will be outcast men/And outcasts always mourn".

So, I asked the outcast Mr Morrissey of Manchester, don't you feel responsible in any way for the desecration of Wilde's grave?

"I think it's a great tribute to Oscar and it's a great tribute to The Smiths and to me. I think if anybody can feel any inclination to write any funny words on a tombstone it's a great compliment to the body enclosed. I mean, how many people will sketch on your grave?"

Someone will probably urinate on it.

"If you're very, very lucky."

Part One: The Smiths

1.

The Past Is Another Country

"It was a special musical relationship. And those are far and few between. For Johnny and I it won't come again. The Smiths had the best of Johnny and me. Those were definitely the days."

— Morrissey

"The people that mourned, and are still mourning, the demise of The Smiths can just lock themselves in a basement for the rest of their lives without running out of Smiths stuff to hear. That's what I say to people — 'Isn't there enough there?' We did so much work. So many songs."

— Johnny Marr

IT's hard to overstate the importance of The Smiths in British popular music. Apart from The Beatles — the pioneers who changed the nature of pop music, writing and performing songs which first spoke for and about British youth — Morrissey and Marr's band emerged in the Eighties as creators of the most original and provocative pop music of the late 20th century. Their output of strong singles and extraordinary albums continues to feature high in readers' and viewers' polls and, 25 years on from their first invasion of the airwaves, their art sounds fresh and relevant, and still inspires legions of new artists.

"The years 1983 to 1987 were industrial light and magic. The Smiths were the first post-punk upshot to lace misery with wit, verve, invention and an almost surgical sense of occasion," claimed Andrew Collins in *NME*. "They rejected the hedonistic glitter of the early Eighties pop machine and instead produced an acclaimed catalogue of angst and realism, the perfect soundtrack for a lost generation of teenagers," argued *Rage* magazine. According to one of their many 'managers', the late Scott Piering, "They were an incredibly subversive band. They had all sorts of themes and, as articulated by Morrissey, were completely radical. That was the beauty of The Smiths. It had fire, it had passion." When reviewing *The Queen Is Dead* in 1986, legendary *NME* writer Nick Kent described the band as "the one truly vital voice of the Eighties".

Yet although The Smiths always had great expectations and great obituaries, and throughout their lifetime were undisputed champions of the British Independent music scene, the fact that they had only two top ten hits in the main UK charts during their lifetime (1982–87) spoke volumes for the cloth-eared closed attitude of mainstream British radio and television during this period.

Even if they're now universally regarded as the most innovative British group of the Eighties, the UK Top 40 never reflected this at the time; even the more-Gothic post-punk work of Siouxsie & The Banshees and The Cure fared better than The Smiths in an arena increasingly dominated by dance music, Madonna, Michael Jackson and Prince.

To their detractors they came to symbolise "all that was twee, pathetic and reviled about indie music, conjuring up images of sad, lonely teenagers poring over lyric sheets in their box bedrooms" (*Rage*). But for those of us who religiously, devotedly followed this exceptional band, their acrimonious collapse (and the subsequent legal battles) still seems hard to believe today. Without doubt, the fall-out from The Smiths plagued Morrissey's solo career to the end of the 20th century.

When we first met, in early January 1988, Morrissey himself had come through a personally traumatic time. The Smiths were freshly buried; it was barely six months since their demise, and only five since I'd written the "Tomb It May Concern" *NME* obituary that had also marked the release of their posthumous studio album, *Strangeways, Here We Come.*

"There is nothing even approaching 'acrimony' between myself and the other members of the band. I've known them all a long time and I love 'em," Johnny Marr had told *NME*, confirming his departure from The Smiths the previous August. But, as time would tell, this was just the start of the increasingly acrimonious relations between Morrissey, Marr, bass player Andy Rourke and, particularly, drummer Mike Joyce.

Contradicting Marr's statement, Morrissey told me he hadn't seen or heard from Johnny Marr since May 19, 1987, and that he hadn't heard from Mike Joyce or Andy Rourke since the previous July. Marr would later beg to differ: "I talked to him (Morrissey) once more, a month or two after the split. He rang me to see if I'd be interested in doing a Smiths farewell gig in London." (*NME*, April 1991)

Whatever the truth, The Smiths had been together for five years until their collapse; five years in which they proved themselves to be the most innovative band Britain had produced since The Beatles. And "like The Beatles", to quote Nick Kent on October 1987's ITV *South Bank Show* profile of The Smiths, "they epitomised their time and place". Elsewhere, Paul Morley would describe their art as "songs that might comically diagnose the English tragedy".

"The Smiths were almost like a painting," Morrissey told me, with genuine sadness, "every month you'd add a little bit here and a little bit there . . . but it wasn't quite complete and it was whipped away. And I find it quite hard to adapt to that. Those people who patted me on the back and said, 'Oh! Smiths split! Very clever, very wise, very cunning' . . . I hadn't a clue what they were talking about.

"Even people who enjoyed the music thought the split was very timely; it's a very popular attitude that the split occurred at the right time. I get quite violent when people say that to me."

Morrissey didn't know about The Smiths' official demise "until I read it in the *NME*". Although the report of August 1, 1987, claimed that one of the reasons for "the personality clash between Morrissey and Johnny Marr" was the latter's trip to the States to record with Talking Heads, Morrissey claimed he had no knowledge of Marr's travels or his travails until he saw that *NME* news story.

Likewise, Morrissey's hopes of continuing to use the name 'The Smiths' were shattered when he read Marr's comment, in the August 8 issue of *NME*, that use of the band's name was "tied up in a whole load of legal things". So Marr stopped Morrissey re-launching The Smiths "but," said Morrissey, "I like to think he was ill advised."

Although Morrissey admirably refused to point the finger, the advice almost certainly came from former Smiths manager, the American Ken Friedman. For a period after the split, Friedman remained Marr's personal manager and, to Morrissey's mind, he'd driven a wedge in the friendship between Morrissey and Johnny. (Friedman would dispute this and, by March 1988, Morrissey would be refusing to talk about the subject, implying that 'the affair' had already gone legal.)

"Within The Smiths, the reason it worked so well was that everybody knew their place and their capabilities and each other's position," continued Morrissey. "It was such a tight unit, and nobody it seemed could penetrate The Smiths' little secret private world. On the occasion that

25

somebody did break through the mould everything fell apart in 25 different directions."

In time I'd learn, of course, that it was much more complicated than this. Apart from the legal minefield of contracts and royalties which would eventually rip inter–Smiths' relations to shreds a decade later, the personal friendship and professional relationship between Morrissey and Marr had irrevocably broken down by the time they assembled to record *Strangeways, Here We Come* in Bath in early 1987.

Other reported problems within the band – bassist Andy Rourke's battle with heroin addiction and ill-founded rumours of Johnny Marr's 'rockist' tastes – were perhaps of less significance in the band's demise. After four years of great creativity and productivity, weakened by a lack of managerial continuity, exhausted by the constant pressures of recording, touring and promotion, The Smiths had simply reached breaking point. Added to this, the old band–splitting cliché of 'musical differences' had made an unwelcome appearance. Johnny Marr felt restricted, now wanted to explore new musical horizons outside The Smiths, and certainly didn't want to cover obscure Twinkle or Cilla Black or even James tracks for use as B-sides to Smiths' singles from *Strangeways, Here We Come*.

Helpfully, at least that's what I thought at the time, I tried to make Morrissey see things from Johnny's point of view. For example, had Morrissey opposed the use of Marr instrumentals on the B-sides of Smiths' singles?

"No! Initially the very notion of instrumentals was motivated by me. I suggested that 'Oscillate Wildly' should be an instrumental; up until that point Johnny had very little interest in non-vocal tracks. There was never any political heaveho-ing about should we or shouldn't we have an instrumental and it was never a battle of powers between Johnny and myself.

"The very assumption that a Smiths instrumental track left Morrissey upstairs in his bedroom stamping his feet and kicking the furniture was untrue! I totally approved but, obviously, I didn't physically contribute."

But you did refuse to write lyrics for 'Money Changes Everything' (which, soon after the split, appeared as a Bryan Ferry/Johnny Marr song titled 'The Right Stuff' on Ferry's *Bette Noir* LP)?

"Yes, but I was also asked to write words for 'Oscillate Wildly' and 'The Draize Train', which I thought was the weakest thing Johnny had ever done. Geoff Travis came to see me one day with the tape of it and said, 'It's the best thing Johnny's written and it's a Number One single if you put words to it.' But I said, 'No, Geoff, it's not right.' So, yes, there was pressure to write lyrics, but I thought they were better as they were."

With The Smiths' death in May '87, and with the imminent release of Morrissey's single 'Suedehead' and his debut solo album *Viva Hate* in Spring 1988, it looked as if Morrissey might have already lined up his new collaborator, ex-Smiths producer Stephen Street, before Marr's departure.

Was Johnny jealous of your growing friendship with Stephen Street?

"I didn't have a better relationship with Stephen Street. Stephen, as you know, had been working with The Smiths since 'Heaven Knows I'm Miserable Now', quite a long time ago. So Stephen's relationship with the Smiths as a group was totally harmonious and very natural.

"There was no undercurrent of awkwardness at all. As far as writing with Stephen is concerned, he sent me a tape in late August when really the news was quite national. It was the last thing on Earth I expected. He simply sent a tape of his songs and said, 'Would you like to go in and record these?' He was very shy about it."

From the outside – as a fan on the terraces and an observer in the press – I felt that The Smiths' demise had been heralded by the transfer from the uncomfortable but fashionable shoes of the independent record label Rough Trade to the corporate, cashed-up jackboots of EMI. After four years dominating the independent charts and making several triumphant, commando-style raids into the higher reaches of the UK Top 20, when the deal was announced, in the March 1987, it almost seemed treacherous; an unbelievable betrayal of The Smiths' 'manifesto'.

But in the context of the band's interior crises during *The Queen Is Dead* tour of the UK and America in 1986 – personal quarrels, drink and drug problems, musical differences, lack of decent management – Morrissey and Marr clearly felt that support for further progress, nationally and more important internationally, could only come from a major label.

Was Morrissey glad to be free from Rough Trade?

"In all honesty, yes! 1985 with Rough Trade was horrendous, the duels were unspeakable. Throughout the release of *Meat Is Murder* and the non–Top 20 singles I think Rough Trade were too aggressive towards The Smiths. We were being treated like some untried independent group from Harrogate and it was not acknowledged at all, in the Rough Trade network, that The Smiths were saving their skins, that The Smiths were also lining their pockets. We were in such turmoil that we had to be something.

"Because of lack of management I would personally have to fight for any promotion The Smiths ever received; it wasn't until the ninth single that they even conceded to fly-posting, even though the first album had entered the charts at Number Two and there had been a string of successful singles.

"There was always the sense with Rough Trade that they were ready to back off and just be quite happy with what they had accumulated without speculating in any sensible direction. Like the quiz show contestants who are quite content with the £5 and don't want to try for the £5 million, even though it actually cost them £20 to get to the studio in petrol."

How did signing to EMI affect the band? Were you all perfectly happy with the decision?

"Not at all! Not at all! But when The Smiths signed to EMI life with Rough Trade became much easier and blossomed in a way it never had done before.

"Although there's no pleasure for me in smearing Rough Trade – I can see their dilemmas and I understand them – I simply feel that, in the final analysis, The Smiths were not looked upon as the little treasures that they actually were. I certainly feel I was the only group member who was ever treated with any respect. I don't think there was any for Johnny, Mike or Andy."

Did that grate with them?

"With them and with me, yes. Also, when The Smiths signed to EMI Geoff Travis made a statement in *The Guardian* that the signing had only occurred due to The Smiths' greed. He didn't really believe that but it was absolutely the final straw. There had been several final straws but that was the last straw among final straws!"

So was 'Paint A Vulgar Picture' an attack on Rough Trade?

He laughs: "No, it wasn't about Rough Trade at all. So I was a bit confused when Geoff Travis, the Rough Trade big boy, despised it and stamped on it. It was about the music industry in general, about practically anybody who's died and left behind that frenetic fanatical legacy which sends people scrambling. Billy Fury, Marc Bolan . . ."

What about 'You Just Haven't Earned It Yet Baby'?

"Obviously Geoff was staunchly against it because he thought it was a personal letter addressed to him."

Well? Was it a personal letter addressed to Geoff Travis?

He laughs loudly. "I never said it was a personal letter addressed to him. That's just a very, very cruel assumption on your behalf."

Were you disappointed the final Rough Trades singles weren't more successful?

"I expected them all to be bigger hits. Obviously I believe that Smiths records should be heard. It would have been quite easy for me, in the circumstances, to have said 'let's not release anything' but I am very proud of those songs.

"I approved in the sense that I believe Smiths records should be heard. 'Last Night I Dreamt That Somebody Loved Me' and 'I Started Something I Couldn't Finish' were great songs but, quite obviously, there weren't acceptable B-sides and quite obviously there was no acceptable reason for a CD and cassette single, but they occurred nonetheless. It's difficult because I wanted those songs to be heard, the death of The Smiths was far too convenient. If there was a last opportunity to invade and infest the airwaves I thought it should be done.

"I do feel The Smiths also extended the language of pop music by introducing words that had never been spotted in a Top 40 context before. And that's very important. I can't think of one other band that does that at the moment."

How did you feel about the poor B-sides – old mixes and live tracks – on the last Rough Trade singles?

"I'm not embarrassed. They're not that bad. But 'Pretty Girls Make Graves' I thought was . . . [grimaces]. I didn't actually play it until weeks after it was released. And I never heard the live 'Some Girls Are Bigger Than Others' until the record dropped out of the charts."

I remember you doing it, at Brixton Academy.

"Not really a good vocal, not at all, but it's not *that* bad."

What about the cover of James' 'What's The World'?

"In another age, with a full living group, that would never have occurred. That was just a matter of trying to suspend 'I Started Something I Couldn't Finish' in the . . . lower fifties."

And Rough Trade's forthcoming Smiths live album?

"Well, it's very good so therefore I'm quite pleased for it to come out. And since none of those songs will ever be heard again it's quite interesting to have them documented in some way."

Could Rough Trade keep bringing out Smiths' singles?

"Yes they can. I believe they're going to re-release 'This Charming Man' which has been deleted since 1932 or something."

Why was 'There Is A Light That Never Goes Out' not released as a single? That could have been your biggest hit.

"In Rough Trade's favour they did want it to be *the* track on *The Queen Is Dead* but within the group that wasn't a popular decision. We did want

29

'Bigmouth Strikes Again'. I suppose it should have been followed by 'There Is A Light That Never Goes Out' but by then we'd written 'Panic' and we were very eager to have it thrown out into the . . . pop wilderness."

But what's to stop Rough Trade repackaging singles until the end of time?

"I don't think they can feasibly, I think it really is over. They were pushing it with the last Smiths release and I think Rough Trade is quite realistic in the knowledge they can't really go any further. If another compilation appeared I think people would descend on them and stone Geoff Travis to death."

Would you be happy about that?

He giggles. "No, I wouldn't cast any stones at all. I'm generally a peace-loving citizen." (Years later, he would compare the re-heating of The Smiths' back catalogue to "a fish dying very slowly on a harbour wall".)

Whatever happened to the 'Stop Me If You Think You've Heard This One Before' single?

"I desperately, desperately wanted that to be released. Rough Trade sent white labels along to Radio One but they said they would never under any circumstances play it because of the line about mass murder. They said people would've instantly linked it with Hungerford and it would've caused thousands of shoppers to go out and buy machine guns and murder their grandparents. I think Rough Trade should've released 'Death Of A Disco Dancer' just to be stroppy."

Because you played piano on it?

He giggles. "Exactly! What better reason. Move over Lieutenant Pigeon!"

Is that because the Lieutenant Pigeon leader's mother played piano on the track?

"Yes, but do you remember the follow up? It was called 'Desperate Dan'. Same song but without the whistle."

In the winter of Eighties Pop, with its throwaway icons and its bankrupt penchant for cannibalism, the importance of Steven Patrick Morrissey should never be underestimated; with The Smiths he proved himself to be the most provocative commentator and articulate lyricist of the Eighties. But already it felt like we were conducting a post-mortem, a pathological examination on a beautiful being that Morrissey and Johnny Marr created together (not forgetting the energetic input of henchmen Rourke and

Joyce); a body that I, along with many others, loved and now mourn.

Whether Morrissey & Marr would be regarded as comparable composers to Lennon & McCartney, Leiber & Stoller or Goffin & King (or even Flanders & Swann) time alone would tell, but clearly Morrissey hadn't come to bury The Smiths but to praise them.

"The Smiths as a live entity were so powerful and, for me personally, almost untouchable. The Smiths as individuals were very hard people in a physical sense, and Johnny, Mike and Andy played their instruments in a very aggressive way. The feeling of power onstage was just like having a vacuum cleaner shoved up your . . . blazer! Which I'm sure you've experienced many times."

Johnny Marr had started working with The Pretenders – "I'd be very surprised if he gained the same degree of interest and urgent momentum he received from The Smiths" – and Rourke and Joyce were playing together with either The Adult Net or Sinead O'Connor. So the prospect of The Smiths reforming already seemed unlikely?

"I think about it all the time," Morrissey tells me, sadly, "and I'm not really impressed by negative public opinion or lofty artistic approval of The Smiths' disintegration. I would be totally in favour of a reunion – which isn't to cast doubts on the solo album or the immediate future; but if a reunion never occurs I'm sure I'll be quite happy as I am. But yes, I do entertain those thoughts and as soon as anybody wants to come back to the fold and make records I will be there!"

Well, there's hope . . . Marr's young . . .

"He's a mere child, he's 24."

There's plenty of time.

"No, because I'm nearly 29. I'll be dead in a couple of years."

So you won't be the Bing Crosby of our generation?

"The Janet Street-Porter, maybe."

2.

The World Changes

"Them was rotten days"
　　　　　　　　　　　　　　　 – Aunt Ada, *Saturday Night And Sunday Morning*

MORRISSEY and The Smiths arrived at a critical time for me. The early Eighties were bleak politically and personally. Having been brought up in economically declining Newcastle upon Tyne since the early Seventies, in 1979 my younger brother Don and I moved South to start a new life in London with our older sister Kath. Eventually I found a job as a sports reporter on the *East End News* (this included covering West Ham matches and Repton Boxing Club fixtures at the York Hall in Bethnal Green) while Don went to University College London to study Classics.

Hard times. Alongside mass unemployment, inflation, rising-Thatcherism and the growing lack of remotely interesting career opportunities, there were plenty of other events to hammer the sensitive. The violent death of John Lennon towards the end 1980, Bob Marley's passing in May 1981, the starvation of Bobby Sands and the death of peace in Ireland, not to mention the arrival of Ronald Reagan in the White House. Could things get any worse for the idealistic youth of Britain? They could and they did. Apart from the escalating conflict in the Middle East, Margaret Thatcher led Britain into war with Argentina over the Falklands Islands. Cue more anthems for doomed youth.

In the early hours of May 27, 1982, while the Battle Of Goose Green raged thousands of miles away in East Falkland, my brother took his own life. A Joy Division fan, Don had never recovered from Ian Curtis' suicide two years earlier. He was 21 years old and, quite simply, no longer wanted to be part of this world.

As a family, we were utterly shattered, heartbroken by Don's death; it was as hard as hell to simply carry on. To say I was numb with grief would be an understatement. To steal a line from the Biff cartoon of the time, I truly felt like a lost sock in the laundromat of oblivion.

Emotionally I was paralysed for months, dependent initially on sleeping pills, then gradually turning to alcohol. I didn't go off the rails, there were no rails. Increasingly, I confined myself to a small attic room in a Camberwell student house, where I'd been moved by my good friend, the photographer Tim Jarvis, in the difficult months after Don's death.

For the rest of 1982, I tried to blot things out and keep the real world at arm's distance, accepting Pascal's view (as quoted by Huxley in *The Doors Of Perception To Heaven And Hell*) that the planet would be a better place if men learned to sit quietly in their rooms alone.

Desperately, I tried to keep Don's memory alive; spending those early grieving, guilt-wracked months trawling through his dog-eared annotated books (Beckett, Eliot, Brecht, Orton, Greek Tragedies . . .) and listening to his precious record collection of Peel-inspired, ridiculous and weirdly original music: The Fall, The Twinkle Brothers, John Dowie, Gregory Isaacs, Postcard bands, Michael Smith, Blondie, Wavus O'Shave, The Modern Lovers, Fela Kuti, Buzzcocks, Nico, Rastafari In Dub, Talking Heads, Trinity, The Pop Group . . . ; eclectic music rarely reflected in the mainstream charts.

In truth, the commercial soundtrack of 1981/82 had limited connection to the downbeat mood of the times. Pop music, post-Punk, again seemed to be as much about self-indulgent escapism – aspirations to love, lust and material wealth – much as Glam and Prog Rock had been in the early Seventies. *Like Punk Never Happened*, Dave Rimmer appropriately called his book on Culture Club and the New Pop.

It was the Thatcherite and Reaganite era of Me-Me-Me Generation music starring Duran Duran and other cashed-up pretty boys; danceable pop music, radio friendly tunes, that worked hard to pretend the world was a fine place. Perhaps these times would best be summed up later in the Pet Shop Boys' ironic 'Opportunities (Let's Make Lots Of Money)'.

After Don's death I couldn't stomach the vast majority of synthesised keyboard-created, unhuman or inhuman, unemotional pop music of the early 1980s. The Punk visionaries who made it commercially were branded sell-outs; the rest faded with a whimper not a bang. Popular music, the New Romantic movement in particular (which I'd hedonistically enjoyed just a year earlier), now seemed incredibly trivial, meaningless and empty. It became more about cosmetic presentation than artistic creativity; how you looked was more crucial than what you said. The dawn of celebrity and the rise of MTV, from *Thriller* onwards, meant that video usurped audio as the new God.

With hindsight, I was desperately looking for someone, something, to convince me that pop music could be important and uplifting and beautiful again; that it could still mean something. Anything.

Of course, I read *New Musical Express* religiously. Maybe it was the only faith I had left; those gospels of Paul Morley and Ian Penman, Charles Shaar-Murray and Tony Parsons. Encouraged by friends and inspired by my lost brother's record collection, I started to write with the vague, half-hearted notion of becoming a music journalist.

In early 1983 my live review of Gaspar Lawal – the African drummer played by John Peel and admired by my brother – appeared in *NME*. This was followed by a piece on the debut album by a band called The Box, created from the ashes of Sheffield's impressive Clock DVA ('4 Hours' on Fetish is one of the great forgotten singles).

It was a start, although I felt like a crash victim getting back on his bike, and I still needed stabilisers. I was struggling to enjoy life, still crying at bus-stops, still drinking to numb the pain; clinging to the wreckage of a past that had already broken up. I hated the way the world just went on, as if nothing had happened, and even felt guilty trying to continue myself. As Samuel Beckett wrote at the end of *Malone Dies*, "I can't go on. I go on." (In my brother Don's copy he'd scrawled the word "irrational" after this.)

By the summer of 1983, an ex-girlfriend, Rose Rouse, was writing for *Sounds*, which seemed to me just like *NME* but without the taste, purpose, intelligence or decency. It was struggling to throw off its Seventies rock past, when it memorably pleasured adolescent boys with tits and bums on the 'Live' pages. Typically, as a artful feminist, Rose regarded *Sounds* as a real challenge. She'd started writing about acts the *Sounds* regime regarded as of minority interest, and championed more creative artists such as Thompson Twins and Eurythmics.

One autumn evening, in late September 1983, she tried to persuade me to go to the Venue near London's Victoria. "A new Manchester band," she told me, "strangely called The Smiths." I'd already heard about them but, negative to a fault, I couldn't really see a band named "The Smiths" getting very far. What were they thinking about? Most chart acts at the time had complex mysterious monikers like Depeche Mode, Blue Rondo A La Turk, Orchestral Manoeuvres In The Dark, Spandau Ballet, even Kajagoogoo. But The Smiths?!? I even wondered if they were anything to do with the ubiquitous Robert Smith from The Cure, who'd also played with Siouxsie & The Banshees.

I'd remembered reading a Jim Shelley's review in *NME* which had ticked all the right 'Independent' boxes but, cynically, I'd assumed it was just another Manchester writer enthusing about some of his post-punk mates. (Shelley received thanks on the sleeve of The Smiths' debut.)

At first, I declined Rose's invitation. It wasn't just lack of money and enthusiasm, more the doom-laden word 'Manchester'. I hadn't articulated the notion but obviously I associated the city with my brother Don's addiction to Joy Division and New Order, with the Hacienda, with the scary Granada Television images of Ian Curtis dancing madly and dead-eyed, to 'Shadowplay' or 'Transmission'; with the closing door of the 'Love Will Tear Us Apart' video; with the deathly beautiful but darkly funereal pulse of 'Atmosphere'.

Frankly, I wouldn't have gone out that night if it hadn't been for Rose and, equally important, The Go Betweens. Don had left me their Postcard singles and 'Hammer The Hammer' had been one of the best things on Rough Trade Records earlier that summer. I'd grown fond of the Australian band and had recently bought 'Cattle & Cane' and 'Before Hollywood'. (There was something more than relevant about Grant McLennan's 'A Bad Debt Follows You'.)

My plan, on the bus to Victoria that night, was to catch The Go Betweens, cadge a few drinks from Rose, then briefly check out these Smiths. But, it did cross my mind as odd that the relatively well-known Go-Betweens, with their still-rising Indie-label pedigree, were now only supporting a Northern band beginning to make an impact. In truth, I knew next to nothing about The Smiths' debut single, 'Hand In Glove', except that its cover flaunted a photograph of naked male buttocks. How very odd.

The Smiths, I soon learnt, had started out in Manchester a year earlier and had recently signed to Rough Trade Records. They'd just recorded a John Peel session and also appeared on the Kid Jensen Radio One show, but 'Hand In Glove' had failed to make any serious impact on the mainstream British charts. Reading the press, they didn't sound like my sort of group at all although, intriguingly, Barney Hoskyns in *NME* described the song as "a pure redemption of all the suffering that's ever been poured down love's drain".

That night, entering the Venue, everything felt different. There was a huge sense of anticipation and great expectation; the atmosphere was extraordinary. A diverse crowd too, not exclusively the purist New Romantic brigade from the Beat Route or Billys, or the gay scene regulars of Heaven and Hell. There were also lots of students, plus many younger teenagers in charity shop chic, wearing second hand American clothes from Flip or Lawrence Corner, mingling with Jo Boxer fashion victims and other renegade elements of the 1983 London music scene.

The Go Betweens were really entertaining – they always would be – performing those sweetly-crafted, slightly weird, Antipodean-skewed songs. When their set ended, I half-expected the atmosphere to change. Surely, the crowd would thin out as, like me, the majority probably expected The Smiths to struggle in the wake of their confident Rough Trade label mates.

I remember being at the bar with Rose, briefly being introduced to David Dorrell – then an *NME* journalist and early champion of The Smiths – as the mood began to change. Clusters of pale love-sick youths started to creep forward, and the initial anticipatory hush was followed by whistles and screams of first rapture, then applause, as four young Mancunians sloped, almost shyly, onto the flower-strewn stage.

It's all about time and place, isn't it? Rarely in life will music alter or affect you in a dramatic way. Maybe it was like watching Elvis live in 1956, or The Beatles at the Cavern, or The Stones at the Crawdaddy. In a flash, mentally and visually, music becomes important; as if, as the cliche goes, what's happened before is black and white in your memory and then, suddenly, it's all colour; not the MTV-contrived, storyboarded version but the raw, in-the-flesh moment when the art form truly begins to make sense. Suddenly you see the point and believe what you're hearing. As if it has some magical power to change you. For that moment onwards you feel you're part of something different, something original. It gives you hope.

That's how I felt when I saw The Smiths that night at The Venue. Still in their teens, Mike Joyce (The Drums) and Johnny Marr (The Guitars) looked born rock stars, with the right working-class faces and the right haircuts. Even Andy Rourke (The Bass) looked less primeval, more integral, than other bassists I'd witnessed.

Above all, the sound they made together was extraordinary and magnificent and unfashionably free from synthesisers. From the opening frenetic, inspiring burst of 'Handsome Devil', it became rapidly clear that here was something unique and passionate but also aggressive.

Every band needs a focal point. How often have you heard a strong, intelligent song on the radio and been driven by curiosity and optimism to see the artist live, only to be savagely disappointed when the creator in question churns their uncharismatic way through a 'performance' (see Dylan, Bob). All great live "acts" depend heavily on a showman, someone you can't take your eyes off, someone blessed with charisma – whether it's Jagger or Bono or Lennon or Van Morrison or Youssou N'Dour or Madonna or Hutchence or Prince or Ian Curtis or Rotten or Strummer or Docherty.

It's not about simple beauty or straightforward sexuality. It's perhaps more mystical and mysterious than that. There's a magnetism that can't be manufactured or stage-managed. Precious few have it. As a spectator, even when you attempt to survey the wider scene, like moths to flames, your addicted eyes are drawn back, irresistibly, towards one particular bright spark.

Morrissey was like that from the moment I saw him. Initially he seemed ridiculous; an early, exaggerated, cartoon version of the person he would become. I can't remember whether it was the cliff of hair – I'd caught the weird and wonderful Split Endz in the late Seventies (as had Morrissey!) and, believe me, the Mancunian lead singer's locks in '83 were definitely drifting into that madly hirsute beyond-rockabilly territory – or the desperately ill-fitting jeans, or the big girls blouse from Evans (purveyors of clothes for large women) that intrigued me first, or maybe just the strange unhealthily thin carriage of the man. (Jessica Berens in the American rock magazine *Spin* would later describe his topiary-style features as "albescent, almost greenish . . . the hair could have been designed by an imaginative hedge trimmer.")

What Morrissey was wearing might not sound outrageously significant, but at the time it was strangely radical in an utterly anti-fashion sense. We were still in the throes of rampant New Romanticism with all the trappings. Steve Strange, Boy George, Marilyn and Spandau Ballet were the peacock punks of London's nightlife.

Pop music was a circus and everyone in the charts in 1983 looked comically ridiculous, from The Thompson Twins to Duran Duran; glamorously made-up and dressed to impress after the anarchic bondage and bandages of punk or the heavy overcoats sported by Joy Division's young men ("the weight on their shoulders"). In this ridiculous context, an underfed scrawny bloke in baggy-bottomed jeans with a Billy Fury hairdo looked like a creature from another planet.

"Morrissey" – how oddly pretentious, why didn't he want to be called

Steven? – moved awkwardly, differently. In a way he wasn't right, he wasn't normal, and yet he looked so right up there onstage; an odd combination of self-consciousness and outrageous confidence yet without arrogance; like a showman in a straitjacket, screaming to get out . . . or back in.

Then there was the voice; so distinctively, proudly, un-mistakenly Northern; weather-beaten and world-weary, slightly lispish in delivery, a naturally soft tenor, prone to adventure towards the upper register and even climax in falsetto. Few white pop stars – only Sparks, Bowie and Billy Mackenzie of The Associates sprang to mind (the yodelling love children of Frank Ifield) – had carried this off before.

What he was saying, the words to these strangely structured songs, couldn't be readily understood that night in the Venue and yet seemed instantly poignant and humorous and confessional. Without being utterly ridiculed, no one else involved in the confidence trick of pop music could or would have sung a high-pitched line about the mess he'd made of his life, without inviting total ridicule.

Or admitted he was jobless purely because he didn't want to work. Or shrilly piped that nobody ever looked at him twice. This extraordinary lyrical, strangely sexual, musical poetry poured forth sounding freshly invented even when obviously half-stolen.

The onstage chemistry was remarkable too. From the outset there was a clear, strong sense of partnership to the central Morrissey and Marr relationship but also a visual unity between all four members of The Smiths; perfectly in tune, musically, stylistically and artistically, and – in contrast with so many other acts I witnessed back in the early Eighties – this combination conveyed a real sense of original talent at work.

These were songs so different from what had gone before, such a contrast to the spitfire anger of punk or the self-indulgent twaddle of New Romanticism (e.g. "Se tourne pour se cacher, We fade to grey"). Sounding proudly "Independent" rather than manufactured and "Major" (at a time when the label a band signed with was regarded as a political and philosophical statement), The Smiths created uplifting guitar music that acted as the perfect backdrop to Morrissey's realistic rather than pessimistic poetry.

Believe me. 'This Charming Man', performed live for the first time that night at the Venue, was breathtakingly brilliant, instantly addictive, a work of art you wanted to have and hold from that moment onwards. Johnny Marr – this young guitar hero, the George Best of Independent music, at a time when such a craft was unfashionably vilified outside the big hair arena of Heavy Metal – stood and played with such mastery and confidence and sheer style that it was hard to believe it all chimed forth from him alone.

It was, and is, and ever more shall be, a marvellous two–minutes–forty–seconds wonder of a pop song, dripping with echoes of great guitar music from the past, yet fresh and new and awe-inspiring. Above the beauty of this complex music, Morrissey's chorus about the emptiness of his wardrobe was instantly unforgettable, theatrically camp, extremely funny and clever, particularly at the point in pop culture when clothes (in an almost quasi-Mod way) were supposed to be more important than life itself.

True, I was young and impressionable then, in desperate need of something to believe in, but among the congregation on the Venue floor, we all seemed to be aware we were witnessing the beginnings of something really special.

Apart from the sheer quality of the music live what remains in the memory is the warm sense that we were like-minded spirits. There was no aggression, no spitting, just the occasional volley of gladioli or cut-price daffodils flying overhead.

Accepting The Smiths, we felt we were embracing a more tolerant and tolerable world, that we were being realistic about life and death, focusing on what's vital but prepared to address head-on the problems we were all facing: fear of the future, a physical lack of confidence, the unrequited desire to be ourselves, to be unconditionally loved for who we really were. (Our close friend Andy Martin still believes that, if The Smiths had come along a year earlier, they could have helped save my brother's life.)

Other songs pierced my ears and stuck in my heart. 'Still Ill', 'What Difference Does It Make?', the absurdly confident calling-card first single 'Hand In Glove', and 'Reel Around The Fountain', with its echoes of Andy Warhol in its famous desire for fifteen minutes of fame.

Not that this Morrissey character said much between songs. His shyness and awkwardness seemed to return whenever the music stopped, as if his self-confidence was struggling to play musical chairs. "Hello you gruesome devils," he quipped, theatrically, after the opening songs then, during the inevitable encore, he urges: "You'll have to do it eventually so do it now . . . accept yourself."

Before the death he encouraged a shambolic second-hand student stage invasion, but even this was an affectionate pacifist affair, almost a love-in rather than a Sham 69 scrum. Security looked uncertain, embarrassed, emasculated even, because there were grown men onstage unashamedly hugging the lead singer. But the only danger Morrissey faced was of being smothered with flowers and kisses. What a way to die. I'd never seen anything like it.

Although as far removed as physically possible from the excruciating closing sequences on Seventies' *Top Of The Pops* – when dolly bird punters in mini-skirts or hot pants danced along with ageing DJs in tank-tops – the chasm between performer and audience was beautifully bridged. Finally, Morrissey departs graciously with the words "stay handsome".

It was a fantastic, memorable evening. The effortless brilliance of The Smiths had made the fine Go Betweens seem unexceptional, even run of the mill. I'd been moved by live performances before – T. Rex in 1974, Talking Heads in 1978, The Clash in 1979 – but there was a much stronger, warmer, lasting glow of connection between The Smiths and their growing band of fans.

Ian Curtis may well, in vain, have been "waiting for a guide" to take him by the hand. In Morrissey, that night in Victoria, it seemed we had found someone like us. Not so much a leader, but more a voice in the wilderness, for the uncertain, the outcasts, the equivocal, the misunderstood.

For all we cared, they could write us off as social inadequates, as the broken-hearted bed-sit brigade, or as unambitious underlings gently trying not to be crushed by the wheels of Thatcherism. If you didn't want to sell your soul to capitalism or dedicate your life to the pursuit of money, or perhaps if you were struggling with love and self-love, then in Morrissey and his Smiths you were offered an alternative, bearable path through the political chaos and the musical mediocrity of the Eighties; a self-help group with great pop songs.

I thanked Rose Rouse with all my heart and took the long walk home alone, over Vauxhall Bridge towards Kennington, back to my rented room in Camberwell.

I felt rejuvenated by The Smiths. It wasn't quite a religious experience but, when you're at your wits' end and need something meaningful to cling to, works of art come into their own. I'd always believed in the healing power of music – Gil Scott Heron's 'Lady Day And John Coltrane' summed up its important, uplifting powers – but invariably it had been the music of the past, nostalgic reminders of my happy childhood. There'd been exciting times during my teenage years watching Bolan and Bowie, The Faces and Slade, Sparks and Cockney Rebel, but much of that could now be catalogued as simple escapist entertainment.

For the first time, through the creative art of Morrissey and Marr, I felt I'd witnessed something more substantial, more important in terms of British contemporary music. It meant something. Elsewhere, U2 were growing in stature (*War* and *Under A Blood Red Sky*) and R.E.M. was on the rise (*Murmur*), but little else seemed worth writing home about.

Certainly not, in my subjective opinion, The Alarm, Lloyd Cole & The Commotions or Big Country. Definitely not Duran Duran or Spandau Ballet. They said nothing to me about my life. And, despite all the loveable youthful quirkiness of Orange Juice, Prefab Sprout and even Aztec Camera, they were hardly saying anything profoundly philosophical or original or life-changing with any great degree of passion. In fact, lyrically, did anyone in popular music have anything fresh or different or controversial to say?

Maybe I was searching too desperately for someone to make sense of it all, someone attempting to use popular music to make statements about how we should live our lives. Early Eighties mainstream pop music was all about escapism, going out, getting out of it and having a good time. I'd already tried that. It wasn't enough.

But for those of us who wanted more, post-punk, post-Joy Division, Morrissey was a breath of fresh air. He was oddly attractive and likeable. A sex symbol you wanted to be like but, if you were heterosexual, you certainly wouldn't want to have sex with. (Although his art "speaks to the homosexual component in heterosexual men," according to the writer Will Self.) Importantly, in terms of Eighties pop music, Morrissey wasn't another mullet-haired frontman saying, 'Look at me I can have all the sex I want and you can't.' Instead, he seemed philosophically more substantial, more worthwhile, than other 'rock stars' of our time.

It wasn't just this strange self-deprecating showmanship that drew me to him. The reference points in songs and interviews, and the visual imagery he used on singles and album covers, immediately struck a chord. They were different, provocative, clever and yet instantly understandable and relevant. Sure, all of the carefully chosen central characters seemed to be either gay or strongly feminist figures, but they added to the different, exceptional nature conveyed by Morrissey and The Smiths. Musically he seemed to be speaking for outsiders generally; for young people who for various reasons didn't comfortably meet society's pigeonholed expectations.

His cover stars would always be characters from film or television or literature who'd struggled against the status quo, particularly in terms of sexuality. Some had been judged and broken by the moral code of their time, but, nevertheless, had achieved fame or notoriety or had created great art despite the general prejudices.

It would emerge that clearly taste, Morrissey's personal artistic aesthetic taste, played an enormous part in the selection process of Smiths' icons. Although creatively I knew it was a musical partnership with Johnny Marr, Morrissey was clearly the instigator of The Smiths' manifesto. While there was often a reason behind the choice of a particular image to grace the cover of each single and album, it was also about the style and presentation of these artistic images. Unless circumstances dictated otherwise (as in the case of 'What Difference Does It Make?'), the purpose was clearly to celebrate or highlight someone other than The Smiths themselves. This in itself was radical, unselfish, almost self-deprecating.

From 'This Charming Man' onwards – it would be their first Top 40 single, but a lack of Radio One play meant it reached a criminally disappointing number 25 – the release of each Smiths single was a hugely anticipated event. (Paul Morley in *NME* declared that 'This Charming Man' was "unique and indispensable, like 'Blue Monday' and 'Karma Chameleon'.")

But it wasn't just about hearing these tracks for the first time – those deliberately different, almost bloody-minded, brilliantly brief, Radio One un-friendly singles – it was also about the superbly crafted B-sides (like 'Jeane' and 'Back To The Old House'), the artful packaging, and the scratched messages on run-out grooves: "Kiss My Shades", "Slap Me On The Patio", "Forever Ill", "Will Nature Make A Man Of Me Yet?"

The 'Hand In Glove' buttocks image from Margaret Walter's *The Nude Male* was followed, on 'This Charming Man', with the narcissistic shot of Jean Marais in *Orphee* staring at his own reflection as if the throes of passionate autosexuality – the love of oneself.

Importantly, the third single, 'What Difference Does It Make?', with its confessional opening lyric, seemed to confirm their passage into the mainstream by reaching number 12 in January 1984. But this move from relative obscurity towards commercial success brought its own problems.

Having set the standard for original artistic covers, Morrissey had decided on an image of one of his favourite actors, Terence Stamp from the film of John Fowles' novel *The Collector*. In the film, Stamp's character is a butterfly collector who turns his focus on women, inspiring the 'Reel Around The Fountain' lines about pinning and mounting.

Stamp initially refused permission, and, as a result, Morrissey himself stood in for the official release, trying to look like a grinning Stamp but holding a glass of milk instead of chloroform. Morrissey later told me, "I didn't want to be on the cover, and it was the ugliest picture I'd ever set an eye upon." Eventually Sandie Shaw intervened on The Smiths' behalf and Terence Stamp changed his mind, but this wouldn't be the only problem raised by the band's first Top 20 hit.

Johnny Marr hadn't even wanted 'What Difference Does It Make?' released and also talked candidly about the problems recording the album; he'd had reservations about the original mixes by Troy Tate ("it just sounded like demos") and they'd brought in ex-Roxy Music man John Porter to salvage The Smiths' debut.

Singles were still important in the 1980s, but they were too often here-today-gone-tomorrow products. Albums, in contrast, needed to have weight and longevity. They had to be more substantial than a cobbled-together collection of 45s; they needed to make a grander statement in order to consolidate a following; to set the artists apart from the many transient pop stars of the day.

It couldn't simply be about production or selling a glamorous lifestyle (like Duran Duran's 'Rio'); landmark albums needed to offer something special. Not necessarily a concept in the style of *Sgt. Pepper's Lonely Hearts Club Band* or, gawd help us, themed like ELP's *Pictures At An Exhibition*, but more a sense of emotional unity, a genuine style that draws the listener in and keeps you there, thirsting for more. Equally important, an 'independent' album had to sound distinctly different from mainstream music of the early Eighties and could not be awash with pointless guitar and drum solos or tarted-up with sythesisers and layered vocals. It needed to be more human than that.

I remember buying *The Smiths* from J.G. Windows record shop in Newcastle's Central Arcade and taking it back for a first spin on my mum and dad's old Sharp music centre in the front room at Bentinck Road.

Sitting there, watching the grey label revolve and the worn needle drop noisily onto the static plastic, I was prepared to be disappointed. Early on, I'd questioned whether Morrissey was a strong enough character to survive the rising tide of negative criticism and ridicule – the way he looked, the way he sang, the way he spoke, the controversial things he said – and I also doubted The Smiths would be able to deliver an album worthy of their early singles. Plenty of other acts (certainly The Police) seemed to me to be just "singles bands", assembling their 45s together to make albums; there didn't seem to be an overall message conveyed by the record as a whole.

The Smiths proved that they were so much more than purveyors of fine (yet, for various reasons, commercially unsuccessful) singles. The music was beautiful, complex, emotional and powerful. Above all this, there was a lyrical vision that offered a different, sympathetic yet encouraging, view of difficult times.*

Listening again and again, everything about that first album sounded and felt like the perfect statement of intent; controversial, sexually ambiguous, provocative and, at the same time, original and stylish. Importantly, the cover revealed one of Morrissey's obsessions, Andy Warhol, by using a topless, muscle-rippling still of gay porn pin-up Joe Dallesandro, star of Warhol's *Flesh*, significantly directed by 'Steven's' namesake Paul Morrissey in 1968. The Warhol theme also appeared in the lyrics to 'Reel Around The Fountain', which seemed to deal with loss of virginity and innocence rather than under-age sex. ('Reel Around The Fountain' was set to be the follow-up single to 'Hand In Glove' before the immaculate 'This Charming Man' came along.)

Elsewhere 'The Smiths' moved easily from the *Carry On* underwear-obsessed comedy of 'Miserable Lie' to the sweet poetry of 'Pretty Girls Make Graves', which happily dealt with failed passions, rejection and mortality, and the truly beautiful lyricism of 'The Hand That Rocks The Cradle'. The latter, building on a line from Al Jolson's 'Sonny Boy', was written from the perspective of a doting parent or guardian angel, and dealt, in an almost spiritual way, with the protection of a vulnerable child while fearing that the corrupting outside world would soon come crashing in.

Symmetrically (in terms of the two sides of the original vinyl album) 'The Hand That Rocks The Cradle' was the protected twin of the controversial, chilling yet moving final track, 'Suffer Little Children'. One of The Smiths' most sensitive, haunting and controversial early songs, 'Suffer Little Children' lyrically rekindled the absolute horror of the Moors Murders; the torture, sexual abuse and murder of five Mancunian children by Ian Brady and Myra Hindley between 1963 and 1965. The young Steven Patrick Morrissey, only six or seven years old when the full sordid details of the crimes emerged, would be greatly scarred by these events on

---

* 'Suffer Little Children' also refers to the Edwardian working-class drama *Hindle Wakes* by Mancunian playwright Stanley Houghton.

his doorstep, on the streets where he ran. (He would return to equally murderous themes in later lyrics such as 'Michael's Bones', 'Ambitious Outsiders' and even, in 2006, 'The Youngest Was The Most Loved'.)

Although most people accept Morrissey and Marr's early statements that the band's name was chosen because of their mutual love of Patti Smith – Smithdom and The Smith Family were also considered – it's always seemed significant that one of the early chapters of actor Emlyn Williams' influential 1968 non-fiction work *Beyond Belief (A Chronicle Of Murder And Its Detection)* begins with the words "The Smiths . . ."

Why did Morrissey tackle this taboo subject? Wasn't it career suicide, particularly after he'd been falsely accused in the tabloids of apparently promoting under-age sex or paedophilia in 'Reel Around The Fountain' and 'Handsome Devil'. (A headline in *The Sun*, August 25, 1983, had read "Child Sex Song Puts The Beeb In A Spin".) Following a negative news story in the *Manchester Evening News*, complaining of the emotional pain the song had caused the families of the victims, Rough Trade would later issue a press statement in which Morrissey explained that 'Suffer Little Children' was "a memorial to the children and all like them who have suffered such a fate". (Royalties were donated to the NSPCC and Ann West, the mother of Lesley-Ann Downey, would be thanked for her understanding on the sleeve of 'Meat Is Murder'.)

From the outset Morrissey seemed determined to cause maximum provocation, to be intensely irritating for those who didn't 'get' him or like him or understand him, particularly those one-dimensional characters who tended to dominate the British media; those upright homophobic males, conditioned to oppose feminism, who refused to accept the value of any of Morrissey's icons.

For all the chilling hardness of such subject matter – this peculiar focus on endangered children and the Moors Murders, which haunted the born-in-the-late-Fifties generation much as the James Bulger case haunts children born in the late Eighties and early Nineties – the album still contained a great deal of hope and warmth, particularly for those of us struggling to find jobs or make enough money to survive; those of us confined to our bedsits, thoroughly discontented with the state of the world and, specifically, the state of popular music.

Was *The Smiths* as bleak an album as many suggested? Did it wallow in its own miserablism? Paul Du Noyer in *NME* described it as "economical beat music" and, at the time, it was the perfect statement of independent production values; that uncluttered Rough Trade sound, sticking two fingers up at the layered, electronic music that spewed forth from major labels. Du Noyer did go on to point out that, "The Smiths make a music which is perfect for that abiding constituency of British youth which is disaffected with the discotheque imperatives of dance and impervious to the appeal of escapist glamour."

Again, the importance of Morrissey's different world view was heightened by the political and economic situation in Britain during 1983 and 1984. Thatcherism in all its dreadful brutality was in full swing after the post-Falklands election victory. "I just pray there's a Sirhan Sirhan somewhere," Morrissey hoped in early '84, referring to the assassination of Robert Kennedy. Unemployment was rising while traditional Northern industries such as steel, shipbuilding and coal-mining were collapsing, as were the working-class communities that depended on them.

Importantly, political commentators convincingly talked about the North-South divide and noted that Thatcher could rule the land by governing for the benefit of only the twenty per cent of the electorate who'd actually voted for her party, primarily in the South and the Home Counties. Let's not forget these were days when, like some unpopular medieval king or tin-pot 'developing-world' despot, Thatcher was unable to visit parts of her own nation without military-style protection.

Morrissey might not have been a card-carrying member of a Left wing party or politically correct or unequivocally open about his own sexual politics but, with the Labour Party in utter disarray following the launch of the Social Democrats, at least he was a questioning, critical and genuinely Northern voice.

In fact, Johnny Marr would seem the more politically committed partner and The Smiths would go on to support Glastonbury, the Greater London Council's Festival For Jobs and later the socialist music-meets-youth-politics organisation Red Wedge. Morrissey would be more supportive of the women protestors of Greenham Common, the vegetarian lobby and the animal rights movement.

Unbelievably – given his shyness, his background and frequent pronouncements about his debilitating childhood – Morrissey was developing into a strong, vocal and at the same time (to my mind at least) extremely humorous individual. He seemed to talk more sense than most of his contemporaries and also had a strong sense of disappointed realism (which others branded pessimism) about the troubled world that we lived in. He wasn't comfortable or confident, but he was forthright and opinionated. Crucially, he didn't seem to care about offending people.

As an Irish Mancunian, with the deaths of the IRA hunger strikers in painful recent memory, it was perhaps inevitable that Morrissey would express disappointment that Thatcher did not die when the IRA bombed the hotel which housed delegates to the Conservative Party Conference in Brighton on October 1984: "The sorrow of the Brighton Bombing is that Thatcher escaped unscathed. The sorrow is that she is still alive." Maybe pop stars can't change anything but, this seemed bravely outspoken at a time when, to meddle with Yeats' fine words, the best lacked all conviction, while the worst were full of passionate intensity.

Unavoidable – in the box in the corner of your room, on the radio, in the press – and full of great quotes, tackling complex and controversial subject matter in his lyrics, stealing from great writers and obscure films, he didn't behave like other rock stars who were generally detached from reality under the influence of drink or drugs or lust or wealth or apathy (or all five). "I'm not a manic depressive just a realist," he said in 1986. "I'm just not someone you'll see romping about in a haystack, singing and swigging a bottle of cognac."

As Prefab Sprout would satirically point out, most pop stars were happy to write radio-friendly songs about cars and girls and, even if their political viewpoints were radical to begin with, they'd soon be mellowed by the flow of royalties and the trappings of fame. Then they'd collect sports cars and open trout farms.

Not Morrissey. No sooner had they (whoever *they* may be) let him out of his box and onto the stage, and he was opening cans of worms by celebrating unemployment, sexual deviation, crooning about the loss of innocence and reminding British society of shocking beyond evil crimes and their perpetrators.

From somewhere he seemed to find the courage to make controversial, comical statements that most public figures would have avoided. For example, when the anti-famine Band Aid single 'Do They Know It's Christmas' was released in late 1984 Morrissey remarked, "One can have great concern for the people of Ethiopia, but it is another thing to inflict daily torture on the people of England"; wildly funny, if not politically correct or remotely supportive of Geldof's campaign to Feed The World.

Against the divisive cash-hungry tide of Thatcherism, Morrissey made it seem positive to openly admit unhappiness with the way things in Britain were going. Throughout 1984, the Conservative government was in increasingly bitter conflict with the National Union of Mineworkers led by Arthur Scargill. Living back in the North East, without a girlfriend, drinking too much, staying with my still-grieving parents while working on an evening paper called *The South Shields Gazette*, the perfect sound-track to my deeply troubled summer of the Miners' Strike was The Smiths' 'Heaven Knows I'm Miserable Now'.

It sounds overdramatic but The Smiths definitely helped me, even changed me. From The Venue concert onwards I felt like I was part of some fantastic new and exclusive underground cult. Musically it was like nothing I'd experienced before (or since), and at the heart of it was this strange sexually equivocal character, the scourge of the airwaves, the man most likely to have you spluttering in your soup or choking with laughter on your spaghetti hoops as you watched him cavorting in pearls on *Top Of The Pops*.

There would be no middle ground, no sitting on the fence when it came to Morrissey; with his over-sized clothes; his back-pocket floral tributes to Oscar Wilde; his naked stomach tattooed in lipstick with the phrase "initiate me" or his neck with the word "Bad"; the Johnnie Ray hearing aid; the care-in-the-community sticking-plastered NHS specs. What a strange, singular, different yet awkwardly handsome creature he was back in the early Eighties. Gay men wanted to sleep with him, women wanted to mother him, sensitive straight men wanted to be like him or liked by him. Studying Morrissey's lyrics, I wondered who on earth this man was and where the hell had he come from?

Was he really so strange? On further investigation Morrissey seemed to have emerged from some Caspar Hauser-like Mancunian cave, where he'd apparently spent years (a) watching *Coronation Street*, (b) consuming Sixties Social Realism films, (c) refusing to accept the demise of James Dean, (d) chuckling at the schoolboy crudity of *Carry On* films, (e) relish-ing the shock-rock tactics of the New York Dolls and followed by the anti-establishment aggression of punk, (f) kissing the feet of Sandie Shaw and worshipping at the ample bosom of Diana Dors, (g) falling in love with the androgyny of Bowie and Bolan and, above all, (h) feasting like a panther on the life and works of Oscar Wilde.

In the late summer of 1984, as Sandie Shaw kicked her legs in the air on *Top Of The Pops* performing 'Hand In Glove' in front of The Smiths (without Morrissey) and while their fourth single 'William, It Was Really Nothing' crept into the Top 20 (with a truly astonishing song called 'How Soon Is Now?' buried on its 12″ B-side), I sat down and applied for a *Guardian*-advertised sub editor's job on the *New Musical Express*.

3.

Used To Be A Sweet Boy

*"It's nothing unique. Millions upon millions of people come from
'damaged backgrounds', shall we say. Mine wasn't so much damaged as
merely nothing at all"*

— Morrissey, 1994

IF the child is the father of the man, what a very unusual and sensitive
soul the young Steven Patrick Morrissey must have been. Born on
May 22, 1959 in Davyhulme, at the Stretford end of Manchester, he was
the second child, his mother's only son (older sister Jacqueline is rarely
mentioned) of Irish Mancunians, hospital porter Peter Morrissey and his
librarian wife Elizabeth Dwyer.

From an early age, perhaps seven or eight, Steven seems to have been
painfully aware that his parents were incompatible and, clearly, if a song
like 'Dial-A-Cliche' can be interpreted as in any way autobiographical and
about critical paternal advice, his closest relationship would always be with
his mother. He'd later say, of the effect of his parents inevitable separation
and eventual divorce when he was 17, "even if you can overcome it, its
very debilitating."

The portrait he's painted of his formative years is poetically and theatrically grim. From St Wilfrid's Roman Catholic primary school onwards he
seems to have been regarded as a complete oddity, someone who simply
didn't fit in any conventional way. From there he went to St Mary's
Secondary School in Stretford, where he struggled and failed to integrate
with others. "The key incident for me was that I never had any real
friends. And I realised that in order to have friends and impress people I
had to do something extraordinary. In a way, it's a type of revenge. You
hate so many people . . . it sounds very juvenile now, I suppose, like
smashing someone's window. But then, what else can you do? It was like a
weapon, something to make them gnash their teeth."

When we've spoken about his childhood and its influence on his lyrics it's become obvious that he's been realistic rather than nostalgic about the gloomy Manchester of his youth. After all, he was born just over a year after the Munich plane crash, in which many of the great young Manchester United footballers of the Fifties, the Busby Babes, died. The tragedy haunted young Morrissey's home city, fifty years on it still does, and inspired his own moving tribute to those lost boys in red such as England Internationals Duncan Edwards and Tommy Taylor ('Munich Air Disaster 1958').

More affecting still, while he was at junior school the full horror of the Moors Murders came to light, revealing how five vulnerable youngsters were stolen from the city's streets and suffered horrible deaths at the hands of the sadistic Ian Brady and his accomplice Myra Hindley.

The Salford of Morrissey's youth – the tough working class, heavy industrial post-war declining Manchester – was captured in L. S. Lowry's paintings and, particularly, the photographs of Harold Riley. It's the warts-and-all Salford of Hanky Park, Seedly, Brindle Heath and Pendleton and it seems as if Riley's images in particular burned their way into young Steven Morrissey's imagination. Clearly photographs such as 'The Cemetery Gates' (1971), a misty portrait of the entrance of the Weaste graveyard, inspired a track on *The Queen Is Dead*, although most of Morrissey's own teenage boneyard tourism seems to have been to Southern Cemetery in Chorlton. (In the opening episode of the TV comedy *On The Buses* in 1969, Stan's number eleven bus ran from the Luxton & District depot to the "Cemetery Gates".)

Elsewhere in Riley's work you find still-shocking portraits such as 'Strangeways, 1970' in which a down-and-out meths drinker stares up at the camera from a piss-stained mattress in a Salford back street, and 'Sunbathers, 1964', in which two children lie face-down on hot flags near Chimney Pot Park, a possible inspiration (along with Wilde's "The Tired Hedonists") for the *Vauxhall & I* track 'The Lazy Sunbathers'.

Riley also captured Salford's real *Coronation Street* with its wrestling impoverished kids, the chimney sweeps and the rag-and-bone men, the clog maker, the nattering old dears in curlers, the "Woman with a club foot, Hodge Lane, 1966", the back yards with washing, the passageways and wild dogs, the iron bridges . . .

Although it's hard to mourn the passing of this urban landscape, particularly amid the regeneration and ongoing PR spin to drastically improve the image of parts of Manchester, it clearly lives on in Morrissey's memory and his lyrics, in his titles and images.

But I don't believe he remembers to celebrate depression or just to be deliberately reflective on some imaginary golden past. I think he's just holding up the portrait and saying, "This is how it was, this is how I remember it, perhaps we shouldn't forget this world that some of us came from."

Again, it's realism rather than pessimism. The old Salford has been demolished, much of it for the better, but maybe Morrissey's saying that something has been lost in the process; parts of Manchester increasingly look like American trading estates. Many of Riley's photographs capture children and old people on the streets of Salford. (As Morrissey later remarked, in revamping Manchester the planners seem to have eradicated old people from the city centre altogether.)

LB: Tell me about your school years?

Morrissey: "I went to a very violent school."

St Mary's in Stretford?

"Yes, it was insane really."

How did you deal with it?

"I didn't go to school." He laughs. "I turned left instead of right. I walked round the shops. Quite seriously, the last two years were quite bad. It was very annoying. The teachers were very annoying. The tattiness of the whole school. There was nothing to do. There were so many strikes in the early Seventies. Blackouts, not electricity, no coal, so I just thought 'well, why bother?' I sat at home and planned the promo campaign for *The Queen Is Dead*."

You've drawn on that period of time a lot in your lyrics.

"Well, they were very graphic times. It was like living through the war and people who lived through the war can never quite forget it. It was horrendous and encouraging and it developed the character. But it was tragic. Interesting to be entering teenagedom at that time but certainly not easy or affluent by any means. Everyone I knew was desperately poor."

It's obvious that his educational experiences have provided a rich seam for his lyrics with The Smiths ('The Headmaster Ritual') and throughout his solo career ('Late Night, Maudlin Street') – the working title for *Viva Hate* had been 'Education In Reverse' – but at the time they clearly scarred him deeply: "If you're too smart, they hate and resent you and they will break you . . . they succeeded in almost killing off all the self-confidence I had."[*]

---

[*] In 2004, when he returned to Salford to play Old Trafford Cricket Ground, supported by his beloved New York Dolls and billing himself as "the local boy made bad", onstage he celebrated the recent death of his former headmaster Vincent Morgan.

He'd celebrated the importance of literature in his own life on The Smiths' early track 'Handsome Devil' and, given the unfavourable circumstances of his childhood, inevitably his mother's library and her love of reading rubbed off on the impressionable, shy, young Steven.

"I swam in books as a child and at some point it becomes quite ruinous. It gets to the point where you can't answer the door without being heavily analytical about it."

Early on his imagination would fired by the works of Thomas Hardy and particularly Charles Dickens. "Dickens is very exciting to me, because he was a terribly gloomy character, terribly embittered and quite depressed . . . I love the grim, dim description of the East End, all those murky, winding passages, full of desperate characters . . . like our friend Fagin". On another occasion, objecting to the way that he was often presented in the media, Morrissey declared, "people always assume that I'm covered in dust, sat in a corner, reading *Hard Times*."

The young Morrissey also embraced the plays of local girl Shelagh Delaney, whose *A Taste Of Honey* he found hugely inspiring and who would be celebrated on several Smiths' covers (notably *Louder Than Bombs* and 'Girlfriend In A Coma'). Then there were more challenging writers, in terms of sexuality, such as Radclyffe Hall and Djuna Barnes. Hall's central character, in *The Well Of Loneliness*, is a confused girl who's been named Stephen by her father because he'd wanted a boy. Barnes' *Nightwood*, published in 1936, is now regarded as one of the early classics of lesbian literature. Further towards adulthood, openly gay writers such as Edmund White (*The Farewell Symphony, A Boy's Own Story, Our Paris . . .*) and Germaine Greer would also influence Morrissey. But, all along, the life and works of Oscar Wilde would have the greatest impact on his formative years.

Encouraged by his mother, Steven became obsessed with Wilde's childrens' stories from the age of eight but later admitted, "It's a total disadvantage to care about Oscar Wilde, certainly when you come from a working-class background. It's total self-destruction almost."

It was Wilde who once said, "I'll be a poet, a writer, a dramatist. Somehow or other, I'll be famous, and if not famous, notorious." Morrissey seems to have read this as gospel and, once living in the unfashionable Hulme suburb of Manchester, decided to burn what little teenage energy and enthusiasm he had in the pursuit of fame. "I always thought being famous was the only thing worth doing in life, and anything else was just perfunctory. I thought anonymity was easy; it was easy to be a simple nodding individual who got on the bus. I wasn't terribly impressed with obscurity." This growing appetite for notoriety would be confirmed in his mid teens when he wrote: "I'm sick of being an undiscovered genius, I want fame now not when I'm dead."

Nevertheless, the journey from anti-social adolescent – "If I hadn't found my social position when I was a teenager so amusing, I would have strangled myself" – to internationally infamous rock star would be a long and bumpy one.

In your youth, didn't you have any optimism at all?

Morrissey laughs, desperately, as if astonished by the question. "I've never been optimistic. The late Seventies became gradually worse and I was quite literally bedridden for years. I found the prospect of turning 20 alarming and I hadn't a clue what was going to happen. When I'd go to bed at night I'd have terrible palpitations because I was so worried. I'd wake up at 3 o'clock and begin to pace the bedroom.

"It was really the beginning of the severe unemployment situation, and people at that time really believed that if you didn't work you were slovenly and lazy and all those other interesting things. They still do but it's less aggressive now because we realise there's world crises, whereas then it was a terrible physical disease to stay at home . . . and paint . . . your face."

Didn't you consider going on to college or university?

"I had no interest in further education because I've never been interested in education in any way. I've never been interested in school! The useful things that I've acquired are by accident or my own personal investigation. I could never retain any degree of information that was placed before me and I still can't really. The prospect of working in a job that pleased me was nil."

Do you regret not having a better education?

"No, I've not done badly, Len. I know I don't have shares in British Gas or don't have a decent pair of football boots but on the face of it I've done all right. I've got a nice coat and I'm sitting in the Cadogan Hotel. What more do you want?"

Even outside of school hours, life wasn't easy for the teenage Morrissey. He once told me how he'd received the unique accolade of being expelled from the Stretford Cubs. More alarming still, his adventures into the rough and tumble real world of fairgrounds, speedway tracks, pop concerts, youth clubs and football matches – the *Clockwork Orange* world of violent "beer monsters" – would have an even more debilitating effect.

"On threadbare Manchester council estates once a year fairs would come round. It was a period of tremendous violence, hate, distress, high romance and all the truly vital things in life.

"I remember being at a fair at Stretford Road, it was very early, about 5 p.m., and I was just standing by the speedway. And somebody just came over to me and head-butted me . . . I was dazed for at least five minutes . . . I don't think it was even that I looked different in those days. There never needed to be a reason."*

An early visit to watch his local team at Old Trafford also affected him badly: "I've been seen once or twice on the terraces. I once bought a Manchester United hat, which I think was 12 shillings, and somebody ran up behind me and pulled it off and just ran ahead. So I thought, 'It's a very cruel world, I'm not prepared for this.' And I decided to get my revenge on society."

While the schooling, scouting and the extracurricular adventures of his Manchester youth only designed him for the dole queue in the summer of 1975 – his curriculum vitae would briefly list him as an Inland Revenue clerk and hospital porter. His religious background also failed to offer any lasting comfort.

LB: You were brought up as a Roman Catholic?

Morrissey: "A roaming Catholic. I stopped going to church when I was ten. Before then I only went because I was forced to. I had such overwhelming doubts that it seemed quite logical that I step away once at the age one is allowed to make these decisions."

So you can't offer any spiritual solutions? In 'Asleep' you suggested you believed in another world, a better world?

"No I find I'm bereft of spiritual solutions. I do believe there has to be a better world, but that's rather simple. I don't meditate and I don't concentrate on particular religions or any bad cults. I'm quite provincial and I'm quite standard really."

As he once explained to Manchester's *City Life* magazine: "I scan the surface of the world, which I do every night before I go to bed, and find that all the wars and all the disturbances in the world are because of religion. And I really was led to believe that religion is all about peace, stretching one's hand out to one's neighbours . . . and stealing milk bottles. It isn't. It seems to divide people, and cause a lot of ruffled hairs."

---

* Perhaps this explains why one vinyl side of *The Queen Is Dead* would be etched with the words "Fear Of Manchester".

Portrait of the artist as a young Mancunian.

The Smiths: unfashionable indie guitar band in a sea of New Romanticism. (MIRRORPIX)

The Bedsit Byron and the rebel outsider...James Byron Dean. (LFI)

Room for Oscar – Morrissey with his greatest influence: "he left you lying on the bed...panting. He was so real and truthful". (LFI)

'Under The Influence.' Pasolini (HULTON ARCHIVE/GETTY IMAGES), 'The Factory' (HULTON ARCHIVE/GETTY IMAG
Kenneth Williams (LFI), Billy Fury (LFI), Diana Dors (POPPERFOTO/GETTY IMAGES),
Magnani (HULTON ARCHIVE/GETTY IMAGES), Patti Smith (LFI), Oscar and Bosie (HULTON ARCHIVE/GETTY IMAGE
Jobriath (MICHAEL OCHS ARCHIVE/GETTY IMAGES), Charles Hawtrey (FREMANTLEMEDIA),
Jimmy Clitheroe (BOB THOMAS/GETTY IMAGES), Dick Davalos (JOHN SPRINGER COLLECTION/CORBIS),
Pat Phoenix (BOB THOMAS/GETTY IMAGES)

Manchester's answer to Johansen and Thunders – "a rare gift and a salvation to each other" (James Maker). (MARK ALLAN)

The Smiths break the UK Top 20 with 'What Difference Does It Make?' The Oxford Road Show, Manchester, February 1984. (MARK ALLAN)

Morrissey poses as shoe-shop worker Jo in *A Taste Of Honey*. (LFI)

Morrissey in 1984 with his Dagenham Diva
Sandie Shaw: "even though we've had many
a fist fight I still think she's great". (LFI)

Rourke (The Bass) and Morrissey (The Voice):
"camping" for nuclear disarmament at
Glastonbury, June 1984. (TIM JARVIS)

London's Royal Albert Hall, April 6 1985: 'Barbarism Begins At Home' featuring Pete
'Dead Or Alive' Burns. ("Morrissey's anybody's for a lupin," according to Burns.) (PHIL DENT/REDFERNS)

Death at one's elbow: Morrissey as
George 'Anarchy In The Ukulele' Formby.
(LAWRENCE WATSON)

Shadow Of A Gunman. (LAWRENCE WATSON)

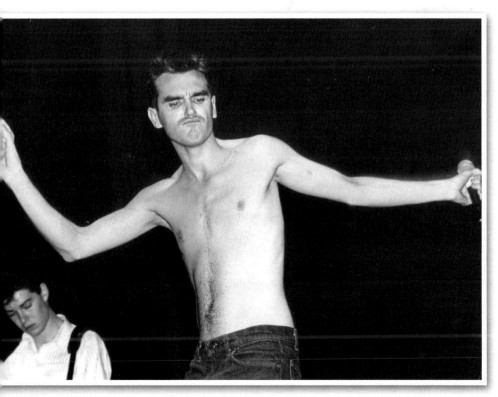

The body rules the mind. (LFI)

Salford Lads: The Smiths in 1986 outside Albert Finney's bookmakers circa *The Queen Is Dead*.
(LAWRENCE WATSON)

The unfavourable circumstances of his childhood tie in with Paul Morley's memories of Morrissey in the Seventies as a misunderstood, almost unwelcome outsider: "Morrissey was always laughed at in Manchester when we were kids. He was the village idiot. That's the ironic thing. Now he's the poet of a generation. But in those days he was 'that one in the corner, Steve the Nutter'." To the influential boss of Manchester's Factory records, the late Anthony H. Wilson, "anyone less likely to be a pop star from this scene was unimaginable".

Inevitably perhaps there came a point in the mid to late Seventies when, confronted with unemployment and ridicule from his peers, and with the break up of his family life, "the nutter" sought to escape from Manchester. Years later, when he was successful and comfortably living in swinging London, I wondered whether he shouldn't have escaped from the North sooner?

"No, I had no capacity to leave. I didn't have money. I only had one friend in London. I came down many many times on a National coach. But obviously I had to go back. I was constantly at Chorlton Street Bus Station in Manchester with £5.50, going away for two weeks.

"I remember once coming to London to live in 1978. I had about £9.50 and stayed in a guest house in South Kensington. The horror was just unrepeatable. Just me, a teapot and a bottle of water."

What would become of him? In terms of youthful ambitions initially he dreamt of writing for *Coronation Street*, the Salford-based soap opera made for ITV and recorded at Manchester's Granada Television Studios on Quay Street off Deansgate. From the age of 12, he'd submitted scripts and plot ideas, and even started a correspondence with one of the main writers and producers, Leslie Duxbury. The small-screen equivalent of Hollywood on your doorstep, it's hard to imagine the impact *Coronation Street* must have had on the impressionable young housebound Morrissey.*

Typically, rather than being drawn to any of the youthful characters, it was the "first of the anti-heroines", the formidable figure of Elsie Tanner who attracted him. Portrayed by Patricia Phoenix, a fiery, brassy, Irish Mancunian redhead – who'd joined the Street cast aged 36 in 1960 and who had also played the controversial role of Sadie Thompson in *The L-Shaped Room* (1962) – Elsie's passion inspired Morrissey. He'd later celebrate *The L-Shaped Room* by sampling Cicely Courtneidge singing 'Take

---

* Street writers in the early Sixties also included Jack Rosenthal and John Finch, former assistant to Jacob Epstein, creator of Wilde's Parisien tomb.

Me Back To Dear Old Blighty' from the film (which also featured Anthony Booth, Tom Bell and *Beyond Belief* Moors Murders author Emlyn Williams), and using it on *The Queen Is Dead*.

When Morrissey interviewed Pat Phoenix in May 1985, for *Blitz* magazine, his character description of Elsie spoke volumes about his own world and explained why he so admired her: "Elsie was the screen's first angry young woman; a wised-up, tongue-lashing, cylindrical tempest, sewn into cheap and overstuffed dresses, harnessed by severe poverty, staunchly defending her fatherless children, devouring a blizzard of temporary husbands in dour Salford council dwellings."

Beyond *Coronation Street* and the books that his mother supplied him with, his deep love affairs with film and popular music would eventually be the making of Morrissey. He grew addicted to cinema that reflected the real world rather than an imagined or hoped-for existence, embracing the social realism of British films in the late Fifties and Sixties: "I'm completely handcuffed to *Saturday Night And Sunday Morning*, which I will never tire of . . . I can't describe the poetry the film has for me, especially that of Albert Finney in the Arthur Seaton role."

Classic Northern working-class British films such as *A Taste Of Honey, A Kind Of Loving, The L-Shaped Room* and *Billy Liar* convinced him that there was a place in the Arts for someone from his background and, crucially, with his accent. "For the first time in British films we had people who were speaking in very down to earth voices. Before that everybody had a very clipped, theatre-school way of talking." Mick Ronson, Bowie's guitar hero sidekick and a Hull-born Spider From Mars (who later became the producer of Morrissey's *Your Arsenal*) once commented on the importance of Morrissey's Northernness: "That matters to him, it matters to anyone. It affects the way you look at the world, the way you deal with people. It affects everything."

After failing to write for *Coronation Street*, further flowering literary ambitions would be crushed when his early attempts at pop criticism were rejected by his favourite music weekly, the *New Musical Express*. Although he did scribble several record reviews for *Record Mirror* under the name Sheridan Whiteside (borrowed from *The Man Who Came To Dinner* character who torments Bette Davis in the 1941 film) the *NME* rejection hurt: "I remember once, a long time ago, somebody at the *NME* slamming the phone down when I called, and that seemed to be the last straw in a bucket of many, many straws."

Determined to become a writer, believing the stock literary advice to "write about what you know", he compiled a book about one of his deepest obsessions – his passion for the beautiful lost boy of American cinema, James Dean. Dean had died in a car crash in 1955 aged 24, but Morrissey seemed reluctant to accept this mortality. *James Dean Is Not Dead*, would eventually be published by Babylon Books in 1981.

Dean's life, portraying the original struggling troubled outcast American youth, struck many chords with Morrissey, and the actor's influence has been a recurring theme throughout his artistic life. Most obviously, Dean became a Smiths' cover star; the bespectacled motorcycle boy on 'Bigmouth Strikes Again'. Another Smiths' track, 'Stretch Out And Wait', echoed Sal Mineo's questioning lines, from Dean's most famous film *Rebel Without A Cause*, about the end of the world. In exile in the Nineties, Morrissey would be photographed in Los Angeles at the Griffith Observatory, scene of the knife fight in which Mineo's character Plato dies.

When Morrissey made his 'Suedehead' video in 1988 he travelled to James Dean's home town Gary, Indiana, and reincarnated himself as Dean as photographed by Denis Stock; playing the bongos and driving a tractor. In the video, Morrissey carries a copy of Antoine De Saint-Exupery's *The Little Prince*; one of Dean's favourite lines from the book – "What is essential is invisible to the eye" – was carved onto his memorial in Cholame, California.

Dean's character from *East Of Eden*, Cal, a young son starved of parental love, also seems to have attracted the young Morrissey and the image of Dean's co-star Richard Davalos would be used on the cover of *Strangeways, Here We Come*. (Dean's face was cropped from the still.) Later in his solo career, Morrissey released the single 'Alma Matters', partly based on Dean's uncredited performance in the John Wayne movie *Trouble Along The Way* (1953). The film's original title was *Alma Mater*. Silent images of Davalos and Dean in a screen test for the film would be screened before Morrissey's 2006 tour.

Once Morrissey asked me if I'd ever seen the French film *Bande A Part* (*Band Of Outsiders*), directed by Jean Luc-Godard in 1963. I had but didn't think it was one of Godard's best, although it starred Claude Brasseur. Although I knew of Morrissey's great interest in French film – the covers of 'This Charming Man' and *The Queen Is Dead* confirm this – it was only when I stumbled across Francois Truffaut's book *The Films Of My Life* (1978) that I understood this "outsiders" connection. Chapter Five is called 'Some Outsiders' and contains an essay titled 'James Dean Is Dead'.

According to Truffaut (who also directed *L'Enfant Sauvage, The Wild*

Child), "Young people today are completely represented in James Dean . . . the adolescent's eternal taste for experience, intoxication, pride, and the sorrow at feeling 'outside', a simultaneous desire and refusal to be integrated into society, and finally acceptance and rejection of the world, such as it is."*

Despite Morrissey's youthful achievement in writing and eventually publishing fanzine-style books about James Dean, The New York Dolls and also a strange compendium about dead actors (*Exit Smiling*), they give little indication of the latent talent that would soon transform him into a British icon, lyrical genius and rock'n'roll poet? Importantly, he became infatuated with pop culture and particularly the pop single from an early, impressionable age. He bought Marianne Faithfull's 'Come And Stay With Me' when he was barely six and, from then on, collected pop music with an insatiable, insane passion.

"There was just something about the pop single. The two minute ten, the cramming of so much emotion into so little time – verses, chorus and fade out . . . All of the great Elvis Presley singles were under two minutes, and in those two minutes you just felt this tumultuous, massive human sexual emotion."

As with his favourite films, his favourite pop stars, chiefly girl singers led by Sandie Shaw and Cilla Black, would speak to him in a distinctly British working-class way: "Most pop has that transatlantic tinge but I prefer the camaraderie of the North . . . I preferred the disposable cheap types . . . I worship every belch of Cilla Black."

Later he'd admit: "I really, really did love those people. I gave them my life, my youth. Beyond the perimeters of pop music there was a drop at the edge of the world." Maybe that's his problem in relationships? Maybe in the real world love can never be as intense, as pure, as perfect or as emotionally focused as in a three minute pop song?

It was the British female voice and also the softer, more vulnerable male voices like Billy Fury's, which spoke most truthfully to the pre-teen Morrissey. Fury – one of his greatest influences, in terms of style and showmanship, and who'd be celebrated on the cover of 'Last Night I Dreamt That Somebody Loved Me' – had transformed himself from the sickly Liverpool lad Ron Wycherley into arguably Britain's greatest rock'n'roll star of the late Fifties and early Sixties.

---

* Alain Delon, often regarded as the French 'James Dean', would adorn the cover of *The Queen Is Dead*.

Inevitably, approaching manhood, Morrissey's musical horizons widened. In 1972, as David Bowie toyed with the notion of bisexuality, the hugely influential New York Dolls arrived to perform on BBC2's *Old Grey Whistle Test* and Marc Bolan led the Glam pack onto *Top Of The Pops*. This sequence of events finally lured the 13-year-old Steven Morrissey from the safety of his bedroom full of books and singles to experience his first live concert: T. Rex.

How important was Marc Bolan to your musical development?

Morrissey: "Marc Bolan was very important to me. Extremely important. He made some great records, even before he became famous, before he became the teeny bopper star. His earlier stuff, with Tyrannosaurus Rex, I found really moving. These records are still very important to me.*

"Lots of people talk about T. Rex being their first musical love affair. The thing at the time was they were the first sign of hysteria since The Beatles. I saw them in '72, in Bellevue in Manchester, and it seemed to be true because you couldn't hear the music. It was just a complete mess. A very exciting mess but people just kept screaming. These things are great memories."

Do you remember seeing him for the first time on *Top Of The Pops*?

"The first time was 'Ride A White Swan'. Nobody ever understood the lyrics. That was never important. He didn't know what he was singing about I'm sure. It just sounded good, and there are certain pop artists who go beyond explanation. You can't really explain how you felt or why you liked them.

"I suppose in a way a part of you just falls in love with them. And when you fall in love with someone it leads you. You don't know why it's happening until it's happened. And that was the way with Marc Bolan. To me he was pretty inexplicable and he seemed very lonely and mixed up and confused. And I'd never seen that in pop music before."

Was 'Cosmic Dancer' always your favourite track? (In 1991 he'd perform it live at The Forum in Los Angeles with David Bowie.)

"I thought it was a very sad song. Around the time of *Electric Warrior* I remember feeling very sad and empty. And, of course, "I danced myself into the tomb" has some weight now because, in effect, that's what he did. I recently heard a very old record from the Fifties which used the same line, which also interested me."

* 'Great Horse' would appear on Morrissey's 2003 *Under The Influence* compilation.

Was Marc the original glam rocker?

"It's hard to say. If you see very early Alice Cooper albums or early Iggy Pop photographs and so forth . . . He seemed to be the first one who actually broke through to the mainstream, obviously wearing make-up and women's shoes, etc, even though The Stones had dragged up and so forth and flirted with interesting satanic things. But Bolan was the first one to appeal to children and appeal to young people, and he definitely had an ambisexual image if not an autosexual image. Of course, nobody will know what autosexual means. To me it was absolutely fascinating, truly fascinating, but I won't explain why!"

Were you a devoted fan right to the end?

"Well . . . I think he's been quite largely forgotten and I think the reason behind that is he deteriorated so quickly. He went downhill very, very fast. He really did lose the plot. It's terrible to say something negative about someone who was once so great when most people in life are never great. If someone can give you greatness for a few years you should be happy with that. But . . . I'm afraid he did really go a bit potty and he wrote some terrible songs towards the end."

Where were you when you heard he'd been killed (September 1977)?

"I was in Manchester listening to the radio and they played five songs in a row. And I thought 'that's very weird, is he dead? Why would they do that?' And then came a voice and it said, "Marc Bolan, who died this morning." I actually didn't feel sad, I didn't feel shocked. I accepted it very easily even though he had been such an important part of my life. I just thought, 'Well, off he goes, dancing himself into the tomb.'"

Have you pilgrimaged to the tree where the car crashed?

"Yes, I have, a couple of years ago. It's still emblazoned with old pieces of satin and tat. Does it mean anything? It's like a gravestone. Does the gravestone mean anything? Is the person there? I don't know. But yes, I've been to Barnes."

Daft question but, in terms of your youthful heroes, were you more upset by Marc Bolan's death or by Billy Fury's?

"It might be considered for both people that it was really over at the time. The death has less impact. If Bolan's death had occurred two years earlier it would have been extremely dramatic, extremely lamentable. But when you're a pop star there really is a right time to die and there's a wrong time to die. And I think Marc was just a bit too late really. Billy Fury also. He had retired and gone to live in Wales on his farm."

While David Bowie and Marc Bolan were influential figures in

Morrissey's teenage years, he'd also embrace other artists such as Mott The Hoople. In May 2006, when he played Manchester Opera House, he revealed he'd seen Mott The Hoople, supported by Queen, there in November 1973.

"I'd first seen Bolan and Mott The Hoople in 1972," Morrissey told me. (Mott had played Manchester's Free Trade Hall in February 1972.) "And also Bowie pre-*Aladdin Sane*. I was less enamoured with *Aladdin Sane*. 'Starman' was the beginning and then instantly the back catalogue, the previous three albums I thought were more appealing. There are some tracks on *Ziggy Stardust* I can live without."

But it would be the camply outrageous New York Dolls (briefly managed by Sex Pistols' svengali Malcolm McLaren) who really stunned Morrissey and spurred him into action to become the UK president of their fan club. They had been due to play Manchester's Hard Rock in November 1972 but drummer Billy Murcia died suddenly aged only 21, depriving Morrissey of the chance to see his new heroes. He later recalled, "Back in 1973, the Dolls were total outcasts."

Although he once stated that he "always saw them as an absolutely male group, I never saw them as being remotely effeminate", his 1981 book *The New York Dolls* described them as "transsexual junkies . . . downed out highschool toughs posing as bisexual psychopaths . . . That they looked like haggard hookers from a Fifties B-movie became immaterial. Nothing could detract from *that* music." In a 2006 documentary about Arthur 'Killer' Kane, the recently departed Dolls' bass player, he'd describe them as looking like "male prostitutes".

If Billy Fury was a tragic solo figure, then bands didn't come more doomed than The New York Dolls. Johnny Thunders and Jerry Nolan – who left the Dolls to form The Heartbreakers with Richard Hell – also died relatively young. (The Smiths would support Richard Hell at Manchester's rafters in early 1983.)

"The New York Dolls were my private 'Heartbreak Hotel', in the sense that they were as important to me as Elvis Presley was important to the entire language of rock'n'roll," Morrissey later explained. "The New York Dolls were the best group ever to come out of America, and they were loathed by America at that time. They were an early version of The Sex Pistols, and if America and the American music industry had been alert enough in 1972 and 1973, The New York Dolls could have changed so much.

"There's this enormous capacity (within the music press) not to recognise anything until it's gone. They're never quite there. They were never there for Patti Smith. They were never there when The Ramones were making incredible records. They were never there for the New York Dolls. For Motley Crue yes, but not for the New York Dolls."*

One of the driving forces behind Morrissey's own career has been this desire to educate and enlighten others about the importance of his own particular musical passions. Once success arrived he would generously encourage new talents, from Phranc, Easterhouse and James through to The Killers, The Ordinary Boys and Kristeen Young. Certainly he refuses to forget the key musical influences that inspired him and, with The New York Dolls in particular, he'd strive to keep their name alive. In 2004 he reunited them for the Meltdown festival he curated at London's Royal Festival Hall and they supported him on tour that summer. An email he sent me from Chicago in July 2004 expressed his great sadness at Killer Kane's death.

Although Morrissey has always stressed the importance of his eclectic musical tastes – "If I was simply a hard-edged Stooges, Dolls buff . . . I'd probably be in The Alarm playing bass. I'm not because I can also appreciate Buffy Sainte-Marie." – in his youth the Dolls changed him and, arguably, changed British music too by hastening the slow death of Prog Rock and heralding the dawn of Punk. Certainly Morrissey's attention turned towards America and the New York New Wave scene that grew up around CBGBs, featuring acts such as The Ramones, Blondie and particularly Patti Smith.

Like The New York Dolls, Patti Smith's role in the creation of Morrissey cannot be overestimated. Her extraordinary album *Horses* would be one of the main musical connections between Morrissey and Johnny Marr and their joint passion for her art inspired the choice of The Smiths as a band name. Songs like 'Piss Factory' and 'Radio Ethiopia' made a great impression on Morrissey and her close associations with figures such as Allen Ginsburg and Robert Mapplethorpe would inspire the teenager on a teenage tourist visit to New York.

Morrissey would later cover Patti's 'Redondo Beach' and also followed in her footsteps by celebrating the life and work of Pier Paolo Pasolini.

---

* Most music critics at the time, especially those working for *NME* and *Melody Maker*, supported the Dolls in the face of industry neglect, while the only magazines that supported LA's 'big hair' bands were those devoted exclusively to Heavy Metal. Also, the Dolls were signed to Mercury by A&R man Paul Nelson, a former rock critic.

Mapplethorpe once photographed Patti Smith in front of an image of Pasolini scrawled with the graffiti "Pasolini est vie". Morrissey paid tribute to the murdered *Accatone* director on 'You Have Killed Me' and also used an almost-spiritual image of Pasolini as the backdrop to his *Ringleader Of The Tormentors* tour in 2006.

Patti Smith had come out of another scene that fascinated Morrissey; the Andy Warhol Factory set that dominated the New York art scene in the Sixties and Seventies. Crucially, one of Warhol's closest associates was another Morrissey, Paul. It's worth noting here − given the title of Morrissey's 1993 solo live album *Beethoven Was Deaf* − that Paul Morrissey also directed an art movie titled *Beethoven's Nephew*, in which the deaf composer was also portrayed as an unlovable uncle. Another Morrissey film, *Women In Revolt*, starred the transsexual Candy Darling (cover star of The Smiths' 'Sheila Take A Bow').

The vibrant New York music scene, which predated the British punk movement by almost two years, had attracted future Sex Pistols manager Malcolm McLaren who brought some of its imagery back to London. He'd been impressed by the sight of Richard Hell in Television, the first 'punk' to display his credentials with cropped spiky hair, a torn T-shirt, sunglasses and a blank expression, and tried to persuade him to relocate to London. Unable to do so, McLaren had fed the same look to the Pistols in 1975. Famously, Morrissey would be one of the few brave Mancunians who attended the Sex Pistols' gig at The Lesser Free Trade Hall on June 4, 1976. (The Smiths would perform there on March 13, 1984 and October 30, 1986.)

"It was a fantastic night. Nobody moved. People sat in awe. Those early appearances in Manchester by The Sex Pistols and The Buzzcocks were truly. . . . I hate to use the word 'magical' but I have to use it I suppose . . . I seem to recall being a spectator at almost every seminal performance in the movement's evolution, especially in the North."

Apart from the impact of The Sex Pistols, Morrissey was also impressed by The Ramones and The Buzzcocks in particular because they were "the only ones who possibly sat down beforehand and worked out what they intended to do". By and large he regarded Punk as "a musical movement without music", between 1976 and 1977; "a nice interval, criminally short, very useful".

Although the Punk movement seems to have given him the self belief, or simply encouraged the expectation, that he might one day make the journey from the audience to the stage, it would still be another six years before he found a real musical soulmate. Following his parents' eventual divorce, Morrissey left home and lived in a rented room in Whalley Range ('Still Ill') with the artist and Ludus singer Linder Sterling. Side-stepping conjecture about the nature of their relationship, Nick Kent later wrote in *The Face* that Linder Ludus "had a pretty severe effect on the young aesthete". Kent suggested, with limited evidence, that Linder had inspired two of Morrissey's earliest lyrics, 'Wonderful Woman' and 'Jeane'.

James Maker, one of Morrissey's few stalwart friends at the close of the Seventies, later offered a useful snapshot of the young Morrissey at this time: "At the age of 17 he was possessed of great intellect and humour. He breathed for art. He relied and depended on nobody but himself". However, this would contrast somewhat with Morrissey's later self-portrait of the artist as a young man: "The sad obsessive loner. The idea of me becoming what I have become was unthinkable . . . I was a very deep, to say the least, teenager."

By now, significantly, and in truly Wildean fashion, he would soon sever his Christian name. "Steve The Nutter" would die and people would have to refer to him solely as 'Morrissey'. "I just felt this absolutely massive relief at not being called Steven anymore," he explained, as if the act in itself distanced him from that awkward Stretford youth, that unfortunate Salford lad. Maybe the name Morrissey gave him more authority, more confidence as he began his assault on the Manchester music scene; clearly he felt post-Punk music – populated by assorted Mancunian eccentrics such as Howard Devoto and Vini Reilly – would be the best, perhaps only, route out of his personal ghetto. Traditional paths, such as boxing or professional football or snooker or darts, weren't really options.

Inspired by Punk's democratic or anarchic notion that anyone with or without a smidgeon of musical ability could just stand up, perform and even penetrate the charts, Morrissey had a brief stint with The Nosebleeds (supporting Magazine at Manchester's Ritz in spring 1978 with Billy Duffy, later of The Cult, on guitar) and also auditioned for Slaughter & The Dogs. Devoto, the ex-Buzzcock and Magazine leader, would recall seeing Morrissey singing 'Needle In A Haystack' by The Marvellettes.

As Morrissey later observed, "Perhaps the unfortunate aspect of being a pop artist is that, up until the point where you fulfil your obsessions, it can only be recognised as madness. Making records seems to legitimise one's insanity, which is very useful."

Speaking to him over the years, it still seems astonishing that he has triumphed as a performer. Apart from the likeable shyness, the slight physical awkwardness, the self-deprecating sense of humour and the negative self-analytical mangle he often puts himself through, there must be some unfathomable special quality inside him; something that sets him apart the millions of us who've had dreams of becoming a pop star but have inevitably settled for something more realistic. Deep down, whatever this quality is, whether you brand it as an irritating talent or an extraordinary genius, some inner inexplicable force has driven him forward and transformed him into a remarkable poet and showman.

Or could it just be that, through serendipity or perhaps some magnificent, chemical reaction, the coincidental arrival of another person in Morrissey's life caused this strange metamorphosis? Certainly, in the words of James Maker, "when Johnny Marr and Morrissey met, they were a rare gift and a salvation to each other".

Morrissey himself later reflected of his depressing struggle to find a musical soulmate: "The main reason for my not being able to do anything really constructive before Johnny's arrival is that with all the desires I had been harbouring for years, if anyone else existed out there who shared the same creative urges that person was invariably incredibly depressed, totally disorganised and somehow unsalvageably doomed. In other words, a complete slut."

Johnny Marr (John Maher, born October 31, 1963), from Ardwick Green and later Wythenshawe, was working in a shop called X-Clothes next to Joe Moss' Crazy Face boutique. Moss played an important role in the early development of The Smiths and, to begin with, acted as their chief financial supporter and early manager. (Johnny changed his name to Marr to avoid confusion with Buzzcocks' drummer John Maher.)

Marr recalled in *NME* in early 1984, how "round about 14 or 15, I came into contact with Morrissey through a couple of friends who knew him because of the New York Dolls infatuation, and I was just sort of completely struck by him . . . I'd known of him a couple of years because of his involvement in groups with Billy Duffy."

Inspired by a Lieber & Stoller South Bank Show, Marr "just decided to go round and knock on his door" in May 1982. During their brief, inevitably awkward doorstep conversation, Marr recalled using the confident phrase, "I know who you are. I'm a fabulous guitar player and I'm interested in forming a group . . . let me in!"

Within weeks, early demos of extraordinary songs such as 'Suffer Little Children' and 'The Hand That Rocks The Cradle' had been recorded.

The partnership was initially built on shared musical interests: Marc Bolan, David Bowie, American girl groups like The Shangri-Las and The Shirelles, the New York Dolls, Patti Smith, The Stooges, Lou Reed and even the early Rolling Stones singles. Marr already had a track record as a musician in Manchester having played with funk band Freak Party and been involved with other Manchester bands such as White Dice.

Morrissey recalled their first meeting: "I was so utterly impressed and infatuated that even if he couldn't have played it didn't matter somehow because the seeds were there and from those seeds anything could sprout. He appeared at a time when I was deeper than the depths . . . he provided me with this massive energy boost. I could feel Johnny's energy just seething inside me."

Marr was equally impressed with their early attempts to make beautiful music together: "It was the first time I heard Morrissey sing as I thought he could. From that moment on I knew we were different, and very, very good . . . every word had such real impact that once I'd recovered it suddenly hit me that before this moment I'd never really listened to a lyricist before . . . I felt we were making rock music with some art in it . . . we didn't do any mundane songs and we were making music that said very different things about sex, politics and society."

Early doubts about this odd combination would be dispelled when they took the stage at Manchester's Ritz ballroom in October 1982 supporting the New Romantic chart act Blue Rondo A La Turk, and also sharing the bill with a local drag artist. According to Joe Moss, "They were absolutely incredible. There was only one place they were going."

Although Dale Hibbert played bass at this debut gig, the famous Smiths line-up was soon completed when a schoolfriend and Freaky Party bandmate of Johnny Marr's, Andy Rourke, joined to play bass alongside former Victim drummer Mike Joyce. While Morrissey was already well into his twenties, the other three Smiths wouldn't leave their teens until after the release of their first single 'Hand In Glove'.

Live, the early Smiths would also sometimes feature James Maker as a male go-go dancer – in the style of Warhol's Factory/Velvet Underground – a decade ahead of Happy Mondays' Bez and the Stone Roses' Cressa.*

---

* Maker went on to form the Rough Trade band Raymonde and, 20 years later, would be one of Morrissey's first signings to his Attack label. Morrissey also covered Raymonde's 'No One Can Hold A Candle To You' and featured the original track on his 2004 compilation CD *Songs To Save Your Life*.

After further Manchester gigs at venues such as Manhattan, Rafters, and the relatively-new Hacienda twice (on February 4 and again on July 6, 1983, the Factory club adorned with flowers), The Smiths made their first London appearances at the Rock Garden and ULU (University of London Union). It was here that Rough Trade's Geoff Travis decided to sign them, stealing the band away from the obvious deal with Manchester's own Factory Records, fronted by Tony Wilson and home of Joy Division, now New Order. (Rob Gretton, New Order's manager, had been un-impressed by The Smiths' demo.)

Travis had already heard a tape he'd been given by Johnny Marr of 'Hand In Glove' and 'Handsome Devil'. Travis later remarked: "What was brilliant about Johnny was the fact that for someone of his age, his knowledge of music was breathtaking. He knew who John Renbourn was. He knew who Richard Thompson was. I always thought he was an extraordinary guitar player because he had that lightness of touch, which is what made him really unique."

For better or perhaps worse (with the glorious benefit of hindsight), the deal between Rough Trade and The Smiths was signed in June 1983. Clearly, at the time, they'd decided to follow in the footsteps of bands like Aztec Camera, The Monochrome Set, The Slits, Scritti Politti and The Fall, attracted by the independent philosophy behind the label and guaran-tees of artistic control. Initially it would seem the right decision when record plugger Scott Piering secured the early, crucial Radio One sessions on the John Peel and David Jensen shows that helped propel The Smiths to the top of the Independent charts. But although the terms of the deal were extremely favourable to Morrissey and Marr – the only two Smiths' signatories – years later the details of the deal, which excluded Mike Joyce and Andy Rourke, would prove to be a legal minefield.

What set The Smiths apart from all other bands on the Independent scene in 1983? Apart from Johnny Marr's way with a guitar and Morrissey's way with words, Joe Moss thought The Smiths "a very well calculated operation" while Marr clearly agreed that Morrissey had care-fully plotted their route to success: "It was almost like he was just waiting for the group to form. A lot of his output and decisions had been decided years ago, without a doubt . . . obviously he'd been working on the artwork for years and honing his own art." Paul Morley, writing in *Blitz* magazine, later paid tribute to the vision behind the campaign: "Morrissey has been very carefully worked out as if it was all planned in the bedroom."

Without doubt The Smiths were utterly different, completely unlike anything else in the British music industry in the early Eighties. Against all the odds, stacked against him throughout his childhood, Morrissey was emerging as a charismatic frontman, a provocative spokesman for an independent generation. The Smiths knew where they were going but had they signed to the right record label to get them there?

Interestingly Morrissey later told me that Rough Trade weren't the only London-based label initially keen to sign The Smiths. Before signing with Geoff Travis, the band had come close to joining EMI Records.

"It's hard to say what would have happened if, for instance, The Smiths had been on a major label initially. Interestingly, EMI were the first record label that were ever interested in The Smiths and actually put The Smiths in the studio in 1982 and consequently rejected the outcome."

What tracks did you give them?

"We gave them 'What Difference Does It Make?', 'Handsome Devil' and 'Miserable Lie' which they deemed unsuitable. It's quite interesting that two years later one of those songs was a Top 20 hit."

4.

The New Morrissey Express

"Let me assure you that nothing is as guaranteed to set the NME ablaze with hyperbole, insult, slander, accusation and threat as this man."

– Stuart Maconie

BY the time I joined the staff of *New Musical Express* at the Carnaby Street offices in the autumn of 1984, The Smiths were definitely the readers', if not the writers' favourite new band. It had been their break-through year. The debut album, *The Smiths*, had reached number two in the UK albums chart, confirming their status as much more than an 'Indie' band with a cult following, plus their triumvirate of striking, original singles 'What Difference Does It Make?', 'Heaven Knows I'm Miserable Now' and 'William, It Was Really Nothing' had all graced the Top 20 and *Top Of The Pops*. Clearly Morrissey felt a huge sense of victory and vindi-cation appearing on the cover of the music paper who'd rejected him so insensitively a few years earlier.

While *Sounds* still struggled to cast off its macho rock past, and *Melody Maker* remained the place to advertise for "frontman into Flock Of Seagulls", for me the *NME* was the only place to be if you wanted to learn to write passionately, radically and poetically about popular culture. Mid Eighties, philosophy, politics and pop music all co-existed peacefully within the pages of "The Enema"; Brecht and Rimbaud rubbed shoulders with Bono, Madonna and Rambo.

I entered the fray as a back door man, joining the production team on November 12, 1984, which would have been my brother's 23rd birthday. Surrounded by extraordinary characters and excellent writers – Charles Shaar Murray, Richard Cook, Barney Hoskyns, Chris Bohn, Paul Du Noyer et al. – I soon realised *NME* was going through a difficult period of transition, struggling to adapt, post-Punk, to the challenge of New Romanticism and the New Pop, then to intense competition from freshly

69

launched magazines as diverse as *Smash Hits* and *The Face*.

Many of the infamous old guard such as Nick Kent, Paul Morley, Danny Baker, Tony Parsons and Julie Burchill were moving on for various reasons – Morley to ZTT and Frankie Goes to Hollywood, Murray to write *Crosstown Traffic*, Burchill to assorted right-wing rags where her antagonistic columns would create a storm – but new writers were coming through, particularly Gavin Martin, Adrian Thrills, Lucy O'Brien, Paolo Hewitt, Mat Snow, Sean O'Hagan, Stuart Cosgrove and Alan Jackson. Soon diverse characters such as Danny Kelly, David Quantick, Steven Wells, Andrew Collins, John McCready and Stuart Maconie would also be cluttering up the office.

I didn't appreciate it at the time but most of us had our problems, or saw ourselves outsiders in one way or another. Perhaps, like Morrissey, this intense passion for music – this love of seeing a band live and being part of some madding crowd, this passion for direct contact with musicians via a needle on revolving vinyl – cloaked other failings in our lives? Take away the music, you'd be left with a borstal for overgrown boys or an orphanage for wayward waifs and strays.

Despite the likeably gentle leadership of first Neil Spencer and Tony Stewart, and later Ian Pye, there was a growing sense that this once radical paper was gradually being brought to heel by the management. Within a year we'd be moved from Carnaby Street into the soulless premises of Commonwealth House on New Oxford Street en route to a fate worse than death – incarceration in "the tower", IPC's Kings Reach Tower, where all the managerial suits and accountants sat in final judgement.

Within *NME* there were critics who remained unconvinced by The Smiths and disliked Morrissey, including the departing Tony Parsons (a future supporter) who savaged 'William, It Was Really Nothing' on the September 1984 singles review page: "The main manchild's self-adoring ennui sticks in the craw once you realise that this is what he's going to be doing on his death bed."

In editorial meetings there were increasing doubts about The Smiths' ability to deliver the notoriously "difficult second album", the graveyard of so many unproved bands before and since. When it became clear, in November, that Rough Trade were releasing a cut-price "interim" compilation album of Radio One sessions and alternate takes of familiar tracks and B-sides, Morrissey's enemies had a field day. Rather than another independent statement of intent, at first glance *Hatful Of Hollow* looked more like a major cash-in.

It was hard to defend but nevertheless, *Hatful Of Hollow* is still rated as one of the best of all The Smiths' album releases; Q magazine even listed it at 44 in their turn of the century 100 Greatest Albums Ever. With new improved versions of some of the early tracks on *The Smiths* and the inclusion of the moving 'This Night Has Opened My Eyes' (another lyrical re-working of *A Taste Of Honey*) it looked great, featuring a French model with a Jean Cocteau drawing tattooed on his shoulder. Cocteau had directed another Smiths' cover star, his close friend Jean Marais, in many films including *Orpheus* and his 1946 surreal fairy tale *La Belle Et La Bete*. Yet again it was an example of Morrissey's fascination with French cinema and French culture. His 2007 song, 'I'm Throwing My Arms Around Paris', would be further evidence of his ongoing affection for the city which offered Oscar Wilde a safe haven in the last years of his life.

Maybe I was wrong but at the time it struck me that the hard core of journalists at *NME* were from the South. Perhaps in step with the fashionable North-South divide of the time, some of them just didn't 'get' Morrissey and found some of his reference points too exclusively Northern, chiefly *Coronation Street* and working-class social realist films.

By early 1985 there were growing divisions within the paper concerning the importance and relevance of the band. Despite his anti-Thatcherite and Republican leanings, Morrissey was already arousing the hostility of more politically committed journalists, who seemed to think that he wasn't being honest about his true sexuality.

More critical still, the Rap, Go-Go and early House music lobby was rapidly growing in strength, arguing that *NME* should be more cutting edge rather than promoting a character such as Morrissey who they regarded as, at best, traditional and backward-looking. Already the hostile anti-Smiths letters were coming in from readers – usually variations of "why don't you just change the name of the f***ing paper to the New Morrissey Express?!" – although Smiths' supporters among us suspected most of them were written by peeved soul boys within the office.

Unlike most other artists of the time, The Smiths were incredibly productive so, unfortunately for his detractors, Morrissey just wouldn't go away or even give it a rest. Apart from the fact that he always gave good interviews and would invariably have something controversial to say, there were clearly good reasons to put The Smiths on the cover. Between early 1984 and the late summer of 1987 their output was extraordinary. Yet history also reveals the strength of the anti-Smiths lobby; far from being regulars on the cover of the paper, The Smiths made *NME*'s front page only four times during their five year career.

For those of us who admired The Smiths and were always greedy for more, the arrival of their first single of 1985, the astonishing 'How Soon Is Now?' was something of a surprise. As an advance warning of the imminent release of *Meat Is Murder*, 'How Soon Is Now?' remains one of The Smiths' finest musical and lyrical achievements; arguably, alongside 'This Charming Man' and 'There Is A Light That Never Goes Out', one of their truest creations. Backed by the heartbreaking, rain-soaked beauty of 'Well I Wonder' (and the classic instrumental 'Oscillate Wildly' on the 12-inch), 'How Soon Is Now?' increased confident expectations of The Smiths' inevitable lurch towards world domination; particularly after Sire Records boss Seymour Stein branded it "the Stairway To Heaven of the Eighties". (Sire even created an authorised video to promote the track on MTV.)

However, the track had already graced the B-side of 'William, It Was Really Nothing' the previous September and had also been included on *Hatful Of Hollow*. Were cracks emerging in The Smiths' game-plan? Were they already running out of songs or was there some problem in their relationship with Rough Trade?

Later on, Smiths' associates such as soundman Grant Showbiz and producer John Porter seemed to signal the band's annoyance with Rough Trade. Boss Geoff Travis, it was claimed, had underestimated the song's potential and, as a result, had thrown it away as a B-side. So, when it was released as an A-side in February 1985, it achieved a credible 24 chart position in the circumstances.

Across the Atlantic, a young Jeff Buckley would later reminisce about the importance of 'How Soon Is Now?': "The song completely blew everything away. At the time you've got pretty much nothing, except Prince and Heavy Metal hair bands . . . it was like, whoosh, and I went out and got *Meat Is Murder*."

If anyone needed confirmation that The Smiths were one of Britain's biggest bands, on an independent label or a major, then it came in late February 1985. Their "difficult second album", or at least, their second studio album, entered the UK charts at number one displacing Bruce Springsteen's *Born In The USA*.

I'd been given an advance preview of the album at a Rough Trade launch party; a lively event typically rewarded by the non-appearance of Morrissey. But it was great to be there, at the hub of things, listening to

Meat Is Murder for the first time, then free to shoplift advance album posters and artwork. (Perhaps there's still a price to pay for these listed crimes?)

For Jeff Buckley again, *Meat Is Murder* "was the first time I'd ever heard writing like that over music like that . . . Morrissey's lyrics were so great . . . like completely freaky unique. It was just a better world than what I'd been hearing, and clever in a real admirable way, not in an annoying way. It really felt like the steam of teapots and uniforms and public schools and private schools, some sort of distant romantic vision of what it meant to be English."

Although *Meat Is Murder* suffered from a lack of hit singles, it featured some of Morrissey's funniest and most aggressively political lyrics and remains a great statement of The Smiths' philosophy. Self-produced by Morrissey and Marr, with the aid of a young engineer called Stephen Street, *Meat Is Murder*'s cover image was adapted from Emile de Antonio's documentary *In The Year Of The Pig* (1968), in which a Vietnam soldier's helmet read "Make War Not Love". Morrissey replaced this with his own pacifist, animal rights statement: "Meat Is Murder".

Although 'Nowhere Fast' would be an early indication of Morrissey's addiction to the comic protest art of mooning – later in 'Moon River', 'The World Is Full Of Crashing Bores' and on 'I Have Forgiven Jesus' – overall it's an album about violence. Violence towards children ('Barbarism Begins At Home'), the violence of the education system ('The Headmaster Ritual'), the violence of fairgrounds ('Rusholme Ruffians', which shoplifted from Victoria Wood's 'Fourteen Again') and Morrissey's own fascination with murder ('I Want The One I Can't Have') – and particularly his anger at violence towards animals. In one of his most powerful political statements he memorably outlined the source of his vegetarian beliefs: "I think as long as human beings are so violent towards animals there will be war . . . People don't realise how gruesomely and frighteningly the animal gets to the plate."

I already knew Morrissey was a campaigning vegetarian but the power of the track – Johnny Marr's chilling guitar combined with the graphic lyrics – would have a lasting impact on a generation of guilty meat-eaters.

Some might say that popular music never changes anything. But the release of *Meat Is Murder* – coupled with supportive articles such as Sean O'Hagan's well-argued *NME* piece "Why I'm Not A Fine Young Carnivore" – encouraged many Smiths' fans, including me, to commit to the cause. Even a proudly hardened flesh-eater like Paul Du Noyer, reviewing *Meat Is Murder*, commented that "pop progaganda has rarely come so powerful. What difference will it make? Not a sausage, as far as my diet goes, I'm afraid, yet the roast beef of Old England will never taste quite so good again . . . Whatever, on that track and the record as a whole, The Smiths' artistic achievement is genuinely beyond doubt."

In interviews throughout his career, Morrissey would preach passionately, consistently and aggressively against the meat industry: "I do see McDonalds as the core of modern evil because it is the death industry. I just feel rage that they will promote themselves from every possible angle, but they will not show the process by which the hamburger is made. They will not show the cows' throats being slit, the bull trying to commit suicide by banging its head against the stone floor." Although he would be criticised for supporting the Animal Rights Militia, which targeted those involved in animal experimentation for research purposes, he'd always articulately defend his position, telling *NME* in 2003, "Why not use human beings? The life of that animal is just as important to that animal as your life is to you, so why do we feel we should dominate animals just because we can? Enough animals have been experimented on over the last 40 years, enough is enough."

Morrissey's early, revealing interview with his heroine Pat Phoenix in *Blitz* magazine in May 1985 reinforced these firm beliefs. The interview confirmed Morrissey's deep affection for this strong woman, as if she was the surrogate mother he desperately wanted to be smothered by. Importantly, it touched on their mutual belief in animal rights. Morrissey: "You are a patron for Cruelty Against Circus Animals." Pat Phoenix: "Cruelty against ANY animal! And if you're going to ask me if I've got a fur coat the answer is YES. I've had it for 25 years."

Aside from the growing effect *Meat Is Murder*'s success had on The Smiths, these were also very heady days for the band's fans. Suddenly we were no longer standing in Eastern-European-style student venues or echoing leisure centres or even old sprung dance floors such as Manchester's Ritz, but were now gracing more respectable establishments such as city halls, famous theatres and, memorably on April 6, 1985, London's Royal Albert Hall.

Apart from being a momentous occasion, launched by Prokofiev's 'March Of The Capulets' and admirably supported by the Factory band James – The Smiths would soon cover James' 'What's The World' and Morrissey would later tease singer Tim Booth with his 1992 solo single

'We Hate It When Our Friends Become Successful' – the RAH show also featured a Morrissey duet with Dead Or Alive's Pete Burns on 'Barbarism Begins At Home'. The rumour machine would have it that Liverpudlian Burns, extremely camp and with a fine line in drag, was close to Morrissey in the early days of The Smiths. As usual, there would be little evidence to support these suggestions and, given Burns' decision to don a gorilla or monkey hair coat on Channel 4's *Big Brother* some 20 years later, with hindsight he hardly seemed a suitable soulmate for Morrissey.

One of the many highlights of The Smiths at the Royal Albert Hall, was the extraordinary moment when, midway through 'Meat Is Murder', Morrissey held his tambourine over Marr's head like a halo. It seemed to signify the importance of their relationship, personally and professionally. Centre stage they looked like the perfect double act, the creative power-house behind The Smiths. Increasingly, in interviews if not in live performance, it began to look as if Andy Rourke and Mike Joyce were being sidelined as minor players in this masterplan, even though they were physically crucial to The Smiths' sound.

Years later it would emerge that, contractually, Rourke and Joyce were employed by Morrissey and Marr as jobbing musicians, rather than treated legally as full members of The Smiths. Although Marr would explain that "from day one Mike and Andy knew that they didn't have to do 25 per cent of the work . . . it was me and Morrissey that ran the group", as the band's music became internationally successful (particularly after the deathly split) this unsettled situation would lead to problems. I remember once walking into the production office at *NME*, where the talented art editor Joe Ewart was designing the coming week's paper, looking at colour transparencies of The Smiths taken by photographer Lawrence Watson. The photos were of all four Smiths but Morrissey must have had approval over which of the frames could be used. Next to a preferred shot, written in Morrissey's familiar, half-childlike-half-serial-killer-style hand-writing, it simply read: "Yes, but lose Bill and Ben."

In many ways, the *Meat Is Murder* tour would be a turning point for The Smiths. With the rising fame and the critical and commercial success came additional stresses and strains; the combined pressures of being creative by day and performers by night, accompanied by the perpetual demand to promote their message and music in the media, plus the problems caused by the band's flawed managerial structure. Behind the scenes, known only to Johnny Marr, bassist Andy Rourke was now struggling with serious drug addiction.

Explaining the need for secrecy, Marr would later reveal: "I was his best friend, and he was my friend, so that's what you do . . . we were terrified because we had an anti-drugs policy". With hindsight, Rourke's problem would eventually mean an end to the famous four-piece line-up and the recruitment of a fifth member to cover for him the following year. In a later interview with Johnny Rogan, Marr would recall that "our families' lives were changing because we'd become successful so quickly. Their lives had been turned around as well. In mine and Andy's case, it was the first time the family had something to be proud of. No one wanted to screw that up for Andy. And, an important point, we didn't want to screw it up for Morrissey."

The drug problem was kept from the fans, the media and from Morrissey, as the band battled on with the hard-edged Virginia Woolf-inspired single 'Shakespeare's Sister' and the live spectacle captured in March of 1985 by the BBC at the Oxford Apollo Theatre. But the disappointing chart position for 'Shakespeare's Sister', after the relative failure of 'How Soon Is Now?' and followed by another flop single 'That Joke Isn't Funny Anymore' (number 49 in July), further convinced Morrissey that either The Smiths were being gagged by Radio One or Rough Trade were failing the band in terms of promotion. (In retaliation, Geoff Travis of Rough Trade blamed the quality of the songs: "I don't think EMI could have done any better.")

By October 1985 it seemed that The Smiths were already moving in a new musical direction. 'The Boy With The Thorn In His Side', featuring some of Johnny Marr's most inspired guitar work, made it into the lower reaches of the UK Top 30 and, importantly, looked forward to the next album rather than harking back to *Meat Is Murder*.

Again, it can't be overstressed how prolific The Smiths were; perhaps too creative for their own good and longevity in terms of their intense writing, recording, touring and promotional schedule. Three studio albums in less than two and a half years plus three compilations featuring many non-album tracks (*Hatful Of Hollow, The World Won't Listen* and *Louder Than Bombs*) within a grand total of four years. Perhaps only R.E.M. and Prince matched this level of productivity. (More sensibly perhaps, U2 would take 18 months between *War,* released in March 1983, and *The Unforgettable Fire*, which entered the UK charts in October 1984, followed by *The Joshua Tree* in March '87.)

It's also important to note that, in addition to this studio-album-a-year output and the stream of original singles – three in '84, four in '85, three in

The New Morrissey Express

'86 – The Smiths also prided themselves on the extraordinary quality of their B-sides, which were like thrown away bits of paradise.

'The Boy With The Thorn In His Side' 12-inch perfectly illustrated this. One of their best-loved creations, 'Rubber Ring', leads beautifully into another song that saved my life, 'Asleep'; an astonishing track that deals with suicide in a poetic and understanding way.* As someone bereaved by suicide, still one of the great unspoken taboos in British Christian society, I'll always admire Morrissey for even attempting to tackle such a difficult subject, let alone succeeding so sensitively.

Unfortunately, the high standards Morrissey and Marr set for themselves, even in terms of the quality of (what most other artists would consider) less important tracks, added further pressure to their partnership. Regardless of the ongoing problems behind the scenes, in 1986 The Smiths were approaching their creative peak. They started the year by performing at the From Manchester With Love concert at Liverpool's Royal Court Theatre, a benefit for the city's councillors who were in legal conflict with the Thatcher government over the rate-capping policy (designed to force Left-wing local governments to reduce the cost of public services).

Morrissey was a somewhat reluctant participant in these political fund-raising events but it's significant that both The Fall and New Order were also on the bill. Johnny Marr would later go on to work with New Order's Bernard 'Barney' Sumner in Electronic in the early Nineties, while Andy Rourke and Mike Joyce were already doing extra-curricular work with Brix Smith's Fall spin-off The Adult Net; two years later, when The Smiths collapsed, it was a connection they'd both pursue.

Despite Morrissey's suspicion of benefits and political fund-raising events, he was still developing into one of the most provocative pop stars since the two Johns – Lennon and Lydon. Shy and reticent in person but amusing and controversial in interviews, he had strongly held passions for the iconic cover stars he wanted to promote, and also had uncompromising views on other artists and other forms of music. For example, "Reggae is vile", "Rap is the degree zero of music" while "Acid House was never about music but a doorway for the drug culture . . . It was, if you asked me, the only thing Acid House achieved. The music was rubbish, just like the people who made it."

---

* In 2005, Manchester Metropolitan University staged an academic conference titled *Subjectivity, Suicide And The Smiths*.

Some critics seemed to find it annoying that so many of his statements sounded rehearsed, practiced, even scripted for maximum impact. He'd always deny this but, again, it's worth noting the influence of Oscar Wilde's conversational style here. Wilde's perfect sentences seemed to his countryman and friend Yeats to have been written "overnight with labour and yet all spontaneous". Morrissey, naturally, responded perfectly to any suggestion that he'd theatrically contrived everything: "Well, I don't slip into a suit and practice a certain tone of voice, no. There's no persona as such. It's just what you see across the table."

His detractors would claim that Morrissey was too ubiquitous for The Smiths' own good in early 1986. The chief argument against him within *NME* was that if The Smiths were really a band of equals then, for the good of Marr, Joyce and Rourke, Morrissey should now relinquish media control, step back and share the limelight. The chief soul brothers within *NME* (Stuart Cosgrove, Paolo Hewitt, Simon Witter, Denis Campbell . . .) naturally embraced Johnny Marr rather than Morrissey – who'd also described reggae as "the most racist music in the entire world" – arguing that Marr was the more positively political of the two, as proved by his friendships with Billy Bragg and Matt Johnson of The The.

This probably sounds of minor importance now but, at the time, during the chill of Thatcherism, it seemed crucial. It definitely contributed to a sense that Morrissey and Marr might be growing apart or could become incompatible and that, perhaps, Morrissey was holding Marr back.

It was a time when everyone – artists and journalists – seemed to be asking the question (politically and sexually) 'Whose Side Are You On?' Morrissey insisted on being individual, different, apart from the crowd, a card-carrying member of nothing but the cult of his own personality. He fell into half-hearted conflict with Red Wedge – I'd attended and reviewed for *NME* The Smiths' brief but brilliant Newcastle City Hall Red Wedge performance in January 1986 – and also with outwardly gay artists who implied that Morrissey was being too non-committal about his political beliefs against a background of government-inspired homophobia via the anti-AIDS campaigns.

Given the quality of the song, it still seems astonishing that 'Bigmouth Strikes Again' only reached number 26 in the UK charts. Arguably one of the catchiest of the band's singles with some of Morrissey's funniest lyrics, although The Smiths performed it on Channel 4's *The Tube* it received little Radio One airplay and confirmed Morrissey's belief that Rough

Trade lacked the clout to promote the band successfully. In the song Morrissey seemed to be responding to his tormentors, those critics who clearly felt he should learn to hold his tongue.

This wouldn't have been in keeping with the subject matter of *The Queen Is Dead*, The Smiths' third studio album, a proudly anti-royal record that's often regarded as their masterpiece. Although it reached only number two in the UK album charts in June 1986 (and failed to make *NME*'s Top Five albums of the year), in a Channel Four viewers' poll in 2005 it was voted number 20 in the Greatest Albums Ever. A similar ballot in *NME* in 2006 placed it second after *The Stone Roses*.

Despite the dying shot of French movie star Alain Delon on the cover (from *L'Insoumis*, 1964, aka *Have I The Right To Kill?*) it's a vibrant and uplifting collection of British and Irish pop songs, from the homesick lament for lost England of 'Take Me Back To Dear Old Blighty' (which is sucked into the powerful title track) through to the light-touch of Marr's fading guitar in the *Carry On Cleo*-inspired comedy of 'Some Girls Are Bigger Than Others'. Naturally, the inner sleeve is Mancunian through and through; Steven Wright's now legendary photograph of The Smiths outside Salford Lads Club.*

Along the way there are several of the most poetic songs in British popular music, notably the mortally ill 'I Know It's Over' and what would become The Smiths' (and later Morrissey's) most emotional live anthem 'There Is A Light That Never Goes Out', with its echoes of W.H. Auden's "affirming flame" on the edge of World War Two in *September 1, 1939*.

There's also 'Frankly Mr Shankly', rumoured to be an attack on Rough Trade's Geoff Travis (particularly the closing demand for more money), but which reminds of *Billy Liar* and also the brutal death of Joe Orton, fatally battered by his fame-jealous lover Ken Halliwell. (Morrissey later told me that he'd considered Orton, like Charles Hawtrey, as a possible Smiths' cover star before the band split up.) 'Cemetry Gates', complete with mis-spelling by the Salford bard, is a funny defence of plagiarism, with a nod of recognition to Manchester photographer Harold Riley and also a celebration of Oscar Wilde's pre-eminence among Morrissey's influences. Meanwhile, 'Vicar In A Tutu' mocks men of the cloth yet makes cross-dressing and trans-sexuality sound positively normal.

Amid this rich seam of unusual subject matter, *The Queen Is Dead* – its

---

* In January 2008 Morrissey pledged £20,000 to refurbish this Manchester landmark.

title lifted from the Hubert Selby Jnr's novel, *Last Exit To Brooklyn* (prosecuted in the UK in 1966 under the Obscene Publications Act and banned to protect women from "homosexuality, prostitution, drug-taking and sexual perversion") – would cause most controversy, particularly as it elevated to cult status Michael Fagin, the unemployed burglar who visited the Queen's Palace bedroom in June 1982 before being carted off to Bow Street.

If the subject matter itself is largely humorous, despite the menacing double-guitar rock it's founded on, Morrissey's comments about royalty pulled few punches: "The royal family is an institution which is built entirely on murder and deceit and fraud and hate and we should never forget these things. We shouldn't feel that simply because it's an English tradition that it's good."

While 1986 saw The Smiths at their creative peak, one of the main criticisms at the time seemed to be that Morrissey, eternally destined to be branded a control freak, was now dominating every aspect of Smithdom. Whereas before he'd simply discouraged Mike Joyce and Andy Rourke from doing interviews, now it looked as if Johnny Marr was also disappearing from view. Was this another case of the Rod Stewart-style rock disease Lead Singer Syndrome, the chief symptom being an increasing desire to treat friends and colleagues as little more than a backing band?

Andy Spinoza in Manchester's *City Life* even drew conclusions from the inner sleeve artwork of *The Queen Is Dead*: "Johnny Marr, whose evocative guitar is as much The Smiths sound as that voice, is almost totally hidden by the supreme being himself, serene against the gloom and the decay. It's a good example of how Morrissey has final say over how The Smiths are sold."

Later, Morrissey would assure me this wasn't the case: "Well, Johnny didn't have a passionate interest in the media generally, and he was always free to do whatever he liked as far as interviews were concerned. He made personal choices on each occasion to step back, so there was never any friction there.

"I think within The Smiths the reason why it worked was that everyone knew their place and knew their capabilities. Everybody understood each other's position. And that's why it worked so well until meddling hands at the end really."

It would be the arrival of another Mancunian on the scene that provoked surprise and concern in the fanbase and, several years later, to Morrissey himself. Before the completion of *The Queen Is Dead*, and while

Andy Rourke was struggling with his addiction, in April 86 Craig Gannon joined The Smiths, initially as a replacement for the ailing bassist but then, when Rourke was able to continue, as second guitarist; Gannon, with his quiff and his strange silent movie star looks, had long been hailed for his teenage guitar work with The Bluebells ('Young At Heart'), Colourfield and Aztec Camera. Arguably, if Rourke had been sacked, the decision could have broken the Morrissey-Marr partnership, particulary given Marr's closeness to his old schoolfriend. In retrospect Morrissey would say that Rourke's "leaving seemed more wrong than his staying".

Clearly Morrissey and Marr recruited Gannon to bolster *The Queen Is Dead* line-up but his membership would be short-lived following accusations of "rockism" in the music press. It was a time when r★★k was regarded as another dirty four-letter word in *NME* so now The Smiths were accused of metamorphosing into The Rolling Stones.

Victims of their own success, and with Morrissey flaunting a 'Panic' hangman's noose (promoting the new DJ-hanging single) plus a Ramones' style placard which read "The Queen Is Dead" or "Two Pints Of Light Ale Please", Smiths gigs now became more anarchic and unruly, with the trademark formerly-pacifist, stage invasions increasingly more difficult to control. Violent shows in Newport and Preston, resulting in hospital treatment for soundman Grant Showbiz and Morrissey respectively, were testament to this.

Apart from the smear of 'rockism', which naturally sat uneasily with their Rough Trade Independent image, it also looked as if The Smiths were regrouping in order to try and conquer America. Looking back on the criticisms, primarily pointed in his direction as the musical brains behind the band, Johnny Marr responded angrily, "I never, ever, wanted to turn The Smiths into The Rolling Stones . . . that was just lazy journalistic bullshit" and "There was this thing about me being the touring beast, always wanting to 'take my axe out on the road', which brings us to another classic Smiths' myth. All our tours were instigated by Morrissey. We wanted to do them but he was the instigator."

Morrissey later contradicted this suggestion when he said, "All that rock thing did confuse me. It seemed a preparation for straightforward global success, and in a way I'm quite provincial." Although Morrissey would covet and later achieve, on his own terms, a level of transatlantic success, back in 1986 and early '87 if there was a realistic belief they could conquer America it came from their US label Sire, rather from the band themselves.

As Johnny Marr stated in 1991, "In America I'd have been happy to leave a legacy like The Kinks, Roxy Music or T. Rex". An ambitious target but, without doubt, The Smiths achieved it. Sadly, the praise would be posthumous and the legacy would begin sooner than anyone imagined.

Even their greatly anticipated triumphant return to Manchester in July 1986, to play the Factory Records organised Festival Of The Tenth Summer at the city's converted railway station GMex, seemed to fall flat in Morrissey's view: "I hoped that the atmosphere backstage wouldn't be as I imagined, which was the typical Manchester iciness – nobody really speaks to each other and when they do it's on a really superficial digging nature . . . I didn't really feel any sense of unity or celebration. Nobody put their arms around me and said, 'Isn't this wonderful?' "*

Watching him from the cheap seats, the onstage Morrissey clearly relished his new-found position as either spokesman for a generation, chief source of irritation or, better still, the ringleader of the tormentors. The more controversy he created, the stronger his personality became. His old friend James Maker once said of Morrissey that "in terms of having a clear, concise agenda, implementing it with total prejudice to compromise and executing it, his style was Thatcherite."

Given The Smiths' lack of constant, secure management – they lacked the pressure-relieving continuity of someone like U2's Paul McGuinness or R.E.M.'s Jefferson Holt, a factor which would greatly hasten their demise – perhaps Morrissey decided to toughen up his offstage image and transform himself from the student-thin pipecleaner into something more substantial. One reliable and likeable eyewitness, Dave Harper, who worked for Rough Trade at the time and chauffered The Smiths round in a funeral cortege car, recalled Morrissey's strict fitness regime: "Big man for cake. Cream, you know, creamy tea-shop cake . . . And dumbbells. Big man with the weightlifting."

Managerial difficulties (caused in part by the band's lack of faith in their management) seemed to amplify the faults and also led to frictions with Rough Trade. Caretaker manager Scott Piering later recalled that, "The whole operation was just downmarket. Morrissey was becoming a big pop star and he didn't even have a bodyguard . . . He would get hit with a bottle or something, and his mum would say, 'There's not enough security!' And she was right."

With troubles brewing behind the scenes, when Nick Kent decided to

---

* Morrissey would memorably return to the cavernous GMex as a triumphant solo artist in Xmas 2006.

get to the truth about Morrissey and The Smiths for an article in *The Face* he was gently warned off by Piering who expressed concern he was talking to some of Morrissey's "arch enemies". Morrissey soon confirmed these fears that "at least one of them is a sworn enemy who would get no small amount of pleasure from wilfully misinterpreting my actions."

Without doubt, if a flammable situation needed dampening down you wouldn't call on Morrissey. Trouble, of course, loved him and rather than pulling punches you could count on him to embrace controversy.

Morrissey's relationship with the increasingly soulful, American-addicted music press – *NME* in particular – wouldn't be eased in August by the release of 'Panic', which reached number 12 in the UK charts.

Although inspired primarily by the flippancy of Radio One DJs following an alarming news flash alerting Britain to the Chernobyl disaster – Steve Wright played Wham! – Morrissey's lyrical arson attack on disco was nothing short of incendiary.

The *NME* soul posse regarded it as a deliberately hostile assault on emerging American black DJs/producers from the rising Chicago House and Detroit Techno scenes. The heated debate launched an ongoing weekly battle for control of the cover of *NME* and increased arguments within the paper between Morrissey-hating soul boys in one corner and Morrissey-supporting Indie faction in the other.

It wasn't all Morrissey's fault. In those heady days when *NME* was promoted with the dire advertising slogan "wrap your fish in nothing less", and before it went all shiny and glossy, one senior member of IPC's management even suggested that when black artists were put on the cover of *NME* readers got more ink on their hands. The editorial staff was also confronted with market research implying that white artists always sold more copies of *NME* than black artists, although in reality this issue was more about familiarity versus unfamiliarity, the established against the new rather than issues of race or colour.

Nevertheless, there was growing external pressure to feature white acts from major labels on the cover, chiefly because majors always spent more than the independents on advertising space. This was also a business response to increasing competition from other music magazines (notably *Q*'s appearance in 1986) and also the launch of more general interest men's lifestyle magazines (*Arena*, *Blitz* and *Sky*).

This IPC management interference, fought vigorously by the editorial staff led by editor Ian Pye, certainly exacerbated the internal musical and political differences. *NME* had always prided itself on being at the cutting edge of pop culture; leading its audience rather than simply feeding audience demands. As ever with The Smiths, battle lines were drawn up between those who felt the paper should continue to give the readers their fix of Morrissey and those who thought it was time for *NME* to set a new agenda, embracing the diverse forms of black American music that were increasingly dominating the charts and the London club scene. (Acid House was already emerging following the release of Phuture's *Acid Trax*.)

One memorably heated editorial meeting – always an exciting, passionate and amusing handbags-at-twenty-paces slanging-match between the more fashion-conscious loafered soul boys and the less-elegantly dressed pro-Morrissey brigade – centred on whether the paper should continue its post-'Panic' love affair with Morrissey or become more "forward thinking" by celebrating the presence in Britain of Washington D.C.'s Go-Go kings Trouble Funk with their 'Good To Go' 12-inch.

Against this heated background in the summer of 1986 – God knows, it felt a question of life and death within *NME* at the time but, I suppose, with the passage of time there was perhaps a childish element of over-reaction on my part – that I reviewed The Smiths at the Mayfair Ballroom in my hometown Newcastle.

We're huddled together (2,000 of us) in the home of heavy metal, witnessing the early disturbed sound of 'Bigmouth Strikes Again'. But thankfully they're just warming up; with Morrissey revealed as a shy thin man eternally trying to capture his shirt-tails.

His presence alone makes The Smiths a unique live force; Joyce is buried beneath drums, Rourke's like a zombie, new recruit Gannon's as stiff as a juvenile Ed Collins, while Marr – the boy wonder – calmly controls our changing moods. The new Rolling Stones? Don't talk crap. Jagger never really meant it.

"We know you and you can't sing," we chant at Morrissey during 'The Queen Is Dead' and yet here we are, lapping up his every heartfelt yodel, hanging DJs on his every word; because those of us of a melancholy hue – who are prone to bouts of debilitating self-pity and a little in love with death – find reassurance in these lyrics. His open-hearted poetry is gilded with a passionate humour which only the insensitive, the deaf and the emotionally deformed choose to reject.

Live there's a marvellous bond between us. Perhaps this music is less infectiously danceable, less call-and-response community orientated than, say,

Trouble Funk, but the latter says little to me about my life. For me, Morrissey deals with the very real, very individual concerns. Maybe it's this obsession with uncertainty, with mortality, these intimations of the grave; tonight's rendition of 'I Know It's Over' features his finest live vocal to date.

The music of Joy Division and The Smiths "is a catharsis for the artist and works as a catharsis for the listener" (wrote my colleague Don Watson). Precisely. For here we are releasing our fascination with death ('Cemetry Gates', sic), remembrance for lost loved ones, failed affairs ('I Want The One I Can't Have') and unnatural emotions. Perhaps I'm taking all this too seriously, but the only certainty is that nothing is certain.

Those who have never seen The Smiths accuse Morrissey of being a miserable, egotistical, arrogant bastard. Yet live, in the flesh, these criticisms evaporate because it's all part of his tongue-in-cheek, self-deprecating humour. He's seriously obsessed with the elevation of beauty ("That which the bourgeois call ugly" – Wilde), with overturning conventions and establishing new meanings.

Mixed in are trivial everyday concerns with hair, shoes, the cut of his trousers and the hot breath of the 21st century on his neck. Of course, without the music, few would listen to him. Magical highlights here included Marr's metal groove on 'Panic' and the new 'Ask', Joyce's furious beating on 'Shakespeare's Sister' and Rourke's groin-twanging bass on the 'His Latest Flame'/'Rusholme Ruffians' medley.

But it comes to an end too soon when several phlegm-throwers dampen the sun that shines out of his behind. Perhaps Morrissey's flirtation with a cretin-hopping gabba-gabba-hey banner reading "The Queen Is Dead" transported the resident morons back to barbaric punkdom.

And will fatal fame go to Morrissey's head? The graveyards are full of indispensable people and he can't forget it. But perhaps it's inevitable that an inferior lyric hitched to a repetitive Marr riff must one day turn The Smiths into superstars. Then Fleet Street will hound him and the dream will be over.

"Are you good to go?" Er, maybe, but where are we going and what will we do when we get there?

When this review was published, I was heavily criticised, by Smiths' supporter Adrian Thrills among others, for going "over the top" and inflaming a sensitive situation. Maybe that's exactly what I did but, like many fans, I felt strongly (and still do!) that 'Panic' had been misinterpreted and that these early, smearing suggestions that Morrissey was somehow being racist were utterly unfounded.

What seems more significant re-reading the review is the second last paragraph, which seems in a strange Wildean way – "each man kills the thing he loves" – to will the death of the band I loved. Was I just preparing myself for the inevitable or was there something in the air that night in Newcastle? Perhaps the behind-the-scenes problems within The Smiths had begun to come to the fore and somehow, on the sprung floor of the Mayfair, when Morrissey crooned 'I Know It's Over' to his congregation, we all felt that the end was nigh.

Certainly life didn't get any easier for The Smiths in late 1986, despite the brief success of the addictive new single 'Ask' – a hymn to the shy – which reached number 14 in November, with *Man About The House*, *George & Mildred* television star Yootha Joyce on the cover.*

From July 30 to September 10, 1986, The Smiths toured Canada and the USA. Despite the excellent reception they received, it transpired that relations within the band were deteriorating all the time. Later even Morrissey, trying to put a positive spin on events, gave the impression that The Smiths were now struggling: "Oh, the tour of America was victorious as far as audience attendances were concerned but we could never really breathe when we felt like . . . the product."

More significantly, for Johnny Marr it was the point at which "I just stopped liking the other members of the group, and I stopped liking myself."

On their return, having played another 13 UK dates (including journeys from Carlisle to Cornwall then back to Manchester), exhaustion set in. In November Johnny Marr was injured in a car crash and, as a result, The Smiths' appearance in an Artists Against Apartheid benefit at the Royal Albert Hall was cancelled. Meanwhile, Craig Gannon's brief involvement with The Smiths came to an unhappy end in December.

When I met Craig in Manchester in spring 1989 I must admit I felt some sympathy with him – he seemed to have been brought in to help The Smiths through a difficult patch, then found himself blamed for the 'rockist' accusations and surplus to requirements barely eight months later.

To begin with, he recalled, "I was gonna stand in to play bass (during Andy Rourke's illness) but it went really well with two guitars and Andy stayed on . . . I wasn't a Smiths fan before, I liked the singles but I'd never

---

* The German version featured Colin Campbell from *The Leather Boys*. According to Morrissey's assistant Jo Slee: "I'd say *The Leather Boys* is the third most important film to Mozz after *A Taste Of Honey* and *Saturday Night And Sunday Morning*."

heard their LPs. It went really well, I fitted in and they thought so too. I was just myself." But everything changed, after the recording of *Rank* (at London's Kilburn National Ballroom in October) and on the American tour: "I was just really frustrated, it did work out but things were going on in me head. I was getting really uptight about things, I just decided I've got to get out of this."*

Despite all this unmanaged behind-closed-doors unhappiness, the final moments of *The Queen Is Dead* tour felt totally triumphant to those of us who'd witnessed the five-piece Smiths storming through memorable gigs at Kilburn, the London Palladium and, finally, their last ever UK gig at Brixton Academy; although it did seem unusual that they signed off with two of their earliest compositions – 'William, It Was Really Nothing' and 'Hand In Glove'.

At the death of 1986 it seemed as if the world, chiefly America, was finally prepared to listen and, with Gannon gone, it appeared on the surface that all might be well again with the original four members. Perhaps normal Smiths service would be resumed?

* Although Morrissey would bring Craig Gannon back into the fold for the solo come-back concert in Wolverhampton two years later, by the time I interviewed Morrissey near Reading in 1991, Gannon's legal victory over The Smiths would definitely be a very sore point.

5.

Sex And The Single Male

"Whatever people say I am, that's what I am not. Because they don't know a bloody thing about me. God knows what I am."

– Arthur Seaton, *Saturday Night And Sunday Morning*

"Every song is about sex. I'm very interested in gender. I feel I'm kind of a prophet for the fourth sex. The third sex, even that has been done and it's failed . . . It sounds trite in print but it's something close to 'Men's Liberation' that I desire. I'm bored with men and I'm bored with women. All this sexual segregation that goes on, even in rock & roll, I really despise it . . ."

– Morrissey

IF you've turned straight to this page then I'm very, very disappointed in you. You must have a one-track mind. The truth is that, after you've met Morrissey several times, inevitably the uninitiated – the non-fans, the opponents of The Smiths – always ask the same questions. If it's not the negatively predictable "Is he as miserable as he sounds?" or, post-Madstock 1992, "Do you reckon he's a racist?", invariably, it's the blunt tabloid-style rummaging-through-dustbins approach to his personal and sexual life.

Obviously the carefully chosen images he's used on Smiths covers, the reference points in songs and interviews, plus the celebration of unconventional, equivocal sexuality in his lyrics, deliberately confirm the notion that Morrissey is not your average, run-of-the-mill, *boring* heterosexual rock star. But can his existence really be as solitary as he'd have us believe? Can it be true that "the day always ends the same way, with exactly the same scenario. I'm closing the door and putting the lights out, and fumbling for a book"?

The sexual leanings and yearnings (or lack of them) of the young, before-he-was-famous Steven Morrissey have long been a source of fascination to Smiths' critics. Given his famous statement that "I always thought my genitals were the result of some crude practical joke" (see Orton, Joe) and his devout love of the safely-bawdy seaside-postcard humour of the *Carry On* films, there's naturally been this temptation (playfully encouraged by the man himself) to try to move beyond his frequent No Sex Please I'm Celibate protestations.

For one so self-confessedly pure, so removed from human physical affection, Morrissey in live performance remains a strange-to-behold and sexually charged experience. From the early days of The Smiths there were stage invasions, open gestures of love and adoration from fans of all sexual persuasions. When David Thomas of *Spin* suggested to him in 1992, "maybe you're giving them the hugs they don't get anywhere else?" Morrissey replied, "I thought they were giving me the hugs that I didn't get anywhere else."

From the beginning of his career, Morrissey was being "pushed and prodded" to clearly state his sexual orientation and nail his colours to one particular mast, often by the gay press and gay rights activists. Back in early 1984, even before the first album came out, he was complaining to *NME*, "I hate this 'festive faggot' thing which seems to come through because people listen to 'This Charming Man' and think no further than anyone would presume. I hate that angle, and it's surprising that the gay press have harped on about that more than anyone else."

When Barney Hoskyns responded by suggesting such presumptions were inevitable given his inviting lyrics about exchanging underwear, typically Morrissey's reply refused to defuse the tease. "It's just being honest. It's saying, 'I don't want to sit here for hours and hours talking about W.H. Auden when we just want to exchange underwear or something.'"

Although, sadly, in the 21st century it's clear we do still feel the need to pigeonhole people sexually, back in the dark grim days of the Eighties – that era in which Right-wing Christians tried to convince us that AIDS was a modern plague sent by God to punish the sinful sodomites; that decade of re-ignited Victorian values when opposition to equal rights for gays and lesbians sought to revive the moral climate that destroyed Oscar Wilde less than a century earlier – it was almost impossible for anyone in public life to be equivocal or in denial about their sexuality.

Pat Reid, in his slim volume *Morrissey* (Outlines, 2004) pointed out that "in the Eighties, some gay activists were angered by Morrissey appropriating gay icons for Smiths sleeves" while refusing to become involved in their cause for equality.*

It was a time of social division in Britain – the North–South divide, the divide and rule of Thatcherism, the divisive ruling of Section 28 (basically anti-gay Local Government legislation) – when the press on one side of the fence and pressure groups on the other demanded to know where 'celebrities' (to use the tarnished, 21st century catch-all phrase for 'people in the public eye') stood or, in Establishment cricket speak, which "side" they batted for.

Elton John bore the brunt of the tabloid attacks, such as the infamous *Sun* headline "Good On Yer Poofter" (when he married Renate Blauel in 1984), and his treatment hardly encouraged other artists to be candid. Red top papers at this time seemed obsessed with pigeonholing celebrities into one camp or another, with no allowance for celibacy, so Morrissey's refusal to say where he stood was both provocative and irritating for them. Regardless of his sexual preferences, in Morrissey's case the presentation of a monastic solitary sex-free artistic life must have seemed preferable to the possibility of being targetted by the UK tabloids.

"How strange, then, that the man who claimed to never have sex was also the man who did more than any other to open up discussion and awareness of sex in the Eighties via the medium of music" (Pat Reid).

In 1984 Morrissey had even stated that "I'm just simply inches away from a monastery and I feel that perhaps if I wasn't doing this that I probably would be in one." Twenty years later the song remained the same: "I was never a sexual person," he declared in 2003's Channel Four documentary *The Importance Of Being Morrissey*. Along similar lines, Joe Orton once wrote in his diaries about Kenneth Williams, one of Morrissey's heroes, that "Kenneth W. isn't able to have sex properly with man or woman. His only outlet is exhibiting his extremely funny personality in front of an audience, and when he isn't doing this, he's a very sad man indeed."

When Williams himself was interviewed in *NME* by John McCready, in August 1986, he reflected briefly on his own sex life: "God's said, 'You're not much cop at living how a man should live – there won't be any issue of the loins. We better give you some compensation. We'll make

---

* These were also the early days of Peter Tatchell's OutRage, the direct action group which supported the outing of privately homosexual public figures as part of a political campaign.

you a performer!" Could this be what Morrissey meant when he suggested, in 'Pretty Girls Make Graves' that he wasn't the man we thought he was? Or declared '(I'm) The End Of The Family Line'? Early on in his dealings with *NME* he'd also stated, "I'm not really stimulated by male or female."

In the Eighties, the art of being celibate didn't seem acceptable or even believable to most sections of the British press. Representatives of the music papers tried their best to trowel through Morrissey's past, challenging him to come out of whatever closet he was supposed to be hiding in and simply explain what really buttered his parsnips. *Anything* but celibacy. "I'm just one of those people that God marked on the forehead saying, 'You're not meant to have a happy, fulfilling, physical relationship.'" As ever, Morrissey's reluctance to play the game, his ongoing commitment to doing the opposite of what was expected of him – the slippery gospel of oscillation as preached by Oscar Wilde – amused many, but infuriated others.

With The Smiths approaching their creative peak, and with the inevitable backlash on the horizon in 1986 – provoked by the sheer ubiquity and unavoidable provocative nature of Morrissey's views, politically, sexually and musically – certain writers (notably Frank Owen in *Melody Maker* and Antonella Black in *Zig Zag*) tried and failed to force him to admit where exactly he stood sexually.

Increasingly, the public image Morrissey would project in interviews was part the devout aesthetic celibate, part the stricken lover unable to find a soul mate. "It's not entirely up to you whether you have a relationship with another person. It's either a two-way thing or the other person decides that it will happen. And they don't."

He'd always suggest he was forever searching but never finding; that his enforced celibacy was more down to bad luck than personal choice: "I'm a human being. I live on earth. I go out. I meet a lot of people but nothing ever, ever, ever happens. More than that I cannot do, other than appear on national television in a red suit saying, 'I am said to have a sense of humour, I enjoy Bacharach & David, and I like going for long walks'. . ."

But who, exactly, was Morrissey desperately seeking? Which boxes would have to be ticked before he took the physical plunge? Surely there are clues in his many songs on the subject of sexual love? The fear of romance in 'A Rush And A Push And The Land Is Ours'; the lust-drenched 'Pretty Girls Make Graves'; the flesh-rampage of 'Trouble Loves Me'; the guilty-pleasures of 'Dear God Please Help Me' . . .

At one point it seemed as if the concept of "autosexuality" was of more fascination to Morrissey. When I'd asked him about Marc Bolan, one of his earliest musical heroes, he'd replied, "He definitely had an ambisexual image if not an autosexual image. Of course, nobody will know what autosexual means."

While "ambisexual" is often defined as an indiscriminate attraction to either sex, "autosexual" is different and is generally defined as "preferring self-gratification over other forms of sexual activity". The dictionary goes on to suggest autosexuality "often occurs as a result of numerous failed attempts at interpersonal relationships, leading the individual to make a conscious choice to become autosexual rather than face disappointment and frustration yet again". (Alternatively, "*auto*sexual" could also refer, in Bolan's case, to an unhealthy love affair with automobiles. Not just the Cadillacs, jeepsters and Rolls-Royces featured in his T.Rex lyrics but also the Mini in which he crashed and tragically died.)

When I interviewed Morrissey back in the late Eighties, I politely enquired about his "social life" and wondered whether, somewhere down the line, the subject of any previous "physical encounters" might kiss and tell and reveal the truth.

Has success changed your social life? Have there been any lapses in your meat-free sex-free drug-free lifestyle?

Morrissey: "Yes, it's stricter now than it ever was. I thought I was just getting a bit lax for a while. Social life? That's a difficult term to tangle with."

So you're still alone, still lonely?

"Yes I am and I think as long as I make records I'll be sealed up in this vat of introspection, which is fine because I think maximum attention has to be given to the things that I do. And in order to concentrate absolutely and perfectly on everything I had to . . . give up sausages."

I'm not going to delve into your personal life . . .

"There's nowhere to go."

But, the more successful or controversial you're becoming, isn't there an increasing chance your dirty linen will be washed in public? Don't you fear 'revelations' in the tabloid press? Any scandals? Acquaintances selling stories?

"I have always half expected some fictitious *Sun* spread like 'MORRISSEY INJECTS SLEEPING NUN WITH COCAINE!' but there's really nothing to report, and I'm half humiliated to have to confess such a thing. The only trouble with being famous and being newsworthy is that you have to watch what you say and what you do not just in the public eye but even when you're with friends. Because if you do have a headache and you do take an Aspro suddenly you begin to hear you're a drug-crazed whatever.

"So you do have to tread with caution. Because all your conversations are instantly reportable and interesting to anybody. I've never really worried because if there is ever a *Sun* expose it'll just be pathetic."

So the gossip-hounds haven't started hanging round outside your house yet?

"No I think they only become concerned about people who appear on *Top Of The Pops* and people who are in the Top 10."

Are you astonished by your own success?

"Yes, I've never quite believed it, which I suppose just sounds too persecuted to really believe, but yes I am very surprised by it. Obviously I believe everything I've done has been done with taste but I know the world we live in and I know how simple and intolerant it is. The music industry is incessantly intolerant of me as a living breathing walking sleeping person."

Don't you feel any pressure to write about certain social issues, particularly AIDS? (Various openly gay artists, in the late Eighties, had provocatively tried but failed to enlist his support for their campaigns.)

"Not really. AIDS is something I haven't dwelt upon with any tremendous thought. Other issues have been touched upon but I never wanted Smiths records to become lists of complaints, which was often an accusation."

The Communards had a go at you for not addressing those issues?

"I think that was Jimmy Tattyhead, not Richard Cole."

When I asked him again about his private life, in the early Nineties (in the former monastery, Hook End Manor) Morrissey reaffirmed his commitment to a solitary life: "People have got tired of reading about that. If they read the word celibacy again I'll be physically attacked. Even people who quite like me feel slightly weighted down by all that monkishness, they feel, 'Enough is enough, when is that charade going to end'.

"Unfortunately a lot of people think I did sit in a room with a bit of papier mache and straw and string and created this persona . . . but nothing has changed. There's not very much to say."

The late Scott Piering, who once vainly tried to manage The Smiths, seemed to confirm the state of play in Morrissey's love life: "I personally was with him too often, too long, too much, to believe anything other than what he said (i.e. that he was not interested). There was never one iota, one shred of evidence to the contrary. Yeah it's all true. No drugs, no drink. There were a couple of occasions when he was drinking white wine, which is about the nastiest thing I could say about his vices."

Clearly Morrissey's open admiration for brave literature (Wilde, Genet, Capote . . .) and cinema (like Dirk Bogarde in *Victim*) that explored the struggles of gay men and women against discrimination, plus the use on Smiths' covers of gay icons such as Joe Dallesandro, Colin Campbell from *The Leather Boys* and the transexual Candy Darling, played a huge part in directing Morrissey's agenda for The Smiths. Acting against the narcissistic fashion of the record industry in the Eighties, he cleverly promoted his heroes and heroines (Pat Phoenix, Yootha Joyce, Avril Angers) rather than himself or his band.

At the same time, while provocatively championing these strong characters – the artists he admired and was inspired by – Morrissey was well aware that successful, commercial pop music needed to be universal if not unisexual. The problem in the early Eighties was that, if a celebrity came across as remotely "different" or unconventional, whether by accident or design, he or she might find themselves in the same boat as artists who battled upstream against the creeping homophobic tide of the Thatcher years and, perhaps, eventually become sidelined or ignored by the media.

In the language of popular music, being too specific about love or lust has never been a smart career move. Artists (and their record companies) have fully appreciated that the "record buying public" (whoever they are, if they still exist in these download days) is or was made up of teenage girls eager to spend their pocket money on sexually charged or romantic songs performed by unobtainable objects of desire.

Historically, unlike men writing about heterosexual love, those writing about non-heterosexual love have had to be more careful. In Britain in particular there has long been a popular tradition of great theatrical musical camp, perfected by Noel Coward, in which gay male songwriters used the female voice to express their true emotions. Coward's 'Mad About The Boy' was an obvious example; the song would have been banned had it been released by the artist himself rather than sung by a female vocalist such as Gertrude Lawrence or, definitively, by Dinah Washington.

As Morrissey explained to me in 1997, "Female singers were allowed to be very expressive and dramatic. I think, for example, that in the Fifties and Sixties most people didn't think lesbianism existed, or that it hadn't been invented, whereas male singers couldn't sing in a sexually open way about their heart and how they really felt."

So, in this spirit of the past, while it was crucial that he was equivocal about sex, early on he also realised the great potential in being alluringly vague. For the next 25 years he would be grilled constantly by journalists about his love life or lack of it, allowing him to come out with some of the most revealing, riddled-with-hidden-meaning, lines in the history of the pop interview.

Such as, "I cycle. I have several bicycles. I would like to do more but, I think, you have to know at least one other person in order to, er, indulge, which applies to many things in life." Or, "I don't want to take drugs. I don't, so far as I am aware, want to take part in activities such as group sex. I'm actually a reasonably conservative, boring person." Even, "I don't have physical relationships . . . the amount of activity I have actually experienced in my life could be crammed down to a rather pathetic couple of hours."

Morrissey is a master of this fine art of titillation, side-stepping the crux of the question yet tempting and toying, inviting more questions than answers. "Indulge"? "Group sex"? "Activity"? Further explanations of his lyrics would simply increase the critical fascination with his approach to sexuality: "They're not explicit in a hardcore sex way or in a sensual way . . . I tried to approach it from a different angle, from an angle that could seem wholly innocent, but dramatically known."

Sidestepping his inquisitors, often over the years he's talked about celibacy as preached by Oscar Wilde; although Wilde's aesthetic celibacy, or at least his heterosexual celibacy, was actually enforced on his marriage by syphilis which, according to biographer Richard Ellmann, he'd contracted from a female prostitute while at Oxford University.

Morrissey's expressive confessions of celibacy ('These Things Take Time') have long been used as a shield to keep big-nosed journalists at bay. Yet, assorted contradictory interviews over the years, he's also admitted – or 'intimated', thankfully a less guilt-ridden word – to having had various experiences of a sexual kind.

"I'm not running ahead and leaving clues behind bus-stops," he told Robert Chalmers of *The Observer* in December 1992, before adding that "one of my physical encounters was with a man. That was 10 years ago. It was just a very brief, absurd and amusing moment . . . It wasn't love. I have never experienced that."

Leaving clues behind bus-stops is exactly what Morrissey enjoys doing.

95

Although he once suggested that he lost his virginity at 13 (if *any* of his lyrics can be judged as autobiographical) he perhaps contradicted this in a track on *The Queen Is Dead* – 'Never Had No One Ever'.

Elsewhere Morrissey has claimed that "until I was 28 I never had the urge . . . I just suddenly changed. I do understand that people have physical relationships. And I understand why they need them." Exactly who "the urge" was for has remained a mystery.

Back in 1985, in *Star Hits* magazine, Morrissey had been asked the direct question "Are you gay?" He replied, "I don't recognise such terms as heterosexual, homosexual, bisexual and I think it's important that there's someone in pop music who's like that. These words do great damage, they confuse people and they make people feel unhappy so I want to do away with them."

James Maker, a friend of Morrissey's since their teenage years, told Pat Reid in 2001, "Morrissey is in agreement with Gore Vidal's assertion that one cannot be defined as either a heterosexual or a homosexual – there are only heterosexual and homosexual acts. The extension of which is that we are all, ultimately, sexual." Significantly, both Maker and Morrissey were ardent fans of The New York Dolls, whose lead singer David Johansen had once stated, "Kids are finding out that there isn't much difference between them sexually. They're finding out that the sexual terms, homosexual, heterosexual, bisexual, all those are just words in front of 'sexual'."

On the 1991 *Kill Uncle* track 'Found Found Found', some critics felt the lyrics suggested that Morrissey's celibate days were definitely over and that at last he was involved in a satisfying relationship. Inevitably Morrissey denied this, claiming it was a yearning song of hope rather than a confirmation of love, but also teased, "I'm always slightly exalted by coming across someone with whom one has an instant rapport, an instant harmony . . ."

Once, when Tony Parsons asked him if he'd slept with both men and women, Morrissey replied, "I don't feel like a freak. I never lived in a small town with petty morals. Not all our lives are as cut and dried as they should be." In a more direct way, Robert Chalmers asked him if he'd ever slept with women? Without naming names, Morrissey responded, "Yes, I feel completely open. If I met somebody tomorrow, male or female, and they loved me and I loved them, I would openly proclaim that I loved them, regardless of what they were. I think people should be loved whatever their gender, whatever their age."

Nick Kent wrote, near the end of The Smiths' lifetime, that "detractors attempt to dissect the true sexual urge that might lurk in the celibate's loins" and then went on to guess that some of Morrissey's early lyrics, such as 'Wonderful Woman' and 'Jeanne', were about his love for Linder Sterling, the artist, photographer and lead singer of Ludus who remains one of Morrissey's closest companions thirty years' on.* (Sterling's partner is the writer Michael Bracewell.)

Among Morrissey's few "celebrity" friends have been diverse characters such as Billy Mackenzie of The Associates (a possible source for the song 'William, It Was Really Nothing') and Pete Burns of Dead Or Alive (who had duetted with Morrissey on The Smiths' 'Barbarism Begins At Home' at the Royal Albert Hall in April 1985). Of course, there is no evidence whatsoever that Morrissey was close to either of these men, only that a modicum of camp flirting encouraged the innuendo. For example, when Burns and Morrissey were interviewed for *Smash Hits* in October 1985, Burns revealed, "If I hear he's down or depressed, I'll send him a bunch of flowers. Nothing brings him out like a bunch of flowers. He's anybody's for a lupin." Morrissey replied, "He sent me 26 roses when it was my birthday and I sent him 48 naked sailors."

Another friend in the early Nineties was a boxer/photographer in his late twenties called Jake Walters. One suggested subject of Morrissey's song 'Best Friend On The Payroll', Jake had received "very special thanks" on *Vauxhall & I* and was described by Stuart Maconie as "affable and barrer-boyish . . . driver, gofer, mucker."

There was also the intriguing rumour that Morrissey and Michael Stipe of R.E.M. had become friends. Clearly, there were many similarities in the careers of the groups which they fronted. The Smiths and R.E.M. both started around the same time, were equally prolific and had a similar impact, musically, on either side of the Atlantic. Despite being an artist who sometimes dragged up and wore make-up on stage, Stipe refused to be specific about his sexuality until much later in his career. It's significant that two of the greatest pop writers and live performers of our times have deliberately projected themselves as sexual 'outsiders', making more traditional lyricists and performers seem distinctly one dimensional by comparison.

---

* Linder's photographic book, *Morrissey Shot*, followed hot on the heels of his *Live In Dallas* video, both references to the assassination of US president John F. Kennedy in November 1963.

In Michael Stipe, Morrissey also found someone who'd been as inspired by Patti Smith as both himself and Johnny Marr. As Stipe once recalled, "Patti Smith comes along and it was like a fucking piano landed on my head. I was a teenager, and I was so moved I couldn't sleep . . . It was unbelievable – my life completely changed by a rock'n'roll record." No wonder Morrissey spoke warmly about Stipe: "He just walked and talked and . . . that's always been very difficult for me. Michael is a very generous, very kind person."

There was even serious talk of some sort of musical collaboration, particularly after Morrissey had suggested, "It would be nice to do something unusual, some Righteous Brother type thing. I think it could be one of those funny historic bits of pop television that's so rare these days, especially in England."

Although this never happened, – perhaps in the wake of fall-outs from Morrissey's duets with David Bowie and later Siouxsie Sioux – Adrian Deevoy of Q magazine suggested the Stipe/Morrissey collaboration "sounded promising". Morrissey replied, "Promising? What did you think we were going to do? Become Millican & Nesbitt?"

Yet, later in the same interview, Morrissey teasingly joked: "It's very nice and, who knows, we may even get a cover of *Hello!*"

Obviously, the most important single creative relationship of Morrissey's life was with Johnny Marr between 1982 and 1987. On one of the few occasions when Marr spoke about Morrissey's problems in relationships, he came across as both concerned and amused by Morrissey's inability to find a partner.

"As a person Morrissey is really capable of a truly loving relationship. Every day he's so open, so romantic and sensitive to other people's emotions . . . Try and imagine the hang-ups most people have in bed. All that 'is she enjoying it? Is there something more than this?' confusion. Now magnify that a hundred times and you've got the beginnings of Morrissey's dilemna . . . But I must say that when he gets really upset, frankly I think it's just because he needs a good humping."

Although both Morrissey and Johnny Marr have dismissed the idea, it has been suggested that one source of Morrissey's emotional problems might have been the closeness of his relationship with Marr. Johnny Marr has dismissed all this talk with withering contempt. "Morrissey and I had a super-intense, close relationship, as close as it can get without being physical . . . but for him to have crossed a line would have been a serious misjudgement. For it to be suspected that I would have left my own band for a reason like that would be a complete insult to me and the work I put in."

Johnny Marr had married his childhood sweetheart Angie Brown in 1985 and she received thanks, on the penultimate Smiths' single 'Girl-friend In A Coma', for acting as a conciliatory influence during the recording of their final album *Strangeways, Here We Come*.

It is surely a coincidence that one of the most famous productions by Sixties record producer Joe Meek, whom Morrissey admires, was John Leyton's haunting 'Johnny Remember Me'. The pioneering pro-ducer was responsible for The Tornados 'Telstar' and also of some of Morrissey's favourite British girl singers. Meek, who was gay at a time when homosexuality was still a criminal offence and who was charged with "importuning for immoral purposes" in 1963, took his own life in 1967.

At the end of part one of Radio Two's excellent 2007 Morrissey docu-mentary *Salford Lad*, narrated by Stuart Maconie, 'I Won't Share You' and 'Last Night I Dreamt That Somebody Loved Me' were used to perfectly convey the tragic collapse of the Morrissey-Marr relationship, prompting the death of The Smiths.

Again, it remains impossible to brand Morrissey because he is so wonderfully adept at being elusive, spring-heeled and fleet-footed in interviews, so absolutely determined not to be pigeonholed straight or gay or a third or even fourth way. "I'm not embarrassed about the word 'gay' but it's not the least bit relevant. I'm beyond that frankly," he once stated. "I don't want to be shoved in a box, or put into a category." It's his prerogative. As he told *The Face* in 1990, "I've always said I leave things very open and that I sing about people. Without limitation. And I don't think that automatically makes me a homosexual." On 2006's 'The Youngest Was The Most Loved', he rightly questioned what the word 'normal' really meant.

There's also a real danger in trying to pin down Morrissey – he can tease and tempt as much as he likes but woe betide anyone who tries to categorise him. The late great Tony Wilson, unofficial mayor of Manchester, once described Morrissey as "fair set to be the Jeanette Winterson of the Eighties, the finest young novelist . . . he's a woman in a man's body."

Inevitably Morrissey, who had been riled by Tony's criticisms of The Smiths in the Eighties, responded with some of his most aggressive remarks. First he stated that Wilson was "a man trapped in a pig's body", then later claimed he'd been misquoted: "He's a pig trapped in a pig's body."*

Throughout his solo career Morrissey has continued to deal with the diverse joys of sex within his songs without revealing much about his own sexuality. His first post-Smiths single, 'Suedehead', definitely seems to end with the words a "good lay". But when Shaun Phillips of *Sounds* questioned this, Morrissey replied, "No, 'it was a bootleg'. I mean, good heavens, in my vocabulary? Please!"

"People do try and join up the dots to come up with some kind of answer," Morrissey once told Paul Morley. "There may well be no answer, I have to say, and this sounds rehearsed, I've always felt closer to transsexuality than anything else."

One door closes, another opens. It's always been there, Morrissey's fascination with transsexuals, from the early glam androgyny of David Bowie and Marc Bolan and the camped-up hookers' wardrobe of The New York Dolls; the famous photographs of Oscar Wilde dressed as Salome, the ball-gowned image of Charles Hawtrey, the 'Vicar In A Tutu', the vision of Prince Charles in his mother's wedding dress (very *Coronation Street*!). Then there's *Bona Drag* and the male prostitution subject matter of 'Piccadilly Palare' which celebrates the painted boys of London's West End and is also reminiscent of another of Morrissey's favourite tracks, Jobriath's 'Street Corner Love'.†

This talk of trans-sexuality plus his lyrical games with gender open up further possibilities regarding the meaning of Morrissey's lyrics. For example, in The Smiths' single 'Sheila Take A Bow' he deliberately switches gender at one point, and obviously, within more dramatic circles, it's perfectly *normal* for one outcast male to refer to another as "she" or "her". Responding to Dorian Lynskey's questions about his love life in *The Guardian* (April 2004), Morrissey admitted that he'd "skirted on a few occasions" and even "plunged" but, in dealing with her follow-up "Were all these people women?" he again proved teasingly evasive: "They seemed to be, as far as I knew. They would all be women if they had a choice," he jokingly replied.

---

* Having worked with Tony at Granada Television in the Nineties, I was disappointed in Morrissey's uncharacteristically harsh response. Wilson had, after all, praised The Smiths in the early days – he described their flowery 1983 Whitworth Street show as "one of the greatest moments in the Hacienda's history" – and also interviewed them for Granada Reports when *Meat Is Murder* was released.
† Morrissey compiled and released Jobriath's *Lonely Planet Boy* on his own Attack label.

He once told me of his fascination with drag artists and suggesting there might be a good television documentary to be made on the subject. A 2004 note, sent ahead of his appearance in Bridlington – very *Seaside Special* – had an old poster of Danny La Rue attached to it, appearing at the Casino Theatre in *The Exciting Adventures Of Queen Daniella*. La Rue, another Irish entertainer, is famous for his dragged-up impressions of divas such as Elizabeth Taylor and Dorothy Squires.

On many occasions Morrissey deliberately puts himself in positions – in interviews, in photo shoots, in videos (notably 'November Spawned A Monster') – where he seems to be toying with his audience, almost wilfully being seen in places not previously regarded as comfortable or familiar or congruous to his celibate and solitary image. When Adrian Deevoy suggested in Q that the cover of *Your Arsenal* was "homo-erotic", Morrissey decided to be photographed near Pigalle Place in Paris, the epicentre of sex shops, strip clubs and peep shows.

Around the same time, Morrissey also stated that homo-erotic imagery in lyrics and on album covers should not be taken as a veiled declaration of homosexuality. Even when Paul Morley asked the direct question about the sexual urges lurking in the celibate's loins the intrusion seemed to say more about Morley than about Morrissey.

Morley: "Have you had fantasies of fucking?"

Morrissey: "Yes but they pass . . . I've always felt above sex and love."

But three years later, he would enigmatically declare, "I have had a relationship which opened up a crucial area to me." Is this what he meant when he sang, so movingly, 'Now My Heart Is Full'?

In the 21st century, Morrissey has become more candid, less guarded about his past, as if finally he's content with the cult following he has and perhaps realises that their affection, perhaps adoration, goes beyond the need for clear definitions of sexuality. On a track like 'The Public Image', he seems to imply that the girl he'd once had was a thing of the past.

To add to the deliberate confusion he creates, on 2003's *You Are The Quarry* track 'I'm Not Sorry' he revealed that the woman of his dreams had never existed. Most provocative and publicised of all there was the vivid description of a sexual encounter in 'Dear God Please Help Me' from 2006's *Ringleader Of The Tormentors* in which Morrissey sang about explosive loins and spreading legs. As a result, many critics jumped to the hasty conclusion that Morrissey had finally sprung out of his closet but uncertainty is his stock-in-trade and lyrics can never be read literally, regardless of who wrote or sang them.

All this begs the long drawn-out and convoluted question – do we really need to know? And if we did know, would it, should it, affect our judgement of Morrissey and his art? Perhaps it mattered briefly in the Eighties, when political activists were manning the barricades against anti-gay propaganda – but surely in the 21st century it's more important and enticing that this extraordinary man remains a sexual enigma?

Perhaps by constantly trying to uncover, uncloak his sexuality, we overlook the most vital ingredients in Morrissey's life. Beyond sex, passion and love seem to be the main recurring themes in his lyrics, or rather his ongoing struggle to find passion and true love. Back in 1985 when he interviewed his heroine Pat Phoenix, what emerged from the encounter was the sense that both Phoenix and Morrissey valued passion above everything else.

Tellingly he'd asked Phoenix if, in her work, sexuality was important? She replied, "Very often warmth and compassion are mistaken for sexuality . . . Anna Magnani had what I would call 'sexuality' in the very force of her passion, and I mean passion about LIFE. She was alive and she was living and you felt you could rush into her bosom and she would embrace you." (The great Italian actress Magnani, who starred in Pasolini's *Accatone*, would be celebrated in Morrissey's 2006 'You Have Killed Me'.)

In the past I wondered if Morrissey feared a loving relationship would make him too comfortable, that perhaps it would soften the un-settling quality to his music? As Pete Burns' told him back in 1985, "I think his creativity would go down the toilet . . . Morrissey's appeal is in his public face of loneliness." Again, as Morrissey had told me, back in 1988, "in order to concentrate absolutely and perfectly on everything I had to . . . give up sausages." So, even if he has, in any way, mellowed with age, the public image still has him leading an ascetic life, separate from his 'celebrity' contemporaries, above and beyond the reach of the tabloids: "I'm capable of becoming quite frivolous, which is good for the soul, but I'm not to be found at 6 a.m. lying in the gutter, covered in vomit."

I'm not attempting to make any ridiculous comparison between Morrissey and Mozart but I think Saul Bellow's reflections on art, and the ease with which Mozart created his music might be relevant here: "For it is not a product of effort. What it makes us see is that there are things which must be done easily. Easily or not at all – that is the truth about art. Concentration without effort is at the heart of the thing. Will and desire are silenced (as many mystics have understood) and work is transformed into play."

The crucial thing about Bellow's argument is the line "will and desire are silenced". I believe that this philosophy has been central to Morrissey's approach to life and art and also his attitude towards sexuality. It's a theme explored most beautifully in his 2006 song 'Christian Dior'*, which celebrates the fashion designer's self-disciplined lifestyle and his sex-free focus on his art.

Although the key repeated line suggests that Dior wasted his life (see Wilde, Oscar) what Morrissey's actually saying is that, unlike other mortals, Dior focused passionately and single-mindedly on his art rather than spending his energy on loose women or Neapolitan rent boys.

It's an attack on modern man's sexual weaknesses – a subject Morrissey tackled before on 'Such A Little Thing Makes Such A Big Difference' – which also re-examines and re-evaluates the priorities in life. Although it's about 'Christian Dior', who sacrificed his social life for his art, inevitably the song develops into a self-portrait of Morrissey's self-discipline.

One of his greatest songs, co-written with Boz Boorer, it also offers critics and inquisitors Morrissey's most passionate defence of his pure and celibate or sexually unconventional existence. Basically he seems to be saying, 'I've decided to sacrifice my sexual desires, my chances of physical happiness, for my art and if you want to doubt me or judge me negatively then that's your prerogative.' This deferred gratification or rejection of sexual satisfaction makes him unique and, again, clearly separates him from his contemporaries in pop culture. (Approaching death, when asked if he had any regrets in life, the poet John Betjeman replied "not having more sex". Unlike Morrissey, the rest of us will probably regret not writing more poetry.)

But wouldn't it be funny and typical and extraordinary if it later emerged that, after 25 years of sexual speculation and interrogation, Morrissey wasn't writing about his own life and experiences at all. As James Maker once observed, "Lyrically, he has written from a male-to-male, male-to-female and female-to-male perspective . . . therein lie the provocation and the enigma."

---

* Christian Dior was the creator of "The New Look" in women's fashion as well as star of Morrissey's 2006 paean to self-discipline, self-sacrifice and the pursuit of artistic dreams. Dior's parents had wanted him to study political science but instead he followed his heart and became one of the great designers of the 20th century. Dior died suddenly aged 52 in Italy, in 1957. Some accounts claim he choked on a fish bone, others (Baron De Rede) from a heart attack after strenuous sex.

What if, many of Morrissey's songs – those desperately funny, sad, sensitive, complex, multi-layered works of art, inspired by diverse books, films, songs, individuals . . . – were written predominantly from the perspective of someone else? What if, like a novelist, he's writing 'in character' and the sexual wants and needs, the hopes and fears, the passions in his poetry, are not entirely his own? And if this were true, then who on earth might this central character be?

6.

I Know It's Over

"I think that The Smiths evolved too quickly, too constantly, it just never stopped. It was all very emotional. Constant recording, constant observation, no guiding light at all. No managerial figures, nobody around the group who could offer a really useful, guiding . . . almost parental hand."

— Morrissey

WHEN The Smiths played Brixton Academy on December 12, 1986, none of us, swaying ecstatically in the crowd, realised the significance of the event. A benefit for Artists Against Apartheid, this magnificent live performance would prove to be the band's last ever appearance in Britain. Looking back, listening back to a bootleg tape of that evening, it seems tragic that such an important act, such a crucial artistic partnership – at the peak of their powers performing never-to-be-repeated live versions of 'Some Girls Are Bigger Than Others' and their new single 'Shoplifters Of The World Unite' – should have ended in disharmony less than eight months later.

From a critical fan's viewpoint, The Smiths entered 1987 with great expectations, prepared to build on the growing success of previous years. But we, the fans, still didn't know the absolute truth about the personal problems that had affected Johnny Marr and Andy Rourke during the promotion of *The Queen Is Dead*. Addicted to heroin, Rourke was on the verge of being sacked, while Marr – described by Paul Du Noyer in *Q* as "by far the more rock & roll half" of the songwriting partnership – had been struggling with a drink problem, later admitting to consuming a prodigious amount of Remy Martin brandy per day. Marr later told *NME*, "I guess the real ugly period was the one before, during and after the last US tour (July to September '86). We were, all of us – personally, professionally and in public – a mess."

Nevertheless, the original "Fab Four" line-up had been restored once the unfortunate Craig Gannon had been sacked, and there was renewed hope among the fan base that all the negative, anti-rock, Rolling Stone-style criticisms that had plagued the band in 1986 would soon be forgotten once The Smiths' fourth studio album was released. Even Johnny Marr expressed concern that the band's musical direction and the press' hostile reaction: "I was beginning to get this vision of the group turning into Queen."

From Morrissey's viewpoint, "It became a situation where people around the band began to take sides, and there was even a belief that within the audience there was a Morrissey contingent and a Marr contingent. And critics began to separate, and praise one and condemn the other."

Mea culpa. In the Xmas 1986 issue of *New Musical Express* one of my printed wishes for 1987 included the words "more Morrissey less Marr". I'm still not entirely sure why I wrote this. Of all the members of the *NME* staff I was perhaps more committed to (some might say blinkered by) critical admiration of The Smiths than anyone else. Yet, not knowing the facts behind the expansion of the band and having witnessed the cranked-up power of the five piece "Rolling Stones" line-up at the London Palladium, I obviously felt some strange need to express solidarity with Morrissey rather than Marr.

I now realise that this was unhelpful and acted in many ways contrary to my best intentions. It can't just have been encouraged by the more obvious presence of guitar solos – 'Shoplifters Of The World Unite' would feature one of Johnny Marr's best – or indeed the heavier moments of 'The Queen Is Dead' tour with Craig Gannon on board. It remained important to me that The Smiths moved forward rather than resting on their laurels. But there definitely seemed to be a different atmosphere "on the shop floor", in the congregation, amidst the increasing phlegm being thrown by the new recruits of quasi-Punk Smiths' fans, that all was not well within the Smith family.

Within *NME*, it felt as if minor cracks in The Smiths' perfect art were being exaggerated or exploited to weaken Morrissey's perceived stranglehold on the cover of the paper. Those of us of an Independent persuasion – hostile to the control of music radio and the Top 40 by persuasive major record labels – were being chased down The Beatles' cul-de-sac; encouraged to take sides with either Lennon *or* McCartney, even though individually they might never be as powerful a presence in popular music again. It seemed unlikely Morrissey or Marr could succeed as completely solo artists; respectively they'd need collaborators to write the music or sing the songs.

But further unsettling news broke in the March of 1987, soon after yet another Smiths compilation album, *The World Won't Listen*, had flown into the charts. After barely four years on Rough Trade Records, four years in which they'd proved themselves to be one of Britain's most original and provocative bands, it was announced that (like The Sex Pistols before them) The Smiths had signed for EMI.

It didn't seem right at the time and, with hindsight, clearly it was a desperate throw of the dice by a band in crisis. From the outside it seemed like a far too obvious career move, prompted by Morrissey's belief that Rough Trade Records could no longer provide The Smiths with the necessary backing to place them on the pedestal they deserved.

Morrissey would respond defiantly to the inevitable criticism (not to mention the mirth of some *NME* colleagues) that followed: "If you are an independent person you really don't have to be on an independent record label to prove the fact. I know lots of people on independent labels and they're literally human custard. They really couldn't dress themselves without some serious solicitor's advice. Most of the time the indie scene is an illusion . . . I feel that people are pulling us by the tail and saying, 'come back, come back, stay in this box'."

Apart from making a strong defence of the move to EMI, this statement also revealed Morrissey's growing hostility towards the Independent sector of the music industry. In truth, some of his decisions, his admirable reluctance to jump through hoops like a performing poodle or show pony, had also limited the success of The Smiths. Most importantly, with the rising influence and impact of MTV on record sales, Morrissey's opposition to the pop video proved costly. Perhaps his obsession with the workings of the music industry in the Sixties and Seventies – focusing on radio play and landmark television appearances – caused him to wrongly reject the video it as an art form and marketing tool during the Smiths' years.

Aside from the artful films shot by Derek Jarman for tracks from *The Queen Is Dead*, the only non-performance promotional videos for Smiths' singles would feature Morrissey alone, singing 'Girlfriend In A Coma' and the posthumously released 'I Started Something I Couldn't Finish', again starring Morrissey but this time with a horde of cycling bespectacled doppelganger fans, pedalling round derelict Salford past the original Coronation Street sign and portraits of Oscar Wilde and Shelagh Delaney. Too late for The Smiths, it would only be as a solo artist that

Morrissey would accept (if never openly embrace) the vital importance of the medium.

Aside from the frictions caused by Craig Gannon's hiring and firing, further problems within The Smiths concerned differences of opinion over a proposed world tour. Morrissey later revealed, "Although I had very little passion to do a proposed world tour, and had less passion than any other members, I always thought my opinion was totally, totally valid . . . The Smiths never earned any money touring. We'd come back off remarkably successful tours and have to sit down and sign 80 cheques. Johnny and I would just look at each other and all of a sudden get very . . . old."

A Japanese adventure had already collapsed at the last minute: "We were all the airport, passports in hand," recalled Scott Piering. "Morrissey suddenly decided he didn't want to go. The tour was cancelled right there." Morrissey would later admit that "I don't want The Smiths to be a huge, untouchable mega group."

A coveted slot on BBC's primetime *Wogan* show had also been lost through Morrissey's reluctance to play the predictable pop game, prompting Piering to confess: "I just can't help liking him. On a professional level he's a total nightmare. I don't think if he came to me on bended knee I would ever want to work with him again." Years later, when asked about his unreliability and his skilful avoidance of things he didn't want to do, Morrissey replied, "Sudden illness, never fails!"

Regardless of the problems going on behind the scenes, in the spring of 1987 The Smiths continued to make a stylish impression. Following *The World Won't Listen* compilation and the April release of their Top 10 single 'Sheila Take A Bow' (cover star: Warhol's transexual friend, Candy Darling), Sire's American double album, *Louder Than Bombs*, was also made available by Rough Trade on import. Although there was no sign of their fourth studio long player – we were being *so* greedy, it was less than a year since *The Queen Is Dead* – The Smiths, and Morrissey in particular, seemed to be in great form when they performed 'Sheila Take A Bow' on *Top Of The Pops* and Channel 4's *The Tube* in April.

To the outside world everything seemed to be going swimmingly well within Smithdom. Morrissey, Marr, Joyce and Rourke were all ensconced in Bath's The Wool Hall recording the new studio album, their last for Rough Trade, with Stephen Street, the young engineer/producer who'd joined The Smiths' production team back in 1984 for 'Heaven Knows I'm Miserable Now'.

Back then, Johnny Marr had described himself and Morrissey as "total extremes . . . He's not a great believer in going out because he doesn't have fun when he goes out, whereas I go out every night, so we're two completely opposite cases." While the creative relationship had continued to work to great effect until 1987, their very different lifestyles were now beginning to cause friction.

When I interviewed Stephen Street, in early 1988, he recalled that, "Johnny was on a different hourly cycle to Morrissey at that time. Morrissey tends to get up in the morning and goes to bed at night whereas Johnny was waking up very late. There wasn't much contact, except between five o'clock and whenever Morrissey went to bed." Then, according to Street, "the funk would come out. 'Sign O' The Times' by Prince, put that on full blast." Stephen added to this in 2007 recalling, of the three nocturnal Smiths, "they'd be getting bollocked somewhere and he'd be in bed."

Whereas in the past, those heady prolific days between 1982 and 1986, Morrissey and Johnny Marr had overcome the lifestyle differences in order to make The Smiths great, now there were other sources of irritation and disagreement. In Marr's view, in trying follow *The Queen Is Dead* they put themselves under intense pressure. Although they weren't fighting with each other, they were "under great stress".

In this climate, Marr regarded Morrissey's determination to cover Cilla Black's 'Work Is A Four Letter Word' as an embarrassment. As he told Johnny Rogan, "I didn't form a group to perform Cilla Black songs." Following the version of 'Golden Lights' he felt that "those are the two low points of our recording career . . . and don't deserve a place alongside our material". Meanwhile Morrissey apparently disagreed with Marr's willingness to use sequencers and funkier basslines. Add to this the rows over whether or not Morrissey should have written lyrics to Marr's 'instrumentals' 'Money Changes Everything' and 'The Draize Train', and the well-worn cliché "musical differences" could soon be inscribed on The Smiths' tombstone.

At the heart of the collapse there's the sad truth that Morrissey and Johnny Marr had grown apart. Perhaps, as 'Frankly Mr Shankly' seemed to predict, success and its attendant pressures had gone to their heads.

"I thought we were up our own arses," Johnny Marr told *NME* in 1991. "We had completely inflated senses of our own importance. Ultimately I was giving every single second of my life to somebody else. I started to feel very unnatural and abnormal." When asked if the "somebody else" was Morrissey, Marr replied, "of course". Elsewhere, he embroidered on this changed relationship: "He was my only friend really, my only close friend. And I'm not sure it was such a good thing for him either . . . we worked together for five years, every single day of our lives, and that was getting boring as well as depressing."

As ever with The Smiths, issues such as musical differences and personality problems and stress could have been overcome if they'd had one important factor in common with all other successful bands – strong management. It's universally accepted now that lack of management contributed to The Smiths' demise more than anything else.

In the beginning, before it became too big to handle, Joe Moss managed the band from Autumn 1982 through to the end of 1983, withdrawing just before The Smiths' first dates in January 1984. A Rough Trade insider later suggested that Moss left because "it became apparent that he was getting further and further out of his depth".

A different opinion comes from Smiths' soundman Grant Showbiz, "I think he realised that from now on it was going to be a really heavy fight with a bunch of cold, calculating Southern bastards. We never had another manager, we had this series of people who thought they were managers." According to Johnny Marr, who still wanted Moss to manage The Smiths, "He and Morrissey stopped seeing eye-to-eye . . . it was obvious Joe was feeling forced out." Years later, Marr would admit to Rogan how much Moss' decision affected him, stating that Joe was "the unsung hero of The Smiths".

After Moss' departure, Rough Trade record promoter Scott Piering became caretaker manager. The American (who died in 2000 aged only 53) was a key figure in the careers of KLF, Stereophonics, Prodigy and Pulp as well as The Smiths, but he struggled to manage Morrissey. Scott recalled he'd once gone to collect The Smiths' frontman from his flat. "Morrissey wouldn't answer. He was hiding in the bedroom. After 10 minutes of banging and pleading I had to climb over the ledge from another flat to get at him. I thought he might be dead."

Without a Peter Grant or a Paul McGuinness – a parental and protective figure to take care of business – The Smiths found it extremely difficult to run themselves. Some suggested that Morrissey's mother was too involved in management decisions, while others blamed Morrissey himself for being a control freak. Given the lack of continuity in terms of management from December 1983 through to 1987 it seems even more remarkable that Morrissey and Marr were so creative and prolific. But, in terms of how the group was run financially, Morrissey's hands-on approach to Smiths' business would cause himself and Johnny Marr considerable difficulty further down the line.

As Johnny had revealed in an early interview, great importance was attached to "the Rough Trade aesthetic . . . the running of the group and how everybody got paid. Morrissey had a very healthy outlook on how to run a group financially by not spending money on complete bullshit and nonsensical things, and not being extravagant. His motto was, 'What we make we put in our pockets, and pay everybody from our pocket.' His experience and sense, being a different kind of person from me, was important, and he was older."

Older but not necessarily wiser in terms of business; it would be years before the financial management of The Smiths would come back to haunt them but already the seeds were being sown. Geoff Travis would later tell Q, "I maintain that the reason The Smiths broke up was because they had outside pressure and no management to take care of it."

Apart from Scott Piering, several other figures would try, at various times and with limited success, to fill the management void including Ruth Polski, Matthew Sztumpf of Madness, Martha Defoe and Mark Fenwick.

The last person who'd attempt to manage The Smiths was another American, Ken Friedman, who'd worked for Clive Davis at Arista and had started up as a concert promoter in San Francisco. Soon Morrissey was admitting that the lack of acceptable management was again taking its toll, implying that Friedman had somehow come between himself and Johnny Marr.

"It's an unmitigated disaster . . . We've been through a catalogue of managers. None has really been suitable. And the last one was a great shock because it did seem for once in our lives that everything was going to be ironed out and the future was quite solid. And he lasted five and a half weeks. And he's not going to go down without a hideous great big dirty fight.

"It's very depressing for instance to think that he is going to fight for 15 per cent of everything we earn for the next 12 months. He's not going to get it but fighting him off is going to cost an enormous amount of money and physical hardship."

Later, when asked if the lack of management meant that the band's affairs had been out of control, Morrissey replied, "Oh, it got entirely out of control, totally, totally out of control. This, if anything, was the cause of

The Smiths' death. Especially the monetary side."

Soon after *NME* printed Morrissey's criticisms of Ken Friedman's involvement with The Smiths, I received an angry phone call from Friedman himself. In this Friedman refuted the suggestion that he'd been a primary reason for the band breaking up. "Firstly, I never disliked Morrissey, and I was not the reason Johnny left the band," Ken told me. "Secondly, Johnny didn't leave The Smiths because I told him to. That's totally untrue. Johnny Marr's a very intelligent artist and I think you should give him more credit than you have done."

According to Friedman, it was inevitable that, during the final days in the studio recording *Strangeways, Here We Come*, Johnny Marr would soon quit the band. He argued that the 'musical differences' between Johnny and Morrissey were too great for him to manage. Friedman's argument, in a nutshell, was that he was unfairly being blamed for destroying a partnership that was already irrevocably broken.

Wondering where it had all gone wrong, I later spoke to Stephen Street, The Smiths' young producer and witness to the break-up.

LB: Was it anything to do with Ken Friedman's presence as manager?

Street: "The tension started because Morrissey for some reason started to fall out with the ideas Ken had – that was the only problem I saw argument-wise during *Strangeways*. . . . When Ken first came down he was around as manager but, by the end of it, he'd got the message that Morrissey didn't want to be managed by him anymore. It wasn't tension about the album, more tension about the future.

"I got on fine with Ken. He'd pop his head into the control room to see how things were going but most of the time he'd be on his computer or his phone. I think now people are under the impression there were lots of arguments in the studio but there weren't, it was good fun. By the end Ken had gone back to Los Angeles and the only problem was this business thing in the background."

When did you realise The Smiths were breaking up?

"Two weeks after we'd finished *Strangeways* . . . we went into the studio to do some B-sides and Morrissey didn't turn up. I got there, Mike Joyce and Andy Rourke were there, but Johnny phoned up from Manchester 'cos word had got round that Morrissey wasn't coming."

Is that when Johnny decided to go and record with Talking Heads?

"Johnny's friendly with Steve Lillywhite (who remixed 'Ask') and his wife Kirsty McColl (who sang on 'Golden Lights') and as Steve was doing the Talking Heads album he asked Johnny to come and play. After the

B-side fiasco, when Morrissey didn't turn up, Johnny said, 'F★★k it! I'm off to Paris.'

"I think Johnny must have been at breaking point by the end of *Strangeways* . . . Morrissey's a very private person and it's admirable in some ways, but you can only spend so many years worrying about someone; worrying whether or not you're making them feel included enough. After a while it becomes a bit wearing and maybe that's what happened with Johnny."

Although the news of The Smiths' demise would not leak out until August '87, in mid May, strangely, I found myself interviewing The Cradle, a band born out of the ashes of Easterhouse (who'd toured with The Smiths) and which now featured the recently sacked guitarist Craig Gannon. Although Gannon himself wasn't present, this was the interview in which it was first revealed – via Gannon's bandmate Ivor Perry and the talkative Cradle manager John Barratt – that The Smiths were falling apart.

The rumours about Johnny Marr's drinking and Andy Rourke's heroin problems were gathering pace in the music business, along with alarming talk of "lifestyle frictions" between Morrissey and Marr. My lack of journalistic killer instinct obviously prevented me from getting to the crux of the problem but, with hindsight, re-reading sections of The Cradle interview, there were clues to the seriousness of The Smiths' situation:

LB: What's with Craig Gannon? It strikes me that someone who's been through The Bluebells, Aztec Camera, The Colourfield and The Smiths by the age of 21 must either be exceptionally unlucky or have some severe personal hygiene problem. Ivor (Perry) got Gannon to join The Cradle having seen him 'staggering round, pissed, at the Hacienda'.

Perry: "Craig's very much into being into a band who get on together, who go out together. Like us, we all go out on the beer. But The Smiths, they'd already built the club and he felt like an outsider. He's a great guitarist, he felt he was in a great band, but to be stuck on rhythm guitar obviously disappointed him. He didn't feel any personal animosity, but he hopes he doesn't get ripped off . . ."

Barratt: "Cut! Let's leave it at that . . . except to say that The Smiths are the only commercially viable, valid pop band in the world, ever."

LB: Clearly there are, er, loose ends to be tied up between The Smiths and Craig Gannon. But surely he must be pissed off at being blamed for the 'rockist' phase?

Barratt: "The Smiths are going through great personal turmoil. In that

Danny Kelly interview, Marr seemed to be implying that Craig was responsible for the nun-eating rock monster."

Perry: "Live, you could hardly hear the bugger."

Although Craig Gannon would perform once more with Morrissey at Wolverhampton in the Xmas of 1988 – lead guitar instead of Marr – their brief relationship would be terminally soured by Gannon's victorious court case against The Smiths (over songwriting royalties for 'Ask'); the first in a chain of legal actions that would embroil Morrissey over the next decade.

Little did we know but, on the very day I spoke with The Cradle, Tuesday, May 19, 1987, Morrissey and Marr were meeting in Bristol for the last time in many years. Blissfully ignorant at the time, everyone who loved The Smiths, but who knew there were problems, hoped that peace would break out. All seemed to be well, that July, when the first track of the forthcoming studio album, 'Girlfriend In A Coma' was released.

An infectious acoustic Marr tune, coupled with one of Morrissey's funniest yet mordant lyrics, few of us at the time thought that the "girlfriend" in question could possibly be Johnny Marr, or that the song's final words of farewell might signify the death rattle of The Smiths. But when they failed to promote it on *Top Of The Pops* and instead we witnessed, god forbid, the firsts Smiths' promo video featuring Morrissey solo in front of footage from *The Leather Boys* (starring Colin Campbell, alternative cover star of 'Ask' and Rita Tushingham from *A Taste Of Honey*).

Perhaps the end seemed nigh when Morrissey spoke to Paul Du Noyer of *Q* in early 1987, who asked him if he still enjoyed performing live?

Morrissey replied, "No, for me it's totally totally gone."

Du Noyer: "You aren't about to tell me The Smiths won't tour again are you?" Morrissey: "I'm not trying to say that. Because it sounds like a stamping child."

With hindsight, other aspects of Du Noyer's interview also rang alarm bells, notably Morrissey's unsettled comment that "I feel at the moment that anything absurd can happen. And if I ended up in Strangeways I wouldn't be at all surprised." Then, perhaps more tellingly, "I get letters from people who say, 'When The Smiths break up I will die, I will make a reservation for the next world.'"

With rumours flying from Rough Trade to EMI to *NME*, our news desk followed up, in early August, with a speculative headline "Smiths To Split", which was immediately denied by Morrissey with the famous words: "Whoever says The Smiths have split shall be severely spanked with a wet plimsoll."

The confirmation came days later. "The Smiths announce that Johnny Marr has left the group. However, they would like to confirm that other guitarists are being considered to replace him. It must be stressed that the concept of The Smiths will remain the same and the group will continue to promote their forthcoming single and album releases and are eager to plan live dates once a new guitarist has been selected. The Smiths would like to state that although Johnny's departure is sad they wish him every happiness and success with his future projects."

This statement raised more questions than answers. Why had Johnny Marr left the group? Could any other guitarist replace him, as a performer and tunesmith? What were the real reasons behind the split and, in terms of the band's future, *NME* rightly asked: "Can the concept of The Smiths possibly survive the departure of half of the band's creative force?"

Inevitably, as the August 8 edition of *NME* went to print, Johnny Marr called Danny Kelly "to clear up some inaccuracies":

"There was nothing even approaching acrimony between myself and other members of the band. I've known them all a long time and I love 'em . . . The reason for me going was simply that there are things I want to do, musically, that there is no scope for in The Smiths."

"The stuff we've just done for the new album is great, the best we've ever done. I'm really proud of it. But there are things I want to do that can only happen outside The Smiths."

When Danny asked Marr about Morrissey's intention to carry on with "The Smiths" name, the cautious reply was, "I think that's probably tied up in a whole load of legal things."

Aside from the sequence of events that caused the divorce, it soon became clear that the exhausted Johnny Marr had taken a holiday after the recording sessions, travelling to the USA, and had been there when The Smiths split. Morrissey later claimed that it was Marr's reaction to the *NME* story about the split that actually killed the group. Marr categorically denied this.

"In the final analysis, the thing that used to make me happy was making me miserable and so I just had to get out . . . I'm looking forward to doing new things, and to hearing what Morrissey will come up with. I think the change will actually do him a lot of good. I certainly hope so."

As Stephen Street told me, initially The Smiths tried to continue without Johnny Marr.

"Morrissey received a cassette from Ivor Perry (ex-Easterhouse, Cradle guitarist) and thought he'd like to try it out with Mike and Andy, and I was asked to oversee it. We had two days booked in the studio but only did one. I think it really hit them it wasn't going to be the same. Mike said to me, 'I can't wait for Johnny to walk through the door and for everything to be all right again.' I think it hit Morrissey more than anyone else. The following day I got a phone call from Mike saying, 'Forget it, it's off'. Morrissey had gone AWOL; Mike and Andy went back to Manchester."

I know it sounds laughable, years later – when you're older and greyer and the vast majority of pop music starts to seem incredibly trivial – but, at the time, the death of The Smiths seemed shocking, unnecessary, unbelievable. For those of us who'd followed the band devotedly from the exciting and raw beginnings through to the heights of *The Queen Is Dead* and beyond, it was hard to comprehend.

All our fears about the disastrous decision to move from Rough Trade to a major label seemed to be confirmed when Nick Garfield, Head of A&R at EMI, asserted that the major still had the rights to both Morrissey's and Marr's solo output: "Every contract has a clause which gives the label the rights to any work they do whether the band splits up or not. Essentially we now have two acts for the price of one." For me, there were too many echoes of Colonel Parker's reaction to Elvis' death: "This changes nothing."

Like stricken children, we had to accept that The Smiths had split and – although we hoped it would only be a temporary state of affairs, resolvable marital difficulties, resolvable by arbitration – life at *NME* in the summer of 1987 was becoming unbearable. Apart from the delight of the anti-Morrissey brigade at the prospect of an *NME* without The Smiths ("The No Morrissey Express!" read one joyful letter), the paper itself was going through a time of great turmoil too.

Throughout 1986 and '87 *NME* had backed Red Wedge, the radical musicians' collective led by Billy Bragg and Paul Weller. Red Wedge tried to engage with Britain's apathetic youth to persuade them to vote Labour in the June '87 General Election, thereby preventing Margaret Thatcher's Conservatives from gaining a third term of government. Bravely (outsiders said "disastrously") the eve-of-election pro-Labour edition of *NME* – sexy cover star Neil Kinnock – resulted in increased conflict with our beloved bosses the IPC management, particularly when the Conservatives romped home for a third term.

To make matters worse, an attempt to reprint the controversial poster accompanying the Dead Kennedys' *Frankenchrist* album ('Penis Landscape' by H.R. Giger) gave IPC the perfect opportunity to purge the paper. Overnight we lost our editor Ian Pye – who'd managed the internal Hip Hop Versus Indie skirmishes fairly and with good humour, and had written intelligently on both The Smiths and the Go Go scene – plus two key staff members: the Art Editor Joe Ewart and the Media Editor Stuart Cosgrove; a passionate St Johnstone fan, later Channel Four's King Of The Regions, in fiery editorial meetings Cosgrove often performed like Rab C Nesbitt meets Braveheart.

The new IPC-backed regime – led by Alan Lewis from *Sounds* and introducing the inspirational if politically incorrect James Brown (en route to *Loaded*) – would be less committed to tackling wider social and political issues of relevance to the readership. Through Lewis, IPC demanded *NME* now focus solely on music and pop culture; arguing that Simple Minds should have been on the cover instead of Kinnock and demanding the paper stop supporting radical movements like Red Wedge or the Miners' Strike.

For me, they were dark days. I felt my beloved *NME* – the outspoken controversial and bullish magazine my brother and I had purchased religiously from before Punk and beyond – was being castrated before my eyes. More importantly, the reign of The Smiths, the band I'd followed obsessively since Don's death, was at an end.

Is it possible to grieve over the death of a band? We've all laughed at those television images of girly boy-band fans (from the Bay City Rollers through to Take That to Boyzone to Blue) weeping uncontrollably at the school gates when the news breaks. I went off a girl at school after she cried over David Cassidy's departure from The Partridge Family. Now, despite being older and emotionally in control, was I really behaving any differently?

It was time to go. Partly in solidarity with my colleagues Pye, Cosgrove and Ewart, partly depressed by the unbearable collapse of Smithdom, partly downcast by the relentless tide of Thatcherism – I just couldn't face four more years of that woman and her filling-drilling voice. Also I felt foot-stampingly angry (Freelance In A Tantrum) when the *NME* butchered my article on the demise of The Christians in East Berlin and refused to run my positive 'Secrets Of The Beehive' interview with David Sylvian, I'd already booked my escape to India when the advance cassette of The Smiths' last album arrived. Naturally, regarding myself as history within the *NME*, I was stunned when the album section editor Alan Jackson asked me to review it.

On the eve of my flight, in my Brixton flat, I sat down and listened again and again to the The Smiths' last words and music. *Strangeways, Here We Come* – the title obviously referred to the infamous Victorian prison in Manchester and to the Sixties' 'Strangeways' sequence of photographs of Morrissey's Salford by Harold Riley. The phrase itself was inspired by a throwaway line in *Billy Liar* when a passing juvenile delinquent mutters the words: "Borstal, here we come". It wouldn't be released until late September 1987, entering the UK charts in early October at number two behind Michael Jackson's *Bad*.

As if to confirm that the world had changed but not Morrissey, the *Strangeways . . .* cover featured Richard Davalos, James Dean's co-star in *East Of Eden* (1955) one of Morrissey's favourite films. Davalos would later appear on the American sleeves of the Warner Brothers' 1992 releases, The Smiths *Best* and *Best II*, and mute footage of Dean and Davalos together doing a screen test would be shown before Morrissey's 2006 'Ringleader Of The Tormentors' performances. The back cover image, by photographer Steven Wright (who'd shot *The Queen Is Dead* Salford Lads Club image), is of a Manchester street sign, pointing out that Strangeways is only a quarter of a mile from Salford.

Before I left England, Pat Bellis, Rough Trade's press officer, called canvassing opinions on which track should be The Smiths' final single after the death-knell 'I Started Something I Couldn't Finish'. There was only one choice, as far as I was concerned. The perfect, show-stopping epitaph for a great British band – 'Last Night I Dreamt That Somebody Loved Me'. By the time my review was printed in *NME*, in September '87, under the headline "Tomb It May Concern", I was drinking yak tea with Tibetan exiles on a houseboat in Kashmir.

> *"MAN THAT is born of woman hath but a short time to live and is full of misery. He cometh up and is cut down like a flower. He fleeth as it were a shadow, and never continueth in one stay" – Anglican Funeral Service.*
>
> *The Smiths are, after all the speculation, finally heading the queue for the Crem. Look at the pit they dug themselves: signed to deadly EMI; Johnny Marr – the decade's most original rock guitarist and musical keystone of the combo – had done a runner, and Mike Joyce followed, while bass player Rourke's struggled on with his drug problem. Surely the odds were stacked against them creating another flawed Meat Is Murder, let alone an LP of universally acclaimed quality like The Queen Is Dead?*
>
> *Predictably, in these circumstances, Strangeways, . . . finds Morrissey*

with one hoof heavily into his sarcophagus. From the opening line of the positively raunchy 'A Rush And A Push And The Land Is Ours', it seems as if he's determined to give his fun 'n' money-lovin' critics as much ammo for derision as humanely possible. He even seems to relish calling a song 'Stop Me If You Think You've Heard This One Before'*, in the face of those who perpetually take the piss out of him and reckon that every Smiths song sounds the same.

To my ears the major criticism of Morrissey has been that he's a miserable defeatist who encourages negative, rather than positive, responses from his admirers. There's some truth in this, as revealed here in 'Death Of A Disco Dancer' and 'Death At One's Elbow', the weakest links on Strangeways, *. . . The first is overlong (like 'Barbarism . . .') and, despite Marr's ingenious plinky-guitar crescendo, totally predictable. The second is fast and furious and as much of a slim self-parody of The Smiths' best as 'Sheila . . .' and 'Shoplifters . . .' were.*

But it's the weird balance of Morrissey's mortal humour against Marr's beatific melodies that establishes The Smiths' final greatness. Mozzer as the jilted, unrequited lover who spoils the party with 'Unhappy Birthday' wishes; Mozzer as the agent provocateur *of 'I Started Something I Couldn't Finish', a classic pop song that seems to echo – believe it or not – the treasured oeuvre of T.Rex, Mud and The Glitter Band!; Mozzer as the emotionally dithering laddo in 'Girlfriend In A Coma'.*

The point, of course, is that pop is a confidence trick; it pretends it's a world of harmless entertainment and yet continually bombards us with the we're-having-a-good-time-and-there's-something-seriously-wrong-with-you-if-you're-not philosophy. In response The Smiths tackled bloody serious subjects in tandem with addictive tunes; Morrissey could turn spina bifida into a Top 10 hit and probably will.

Those who believe that Steven Patrick Morrissey should address himself to the political affairs of this nation will again be disappointed. Lyrically he fails to allude to Roy Hattersley's girth or the indignity of Labour, and instead continues to mine that seam of fatal realism. Excuse me, but Saul Bellow observed that "Ignorance of death is destroying us. Death is the dark backing a mirror needs if we are to see anything". And it often seems that Morrissey's

---

* Morrissey's hopes of releasing 'Stop Me If You Think You've Heard This One Before' as a single had been dashed in August 1987 by the Hungerford Massacre in which Michael Ryan shot 17 people dead. The BBC felt the lyric about mass murder could be interpreted as insensitive in the circumstances.

philosophy and humour (like Woody Allen's) arises from a similar obsession with the inevitability of turning one's toes up, of popping one's clogs; hence the emphasis on life's priorities such as love, sex, laughter and bicycles.

Love, sex and death remain constants in The Smiths' Strangeways . . . songs. The universal appeal still stems from Morrissey's comic, deliberate ambiguity about who he can and can't have. He's sexy and risqué but never crude or sordid; he wears his heart on his sleeve, I see no reason why he should have to make clumsy public proclamations about his sexual preferences.

In the same way that he took time out on Meat Is Murder to propound vegetarianism and on The Queen Is Dead to satirise his own Wilde-like plagiarism, on Strangeways . . . it's Rough Trade that get the treatment. 'Paint A Vulgar Picture' is a bitter attack on the label's exploitation of the band's success and on its marketing ploys.

Morrissey also deprecates his own status as 'spokesman for a generation', pokes fun at his fawning fan's alarmingly close identification with him and his beliefs ("I walked apace behind you at the soundcheck, you're just the same as I am")' scoring a direct hit on people like me.

Morrissey's assured us that "it's impossible for anybody to change me as an individual, and it's certainly impossible for a record company to change me". Thus The Smiths had sentenced themselves to that Strangeways, . . . of pop, that long-term institution, EMI; a multinational which seemed to celebrate news of the split (between Morrissey and Marr) with the tell-tale comment, "essentially we now have two acts for the price of one".

Whether Morrissey or Ferry-sidekick Marr can thrive in this new environment remains to be seen but listening obsessively to Strangeways, . . ., I can't help feeling that this is a once in a life-time partnership; a uniquely complementary marriage of talents that's developed from a long established friendship.

Coming to Strangeways, . . . I was half prepared to put the boot into The Smiths. I was sure that mid-production upsets – the breakdown in communication between Mozz and Marr (the absence of Marr's beloved B-side instrumentals from the last four singles and Marr remaining close to sacked Smiths manager Ken Friedman) – would tarnish its quality.*

But Strangeways . . . contains two of Morrissey/Marr's greatest moments since the Fab Four's inception. There's the warm Mersey acoustics of the final

---

* Other music papers were less enthusiastic about *Strangeways, Here We Come. Sounds* suggested "its many flaws were immersed in a moist-eyed funeral gloss . . . even the few excellent moments sound desperately bleak in a way The Smiths never were".

track 'I Won't Share You', which beautifully echoes both 'Back To The Old House' and 'You'll Never Walk Alone'.

And, outstandingly, there's 'Last Night I Dreamt That Somebody Loved Me' – which builds from atmospheric solo piano and madding crowed noises, then explodes into Morrissey's most emotional unlovable vocals, and reaches a 'Wild Is The Wind' falsetto climax coupled with a thousand violins. It's as great as 'I Know It's Over'.

I don't think there's any point in comparing The Smiths with their pop contemporaries; a couple of dodgy singles aside they remained above and beyond the rest, ploughing their own furrow (digging their own grave?), setting their own standards.

I passionately hoped this was not to be their last breath, but nevertheless, in case you haven't guessed by now, Strangeways, Here We Come *is a masterpiece that surpasses even* The Queen Is Dead *in terms of poetic pop and emotional power. Yes, very nice . . .*

Maybe in the next world, I hoped, The Smiths would reform and continue to produce remarkable music. Although, over the years, these heartfelt opinions on their final studio album have been much criticised, even ridiculed for being "over the top", I stand stubbornly by virtually everything I wrote over 20 years ago.

In fact, the only change I'd make would perhaps be to elevate 'Death At One's Elbow', with its Wildely (sic) mortal obsession, from "slim self-parody" to "sublime pointer to lead singer's future rockabilly intentions".

The great debate still goes on. Is *Strangeways, Here We Come* The Smiths' best album? Or is their greatest work, as many suggest, *The Queen Is Dead*? It's worth noting that although *The Queen Is Dead* was universally hailed as a masterpiece on its release in 1986, within *NME* by the end of that year it was regarded as inferior to Anita Baker's *Rapture*, Janet Jackson's *Control* and even Paul Simon's *Graceland*. Yet, over the past 20 years *The Queen Is Dead* has always been the highest ranking Smiths' album in readers' and critics' polls.

When I worked as a consultant on Channel 4's *100 Greatest Albums Of All Time* extravaganza in 2005, made by Granada, *The Queen Is Dead* was voted 20th in the chart behind two Oasis albums, one Coldplay, one Verve and, at number one, Radiohead's *OK Computer*. *Strangeways, Here We Come* failed to even register.

Was I wrong? I'd argue not, based on an independent poll of individuals relatively close to the production. In Smiths' and Morrissey's soundman

Grant Showbiz's view, "I still think *Strangeways, Here We Come* is the best record. I get really pissed off with this critical cliche. Like they've swept *Strangeways, . . .* under the carpet." In difficult recording circumstances, drummer Mike Joyce explained "there was a lot of pressure on Johnny. And that's why *Strangeways, . . .* to me sounds like a total white-knuckle ride. We were very tense. But we were playing together really well, better than we'd ever played before. I wish we'd toured *Strangeways, . . .*"

But what about the two central characters, Morrissey and Marr, the Morecambe & Wise of Eighties pop, whose individual successes would forever more be judged against the fruits of their Smiths' years 1982–87?

In 1991, when Danny Kelly of *NME* suggested to Johnny Marr that *Strangeways, . . .* was the band's "worst LP", Marr totally disagreed, arguing it was their best. Later, he even told *Select* magazine that "*Strangeways . . .* suffers because it was our last record, so people think there were arguments and horrors in making it, but there weren't. Morrissey and I both think it's possibly our best album . . . Last time I met Morrissey he said 'Last Night I Dreamt That Somebody Loved Me' was his favourite Smiths song. He might be right. Over the last few years I've heard 'Girlfriend In A Coma' in shops and people's cars, and I'm always surprised by how good it sounds. 'Unhappy Birthday' I really like."

In tandem with Marr's thinking, Morrissey positively agreed that *Strangeways Here We Come* was The Smiths' greatest triumph: "Well it is. We're in absolute accordance on that. We say it quite often. At the same time. In our sleep. But in different beds . . .

"*The Queen Is Dead* is not our masterpiece. I should know. I was there. I supplied the sandwiches . . . We both sit down and think about *The Queen Is Dead* and a giant question mark appears. *Strangeways, Here We Come* said everything eloquently, perfectly at the right time and put the tin hat on it basically."

Except that, at the time, it didn't say "everything". In addition to the *Strangeways, . . .* singles 'I Started Something I Couldn't Finish' (cover star: Avril Angers) and 'Last Night I Dreamt That Somebody Loved Me' (cover star: Billy Fury) – not to mention the withdrawn release 'Stop Me If You Think You've Heard This One Before' (cover star: Murray Head, also, like Avril Angers, from *The Family Way*) – a *South Bank Show* on The Smiths', mostly filmed before the split, was broadcast on ITV in October 1987.

I was in Calcutta (staying at the YWCA!) when the programme was transmitted and didn't see a copy until the New Year. When I talked to

Morrissey about it, in early 1988, I asked him if he'd had editorial control over the whole production?

"A lot of people erroneously assumed that I entirely tailored *The South Bank Show*; that I chose the people to be interviewed, that I edited it. I didn't have anything to do with it, I just did one lengthy interview and I don't watch my bits. I turn the sound down. I found I couldn't watch it until two weeks after it had been screened, particularly after the pain of the previous months.

"I found it to be the Smiths too simplified. I would rather it had been a presentation to the people who quite intelligently had followed the Smiths since the very early days; instead it seemed to be the most harmless, the most base viewpoint of the Smiths for the uninitiated. And I never ever understand why anyone should produce for the uninitiated. But I thought some of the footage was excellent, such as the cows – that was great, but it seemed a bit old, the same documentary could've been made three years earlier."

But you must have been pleased when Nick Kent compared The Smiths with The Beatles saying both bands "epitomised their time and place"?

"In the sense that they spoke of the simple things of life in a very eloquent or simple way. I think The Smiths totally spoke for now. The most realistic voices, musically and lyrically of the Eighties. And it's not just self-bleatings, I think that's really really true. I've never heard a group like The Smiths."

The Viv Nicholson sequence?:

"Very awkward. A beautiful woman but it was really delving into January 1984, just a little bit late. The actual sequence was so abstract, of me and her just disappearing with no sound. It was like some curious Polish play."

On *The South Bank Show*, Johnny Marr described The Smiths as a "victory for the gawk"? Do you agree?

"Not for the gawk but I think for style and intelligence. I never felt like the nerd, the one that shouldn't really have made it. No, it's always been a victory for taste. Even the low spots were remarkable."

What were the low spots?

"Ooh, I can't think of any."

Part Two: Morrissey

7.

Nineteen Eighty Hate

"It was definitely an amputation of a giant magnitude, not just because Johnny and I were no longer friends, but because all the people I had been involved with up until that point just seemed to disappear overnight . . . But I think I've survived, and I'm sitting here to tell the tale . . . with blood all over my face."

– Morrissey

SKIN and bones from a mild dose of amoebic dysentery, from 10 stone down to a paperweight eight, I arrived home from India and Nepal and, by mid January 1988 – at a complete loss as to what to do with the next stage of my life – I found myself back in the *NME* offices on New Oxford Street.

It was already a very different, less political and, certainly, a less politically correct newspaper from the radical weekly of the late Seventies to mid Eighties. After we'd put Neil Kinnock on the cover of *NME* instead of Simple Minds and Margaret Thatcher had achieved another victory over Labour in the June 1987 General Election, inevitably there had been changes in personnel and policy.

From then on the focus would be solely on music rather than wider, more radical aspects of youth culture; under the new *NME* editorial regime (which admittedly improved the paper's circulation and also launched the grown-up music monthly *Vox*), led by Alan Lewis and fronted by James Brown, who would later go on to launch the original lads' mag *Loaded*.

As Neil Spencer – the *NME* editor who'd employed me back in 1984 – would write in *The Guardian* (2005), "The company's tolerance snapped when the editor (Ian Pye) gave Neil Kinnock a cover at the 1987 election. It was the era of the 'moral majority' and US-led censorship campaigns to clean up pop. Eventually a new editor was installed, the paper carted back to IPC's grim tower and neutered, its politics confined to musing on precisely why Morrissey so loved the Union Jack."

Post-India, but still a committed member of that now-forgotten much-maligned Eighties species the "New Man", I was regarded as old school in *NME*; too PC as opposed to IPC, too unfashionably Left wing. Although I still loved *NME* (and always will, like some battered wives), I was seriously considering my immediate future one late January morning when, out of the blue, I received a call from Murray Chalmers of Parlophone Records (part of EMI).

Following my live review of The Smiths' Newcastle Mayfair concert in August '86, and my positive *Strangeways, Here We Come* album obituary of September '87, Morrissey had decided to give me his first interview since the death of The Smiths. More importantly, and to the great astonishment (and in some cases, immense irritation) of everyone within *NME*, it transpired that Morrissey had already finished recording his first solo album in collaboration with Smiths' engineer Stephen Street.

I had mixed feelings about this news. For Smiths' fans, there was still the hope, even expectation, Johnny Marr would soon return to the fold. The Smiths – the most original and influential band of the Eighties – had lasted less than five years. Although I'd first heard about the turmoil within the band the previous summer and, with Marr still in his early twenties, it seemed musically tragic that his partnership with Morrissey had collapsed so soon. In comparison, U2 and R.E.M. would continue for decades.

The arrival by bike courier of a 'Suedehead' white label further dashed hopes of a Smiths' reconciliaition. Not only did the record cover feature topless Morrissey himself – a shocking departure considering all Smiths' covers had featured carefully chosen icons from film, pop and television (apart from Morrissey's cameo on 'What Difference Does It Make?') – but also, with the opening bars of the new single it became clear that Morrissey had – god forbid – embraced the synthesiser. How the anti-guitar-band, dance aficionados laughed as the 12-inch single span round on the *NME* office turntable. After all, hadn't Morrissey declared back in 1984 that "the synthesiser should be symbolically burned"?

Suddenly it became crystal clear that this wasn't just a stop-gap project while Morrissey and Marr resolved their creative-marital differences. I began to fear it was a hurried, competitive response by Morrissey to Marr's statement that he'd been working on new material and even planned to tour with a new band in early 1988. After the death of The Smiths in August 1987, Marr had said, "I've already recorded some stuff and it's gone really well. If the rest of it goes as well there's every chance I'll be forming a permanent group, though obviously it's a little early to be too certain about that. But I definitely want to have some live dates set up by the New Year at the latest regardless of the situation with other musicians."

With hindsight, this was the dawn of Morrissey's solo career, but in January 1988 it felt too soon for me to embrace such a brave new world. I wasn't even sure, listening to 'Suedehead' and preparing to interview the band-less frontman, that it would be a major hit, despite now having the backing of EMI for Morrissey's revived HMV label. (As it happened, it would be Morrissey's biggest solo hit of the 20th century, reaching number five in the UK charts in March.)

To make things more complicated, the title of the single was already being interpreted as controversial by some within *NME*. The *Q Encyclopedia Of Rock Stars* would, years later, state that Morrissey had taken the title from "Richard Allen's 1971 novel about black-hating, gay-bashing, post-skinhead gangs", but at the time *NME*'s resident skinhead expert, the SWP-loving punk poet Steven Wells (aka Seething Wells aka drag king Susan Williams) rattled off an impressive article about Allen and his varied collection of realistic-but-seedy youth-movement trash titles such as *Skinhead*, *Skinhead Girls*, *Sorts*, *Glam*, *Terrace Terrors*, *Boot Boys*, *Suedehead* and *Smoothies*.

To me, from the outset, it just seemed as if Morrissey was simply writing about the warts-and-all England of his youth; he wasn't celebrating or championing negative youth movements but just felt that such an intolerant, aggressive time shouldn't be forgotten.

The Smiths had been dead for six months when I met up with the solo Morrissey at the Cadogan Hotel. In the midst of a Seventies-style revival, that engulfed Britain up to our snakebelts, it seemed appropriate that Morrissey was bouncing back with 'Suedehead'. Co-written with Johnny Marr's musical successor Stephen Street and performed by Street (the bass), Vini Reilly (the guitars) and Andrew Paresi (the drums), Morrissey's solo debut single was backed on the B-side by 'I Know Very Well How I Got My Name' and also the Ortonesque 'Hairdresser On Fire'.

Complete with those radio-friendly keyboards and human string section, this trio of tracks would prove that, not only was there life after The Smiths, but also revealed that Steven Patrick 'Mother's-Boy' hadn't really enjoyed the sin-free, housebound, bespectacled, club-footed, misery-packed, adolescence he'd wanted us to believe.

LB: For starters, surely 'Suedehead' has something to do with Richard Allen's trash novel of the same name? (Morrissey raises one eyebrow but doesn't reply.) Yet there's no mention of suedeheads in the lyrics?

Morrissey: "No, I'd noticed that. Does the song have anything to do with the title? Well, I did happen to read the book when it came out and I was quite interested in the whole Richard Allen cult. But really I just like the word 'suedehead'."

So it's not even based on an episode from *Suedehead*?

"No, not really."

And it's not about anyone in particular?

"Yes, it is, but I'd rather not give any addresses and phone numbers at this stage."

Did you read all the Richard Allen books? *Skinhead, Suedehead, Smoothies, Glam . . .* ?

"Yes, they were quite risqué little books at the time, certainly for 13-year-olds, who were the only people who read them. They were definitely to be hidden under the pillow."

Did your mother know?

"No, but she wasn't a suedehead. She was heavily into reggae." (He giggles.) "I don't think she even read *Suedehead*! I had a small bookcase in my bedroom and I'm sure that while I was at school she placed a chair in front of it and examined everything, noted the turned over corners."

Weren't the books full of fighting and fornicating?

"Yes, but I skipped those bits. I do remember the fuss they caused but I think they were only really little bits of enlightenment for a certain sector of people."

Were you attracted to *Suedehead* and *Skinhead* because the heroes led very different lifestyles to your own?

"They didn't really because youth cults in Manchester were very strong and suedeheads and skinheads and smoothies were very much part of daily life. I went to youth clubs that were quite violent and youth discos in the afternoons. I have certain fond memories . . . the grime, certain records like 'Double Barrel' and 'Young Gifted And Black'.

"There was a tremendous air of intensity and potential unpleasantness – something interesting grabbed me about the whole thing. Perhaps only in retrospect, not really at the time because on your way home you'd always get duffed up."

How often were you duffed up?

"Well, I was chased occasionally, but I wasn't entirely incapable of running and hiding behind adults, pretending I was with them. A few times I'd have to run up and down people's garden paths and ring on the doorbell."

Were suedeheads the good guys?

"Not really. I don't think there were any good guys. Everybody had several chips on several shoulders. There was a great velocity of hate!"

And what exactly was a suedehead?

"I think it was an outgrown skinhead. But outgrown only in the hair sense, nothing else. I don't mean a very, very large skinhead with a growth on his back. No, an outgrown skinhead who was slightly softer, not meant to be a football hooligan for instance . . . so obviously much less interesting."

What were you wearing back in '71, when the *Suedehead* book came out?

"I fluctuated slightly. I didn't religiously belong to any cult apart from when T. Rex happened and I bought a satin jacket. It was the first independent statement I made and it was extremely important to me."

Flares?

"I did stray into a pair of loons on some occasions. Quite naturally green at the bottom and quite naturally yellow at the top. Extreme horrendous colours. Then later, when The New York Dolls happened, I tried to buy a pair of knee length platform boots but I was very wisely stopped! At the time, just to have a faint platform on a very dull shoe was very risqué. It was tempting disaster."

A Crombie?

"I slept in a Crombie, with a Lancashire rose on it. You could quite easily be duffed up by those wearing a Yorkshire rose. There were constant territorial vicious antagonising reasons for small-time anarchy. Everybody got their head kicked in, everybody! Even at school . . . it's made me what I am today."

Hair?

"With the Bowie thing and Roxy Music and Mott The Hoople I began to hang around with a gang of people in Manchester who were very artistic and very expressive. They dyed their hair."

Hence the reference to dyeing your hair gold in 'I Know Very Well How I Got My Name'?

"Yes, that's me. That's true. When I was 13 I did experiment with bottles of bleach and so forth. I tried to dye it yellow and it came out gold, then I tried to get rid of it and it came out purple. I was sent home from school."

131

How did your mother react?

"She was mildly concerned. Very tolerant, she'd had a lot of practice."

You weren't spanked?

"No, that came much later in life, with the release of *The Queen Is Dead*."

Is 'Hairdresser On Fire' (complete with hair dryer solo!) based on Orton's (and Halliwell's) *The Boy Hairdresser*?

"No, it's just a very simple song about trying to get *hold* of a hairdresser."

Why did you dye your hair?

"I think 'Starman' was the beginning but the whole notion of Bowie being this despised person I found very encouraging. The daily tabloids wrote hateful things and there were only one or two people at school who'd actually confess to liking David Bowie. I don't think that level of outrage exists anymore. People have forgotten how dramatic and serious it really was.

"The Slade and Faces contingents were particularly aggressive people, while those who liked Bowie, Mott The Hoople and Lou Reed tended to be slightly more passive and easily picked on. I remember standing outside concert halls in the early Seventies, especially in the daytime when you'd go very very early to try and spot a coach. People would just walk past you in Manchester and start kicking the queue. Everybody would just cower and hide under a mass of Afghan coats."

And now those happy days are here again?

"Not for me! But I've seen a tramp with an Afghan coat on. I think we'll reach the stage where tramps no longer wear old 1930s overcoats and cloth caps, that they'll actually be going round in platforms and Chicory Tip T-shirts. It will happen! The tramps of the future obviously have to move with the times. They have a certain obligation."

Now you're on a major label, do you think 'Suedehead' will be a hit?

"I have only ever been interested in people who quite faithfully have a keen interest in what you do, otherwise the world doesn't interest me. The obvious chart manoeuvres, the obvious track which would appeal to people who generally wouldn't be interested in me . . . I find it very hard trying to cater for those people, which I suppose is what being on a major label is all about. To reach the uninitiated . . . which entirely foxes me."

The Smiths' story might have been very different if EMI had signed you back in 1982 instead of Rough Trade.

"People often say to me, 'Do you think if The Smiths had been on a major label would every record have been a landmark in sales terms?' I'm not really sure about that. There's a belief that the records would have sold more and had more acceptable chart placings. But I think the celebration of The Smiths being on Rough Trade without financial backing was part of the whole appealing picture in the sense that, when 'Girlfriend In A Coma' entered the charts at number 13 without any Radio One airplay and without any promotion, it was an enormous achievement. I think people sense that. But it was more of a miracle than people generally realised."

How have you found life on EMI so far? What's their attitude towards you?

"They've really agreed with practically everything, which can't be explained; very approving, a total phenomenon. I thought they'd step in and start trying to re-chisel everything. They said, 'It's great and it's going to be huge' . . . So at the time of making the decision about 'Suedehead' – which didn't occur to me as a quite obvious, easy slide-up-the-dreadful-pop-tree as it were – I didn't really mind. It motivated me and that was all I was really concerned about."

Its "radio friendly" isn't it?

"I'll be very surprised if anybody plays it."

The "keyboard wash" will help. (Morrissey winces at this dreaded Eighties phrase.)

"I don't really mind, to be quite honest, if they don't play it. Not because I'm less interested in what I do, I've grown accustomed to that situation where people, if they don't like you, won't accommodate you in any way, regardless of what you do, even if you had a big fat keyboard washy sound. Or if you re-released 'Shakespeare's Sister'. If people are interested they'll play, if they aren't they won't."

You haven't got a great relationship with radio DJs have you?

"They obviously acted unforgivably towards The Smiths. It can't ever be forgiven really."

How do you feel about Radio One's Steve Wright now? Have you heard him mimicking you? (Morrissey had written the lyrics to 'Panic' in response to Wright's decision to play Wham's 'I'm Your Man' immediately after a newsflash about the Chernobyl Disaster in April 1986. In retaliation, Wright later released the single 'One More Week In The Charts' to the tune of 'Oscillate Wildly'.)

"I heard it once, I was in shock. I was buying scented candles in a shop and it came on the radio. I don't take it as a jibe or hurtful. I do see the twisted compliment somewhere. Believe it or not, he hasn't been too bad. He was the only daytime DJ to play 'That Joke Isn't Funny Anymore' so he isn't obviously as bad or ugly as he looks."

What did you think of Bernard Manning's tribute to The Smiths? (The controversial Manchester comic, who died in 2007, had memorably covered 'This Charming Man' and 'Girlfriend In A Coma'.)

"Well I definitely laughed and, yes, I would like to think he was the antithesis of me. I was very pleased that he did it. I thought it was very funny and that it should be released as a single. Very very very humorous."

So, aside from radio, what will you do to promote 'Suedehead'? TV appearances on *Saturday Superstore* or *Wide Awake Club*?

"I can't think of one television programme in the pop field that I'd want to appear on. There just aren't any. I think it's sad that things have reached such a level where the pop industry, television and so forth actually embarrasses intelligent artists.

"Strong intelligent artists should dictate practically everything. If we talk about Tiffany, Belinda Carlisle, the whole influx of Americanised Debbie Gibsons we could easily be accused of being trivial, of giving too much attention to obviously untalented, discountable people. But these people are absolutely ruling British popular music in 1988 and it's a serious epidemic. The Top 40 has never been so dank and depressing and non-musical as it is now."

Morrissey can't help getting annoyed about this. As he once explained, "I care because I have always loved passionately popular music. I think even as each day passes and popular music becomes more and more distasteful, its actual history becomes more and more important."

Perhaps it's caused by the whole *Fame* thing? This American dream that high school girls can become heroines, shop girls can become superstars. It gives everyone the hope that they can easily become a pop artist.

"But I don't think people really buy them, I really don't believe that. We're intelligent people, we all know that the Top 40 chart is a game and is, quite seriously in certain cases, rigged. I don't believe that people are going out and buying certain records in the Top 10. It's impossible, even taking into account the possibility that 30 per cent of the British public might be seriously mentally . . . unspectacular. There's a serious conspiracy going on and I personally blame . . . Jack Charlton."

Are we talking about pop music as escapism rather than an attempt to confront reality?

"No, I just think they're incredibly thick people who are being given free reign. They're being handed the music industry and every degree of national exposure saying 'it's yours'."

Do you think its just pop apathy to go with the current mood of political apathy?

"It is apathy but it's even more serious than apathy. Sometimes I find it hard to believe that anything truly violent can happen again. And certainly we seem to be further away from the possibility of disruption than ever before. Nobody is brave any more. Nobody makes brave records, brave statements. Everybody has just thrown down their arms and backed off.

"Equally, I get very annoyed with groups who are intelligent and groups who are creatively acceptable because I feel that people aren't kicking hard enough. Groups aren't maintaining any real protest. Everybody's just lying back and saying nothing really. I don't understand that. There is a distinct lack of aggression!"

Is that why you called the album *Viva Hate*? Or is it something to do with the car, the Vauxhall Viva?

He looks crestfallen. Then, as if talking to a complete simpleton, "No, no, no . . . it means 'Long Live Hate'!"

Wasn't that a New Seekers' song?

He laughs, desperately. "No, they didn't do 'Long Live Hate'. If they did it wasn't a hit. But did you ever like Chicory Tip?"

Chicory Tip? What, the band that did 'Son Of My Father'?

"It was Giorgio Moroder who wrote the song and I think he played the synthesiser. The follow up was 'Good Grief Christina'. Johnny and I once drove 250 miles to get a copy of 'Good Grief Christina'. And 'What's Your Name', which was the third hit, was excellent."*

So did you embrace the pop side of Northern Soul? What about Wigan's Ovation, did you like them?

"They had three hits, the most famous was 'Skiing In The Snow'. The follow-up was called 'Personally', and the follow-up to that was 'Superlove'. Great! It was actually on the Spark label which was a Northern Soul label."

So you were into all that?

"Oh, completely. As a spectator. Yes, definitely Wigan's Ovation and

---

* I was baffled by this sudden Chicory Tip diversion. I couldn't work out if it was a defence of the synthesiser on 'Suedehead', a nod to gay disco and Northern Soul, or a simple celebration of the work of Moroder. Of course, I later realised 'Long Live Hate' was Morrissey's comic response to Sandie Shaw's 1965 hit 'Long Live Love'. Similarly, he'd stolen the title for The Smiths' 1984 single 'Heaven Knows I'm Miserable Now' from her 1969 45 rpm 'Heaven Knows I'm Missing Him Now'.

Chicory Tip. You don't really believe me do you? You think I'm just jumping on this modern bandwagon for Dave & Ansell Collins."

Well, without wishing to rekindle the old garotte-the-DJ furore, what do you seriously think of Rap and Hip-Hop?

"I really do think it's a great musical stench. I find it very offensive, artless and styleless. To me it's very reminiscent of thuggery . . . pop thuggery. I don't want to hear it at all."

But surely it just reflects a different culture from your own?

"I don't think it has anything to do with culture. Initially it did but I think it's burnt out. I know white people who are obsessed with it and feel it speaks to them but I find it remarkably illiterate, without any degree of cunning and without any degree of confrontation. I don't forgive that regardless of the category."

Yet it's got great appeal and it's powerful music because it's the product of our new multi-racial society?

"I think that's proved to be true, very true, but it says nothing to me . . . about my kitchen."

Do you really think it's fair to slag off an area of music outside your taste and experience?

"Yes, I do."

But Schoolly D's never off your turntable?

"All the time."

Whereas The Wedding Present and The Primitives do say something to you?

"Well, it's definitely my world, but even within that I do have certain criticisms, I do have certain rules and regulations. But, yes, they are very much part of my little planet. The Primitives, if we have to get personal about these things, I was initially very excited by, but no longer see what I first saw. I don't know whether that's the draining process; I can understand the pressures of suddenly being on *Wogan*, of suddenly being on RCA, but a little bit of intrigue has disappeared."

Is that why you refused to perform with them?

"No, I don't think that's very stylish at all, singing with other people, especially as the song in question was 'Ticket To Ride'. I mean, would you?"

You also turned down the chance to record a track for the *NME* compilation *Sgt. Pepper Knew My Father.*

"It was a difficult time when the request came through. I was in emotional turmoil. Even in retrospect it doesn't seem like a terribly interesting idea. Some bits of *Sgt. Pepper* . . . I really like 'A Day In The Life', 'Lovely Rita'. Obviously I'm a great Beatles fan."

Given the effect that the break-up of The Smiths has obviously had on you, have you tried to deal with your feelings in any of the tracks on *Viva Hate*?

"No I haven't because that would be the next expected thing to do. I don't really want to do that. I suppose, whatever way you look at *Viva Hate* it quite elegantly expresses the way I felt instantly post-split because as soon as The Smiths broke up I was practically wheeled into a studio to make that record. Whichever way you examine it that is post-Smiths Morrissey. But there are no bitter references to the past."

Do you intend to tour as a solo artist, or would you find being onstage without the cloak of The Smiths too lonely an experience?

"Loneliness doesn't really come into it. I think there are other stronger feelings which are quite negative. Unless I find musicians who are particularly aggressive I'd be very nervous of attempting anything that was less than The Smiths."

What about the musicians on *Viva Hate*?

"It isn't a set group as such. I hope I can just skip in and skip out of situations, much as I always have done. It's very different. I would rather The Smiths had not broken up but they have and there is very little I can do about it. So I just simply adapt."

If you ever do tour again, now that you've released a song called 'Suedehead', isn't there a danger that you'll attract a more violent element to your concerts?

"I should be so lucky. I kind of predict that but it's not something that would dramatically offend me. I like self-expression and I like the self-rescue of being in a gig/concert environment, expressing yourself in a very strong way."

Even if you're dragged off the stage?

He laughs. "That's why I'm there."

I'd really like to see The Smiths live again.

"So would I. I'd love to see The Smiths live. You've got to be there, to smell the body odour!"

That evening, after the interview, Jo Slee – who'd coordinated the artwork to all The Smiths covers and would now act as a personal assistant to Morrissey – drove us across town in her old Morris Minor Estate to Rough Trade's offices in North London. Arriving at the Collier Street HQ, it seemed very strange to see a solitary plimsoll hanging by one lace from the overhead telephone lines. I reminded Morrissey of his spanking line about the "wet plimsoll" when rumours of The Smiths' split first broke, then, jokingly accused him of placing the plimsoll there. But he wasn't in the mood for humour and, initially, seemed reluctant to enter the building.

There was a party going on but it seemed more like a wake for Morrissey and The Smiths, with echoes of 'Paint A Vulgar Picture'. No sign of Mike Joyce or Andy Rourke or Johnny Marr, of course, but many of the people who'd worked with The Smiths at Rough Trade, including press officer Pat Bellis, were obviously still stunned by the death of the band. Morrissey was treated like a royal visitor but he seemed uneasy in this situation and he definitely struggled to do small talk. He clearly had mixed feelings about the past and there was obviously a strain in his relationship with Geoff Travis. The fruits of the band's success – gold discs, posters, album artwork, etc – were displayed all around us.

The mood was only lightened by James Maker, the ex-Smiths go-go dancer, who was there with his band Raymonde. One of Morrissey's oldest friends, they would lose touch for most of the Nineties. In a later fax to me, Morrissey sounded nostalgic about these days. He'd choose a Raymonde track for his compilation *NME*'s *Songs To Save Your Life* and, when he set up his own Attack label in 2003, James Maker would be one of his first signings.

After the party, Jo Slee drove us back across London, Morrissey in the passenger seat, me sitting like a small child at the end of a day trip out, in the middle of the back seat. The words to 'There Is A Light That Never Goes Out' went through my head as we crossed the city at night, while Morrissey asked me about my home city Newcastle – "an interesting place, uneven place," he tells me – and pointed out several London landmarks once frequented by the ubiquitous Oscar Wilde.

We talked about Manchester and his decision to leave the city. Did he still like the place? "Well I do go back a lot. I hover mainly just outside the centre. Although I physically moved away, imaginatively I never felt I left Manchester behind. It's always with me. I brought it with me in a sense. Obviously I know people there so the ties haven't really been broken."

Didn't he worry about losing touch with his roots?

"People who are left behind themselves always say those things. For me, getting out and getting on, progress always meant leaving Manchester. Suddenly going back almost seems quite wrong."

Jo Slee dropped me back off at Sloane Square, and as I left the car, I was given an advance cassette copy of *Viva Hate* and a 12-inch of Morrissey's second solo single, 'Everyday Is Like Sunday'. Delighted, I shook hands again with Morrissey and this time there was less awkwardness, perhaps more of a relaxed connection. "Be gentle," he laughed as I walked away.

Arriving home in Brixton, I played 'Everyday Is Like Sunday' for the first time, a beautiful, funny, happy-sad anthem with music by Stephen Street. It will remain one of his Morrissey's finest songs and greatest lyrics, both a celebration and also a commiseration of the deserted delights of an out-of-season English coastal resort.

Recognising its lyrical tribute (others would brand it plagiarism) to John Betjeman's *Slough* – "Come, friendly bombs, and fall on Slough, It isn't fit for humans now" – I reached for my Penguin Modern Classics volume *The Best Of Betjeman*. After reading *Slough* again, I let the page turn and found myself confronted with another Betjeman poem entitled *The Arrest Of Oscar Wilde At The Cadogan Hotel*.

This connection or staged coincidence, I would learn, was very typical of Morrissey. There always seems to be another reason why he wants to meet you somewhere, or why he mentions someone or something, as if it's all part of some intricate masterplan. Maybe he's got an underground bunker somewhere, like a Bond villain, complete with complex wall-charts explaining how everything's connected, how everthing leads to and from the heroes or villains he's hell-bent on celebrating or elevating.

Although Morrissey would soon publicly regret the release of *Viva Hate* it remains one his great artistic achievements. By anyone's standards, given the fact that The Smiths' split wasn't official until August 1987, the arrival of his first solo album at number one in the UK albums charts in March 1988 was remarkable. Morrissey would later describe it as "more of an event than an achievement" and even told Nick Kent there were "six tracks on it I'd now willingly bury in the nearest patch of soil".

Nevertheless, in 'Suedehead' and 'Everyday Is Like Sunday', *Viva Hate* contained two of the most commercially successful singles of his entire career (with The Smiths or solo), while he'd continued to provoke political controversy with the hate-fuelled final track, 'Margaret On The Guillotine'; the musical fulfilment of Morrissey's dream that Thatcher would be 'taken out' by some Sirhan Sirhan-style assassin.

Elsewhere *Viva Hate* sounded like an extremely personal album. 'Dial-A-Cliché' explored the awkward relationship between a boy and his father, while 'Break Up The Family' and 'Late Night, Maudlin Street' were too painfully close to home to be about anything but the toughness of Morrissey's troubled teenage years.

'Late Night, Maudlin Street' perfectly conveyed run-down Northern England in the early Seventies, and dealt with the difficult transition from childhood to adulthood, "bad times" complete with power cuts, brushes with violence and the police, leaving home and the loss of friendships. As with 'Angel, Angel, Down We Go Together' and 'Break Up The Family', mortality and suicidal thoughts are referenced in the subject matter of the song.

The title of 'Late Night Maudlin Street', like 'Suedehead', was taken from one of the books Morrissey had consumed in the early Seventies. *Short Stories Of Our Time* (edited by D.R. Barnes, Harrap, 1963) was a standard text book in English schools and featured writers such as H.E. Bates (*Shot Actress*), John Steinbeck (*The Raid*), John Wain (*A Message From The Pig-Man*) and finally Bill Naughton's *Late Night On Watling Street*. 'Maudle' had been a derogatory nickname for Oscar Wilde a century earlier, and Maudlin Street Secondary was also the name of the school in *Carry On Teacher*.*

Elsewhere on *Viva Hate*, there was 'Alsatian Cousin' with its *Carry On Camping*-style sexual shenanigans; its title inspired by a throwaway line in Alan Bennett's *Forty Years On*. Memorably, there's also 'I Don't Mind If You Forget Me' – perhaps the only album track that could be interpreted as a hostile response to either Radio One or Johnny Marr or both.

Another track, 'Little Man, What Now?' focused on the tragedy of a fallen child star – I suggested someone like Oldham-lad Jack Wild (The Artful Dodger in *Oliver*) or even Bobby Bennett or Glynn Poole (*Junior Showtime*) but Morrissey said he preferred "Sixties things like *Petticoat Junction*" (an American sitcom from 1963 to 1970, set in fictional Hooterville with a rockabilly theme tune by Curt Massey) – who goes unrecognised on an afternoon nostalgia show. A classic example of Morrissey's ability to create a moving, sympathetic pop song out of absolutely nothing.

---

* Irish born Bill Naughton also wrote the Sixties sex-comedy *Alfie* and the Northern kitchen-sink dramas *Spring And Port Wine* and *The Family Way*, the latter featuring Smiths' cover stars Avril Angers and Murray Head. Two of Morrissey's favourite performers, Anthony Newley and Terence Stamp, turned down the chance to play *Alfie* in Lewis Gilbert's 1966 film, but Cilla 'Work Is A Four Letter Word' Black memorably sang the famous Bacharach-David title song.

Several years later we'd talk about Jimmy Clitheroe, fondly remembered from Morrissey's youth; the diminutive Lancastrian comedian who starred on BBC radio in the Sixties as *The Clitheroe Kid*, originated the catchphrase "some mothers do 'ave 'em" and was destined to play the overgrown schoolboy forever. While working at Granada Television in 2003, I stumbled across some film footage of an interview with Clitheroe in the early Seventies and sent a copy to Morrissey. In his reply, he informed me that Clitheroe lived with his mother all his life . . . and killed himself on the morning of her funeral.

More controversial than even 'Margaret On The Guillotine', in the longer term at least, was 'Bengali In Platforms', a supposedly light-hearted song in which Morrissey urged a citizen of Asian origin to avoid Seventies fashion crimes, to shelve his Western plans, because life was hard enough for those who belonged here. (At the time, Morrissey told me the song was "really 1988 and the very notion of people coming from one clime and trying to adopt English culture in order to blend in".)

The song would come back to haunt Morrissey during the 'Madstock' controversy of 1992. Although the subject matter clearly reflected Morrissey's own unhappiness with British society in the late Eighties – the sense that he (as an Irish Mancunian) struggled to feel he could ever belong or be accepted – the song would later be used in negative press articles to imply that he was somehow being racist and that he believed in the exclusion or repatriation of ethnic minorities. His conservative, nationalistic but certainly *not* racist views on immigration would cause a further stir in the first decade of the 21st century.

In the summer of 1988 I got further insights into the recording of *Viva Hate* by interviewing Stephen Street, The Smiths' producer who'd stepped into Johnny Marr's songwriting slippers for most of the tracks on the record.

The youthful Street had started working as an engineer with The Smiths in 1984 when they'd recorded 'Heaven Knows I'm Miserable Now'. He'd worked on every subsequent Smiths' release, had observed them surviving *The Queen Is Dead* traumas of Andy Rourke's heroin addiction, the hiring and firing of second guitarist Craig Gannon, and had finally been a key witness as co-producer during the sessions that fermented the collapse of The Smiths.

It was at this point that Stephen Street had humbly proffered his own compositions; not initially as Morrissey/Street solo material but, as B-sides to back the *Strangeways, Here We Come* singles which were to be recorded

141

by Morrissey, Rourke, Joyce and a replacement for Johnny Marr.

"I thought I'd help out. I sent Morrissey a cassette of demos with a letter saying, 'Chances are you won't like them but . . .' I got the impression from Mike and Andy, when I told them, that I shouldn't have interfered but the cassette had already gone.

"At best I was hoping for him to say, 'OK I'd like to use them as B-sides with Mike and Andy' and off we'd go. But I got a letter back from him saying, 'I don't see any point in continuing The Smiths, would you like to make a record with me?' I think the idea was still to use Mike and Andy but Mike put in his notice that he was leaving The Smiths. I think he got wind that it was going to be a Morrissey thing rather than a Smiths thing."

Initially Street sent Morrissey demos of the melodies that became 'Angel, Angel, Down We Go Together', 'Bengali In Platforms' and 'Everyday Is Like Sunday'.

"When he wrote back saying he'd got some great ideas I thought it was just going to be a single. But when he came round to my place and put vocals on my four-track demo it started sounding like it could really work. We did the first session and EMI still weren't happy about me doing the whole album. But at the end of the first week we had 'Suedehead' ready, and they really liked it, so we got down to work."

How did Vini Reilly of Durutti Column come to be involved in the project?

"I introduced Vini to Morrissey which was really frightening because they're both strong moody characters. I thought, 'This is either gonna work or it'll be embarrassing.' Fortunately they got on really well.

"I'm not like Johnny where I could rely on technical ability to make a mediocre song sound really great. I'm not saying Johnny did that but I've got to write a sound song without any great ability. I was worried people would say, 'Oh the songs are OK but the musicians aren't very good' because Johnny's really been put on a pedestal as far as guitar players are concerned.

"That's why I'm so pleased Vini performed well. He would come up with weird ideas; his guitar playing on 'Maudlin Street' gave us a different angle and also his Spanish guitar on 'Margaret . . .'."

Stephen Street's main problem in crafting songs for Morrissey was how to sound original and different from The Smiths while incorporating the great groaner's familiar style. He had the advantage of being free to make the break with The Smiths guitar-dominated sound and flex technological muscles, but he also acknowledged "there's a certain kind of music Morrissey likes writing to.

"You can find yourself going down the same roads Johnny went down. That's why, when I did 'Maudlin Street' and 'Break Up The Family' I wrote from a percussive loop. Morrissey does ask me to write in different styles, he looks to stretch himself because he knows if he doesn't do it now, as a solo artist, he'll never do it. When I gave him 'Break Up The Family' I thought he wouldn't like it because its got soully overtones. But he really liked it and wrote back to say he'd got lyrics for it."

Did Street think Morrissey had been starved of variety by Johnny Marr?

"No, Johnny would always come up with ideas but I suppose when you're as famous as The Smiths there's great pressure. Mind you The Smiths could try any style, because of Morrissey's voice. They were like The Beatles in the sense that whatever they tried it was unmistakeably their sound.

"But I did get the impression on *Strangeways, Here We Come* that Johnny wasn't supplying Morrissey with as much material as Morrissey would've liked. As if they were all pretty tired after the tour of America and Johnny didn't write much."

Despite the positive reviews, the Number One LP success of *Viva Hate* and the Top 10 placings for 'Suedehead' and 'Everyday's Like Sunday', Morrissey himself recently expressed disappointment with the result. Why?

"Morrissey sent me a card saying, 'Don't read the interview.' I think he realised after he'd done it that he'd been a bit negative about things. The idea that he didn't want 'Suedehead' to be the single is utter rubbish, he was just as excited as anyone else about releasing it. And saying *Viva Hate* wasn't a success is a complete load of bollocks, it surpassed many things he's done in the past."

Wasn't 'Disappointed' ('Everyday Is Like Sunday' B-side) just a parody of 'How Soon Is Now?'?

"People say that but only because of the chugging guitar. I think its more like The Fall or Siouxsie & The Banshees, with the drummer leading it along. I deliberately tried to stay away from those rocky fast/mid tempo songs on the album but, afterwards, we felt we were missing them. So I wrote some but, as soon as Morrissey sings, it's bound to sound like The Smiths."

Weren't you really worried about the response to *Viva Hate*? Did you expect a lot of flak for trying to follow in Johnny Marr's footsteps?

"I was really scared, and I think Morrissey was as well. After the LP was finished in December he went through a low period in January and really didn't want the album to come out.

"When you think about it, The Smiths broke up in July '87, I didn't get word from Morrissey that he wanted to work with me till September, and we finished *Viva Hate* in December. That's bloody good going! It just happened and I know it won't happen quite as magically again."

In addition to his thoughts on the creation and release of *Viva Hate*, only four months after *Strangeways, Here We Come*, Stephen Street also offered insights into the delights of working with Morrissey.

"People say he can be difficult but I think I do my best work with him because he really inspires me. He always tends to amaze me lyrically because his timing's totally different to anyone else.

"'I'd write a song, thinking, 'that's the verse, that's the bridge and that bit's the chorus'. 'Disappointed' is a perfect example because he chose to sing over the little bridge bits and I had to chop it and change it all around. He's really very special. I hate to use the word 'genius' but I do regard him lyrically as that."

Is he as miserable to work with as he'd like us to believe?

"No he's not miserable at all, he's really good fun to be around. He's not extrovert but, during the *Viva Hate* sessions there was some very sharp dry Northern wit flying back and forth over the dinner table with Vini. We'd had a good time during *Strangeways*, . . . and, when we went back to The Wool Hall for *Viva Hate*, I think Morrissey was worried he'd miss The Smiths as a group of lads together.

"In fact, I think he felt more a part of it because during *Strangeways*, . . . he'd go to bed about midnight and the rest of the band would all-night party. With *Viva Hate*, we started and finished earlier. It wasn't like, 'OK, Morrissey's gone to bed let's have a good time lads!' He seemed happy. He actually started going down to the gym, to the Health Club near the studio. He really got into it, enjoyed it, doing the old weights and stuff!"

Did he really go dancing with Vini Reilly in Bath?

"Yeah that was a great night. We all went down the disco and had a few drinks. And this girl went over to Morrissey and got him dancing. I couldn't believe it . . . dancing to some normal dance track. I nearly keeled over."

But he's prone to disappearing tricks, as he was during The Smiths' lifetime. Don't you get annoyed when he fails to turn up or keep in touch?

"When it first happens you tend to get worried about it and think, 'I should have heard from him by now.' But you come to accept that he doesn't feel the need to phone you constantly. He might suddenly, out of the blue, call and say, 'OK, I've got these songs can we book some studio time?' That's the way he works but I never presume I will work with him again.

"I'd like to think there'll be another album this year, I'd like to try out new ideas, but you've got to take it a step at a time with Morrissey. You can't suddenly get him to do an Acid House thing."

Doesn't it piss you off that you're still in the shadows? That most people think you must be some spotty, grim-looking Glitter Band figure or you would be out there in the spotlight as Johnny Marr was?

"When we were doing the album I said to Morrissey, 'It'd be nice to be seen doing something with you because I'm sure people think I'm some kind of Trevor Horn, Stock Aitken & Waterman middle-aged producer in the background'. Afterwards I thought, 'Oh no, you've pushed it a bit, Stephen' but I want it to be known I'm not just some old button pusher!"

You could end up playing Bernie Taupin to Morrissey's Elton John – The Man In The Iron Mask.

"It's not my desire to be like that. It's up to him. I was hoping he'd take a band on *Top Of The Pops* but there isn't really a full-time band, that's the problem. But I was disappointed. It was a childhood dream to be on *TOTP*."

Do you think you'll ever perform live with him?

"He's got such fond memories of The Smiths, he's got it into his mind that he can never match that again. I don't agree. I think, as long as we're careful, people'll love him whatever he's doing. Maybe it'll happen after the second album, when we've got more songs. But I think he's worried about not capturing the same spirit of The Smiths live. Going out with me live would be the full stop at the end of The Smiths' sentence."

Whether or not people regarded Stephen Street as either a saviour or a poor substitute for Johnny Marr, without Street's humble intervention Morrissey would have spent a lot longer languishing in a pit of despair. He had, at least, been instrumental in the first success of Morrissey as a solo star.

But would it last? Surely the notoriously paranoid singing vegetarian wouldn't take kindly to Mr Street's 'unauthorised' chat with *NME*?

"Chances are I'll get an angry letter from him, I can't tell. I don't think I've said anything bad about him. I know Morrissey did control what was said by The Smiths. I think Mike once did an interview and Morrissey didn't like the sound of it; after that Mike didn't do any more interviews."

And if it all ended tomorrow, if Morrissey finally disappeared or failed to call, would Stephen Street be surprised?

"No, because I still get the feeling, at the back of my mind, that The Smiths are going to reform at anytime. Since that *NME* interview I've always been aware I can't sit back and expect to always be working with Morrissey. I think if Johnny just phoned him and they somehow resolved whatever differences they've got, they'll reform. But I can't say."

With hindsight, my interview with Stephen Street, published in *NME* in July 1988 – headlined "Hate Male" – almost certainly marked the end of Street's relationship with Morrissey.

It wasn't so much what Street said but that he had spoken without permission; or perhaps had simply ignored the ground rules laid down in advance by Morrissey via his then manager Gail Colson.

When I telephoned Morrissey, on the eve of the interview being published in *NME*, I wasn't entirely sure at first whether to confess my sins (for talking to both Ken Friedman *and* Stephen Street), to be evasive, or to opt for Morrissey's own personal favourite . . . feign sudden illness.

Morrissey: "Please hold on. The Darjeeling's just being wheeled in."

He's on the phone from a Marble Arch hotel. To put it bluntly, he sounded like he was in a bad mood.

I worked out the Betjeman connection, I tell him, nervously, struggling to quote from *The Arrest Of Oscar Wilde At The Cadogan Hotel*.

He laughs but seems defensive. "I'm not really a Betjeman fan. I just liked the poem." (Given his selection of Betjeman reading *A Child Ill* for *NME*'s give-away CD compilation *Songs To Save Your Life* in 2004, it would seem safe to assume that Morrissey likes Betjeman!)

How's it going then?

"I have all but retired . . . although nobody's really noticed. I'm still doing lots of interesting things but the whole thing now is finding somebody to write with. Much harder than it sounds."

What's happened to Stephen Street?

"Well . . . Didn't you interview him recently?"

Er, yes, yes, I did. (Crikey.) It's in this week's issue.

(Coldly.) "I'll buy it tomorrow, what does it say?"

It's not particularly critical of you but . . . (I'm desperately trying to remember anything remotely critical that Stephen Street told me) . . . I did find it strange that he wanted to do the interview. I know you're not very keen on other people talking about you.

"Was it not the fact that Gail (Coulson, Morrissey's manager) told him not to discuss me? Or was that just a rumour that got back to me?"

No . . . I wasn't told that at all. There was . . . inevitably . . . quite a bit of . . . discussion about you. It's quite a big piece. Maybe slightly awkwardly phrased in terms of the headline.

"Why . . . what does it say?"

(I take a deep breath.) The Man Who Saved Morrissey.

There's a stifled guffaw at the other end of the phone. Perhaps it's the groan of a man who's just stubbed his toe, or a stifled scream, or maybe he's just gulping down Darjeeling to give himself strength.

It wasn't my idea! (This sounds pathetic, like a child deflecting blame.)

(Pause, then sadly) "Well . . . it's not really been solid over the last few months . . . It didn't really work out. But he's a very, very amiable chap. Very, very nice."

He did say he thought you and Johnny would soon get back together. That if Johnny just phoned you and you resolved . . . you know . . . your differences . . .

"I wrote to Johnny two months ago. He didn't reply. It was the third time I'd written to him, and I was very hurt by the fact that he didn't reply. He still remains the only person I'd really want to work with. I don't know . . . strange isn't it."

When I was writing the *Viva Hate* article I remember checking back through Johnny Marr's statements when he first left The Smiths. (E.g., on August 8, 1987: "I've already recorded some stuff and it's gone well. I definitely want to have some live dates set up by the New Year at the latest.") It sounded as if he was going to bring new material out in the near future yet, apart from his contribution to Talking Heads' *Naked*, nothing's appeared for over 12 months.

"It's interesting because I've heard that Johnny is working with Barney of New Order and that Ken Friedman is saying 'This is a Johnny Marr record. Johnny's songs are all over it'. It's funny because a person I know . . . connected to New Order, shall we say, has maintained that no demo tapes have been made at all and that they haven't written one song.

"Ken is quite anxious to try and establish Johnny and make him seem as if he's really on his way. And I wish he was. But it isn't really true I don't think." (Electronic's debut single would be released at Xmas 1989.)

Did you see Johnny on telly playing at the Nelson Mandela Concert (June 11, 1988, Wembley, to mark the 70th birthday of the imprisoned ANC leader)?

147

"Oh yes, I did. I thought he looked quite well but . . . why did he do that? I really don't know."

Someone sent me a Dutch copy of 'The Headmaster Ritual' the other day. We stuck it on in the *NME* office and everyone agreed it sounded better than anything around at the moment.

"I listen to The Smiths every single day of my life. I'm really very excited about the live album. It really is beautiful. The sleeve is spectacularly lavish."

Is it you again?

"No it's a person called Alexandra Bastedo."

From The Champions? Wonderful, I used to fancy her.

"Well, didn't we all."

Is it really going to be called *Rank*?

(laughing) "Yes, yes."

As in 'J. Arthur' Rank' (celebrated in Cockney rhyming slang)?

"Yes, yes . . . it's impossible for me to hear it without eating a pillow. Unfortunately the release of that is more exciting than the release of *Viva Hate* . . . which you don't have to comment on."

I protest my affection for *Viva Hate* but Morrissey's winding up now. I finish the conversation hoping that he finds the Stephen Street interview fair and accurate, and wishing him all the best in his search for another songwriter. He sighs deeply.

"I better let you get back to your Shredded Wheat."

Although he'd sounded down-hearted and heading for retirement, 1988 was in reality far from being a doom and gloom year for Morrissey. Apart from the success of *Viva Hate* and the Top 10 singles 'Suedehead' and 'Everyday Is Like Sunday', The Smiths' posthumously released *Rank* (recorded in Kilburn in October 1986) was universally acclaimed as one of *the* great live albums, and made number two in the album charts behind Kylie Minogue's *Kylie*. From the opening bars of Prokofiev's *Romeo And Juliet* through to the glitzy show-closing "Exitus" of Shirley Bassey's 'You'll Never Walk Alone', *Rank* captured The Smiths at their most powerful, emotional and atmospheric best (even with Gannon on "additional guitars"). If, competitively, Morrissey had set out at the start of the year to achieve a higher-profile post-Smiths impact than his ex-partner Johnny Marr, then he'd certainly won that battle.

To witness the climax of his triumphant solo year, on December 22, 1988, I went to Wolverhampton's Civic Hall to cover Morrissey's famous 'comeback gig' for *The Guardian*; his first live performance in Britain since

148

The Smiths had played Brixton Academy two years earlier. Initially it was planned to be something of a Smiths' reunion or a Smiths farewell gesture, but because of the ongoing legal row with Johnny Marr over rights to The Smiths' name, it turned out to be the launch of Morrissey as a live performer instead.

Why Wolverhampton, of all god-forsaken places? Nobody organising the event seemed to know and Morrissey wouldn't explain. Perhaps it was because The Smiths had enjoyed playing there on their last tour, in October '86? I'm none the wiser except to note that Oscar Wilde lectured there on February 10, 1885.

Of course, I'm a great lover of this kind of dramatically staged event; the growing anticipation, the gathering fans, the stipulation that entrance would be free but only gained by those wearing a Smiths' T-shirt, the turned-away truly disappointed teenagers stranded outside once the Civic Hall had reached capacity.

Then there was Morrissey's grand entrance. He arrived at the venue in the school bus originally used in the *St Trinians'* films; probably paying tribute to Alistair Sim's dragged-up headmistress Miss Fritton, or possibly remembering one of the original *St Trinians'* books, *Back To The Slaughterhouse*.

With The Smiths' rhythm section alongside him – Mike Joyce (drums) and Andy Rourke (bass) – plus "ex-Smith 1986" Craig Gannon back on guitar, two people seemed very conspicuous by their absence. There was little surprise that Johnny Marr had declined to appear, but the non-inclusion of Stephen Street still seemed, to say the least, unusual. In fact, given that the set-list was mainly made up of Street's compositions for *Viva Hate*, his non-appearance was perhaps more peculiar than Marr's.

From *The Guardian*, 30 December, 1988

With a soft Charles Hawtrey-style "hullo" and a shower of flowers, Steven Patrick Morrissey returns to the stage. It's two years since his uniquely English band The Smiths played live, and 18 months since co-writer boy-wonder guitarist Johnny Marr's departure for rock'n'roll Hollywood (Simple Minds, Bryan Ferry, Pretenders). Yet now it's as if Morrissey's never been away.

Arguably the most prolific pop lyricist of the Eighties, and certainly one of the most acerbic commentators, Morrissey has managed to pick up the pieces and remodel his remaining Smiths. Drummer Mike Joyce and bassist Andy

Rourke again fire the rhythm section while former second guitarist Craig Gannon has been promoted to lead.

Two thousand people in Smiths T-shirts (the only condition of entry to this free event) celebrate the band's revival, although for legal reasons involving Marr they're unable to call themselves The Smiths.

This is primarily a showcase for Morrissey's New Year single 'The Last Of The Famous International Playboys', but it's also a wildly nostalgic evening; after charging through tracks from the last Smiths LP, Strangeways, Here We Come *and the singer's solo* Viva Hate *work, wave upon wave of fans invade the stage to embrace him.*

With his teasingly confessional lyrics and his comical obsession with mortality ('Death At One's Elbow', 'Disappointed'), Morrissey inspires the sort of rock'n'roll devotion that perhaps only Bono can match this side of the Atlantic.

From the opening salvo of 'Stop Me If You Think You've Heard This One Before' through to a furious encore of the violently funny 'Sweet'n'Tender Hooligan' this was a sweaty, stirring affair. And, although Stephen Street's keyboards were sorely missed on 'Suedehead' and Gannon's live guitar work never quite matched Marr's, clearly Morrissey's solo material can stand alongside The Smiths' best. 'Sister I'm A Poet' works beautifully as does a fresh, addictive unreleased song titled 'Interesting Drug'.

"Johnny Marr is dead," a portly fan screamed in my ear. Certainly few mourned his absence here, but it remains to be seen whether or not Morrissey's men will perform live together on a regular basis. Whatever, this concert was a triumphant, exciting, emotional occasion, the return of one of the few remaining original artists capable of achieving critical and commercial acclaim.

Let's hope it isn't the last of this famous international playboy.

After this extraordinary concert, the hall cleared and, along with my *NME* colleague James Brown (no relation), I was shepherded upstairs to the post-gig party. Morrissey was there, quietly thrilled but modest to a fault about with his return as a showman; overwhelmed by Smiths' fans' physical display of emotion towards him, but humbly accepting the plaudits of the chosen few.

Afterwards, I found out I'd been booked into the same Shropshire hotel as Morrissey, the band and video director Tim Broad plus the Rough Trade and Parlophone entourage (including Pat Bellis and Murray Chalmers, Morrissey's press officers past and present). We sat drinking round a long table in the hotel bar until the early hours, briefly having to file outside when the fire alarm went off.

Unloveable? – the self-styled *Semi-Sorry* (anagram), alone in 1988. (MICK HUTSON/IDOLS)

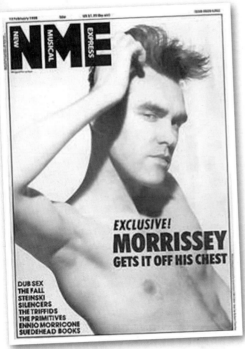

Saint Sebastian gives his first interview as a solo artist (to Len Brown) following the death of "The Six Asterisks", NME 13th February 1988. (PHOTO: EAMONN MCCABE)

Bombed by Betjeman, 'Everyday Is Like Sun on *Top Of The Pops*, Nineteen Eighty Hate (ROBERT HILL/BBC/REDFERNS)

Two years after The Smiths' last UK concert, the Famous International Playboy gets back on the stage at Wolverhampton Civic Hall, Xmas 1988. (STEVE DOUBLE/RETNA)

November Nineteen Ninety. From his monastic cell near Reading, the 'Monster'-e Mozzer describes Madchester as "the reven of the daft". (PHOTO: KEVIN CUMMINS/IDOLS)

'We Hate It When Our Friends Become Successful', especially if they're Northern! With Tim Booth, at the height of James' 'Sit Down' fame, at Amnesty International's 30th Birthday Party, Nottingham, December 1991.

"I needed to rebuild the gang spirit". The Glitter Band, *Kill Uncle*, 1991: Alain Whyte (guitars), Gary Day (bass), "Trouble" (vocal chores), Boz Boorer (guitars), Spencer 'Ringo' Cobrin (drums). (KEVIN CUMMINS/IDOLS)

A Mancunian In Paris, aghast at the top shelf. Pigalle, 1992. (HUGO DIXON/IDOLS)

Pinkie Brown promoting "his best record since *The Queen Is Dead*" (according to *Select*). *Vauxhall*-era personal assistant Jake is on Moz's left. (KEVIN CUMMINS/IDOLS)

Portrait of Whistler, Q magazine's Songwriter Of The Year, 1994. (PA PHOTOS)

The Cantona-loving Manchester United fan? Promoting 'Boxers', 1995. (ADRIAN CALLAGHAN/RETNA)

The row over royalties: Wilde prepares to Mike Joyce and the "Victorian legal system" the High Court, London, December 1996. (PHOTO NEWS SERVICE/REX FEATURES)

The exiled, *Maladjusted* man in San Francisco, *sans* quiff, 1997. (STEVE JENNINGS/WIREIMAGE.COM)

Author Meets Artist (in a Cheshire pub car park). *The Brit Girls*, 1997. (LEN BROWN)

"Cilla Black actually broke The Smiths up...which is...pretty much to her credit" (*The Brit Girls*, 199
(LEN BROWN)

Grosvenor House, London. May 28 1998.
[wit]hout a record deal but with an Ivor Novello
award; presented, for his Outstanding
[c]ontribution to British Music, by one of his
[h]eroes Anthony Newley. Accepting his Ivor,
[he] thanked "John Maher of Wythenshawe…
[for g]etting me where I am today. Which begs the
question, 'Where am I?'". (PA PHOTOS)

Coachella, California, October 16 1999,
with the 21st Century breathing down his neck.
(VAUGHN YOUTZ/ZUMA PRESS/NEWSCOM)

An old southpaw, out for the count, 2001 – three years before his famous
You Are The Quarry comeback. (ROLAND TANNLER/EYEVINE)

"This country's greatest songwriter" (according to Chrissie Hynde). Mozzer and the great Pretender share a light ale at PETA's 20th birthday party, September 2000. (BERLINER STUDIO/PETA)

Bernard Matthews' arch-enemy, Moriarty, with friendly fowl. At PETA (People for the Ethical Treatment of Animals) in Los Angeles, November 21 2002. (CHRIS POLK/PETA)

Morrissey and I talked about *St Trinians* and the *Carry On* films. In the Xmas issue of *NME*, published a week earlier, I'd written an extensive article about the *Carry On* genre and interviewed the producer/director team of Peter Rogers and Gerald Thomas. While he'd loved the headline – "Carry On Dying" – Morrissey seemed shocked by the unsympathetic tone of Rogers and Thomas towards his heroes Kenneth Williams and Charles Hawtrey, who'd both died earlier that year.

Thomas, in responding to my suggestion that there might be a *Carry On* curse (five of the eight key actors all died relatively young), had said about Hawtrey: "You can't really call it a curse when a man in his seventies, pickled with alcohol, is offered the choice of either losing both his legs and living, or dying."

Morrissey, of course, was something of an expert on the *Carry On* series: "There were 27 films made in all, and at least six of them are high art. They finished artistically in '68 but went on, I think to '76 or '78 . . . when you think of Charles Hawtrey, Kenneth Williams, Hattie Jacques, Barbara Windsor, Joan Sims, Sid James . . . the wealth of talent!"

We had talked about Hawtrey earlier that year, before the actor's death, when I'd asked Morrissey if he still saw himself as "Kenneth Williams' understudy"?

Morrissey: "I never said Kenneth Williams, I said Charles Hawtrey, but they printed Kenneth Williams, probably because he's better known."

But Charles Hawtrey was a legend.

"He is! He's still alive, and I believe his father, who's mentioned in the Richard Ellmann biography, acted in some Oscar Wilde things . . . small world!"

But Hawtrey was never a contender for a Smiths' cover?

"Yes he was. I got lots of prints of Charles Hawtrey and I had just narrowed it down to one, when there were no more covers left." (Hawtrey would, of course, later adorn the cover of one of The Smiths' greatest hits compilations.)

In the months preceding Wolverhampton both Charles Hawtrey and Kenneth Williams had died and Morrissey had penned *NME* obituaries for both actors. His tribute to Hawtrey, as the "very last comic genius", claimed that the actor was "60 per cent of *Carry On* appeal. By never giving press interviews, and by all accounts being unfriendly and friendless, Hawtrey's mystique surpasses Garbo".

Of Williams' passing he wrote, "I loved his bomb-shelter Britishness, his touch-me-not-wit, his be-ironed figure, stylishly non-sexual; his facial features were as funny as anything he ever said . . . The passion absent from his celibate existence appeared to the brim, and past the brim in his work. Another irreplaceable strip of Britishness falls away."

Despite my reminding him of these sad *Carry On* losses, Morrissey seemed to be on a real high that night in Wolverhampton, almost as if he couldn't believe such a post–Smiths, post-*Rank*, posthumous performance could have been possible. I honestly don't think, before Wolverhampton, that he had any long term plan to go on, to carry on. But the ecstatic, affectionate reception he'd received clearly proved he could exist as a solo star, having previously described The Smiths as his "life support machine".

As an observer, looking round the table after Morrissey had left the happy gathering, there suddenly seemed to be a definite sense that the break up of The Smiths' wasn't the end of the story and that tonight was a new beginning.

With Gannon, Joyce and Rourke alongside him, Morrissey's future as an EMI recording and performing artist looked assured.

Later I talked to Craig Gannon, who'd stepped back onto the stage with Morrissey after being dumped by The Smiths only two years earlier. He spoke about key moments in his career – Aztec Camera, The Bluebells, The Colourfield, The Smiths – but confirmed Wolverhampton was "one of the greatest gigs I've ever played" and seemed thrilled with the praise he'd received from Morrissey for his guitar work on 'The Last Of The Famous International Playboys' single.

Craig reflected on his disappointing, post-*Queen Is Dead* departure from The Smiths in 1986 and explained how he now felt far removed from the blame he'd received for making The Smiths look and sound like The Rolling Stones. Clearly, for what would be one night only in Wolverhampton, he briefly stepped out of Johnny Marr's shadows: "Everyone says that, you know, 'Craig Gannon – rhythm guitarist', but I hardly ever played just solid rhythm. When I played lead Johnny played rhythm, we just swapped around."

Sitting in that hotel bar, somewhere in deepest Shropshire, I couldn't help thinking about Stephen Street and his expressed desire to tour the songs he'd written with Morrissey for *Viva Hate*. Where was he tonight? Sitting at home wondering what might have been? Above all, I wondered where Johnny Marr was?

Looking from the outside, it seemed as if since The Smiths Johnny Marr had been quietly content to just collaborate and contribute guitar to projects devised by some of his friends and heroes. Perhaps he'd been burnt out by the prolific nature and unstoppable success of The Smiths?

Back in late 1986, music journalists had been making barbed attacks on Johnny Marr's "nun-eating rock-monster" version of Smiths. With Nick Kent's revelation of Marr's "potential alcoholism" during The Smiths last, self-destructive American tour, not forgetting the rock'n'roll car crash which forced the cancellation of their Artists Against Apartheid gig, perhaps it was inevitable that Marr had needed a break from the madness.

Reflecting on his decision to quit The Smiths, he once told Manchester's *Debris* magazine that, "I was ill and away from home and I've no idea what would have happened to me musically . . . ." He added, "I ally myself more with modern musicians. I don't see myself as one in a long line of guitar greats." And also, "what freaked people out was the fact that I was betraying the most perfect pop group of the Eighties . . . They wanted me to die, they wanted to see me die in some rock'n'roll graveyard."

While Morrissey and the remainder of his Smiths' returned to the stage at Wolverhampton, Peter Hook of New Order revealed that "Barney is working with Johnny Marr in the Lake District and getting some stuff together with The Pet Shop Boys." Barney (Bernard Sumner of New Order) himself later added, "Johnny's playing guitar on it. We've done about seven backing tracks without any vocals. What's going to happen is he'll write a couple and I'll write a couple and maybe four we'll write together."

These tracks would, of course, signal the launch of Electronic, something of a supergroup initially involving Barney and Johnny Marr with Neil Tennant of the Pet Shop Boys. Their first hit, 'Getting Away With It' charted in December 1989 and Johnny and Barney continued releasing Electronic albums throughout the Nineties.

In addition to his own band, The Healers, over the years Marr's worked with a wide variety of artists since The Smiths, from The The to Oasis and Bert Jansch to Kirsty MacColl, and would have his greatest commercial success in 2007 after linking up with the American indie rock band Modest Mouse. The album he co-wrote with them, *We Were Dead Before The Ship Even Sank*, entered the *US* Billboard chart at number one – a feat yet to be achieved by Morrissey.

8.

Madchester, So Much To Answer For

"I think my solo situation and achievements have been outrageously undervalued, whilst that of certain other ex-Smiths have been outrageously over-valued."

– Morrissey

ARRIVING back in Brixton from Newcastle in the New Year of 1989 I was surprised to receive a card from Morrissey. I'd sent him a Xmas gift via EMI Records; a copy of *Deep Joy* by Stanley Unwin (the inventor of Gobbledegook, who'd appeared in *Carry On Regardless*) plus a map of the Parisien churchyard where Wilde was buried.

Morrissey's reply, in an envelope covered with stickers promoting the animal rights organisation People for the Ethical Treatment of Animals (PETA)*, was typed on the back of a postcard showing Irishman Frank Stapleton of Manchester United (his team) out-jumping the Newcastle defence (my team). It was a message of thanks for Wolverhampton, Unwin, the Wilde graveyard map and the *Carry On Dying* conversation. Typically, it was signed "Julian Orchard".

Apart from his re-working of Wilde's famous line "we are all in the gutter but some of us are looking at the stars", the obvious question was why Julian Orchard? I remembered the gangling, ever-so-camp terribly English actor from his role in *Carry On Henry* (brilliantly cast as the Duc de Poncenay) and he'd also played Fred in *Carry On Doctor* (significantly sub-titled, terrible pun, *Life Is A Four-Letter Ward*). But I suspect Morrissey also valued Orchard's role as the Red Cardinal in *Can Hieronymus Merkin Ever Forget Mercy Humppe And Find True Happiness*, the sex-mad 1969 film

---

* PETA is the world's largest animal rights organisation. Its slogan is "animals are not ours to eat, wear, experiment on, or use for entertainment".

154

written, directed and starring Anthony Newley – another of Morrissey's heroes.

Back at the *NME*, in early 1989, with Morrissey resurrected from the washed-up pop stars bargain bin and re-established as the *NME*'s top-selling cover star, the irritated anti-Morrissey forces within the paper were manning the barricades again. But their arguments seemed more convincing now. Acid House was in full swing and the ecstasy-inspired Indie-Dance movement was beginning to have an impact on the mainstream charts. Perhaps *Viva Hate* and Wolverhampton had really been the last twitches of The Smiths' corpse? Perhaps Morrissey would now retreat gracefully to his writer's garret and become a novelist?

Maybe it was time I moved on too. In March '89 I got my first television job as a researcher on *Rough Guides To The World* – part of Janet Street-Porter's Def 2 "youth" television unit – and re-located to Chorlton in Manchester.

It was the dawn of "Madchester" and it launched me into a new life, out clubbing at the Hacienda, PSV and Konspiracy, in bars surrounded by Stone Roses, Happy Mondays and Inspiral Carpets. It was a long, hedonistic way from the Manchester I'd hated in the early years after my brother's suicide.

With Johnny Marr working with Barney from New Order (and Pet Shop Boy Neil Tennant) as Electronic, and with Andy Rourke and Mike Joyce involved full-time with Brix Smith of The Fall's Adult Net, Morrissey now seemed like the odd man out, the true outsider. Everyone I met out and about in Manchester would talk of Morrissey fondly but almost in the past tense. If the present and future was House and Rave music then there didn't seem to be room in the charts for old Morrissey any more.

Nevertheless, I fell in love with Manchester. Apart from the social inclusiveness of the place (particularly under the warm glow of ecstasy) and the Cavern-like pull of the Hacienda, I found myself bumping into people who'd stepped straight out of my brother's record collection – Mark E. Smith, Tony Wilson, John Cooper Clarke, New Order – plus all the landmarks featured in Smiths' songs, the remnants of Morrissey's Mancunian history, were scattered monumentally around me: the Church of the Holy Name, Rusholme, the Ritz, Southern Cemetery, Whalley Range, the Salford Lads Club, Strangeways, Coronation Street . . .

While 1989 would be a big year for Madchester and its extraordinary array of baggy bands – the break-through year for important dance singles such as 808 State's 'Pacific State', A Guy Called Gerald's 'Voodoo Ray', James' 'Sit Down', Happy Mondays' 'Hallelujah' from the 'Madchester Rave On' EP, Stone Roses' 'Fools Gold/What The World Is Waiting For' – back in Morrissey land, the bedsit poet laureate seemed to be unaffected and working at his own leisurely pace. He seemed almost a distant presence, utterly, deliberately out of step with everything that was happening in his formerly humdrum hometown.

As Andrew Berry – musician and Manc about town, a friend of Johnny Marr's and former hairdresser to Morrissey and The Smiths – explained to me at the time, "There's a good spiritual vibe in Manchester, particularly at the Hacienda when it's brilliant. Obviously drugs have got a lot to do with it, it *is* a drug culture. There's so many people selling it, it's so easy to get. Rock'n'roll has always been influenced by it, all the great albums. People have sold themselves to make them. Syd Barrett wouldn't have come up with all that if he hadn't been out of his head on acid."

Against this backdrop, Morrissey, with his cups of Darjeeling and two pints of light ale, seemed distinctly quaint and old-fashioned. Although he'd had two Top 10 singles earlier in the year in 'The Last Of The Famous International Playboys' and his gentle critical-of-chemicals track 'Interesting Drug' (complete with graphics of Wilde waving a sunflower), his November release, 'Ouija Board, Ouija Board' barely scraped into the Top 20 and, once again, the negative press (blaring down the phone at me from the *NME* HQ in London) suggested that it was all over bar the shouting for the old Monarch of Manchester.

Caught up in Madchester, living in Chorlton then shifting over to Rusholme, even I had fleeting doubts that Morrissey would regain his throne. I still liked him, still religiously played Smiths' records and still clung to several quality *Viva Hate* tracks, notably 'Everyday Is Like Sunday', 'Angel, Angel, Down We Go Together' and 'Dial-A-Cliché'. But briefly, convinced by many new Mancunian friends that the world had danced on and left Morrissey behind, I almost wrote him off in an article for *The Observer* about the 'sorted' Madchester scene.

It did seem odd that while the Mondays were resurrecting Glam rockers and Sixties singers like John Kongos and Karl Denver, Morrissey was now more interested in re-discovering *Carry On* icon Joan Sims (for the 'Ouija Board, Ouija Board' video). Harsher critics even attacked his decision to cover a Herman Hermits' track, 'East West', on the B-side. In contrast, my only criticism was that he hadn't covered 'Gaslite Street' instead; the flip side of 'There's A Kind Of Hush' on Columbia it was one of the songs

I'd cherished most growing up in the mid-Sixties. (Later, working for Granada Television, I even produced a Channel 4 documentary on Herman's Hermits!)

Although I wasn't in direct contact with Morrissey after my move to Manchester – he was back down in Camden Town living near the playwright Alan Bennett – I'd kept in touch via Murray Chalmers and Lyn Evans at Parlophone. So when I received an advance cassette of his spring 1990 single 'November Spawned A Monster', all my previous concerns were laid to rest and I instantly realised it was a truly remarkable piece of pop music, even in the context of the dance-orientated Madchester music that was dominating the charts: 'Step On', 'The Only One I Know', 'Kinky Afro' . . .

Apart from the extraordinarily brave and challenging subject matter – attacking negative attitudes towards a disabled child and probably inspired by Peter Nicholls' 1967 play *A Day In The Death Of Joe Egg* in addition to *A Taste Of Honey* – 'November Spawned A Monster' would remain one of Morrissey's most powerful and original creations, particularly in live concert.

When I'd written my *NME* review for *Strangeways, Here We Come* in September 1987, I'd jokingly suggested that "Morrissey could turn spina bifida into a Top 10 hit and probably will." Although the single only made number 12 in the charts, without doubt he'd proved my point.

On hearing that Morrissey was recording a new studio album with Madness' producers and, post Stephen Street, writing with the tuneful Mark Nevin of Fairground Attraction (of 'Perfect' fame) I fully expected the fruits of the partnership to be mainstream pop. It would have been utterly typical of Morrissey to take an anti-dance stance and release a much more mellow, limited beats-per-minute, crooning follow-up to *Viva Hate*.

Yet the advance album cassette I received, titled *Bona Drag*, merely turned out to be a water-treading collection of out-takes and oddities plus a new single, 'Piccadilly Palare', about male prostitution. At the same time there were growing rumours in Manchester that legal action was now being taken against Morrissey *and* Johnny Marr by ex-Smiths Mike Joyce and Andy Rourke, in addition to other monetary claims from both Stephen Street and Craig Gannon.

So, when Alan Lewis, the *NME* editor, called and asked me to interview Morrissey again for the cover feature a new magazine, *Vox*, in November 1990, I took the day off from television work and headed towards Reading wondering what on earth Morrissey was up to.

Having first met Morrissey at the scene of Oscar Wilde's arrest at Chelsea's Cadogan Hotel, then followed this up with a second discussion, centred on the desecration or decoration by Smiths' fans of Oscar's grave, I naturally expected – having been summoned to Reading by Terrace Stomp (another *nom de guerre*) – to find him tethered to Wilde's old slop-bucket in cell C33 of Reading Gaol.

Instead, aided by Murray Chalmers, I tracked him down to the sleepy, rural Tudor pile that is Hook End Manor. This former stately home was once domicile to flying fingers Alvin Lee (ex-lead axeman with Ten Years After of *Stonedhenge* fame) and later Dave Gilmour, before becoming a classically English retreat-cum-studio run by Morrissey's latest co-writers, ex-Madness/Costello conspirators Clive Langer and Alan Winstanley.

Wandering round the grounds of this *Draughtsman's Contract*-style rock pile, I stumbled across Morrissey emerging from the orchard. Together we toured Hook End, taking in the rural beauty of the place, before settling down in a comfortable wood-panelled lounge.

"Very peaceful. It's a lifetime away from the stress and grime of being in a horrible, uncomfortable city studio. Some people might say it's too luxurious for any real creativity to take place but I don't think that matters."

Morrissey seemed a long, long way from Madchester, particularly in terms of fashion. While everyone else had gone baggy – even me, in an oldest swinger in Salford sort of way – he now looked like a cross between a mod and a Teddy boy. But in terms of his state of mind, he came across as more defensive than he'd ever been in The Smiths or even his early solo *Viva Hate* days. At one point in the interview, when he was attacked by a wasp, I suggested it might have been attracted by his aftershave. "No," came the sharp reply, "by the Northern tone of bitterness."

But why had he come here, to the middle of England, to record his second album?

"I first came here almost a year ago," explained Morrissey, surveying the rural English scene. "I just turned up with a little cassette of the original piano for 'Ouija Board, Ouija Board' and a little Columbia seven-inch of 'East West' by Herman's Hermits . . . and that was the first time I met Clive and Alan. I instantly went into a vocal booth and sang over this cassette. Alan and Clive were looking at each other sideways, humouring me, which I thought was OK. The first session for 'Ouija Board, Ouija Board' was quite difficult but now I think we have got into a very unique pattern."

Had the Tudor history of Hook End contributed to the spiritual mood of 'Ouija Board, Ouija Board'?

"Originally it was a home for monks," Morrissey explained, as if 'monastery' was a dirty word. "Since I've been here several people have had certain visitations at night time, including me . . ."

Hold the gossip columns . . . "Mozz in monkey biz at monastery!"

"It happened for each person at ten past four in the morning," he continues, in that goose-soft Percy Sugden-style brogue. "It felt like a hand on your chest, as if you were being woken or stirred. The conclusion I've come to is that it's the ghost of some misguided monk going round waking people up for prayers."

What at four in the morning?

"Yes, why not? It's nice and light."

Gathered around him at Hook End – in his ongoing search for musical soulmates to replace Johnny Marr – were characters such as Mark Nevin from Fairground Attraction and Bedders from Madness. But the move to Oxfordshire meant he'd had to kiss goodbye to his old haunt, The Wool Hall in Bath, scene of both *Strangeways, Here We Come* and *Viva Hate*.

"That was enough," he replies, "it was time to try a different bed and the one here's quite comfortable."

Despite the monk?

"Because of the monk!"

Morrissey doesn't like doing interviews – "I'd rather just disappear into the woods and stay there" – particularly when circumstances dictate that he's on the ropes, fighting his corner. With Manchester on the rise, from humdrum town to capital of the music world, Morrissey was clearly worried about his place in the grand scheme of things.

"I'm deeply apprehensive. I know you're fully aware of the current climate that surrounds me in the press. It almost means that flattering articles can no longer be written about me. But, while I admit that 'Ouija Board Ouija Board' wasn't exactly 'Chirpy Chirpy Cheep Cheep', I do think the backlash has been slightly overdone. Now I have to be defensive about the very rock on which I stand."

The previous 12 months by his own high standards, had been a mix of the unremarkable and unavoidable, with perhaps only the strange beauty of 'November Spawned A Monster' reminding us of his uniqueness. Things reached a post-Smiths low with, what he described as, a "condemning, disgraceful" interview in *The Face*.

"I could tell you things about Nick Kent that would take the frizz out of your Afro! Had he praised me blindly, of course, I would not complain about things, that's just human nature. But the piece began with a section where I pick up a guitar, supposedly, then throw it down in disgust saying, 'Oh God you must think I'm Johnny Marr', an event which happened purely in the mind of Nick Kent, which actually saddens me. I begin to feel that people like Nick Kent and Danny Kelly, who always championed The Smiths, curiously seem to have had a hand in the destruction and downfall of The Smiths. I began to feel you can never actually be friends with people like that."

Apart from the run-ins with the press – a theme that would begin to be mined by Morrissey on the track 'Journalists Who Lie' – a more pressing problem seemed to be the decision to scrap his scheduled *Bona Drag* studio album overnight. Instead, EMI had launched a rather obvious compilation LP, also called *Bona Drag*, comprising of B-Sides and singles from 'Suedehead' through to 'Piccadilly Palare'.

Inevitably, I had to state the obvious and spoil the tea party. Without torpedoing the whole interview, I wonderered out loud why he wanted to talk about this compilation, particularly when most critics seemed to think he was struggling and out of step with current pop music.

"People will view it suspiciously in England but not in the rest of the world where all those funny little singles were never released. It was initially for the rest of the world, but EMI were determined to release it here."

It wasn't a bad collection of songs, just rather unnecessary. Why had he included *Viva Hate* tracks like 'Suedehead' and 'Everyday Is Like Sunday' once again?

"Why live? Why dress yourself? Why shave?" he chuckled quietly. "I have no answer except to say that if *Bona Drag* and 'Piccadilly Palare' had not been released the only visible sign of my personal existence this year would have been 'November Spawned A Monster'. So they'll remind people that I'm a faintly living person although I'm not sure about that myself. Let them mock, I don't mind."

As his output had been so prolific over the years, this break in the release of studio albums, between *Viva Hate* in March '88 to *Kill Uncle* in March 1991, would seem like a definite crack in Morrissey's career.

"But if you're examining other artists, they disappear for two or three years, to tour Bangkok or live in large houses. Throughout the Eighties it was so constant – then for a slight second it looked as if there was a lull – let's face it, there was a very attractive lull – so people started saying 'ah-ha, the acrobat falls' . . .

"And yet, if I was turning them out like a cracker factory people would say, 'Why doesn't he go away? Why doesn't he have a slight rest? Pass me that bread knife!'"

It's probably because he seemed to lead such a disciplined life. People probably think, 'Old Morrissey, all that time on his own, he ought to be able to knock out a couple of albums a year. He hasn't got a drug problem, he hasn't got a drink problem.'

"Life would be so colourful if only I had a drink problem."

Many critics, having cremated The Smiths, initially decided that the band's components couldn't succeed apart. Morrissey's single life had clearly upset those arguments although he'd always struggled to achieve a wider audience. Every 45 would charge high into the charts before rapidly plunging downwards like a stockbroker from a city high-rise. 'Piccadilly Palare' would follow suit.

"It's not a particularly strong record," admitted Morrissey, candidly. "It's not overwhelming, the subject is even slightly dated. 'Piccadilly Palare', which will receive blanket horrendous reviews, is a song about male prostitution.

"But I'm not running around in the street saying 'Look at me singing about male prostitution, isn't that incredibly unique!' I don't want plaudits for examining a new subject, but I will say that even coming across a pop record with a reasonably unique situation is in itself interesting."

It seemed as if EMI didn't have particularly high hopes for 'Piccadilly Palare' either, according to Morrissey. There would be no video – an end to his association with video director Tim Broad – and Morrissey himself was realistically confident it wouldn't make the Top Five.

"People often say to me at bus stops, 'Why are you releasing this record?' But I don't mind that 'Ouija Board, Ouija Board' never received an Ivor Novello award. I never believed that sitting on top of the pop arena was a nice place to be."

But was he now going out of his way to be less successful?

"No, but I do hear certain opinions. I think there's always a danger in trying to give an audience what it wants. I think it's more interesting to give an audience something it might not want."

This attitude must have sounded somewhat painful to the bigwigs of EMI. For here was a man who many felt should go *all* the way – hell a Pet Shop Boys-style Elvis crooner would've done it – yet who remained defiantly anti-careerist and, apparently, against success.

Even his old Red Wedge sparring partner Billy Bragg had managed a number one record, covering 'She's Leaving Home' in the summer of 1988 on the Wet Wet Wet 'With A Little Help From My Friends' single for Childline. Wouldn't something like that have made life easier and kept EMI happy?

Morrissey laughs: "I learn from Billy Bragg's mistakes. I saw that *Top Of The Pops*, I heard that record. Thanks Billy. He's possibly spent a little too much time in Hungary."

But serious success like that would have reduced the pressure Morrissey must have felt being a major label signing?

"Sometimes I feel I'm one of the artists who is expected to succeed. It's like the person who's most cut out for the job but has no enthusiasm for the fake intimacy that you have to employ to shuffle further and further. I don't want to criticise record company people but they could never be satisfied. Because as soon as you sell a million they want to sell five million, and as soon as you sell five million they want ten."

So was he happy to hold onto the following he already had?

"Yes I am, even if it decreases I won't mind that much."

There seemed to be an edge of revenge about Morrissey's stance, an affirmation of his staunch individuality against the ever-tightening business demands of being a "pop" star.

"I can only control it by not being approachable, by not being at Stringfellows, by not sitting on somebody's desk at EMI. I came to the conclusion that if, when these sessions are finished, I took the label of the master tapes and put Tina Turner's name on them and sent them to EMI, the results would be staggering. Television advertising, all those things that, if they really happened, I'd hate every minute of it."

His wardrobe would be radically different too.

"Not necessarily!"

If Morrissey needed any reminder of the downside of the music business he'd got it earlier in 1990 when the "Fifth Smith", *Queen Is Dead*-era (and Wolverhampton reunion) guitarist Craig Gannon successfully sued Morrissey and Johnny Marr over songwriting royalties from 'Ask'.

"Yes, he did win his case against The Smiths which was heartbreaking, deeply sad, and an outrage of public justice. His lawyer, my lawyer, everybody involved knew he didn't have a leg to stand on yet, through some perversion of *justice*" (he spits out the word) "he walked away with . . . £42,000.

"It made me very unhappy because it seemed a perfect example of how nauseous this business can become. And it reminds me that, like it or not, however much I kick, however much I back-pedal, that I am finally a part of this business. It's the thing that most wears me down but my opinion is that Craig Gannon didn't really win because . . . he's still Craig Gannon. Ha ha!"

When the laughter stopped and his attack of bitterness subsided, I half mentioned that such cruelty seemed to contradict the spirit of one of Morrissey's great lyrical one liners: *"It takes guts to be gentle and kind"*?

"Oh it does but you know I've never been cruel unnecessarily."

Minutes later, referring to his former friend and hairdresser Andrew Berry, I remarked that Berry had taken credit for that floppy-haired Happy Mondays look.

"Yes, but he probably takes credit for the Zeebrugge Disaster. And rightly so!"

But how did Morrissey, having been so central to Manchester music for so long, feel about the whole Madchester movement which had definitely put the city on an international map. Even on the cover of *Time* magazine. Was it something he now watched with pride and admiration or envy from a healthy distance?

"I think the backlash came at the right time." He's more relaxed now, sitting on the cream sofa opposite me, flicking that cockatoo quiff to one side. "It's been useful, it's proved I'm not part of this whole suffocating wave of Manchester monstrousness. And that's almost unavoidable really if you do happen to come from Manchester. It really emphasises that, whether you like me or not, I remain an individual . . . individually nauseating or individually interesting. The key word in my vocabulary is individualism."

We talked about his decision to escape from Manchester. Did this mean he now got more privacy?

"No I don't. I close my curtains at night and I get a round of applause."

How do you find life in London?

"I have a very jaundiced inaccurate view of London because I've always lived in very comfortable surroundings. But I think to most people who come here, to scratch together a living, an existence, it's probably a very cold place, very impersonal. So I do enjoy it but I'm not tricked by any camouflage."

Flowered Ups and Farms aside, the previous 12 months of celebration had been dominated by Mancunian candidates. Practically every mad sod in the city had swarmed up the charts – Mondays, Roses, 808 State, Charlatans, Carpets, and even Manchester's old guard appeared rejuvenated: The Fall, New Order, James, ACR . . . But Morrissey, some-what predictably, had remained apart.

"If I was herded in with those groups, believe me, I'd emigrate to Norway. I'm not impressed and that's why I'm seen as the person outside the gates with arms folded. When the whole Manchester movement began I've never seen so many people in their late thirties with quaking knees making the most absurd comments about groups who hadn't even time to prove themselves. Certain journalists have become incredibly irritated by the fact that I've kept the whole thing at arm's length."

Someone noted that the floppy hair, favoured by some of the band members in the scene, is reminiscent of Oscar Wilde's . . .

"That's laziness probably. I wouldn't imagine that anyone involved is skilled enough to draw parallels between their own hair and Oscar Wilde's.

"I don't believe it's a real scene or a real movement. Even if it was a movement the last thing I'd do with my life is join a movement. Unfortunately as all those groups are herded together as soon as there's a leak in the boat they'll all go down. It will be interesting to see who is the first figure belonging to that scene who cuts their hair. That'll be the first interesting turning point. Someone will have a short back and sides and down goes the ship.

"I'm not the enemy of those groups but I still have a boring old-fashioned notion of talent. I still believe in songs. I don't want to sound like a member of Fleetwood Mac, however hard that may be, but I just don't hear a commendable impressive voice. I don't want to sing their songs and that's my judge of a good record."

But surely, to their strange supporters, those bands might have the excitement of The Smiths. People needed new things to cling to . . .

"Understandably so. I don't expect people to remain with one hundred per cent memory of The S-S-Six asterisks. People must go on to groups that are alive and kicking. I understand that but I still have not heard a song and I don't believe the groove in inverted commas is enough. I think a lot of groups are getting away with murder, the level of publicity is practically outrageous, and there are no real honest faces or even minor celebrities."

What about Frank Sidebottom?

"Trust you to cripple my argument."

Didn't Morrissey consider the Mondays or the Roses to be significant?

"But to me it's the revenge of the daft. We had a period in Manchester where people were trying to be almost restricted by their own intelligence.

Suddenly it somersaulted and was replaced by this strange thug element, which is mildly interesting, almost worth examining. I'm not saying there's anything terribly inferior about the football mentality or the drug mentality but it's outlandishly limited. Taste has completely disappeared.

"The most interesting aspect about the whole Lancashire movement is that it's remarkably non-revolutionary. There is not one single revolutionary record. To me the reason why these groups have been embraced by the Sunday supplements is because they're very tame. If the music had matched what we'd been led to believe about these groups I'd now be standing in the middle of Market Street in bellbottoms.

"If you examine the new Manchester movement, the music is retrogressive, the attitude is retrogressive and the influences – Hendrix, The Beatles, the Stones, The Doors – are very retrogressive. It actually begins to make my New York Dolls obsession look slightly modern."

So was there nothing in terms of style or fashion that really commended itself to him? Surely the clothes he'd worn back in his teenage years had been equally outrageous and strange?

"But it's an outstandingly unflattering fashion unless the shape of your body is triangular. I firmly understand that if I had run out and bought a triangular top and said, 'Oh yes I'm in with all these' and 'I know that bass player', I would have been shot in the middle of the street. I can see lots of people saying, 'Ah that's because you're too old now' and the measure of wonderful street youthful fashion is that it makes the older generation go, 'Ooh how can they do that?' But I only feel it towards excessive physical ugliness whether you're 50 or 15. I feel I can identify ugly clothing."

Unsurprisingly Morrissey remained happily, unfashionably and consistently hostile towards the House movement in general and he practically spluttered when I regurgitated the old rumours of his supposed liaisons with outfits such as 808 State.

"Somewhere along the line I bought an 808 State record which I quite enjoyed. 'Specific State' or whatever it was called. But I'm an odd person because I think The S-s-s-six Asterisks were *immensely* danceable, even some of the things I've done are enormously danceable! The reason I'm not considered danceable is because there is lyrical content."

But his music wasn't really slotting into the current style of Top 40 dance-orientated records was it?

"The Top 40 has become so important to people, which foxes me, because whoever manages to slide in there they all manage to be several notches below Paula Abdul."

Perhaps taking ecstasy enabled people to be more tolerant of dance music?

"People have told me the major rule in taking ecstasy is never ever to play a record that happens to have my voice on it. It completely dilutes the ecstasy and has the reverse effect. I have been told that, when you're coming down from ecstasy, you should slip on *Viva Hate* and it's like being slapped back to reality with a wet dish cloth."

He'd been outspokenly critical of dance music in the past. But was there anything new he'd heard, Madchester or otherwise, that might have changed his mind?

"I don't believe there's anything new in pop music. Rap, of course, is reasonably new but it's terribly limited."

Didn't he feel like a bit of a novice talking about that musical territory?

"I feel a bit of a genius in that sort of territory. The artists tend to have a curious anonymity. For instance, 'The Power' by Snap can reach number one all over the world, become a global record, but Snap could walk past this window now and nobody would care."

From the way Morrissey often talked, about the ashes of pop being all around us and about his lack of faith in the originality of other artists, you always half expected him to flamboyantly announce his retirement.

Back then, at 31 years of age, it often seemed as if the solitary garret-bound life of a novelist would've been more appealing to him. And yet he still appeared to relish his platform in pop as a lyricist, as a vocalist, and as an *agent provocateur*. What then was his role in this alien culture?

"People find me enormously irritating. If you don't have 100 per cent passion for every move I make then I'm the most irritating person you could hope to hear of. I know this because people write and tell me."

Had he received hate mail?

"Yes, especially after *Top Of The Pops*. It's usually people's parents who write, 'Every time I walk past my daughter's bedroom I hear this person having their legs sawn off, which ultimately leads me to the stereo and it turns out to be you singing.' They say, 'I don't like it! I don't want it in my daughter's life! Leave the country!' It's a tremendous accolade. Inadvertently, accidentally, I still have this unsettling edge and I do think it's a strength."

Likewise the subject matter of many of Morrissey's lyrics continued to provoke hostile reactions. Some DJs deemed the focus on a disabled girl in 'November Spawned A Monster' unsuitable material for a pop song.

"It's that attitude that excludes those people who are inverted commas, italics, whatever, less fortunate than the rest of us. They think they're being protective but they're not, they're being insultive [sic]. They're the type of people who will condemn me for even considering writing a song about a person who is, inverted commas, incapacitated, etc."

Apart from Mary Margaret O'Hara, who joined him on 'November Spawned A Monster' – "she's the oddest most eccentric person I've ever met, I went into the vocal booth and said 'Just simply give birth', which she most expertly did, while I stood behind with a mop and a bucket" – he rather arrogantly suggested that few other lyricists had the capacity, perception or the nerve to tackle such sensitive subjects within the single format.

"I heard that new Prefab Sprout album (*Jordan, The Comeback*) the other day," he says, "which has been bombarded with plaudits. And I literally slipped into a coma, I mean, it was so absolutely lifeless. I met Paddy Ashdowne once and thought he was a very nice person, but that doesn't really excuse the fact that, in a position of national attention, he's released a record that's disturbingly middle-aged."

Whether you prized or despised Morrissey's 'way with words' he was unquestionably unique as a lyricist. His musical partners may have kept changing – the 'November Spawned A Monster' and 'Piccadilly Palare' 12-inchers found him working with old and new characters from Stephen Street and Andy Rourke through to Alan Winstanley, Kevin Armstrong and Mark Nevin – and there may have been a lack of stylistic direction, but he'd always attempted to tackle original, controversial subject matter with a rare combination of humour and sensitivity.

But side-stepping the backlash, the setbacks over *Bona Drag* and the somewhat distinct lack of enthusiasm for 'Piccadilly Palare' from either the artist himself or EMI, Morrissey had thoroughly enjoyed one great moment in the last year. No, not Wolverhampton, or even the arrival of 'Suedehead' in the Top 10, but . . .

"Standing next to Joan Sims when we made 'Ouija Board, Ouija Board'. Mainly because she was so excellent, so enormously gifted, and here I was, a silly sausage from somewhere near Manchester."

And despite the mediocre reactions to his solo work from the uninitiated in Britain, in America Morrissey's star was definitely on the rise. 'November Spawned A Monster' had been universally acclaimed, at a rare radio interview in Los Angeles he had been mobbed by 1,000 Angelenos, and The Smiths' back catalogue was suddenly in "massive ascension".

With his second solo album (excluding the *Bona Drag* collection) scheduled for release the following spring, Morrissey was planning to take to the stage again (Wolverhampton aside) for the first time in four years.

"It's been several years since I've been on stage properly with a real group. If I'd felt the pressure I'd have done more, I'd have been more visible. I feel I want to sing on stage again. Wolverhampton was not really a concert, it was an event at which I didn't really sing. Now I feel a great need to be able to sing onstage again."

In America he was booked to play 26 dates, mainly in stadiums larger than the 5,500-seaters The Smiths had performed at on their self-destructive tour back in 1986. In Britain, thankfully, he would grace less hangar-like, more intimate venues.

"Being English I can see the depressing connotation of me playing Birmingham NEC. I can see the depressing connotation of me racing to Wembley. I don't want people to feel they're coming to visit me in Birmingham NEC, I want people in Doncaster feeling I'm coming to visit them."

In the meantime, he declared his private life as uneventful as ever: "Even people who quite like me feel slightly weighted down by all that solitary monkishness . . . No, I haven't found religion, no I haven't found love. I haven't even got a whippet!"

At last, he seemed to have accepted that Johnny Marr had moved onwards and that it would be unlikely they'd work together in the foreseeable future.

"I'm not a group I'm not even an ex-Smith," he said, clearly a dig at Marr who, while promoting Electronic singles, had the words "Ex-Smith 1982–87" tattooed on his shoulder). "At the moment I don't feel as if I belong within the vast scheme of things. I find it hard to remember a place where I did belong. Ultimately I didn't belong with The Smiths. Within me, and I know within him, everything has been resolved. It almost doesn't matter anymore . . . No, I don't think he'd expect me to enjoy *Electronics!*

"But I still feel enormously protective about The Smiths without being steeped in nostalgia, without being incapable of moving on or living another day . . . Oh God, let's go and pick some apples."

The only real doubts that remained about Morrissey in 1990 concerned the future direction of his music. There was little indication, no evidence on *Bona Drag* or 'Piccadilly Palare', that the post-Madchester Morrissey was going to seriously alter or update his sound.

However, one of the tracks on the B-side of 'Piccadilly Palare', called 'Get Off The Stage' – a 'Knees Up Mother Brown' style pub polka, written with Smiths' bassist Andy Rourke – clearly seemed to attack pop stars past their best.

Who played on it?

"Chas and Dave, Dandy Nicholls . . . someone came in to play the accordion but I didn't catch his name. No, it's not Jimmy Shand."

So was it really a self-portrait of Morrissey now that he'd crossed his thirties on the road towards rock senility?

"No it's about you actually, in case you have any aspirations. It's really about The Rolling Stones, people of that ilk who just refuse to die in the physical sense; all these boring old faces, some of which are on EMI. I don't understand why they're still omnipresent, why they have this *ubiquitousness*.

"But then, come to think of it, I've never had the luxury of experiencing hype, really solid visible promotion, of being pushed. I marvel at the extent of other people's publicity, I become exasperated.

"I even think the memory of The Smiths is ignored, in the way that when The Smiths existed they were ignored by the fat media. The Smiths Convention, if it were for Barry Manilow or The Rolling Stones, would have its own television series on Channel 4. I've never been to one but I understand they're very emotional things."

I put it to him that the artists who'd survived, who'd managed to garner respect amidst the wrinkles, were those who had been able to re-invent themselves, to present different personas and carry music in new directions.

"I know I've reached the stage where other artists would bleach their hair or buy a fancy costume," he replies, tugging at *that* chin. "But I'm not inclined towards either presenting a new persona or even presenting myself as the person Smiths' apostles felt they knew more intimately than their own friends. Inexcusably I can only simply be me, which is a full-time occupation and causes terrible back-ache.

"But there's a famous quote, in *Far From The Madding Crowd* by Thomas Hardy, where Bathsheba Everdene says, 'I shall be breakfasted before you have risen and, in short, I shall astonish you all.' It has no relevance of course but I honestly do believe that, once they've raked away all the nonsense, I'll still be here . . . Stop smiling!"

9.

Napoleon Solo – The Political Animal

"Any pop journalist who wishes to do a savage critique of anything I've done is wasting their time, because I get there before they do."
– Morrissey, November 1992

I LEFT Hook End Manor near Reading in October 1990 reflecting on Morrissey's strange position in pop music. Despite his chart successes between 1988 and 1990 perhaps even he had begun to believe that he'd never regain the heights of artistic success, acclaim and influence he'd achieved with The Smiths. Despite all the cleverness and all the craft of his quartet of 1991 singles – 'Our Frank', 'Sing Your Life', 'Pregnant For The Last Time' and 'My Love Life' – none of them broke into the UK Top 20. He didn't seem defeated – the bubble hadn't burst – but two and a half years on from his remarkable rehabilitation with *Viva Hate*, Morrissey temporarily seemed somewhat deflated.

The release of his second studio album, *Kill Uncle* – within six months of the HMV stop-gap compilation *Bona Drag* – hardly altered the perception that he was treading water. It sounded oddly-out-of-place in the context of the passing Madchester/rising Rave scene that dominated British music in the late Eighties, early Nineties, and deliberately different from Johnny Marr's debut LP with Electronic, which had been critically acclaimed earlier in 1991.*

Written mainly with Mark Nevin of Fairground Attraction, with additional tunes from producer Clive Langer, *Kill Uncle* would come to be regarded as something of a transitional album for Morrissey. It's not *that* bad, just nowhere near as good as *Viva Hate* or several of Morrissey's later solo works. True 'Our Frank' wasn't his cleverest or most controversial

---

* Marr, in a rare moment of harsh criticism for his former Smiths' soulmate, would dismiss 'Our Frank' as 'Alf Wank'.

170

single – after 'November Spawned A Monster' and 'Piccadilly Palare' the subject matter seemed weirdly safe – but 'Sing Your Life' was a strong song and another fine *riposte* to those who constantly claimed he couldn't sing. He'd laughed back at earlier criticisms on *The Queen Is Dead*, when he broke into the palace and HRH also told him he couldn't carry a tune.

Elsewhere on *Kill Uncle* there's the Roxy Music/Mott The Hoople-influenced piano-led track, 'Mute Witness' – possibly inspired by Rita *A Taste Of Honey*, *The Leather Boys* Tushingham's performance as mute wife Eve opposite Oliver Reed in *The Trap* (1966) – plus the throwaway, oddly-unfunny 'King Leer' and the strangely hopeful sounding 'Found Found Found'.

'Driving Your Girlfriend Home', with additional vocals from his closest friend Linder Sterling, is among the few highlights; a melancholy follow-on from The Smiths' leave-taking track 'I Won't Share You'. But it doesn't really lift the lyrical mood of unhappiness and defeat that permeates an uneven collection of songs. Perhaps appropriately, 'The Harsh Truth Of The Camera Eye' suggested he'd prefer to be blindly loved than judged.

The album would be more remembered for Morrissey's latest attempt at dealing with issues of racial tension and cultural integration (or disintegration) through the track 'Asian Rut'. Having been misunderstood on the light-hearted portrait-of-a-fashion-victim 'Bengali In Platforms', here Morrissey seriously tried to put himself in the shoes of a young Asian who seeks revenge for the killing of his best friend. Lyrically, Morrissey writes sensitively about the unfair defeat of the Asian by English boys, and – above the melancholic violin of Nawazish Ali Khan – conveys his helpless horror at witnessing such an uncivilised scene.

Later he would tell me that he felt true artists should have the ability, the vision and the freedom to write about *all* situations in life, however painful. Yet, increasingly in the Nineties, many of his critics would challenge Morrissey's right to write about subjects *they* regarded as far removed from his own personal experience.

With hindsight, *Kill Uncle* was perhaps little more than an attractive lull in Morrissey's career. Generously, David Quantick in *NME* suggested the album "bodes immensely well for the future, not least because this is the first Moz album where half the songs are about someone other than himself". Conversely, that's perhaps the root of the problem. Much more negatively, Steve Sutherland of *Melody Maker* opted for words such as "tragic, turgid" and "pathetic", claiming the LP was "Morrissey revelling in mediocrity" and concluding that he didn't matter any more, "R.I.P."

Following *Kill Uncle* – angered or chastened by the criticism – it began to seem as if Morrissey was committed to pleasing only "the initiated" in the UK and, more ambitiously, was clearly now more interested in seducing a new audience in the States. Previous Smiths' visits to America had been briefly brilliant but troubled affairs (particularly *The Queen Is Dead* tour of 1986), plagued by personal problems and management difficulties. But in May 1991 – promoting the MTV-friendly *Hulmerist* video collection and *Kill Uncle* – Morrissey began to make serious solo inroads into the American market, starting out in San Diego California, appearing on *The Tonight Show* and, most significantly of all, selling out Madison Square Garden. He later complained, "It would have been nice to read somewhere, throughout the world, 'Morrissey has sold out Madison Square Garden!' To my knowledge I've never seen anything that pertained to that particular night in history."

He'd left Britain as a post-Smiths, directionless, unfashionable pop act, but by the time he returned on July 20, 1991 to play Wembley – his first UK gig since Wolverhampton in December 1988 – he'd become the gang leader of a fully fledged rockabilly band. Although the transition single 'Pregnant For The Last Time' (with a B-side cover of Bradford's 'Skin Storm') had been written with Mark Nevin, it saw the beginning of new long-term partnerships with songwriters/guitarists Boz Boorer and Alain Whyte. Against all expectations, these creative relationships would persist well into the 21st century; over three times longer than Morrissey's famous liaison with Johnny Marr.

When I caught up with Morrissey performing at salubrious venues such as Blackburn King George's Hall in late July 1991, followed by Stoke Victoria Hall in October, I was surprised to witness the raw aggressive quality of this new American/Fifties-style band, "composed of tattooed casualties of the British rockabilly scene" (according to John Harris in *Volume*). Even some of the *Kill Uncle* tracks now sounded harder (I nearly wrote "beefier"!) and Morrissey, for the first time since The Smiths, obviously felt comfortable and energised performing in front of them.

Although still living in Manchester, by autumn 1991 I was working for Central Television, TV21 and Working Title, helping to produce a 90-minute ITV "extravaganza of music and comedy" to mark Amnesty

International's 30th birthday that December. We'd already booked 'TV-friendly' mainstream artists like Tom Jones, Seal, Pink Floyd's Dave Gilmour, Daryl Hall, Lisa Stansfield, Rick Astley, Jason Donovan and Kim Wilde but, apart from the 'Unbelievable' EMF (at a hefty push), it was like Madchester (never mind Punk or House) had never happened.

When we approached managers of more 'cutting edge' acts and read out the ITV cast-list, most of them, while wishing Amnesty well, quickly made their excuses. Even old Amnesty stalwarts Peter Gabriel and Kate Bush were reluctant to get too involved in the TV show.

Lord knows why I tried Morrissey. At first it didn't seem his style of thing at all. Neither Murray Chalmers at Parlophone or Morrissey's assistant Jo Slee held out much hope; he'd been away touring in Europe and the States between April and early July and had just pulled out of an Australian tour in September. (Sudden illness, probably.) What chance he'd do a TV special for Amnesty International, alongside Rick Astley and Jason Donovan? It seemed very unlikely.

But I knew he had strong, individual political views. Of the many artists I'd interviewed for *NME* (with the exception of Billy Bragg and Gil Scott-Heron) Morrissey had been the most opinionated and certainly the most provocative artist I'd met. Most bog-standard pop stars would write radio-friendly songs about love and lust and cars and girls; even if their political viewpoints were radical to begin with, they'd soon be mellowed and softened by royalties and the trappings of fame. It's the different, awkward characters the authorities needed to watch, the odd sods who always cause problems. (As Shakespeare's Julius Caesar observed, "Let me have men about me that are fat; Sleek-headed men and such as sleep o'nights; Yond' Cassius has a lean and hungry look; He thinks too much: such men are dangerous.")

Politically Morrissey had always spoken out about issues normally swept under the carpet or regarded 'out-of-bounds' in mainstream popular culture. He seemed to relish commenting on taboo areas of the past and the present from the Moors Murders to the Brighton Bomb, from animal rights to racial violence and Section 28. These subjects would arouse tabloid indignation because, to *their* minds, he appeared to be celebrating negative aspects of the British way of life. This wasn't the Britain they wanted projected to the world; this wasn't their 'Jerusalem', England's green and pleasant land, the 'most civilised' country on God's Earth.

The political context of The Smiths had greatly contributed to their impact. The policies being pushed through by Margaret Thatcher's strong

Conservative government seemed to be in direct opposition to many of Morrissey's personal beliefs. While he would be celebrating and documenting, warts and all, the troubled working-class North of his Mancunian childhood, Thatcherism seemed hell-bent on destroying the *raison-d'etre* for the very existence of those communities.

Morrissey's radical, youthful philosophical statement that England owed him a living couldn't have been further removed from the long-held conservative belief, best expressed in John F. Kennedy's patriotic mantra "ask not what your country can do for you but what you can do for your country". As a statement of intent, coming within a year of the Falklands War and the wedding of Charles and Diana, The Smiths' 'Still Ill' clearly presented the changing, questioning attitude of discontented British youth.

Morrissey had long been a vocal opponent of Margaret Thatcher. While many other pop stars were anti-Thatcher because it seemed a radically sound move, few of them (Elvis Costello, Billy Bragg and Paul Weller would be honourable exceptions) actually put their heads on the block, probably in fear it might smear their lovely careers. In contrast, back in 1984, Morrissey had publicly regretted that the Prime Minister hadn't died in the IRA's bombing of the Conservative Party Conference in Brighton and, of course, 'Margaret On The Guillotine' had been one of the standout tracks on *Viva Hate*.

It certainly wasn't about political correctness but, throughout the Eighties, Morrissey had definitely used Smiths' covers to promote either gay or lesbian or simply strong feminine figures; characters from film or television or literature who'd struggled against social 'norms', usually sexually. Many of his icons had been broken by "The System", the legal and moral codes of the time, but had still achieved fame or notoriety in the face of general prejudices. Musically Morrissey seemed to be speaking for outsiders, for young people who couldn't or wouldn't conform to society's expectations.

His passionate support for the vegetarian and animal rights movements was a case in point. In the early 21st century it might seem a less radical, more personal form of politics, but back in the Eighties, vegetarianism was still regarded as something of a hippie fad, personified by the lentil-loving character Neil in *The Young Ones*. Morrissey's outspoken anti-meat-eating views, coupled with growing concern at the treatment and welfare of animals in 'factory farming' (Peter Singer's 1975 book *Animal Liberation* had been particularly influential), emerged creatively in The Smiths' 'Meat

Is Murder', a controversial and confrontational statement at a time when Britain's high streets were being over-run by American-style fast-food outlets.

It was a political stance Morrissey continued to proclaim from his pop soapbox. For example when asked for his views on Elton John's marriage to David Furnish, Morrissey replied: "I was a bit shocked by the menu, which wasn't remotely animal friendly. Pate de fois gras, which is horrific and lamb! Would you serve curried child at your wedding? Lambs are simply children."

But he would receive criticism for expressing sympathy with the aggressive tactics of the Animal Rights Militia: "I understand why fur farmers and so-called laboratory scientists are repaid with violence – it is because they deal in violence themselves and it's the only language they understand." The Medical Research Council responded, "if Morrissey is truly opposed to barbarism he should condemn any deliberate violent, threatening and intimidating acts, including these against researchers." Regardless of where you stand on these issues, for or against animal rights, the important fact is that Morrissey is again using his art to some purpose other than the popular pursuit of money and fame.

Apart from the militant vegetarianism of 'Meat Is Murder' and his ongoing campaigning work for Animal Rights organisations and pressure groups, notably PETA (People for the Ethical Treatment of Animals –), its important also to note that when we'd met to discuss the creation of *Viva Hate* in "Nineteen Eighty Hate", Morrissey clearly wanted to reflect the climate that existed in the Victorian Britain exactly one hundred years earlier.

In 1988 the Thatcherite legislation preventing local authorities from promoting homosexuality, Section 28 of the Local Government Act, finally became law. Fired up by *The Daily Mail* and against the background of moral panic following the rise of AIDS in Britain, the amendment in question had been introduced in 1986 (the year of *The Queen Is Dead*) by Tory backbencher Lord Halsbury, who claimed that left wing councils were indoctrinating children with homosexual propaganda.

Morrissey had responded, in early 1987, with the criminally comic but controversial Smiths' single 'Shoplifters Of The World Unite'. (Unsurprisingly it would be re-christened "Shirtlifters . . ." by less evolved members of the music industry.) Significantly, a century before, the Labouchere Amendment to the Criminal Law Amendment Act, enabled courts to prosecute homosexual men for "gross indecency" and send them to prison for two years' hard labour. The most famous victim of this amendment was Oscar Wilde.

Back in 1988 Morrissey's political beliefs could loosely be defined as anti-establishment and pro-animals, but he had also suggested that his "innards" were too brittle for party politics.

Morrissey: "I look around me and . . . well, I don't want to break into a Ralph McTell song, but I do feel the light has gone out and that things just get progressively worse in every way. I can't think of one thing which improves."

LB: Does that make you a pessimist or a realist?

"I think I'm a realist. Which people who don't like me consider to be pessimism. It isn't pessimism at all. If I was a pessimist I wouldn't get up, I wouldn't shave, I wouldn't watch *Batman* at 7.30 a.m. Pessimists just don't do that sort of thing."

But you're a socialist, as Oscar Wilde was a socialist? (Wilde set out his vague political philosophy in *The Soul Of Man Under Socialism*.)

"Yes, but I think a humanist before that. I've never had a flat cap and I've never smoked Senior Service."

You're pretty discontented with the world. Why don't you do something positive and run for Parliament?

"I don't think I'd have much chance in a political sense. I don't think I have the intelligence to begin with but also I don't think I'd be very tolerated. Also to be a successful politician you have to have brittle mental innards and I think I'm too much of a sensualist. I care too much about things like conservation and animals, which aren't allowed."

How would you define your political aims with The Smiths?

"I'm very concerned about animal issues. I've donated occasionally but I'm not an active member of any action group, which is something I'm very embarrassed about . . . it's largely a question of time."

Do you believe in Direct Action?

"Yes, I do, I think what we're lacking is Direct Action whether we're discussing Tiffany or nuclear waste. Direct Action is the only thing that can save the world, there's no point in sitting cross-legged round a nicely polished table . . . No, I wasn't referring to us I was referring to political groups, nurses' unions and so forth. I think a few bricks need to be thrown through a few specific windows . . . like Katie Boyle's."

Will you lead the charge?

"Well, I gladly would if I thought there were any troops, but a one man army can get a little strenuous . . . Who would make the tea?"

You could do benefits.

"I don't know about benefits. I'd rather do something a bit more productive than that. Benefits just come and go, they're a bit wishy-washy really. Just musical events with T-shirts."

But you've done Glastonbury, Artists Against Apartheid, the GLC's Festival For Jobs, that benefit for the councillors in Liverpool, you even did Red Wedge . . .

"Yes, I didn't have much enthusiasm for Red Wedge. If Johnny hadn't been initially involved I don't think it would have occurred to us to troop up to Newcastle really. It sounds awful but nonetheless there it is."

I noticed you didn't come on for the grand finale, 'Down At The Old Bull And Bush'-style singsong at the end of the Newcastle benefit.

"No, I missed that one."

Morrissey gave me further insights into his political worldview at Reading in 1990, when the Labour Party was struggling again even though this was barely two months before Britain celebrated Thatcher's resignation.

Speaking against the background of the Poll Tax Riots and the growing Gulf Crisis (which had resulted from Saddam Hussein's Iraq detaining Western hostages in Baghdad in the autumn of 1990), Morrissey said: "I know I'm going to witness Thatcher electioneering. As more hostages are released the look of complete disappointment on Margaret Thatcher's face becomes apparent. For her it's the key to the next election and, mark my words, she'll get it. Heaven forbid that the situation is peaceably resolved. It's the last thing in the world she'll want. And she'll cause enough agitation to make the situation worse."

So your hatred of Thatcher remains undimmed.

"I'm the one who in 1984 said the sorrow of the Brighton Bombing was that Thatcher survived unscathed. So when I see crowds of pop stars running about complaining about the Poll Tax I think 'Well why are you surprised?'"

But the Poll Tax marches were strong statements of opposition to Thatcher.

"Yes but the police are a very strong army. There's no avenue for demonstration. The poll tax demonstrations were incredibly exciting and positively astonishing but basically it's all over now and the British mentality is submission."

Don't you hold out any hope for the Labour opposition?

"I think Neil Kinnock is nobody's idea of a Prime Minister. The only person of real value in the Labour Party is Clare Short. Otherwise I've become confounded whenever I see the face of Paddy Ashdowne on *News At Ten* giving his view when even his wife wouldn't vote for him in a local election.

"Neil Kinnock has had so many opportunities to pounce on Thatcher and underline her basic evilness but he doesn't take the bait. Let's face it, Thatcher has done it in such a brazen powerful way that sometimes you shrink into your armchair and almost admire aspects of her character."

We'd also talked about his painfully brief appearance on an episode of Granada's *World In Action* defending animal rights activists?

"Pretty awful. They (*the journalists*) pretend they're your friend and have a free reign over the things you say but they edit it in such a way that it's unflattering to you. So you look defensive because you don't want to eat animals. The people who made the programme were not vegetarians, not sympathetic to animals."

So, we'd certainly talked politics a-plenty long before I approached him to appear in the Amnesty International benefit but, partly because of his passionate commitment to the Animal Rights movement, I honestly doubted he'd align himself with a *Human* Rights organisation.

As usual with Morrissey, it was something surprising and amusing that made him decide to appear at the Amnesty 30th birthday party. While 'Sing Your Life', 'Pregnant For The Last Time' and 'My Love Life' had all struggled to break into the Top 30 in 1991, his old Rough Trade label-mates (and early Smiths-support-act) James – the Manchester band fronted by Tim Booth – had reached number two in the charts with their re-released classic 'Sit Down'. Only an indie hit back in 1989, 'Sit Down' would be voted one of the top-selling records of 1991.

Clearly Morrissey saw an opportunity to get his own back. When he agreed to join the Amnesty International cast-list, via Jo Slee, there were only two conditions for his appearance. Firstly, that we book James. Secondly, that he would be introduced by Lulu.

James eagerly agreed, although they were initially reluctant to do 'Sit Down' *yet again* and would even try to perform an alternative, reggae version of the song at the TV studio event in Nottingham. Lulu, however, was unavailable. Just as well really, as I later found out that Morrissey had only suggested her because of the 1920s comedy song 'Don't Bring Lulu' (written by someone called Lew Brown).

Wrongly assuming Morrissey had never been serious about appearing and thinking he would definitely cancel when I told him Lulu was busy,

Morrissey next requested Cathy McGowan, presenter of Sixties pop show *Ready, Steady, Go!* Billy Fury, one of Morrissey's great heroes – one of the first British rock'n'roll stars – had appeared on the first episode of the show. Thankfully, for me and for the Amnesty production, McGowan happily agreed to introduce Morrissey in front of the live studio audience.

On a cold December night, a week before Christmas, Morrissey's new band arrived ahead of their leader. At first sight they seemed an uncouth bunch, dressed in black, tattooed and in high spirits, lugging some of their own gear; the two guitarists and songwriters, Boz Boorer and Alain Whyte, followed by the villainous-looking bassist Gary Day and the drummer boy Spencer Cobrin. After showing them to their dressing room, where they seemed over-impressed with a new fangled Corby Trouser Press, I waited in the foyer for Morrissey, half-expecting him to get out of the saloon car, spot Rick Astley and feign sudden illness at the eleventh hour.

Naturally, he arrived fashionably late, carrying his stage outfit. Briefly, as he arrived, it passed through my mind how un-flashy his entrance was. Whereas most of the other acts seemed to have entourages and management teams and record company employees in tow, Morrissey strolled in alone. We shook hands awkwardly once again. "You've aged," he said, encouragingly. "That's television for you," I replied, laughing. As we walked to his dressing room, we heard James begin sound-checking 'Sit Down'.

After dropping his gear off, we headed towards the canteen and watched James' performance on the monitors. I thanked Morrissey for agreeing to appear. He admitted that, while he was sympathetic to the work of Amnesty International, he also regarded it as one of those too rare British television opportunities to perform in a different setting with a variety of incompatible acts.

Above all, I realised, he was there because of James. It soon became clear that his latest Wilde-inspired song, 'We Hate It When Our Friends Become Successful', was targeted at James' recent triumph – not to mention the marketing success of their famous promotional flower-power T-shirts – and specifically at his old friend, the lead singer Tim Booth.

In the canteen, over a mug of Central TV tea, I talked to Morrissey about other important issues of the day, chiefly the state of the music industry and my ongoing fascination with his choice of lyrically different and difficult subject matter.

Morrissey: "If you're a genuine artist you have a very powerful, oh

God, vision of most situations, whether they be painful as in my case they most often are. It's simply writing about what one sees. God, I see almost everything . . ."

LB: You're beginning to sound like Soul II Soul's Jazzy B with his (cue band impression of the Funky Dred DJ-ing supremo) *"now I see everything"* . . .

"Heaven forbid! You're aware of the powerful sadness in most situations. You can see beauty in most individuals as well as the other side."

In the case of 'Girlfriend In A Coma' or 'November Spawned A Monster' or even 'Mute Witness' on *Kill Uncle* . . . is it empathy or sympathy?

"It's one of those words."

But not pity?

"No, that would be horrible. After 'November Spawned A Monster' I had letters from people who were wheelchair-bound and they expressed enormous support and understanding and thanks for the record. It's not just a matter of 'thank you for including us because no one else does' but 'thank you for involving us in the right way'."

My mum's disabled so I was wondering whether you'd based your songs about disability on anyone you know? On the B-side 'At Amber' you sing about an invalid friend?

"Not really, but I don't have to know people. It's a matter of understanding many extreme situations in life. And if you see someone in what we oddly refer to as an unfortunate situation, someone who's wheelchair bound, if you're very perceptive and sensitive you can fully imagine the lifelong frustrations of constantly being discussed by other people, and constantly having people being irritatingly kind to you."

Most other artists in popular music wouldn't choose to create a pop song from this subject matter.

"They don't have the capacity to. And it's the Radio One mentality. Before one examines the level of understanding it's 'Oh, wheelchairs? We don't discuss those things'. And if you want to discuss them you're perverted and you're criticising. It's that attitude that excludes those people that are inverted commas, italics, whatever, less fortunate than the rest of us."

They'd argue they're being protective of . . .

"They're the type of people who will condemn me for even considering writing a useful song about a person who is inverted commas incapacitated. There are people whose job it is in life to condemn."

So, do you think the people who criticised you for tackling such sensitive subject matter, simply misunderstood and got the wrong end of the stick?

"That doesn't matter. The people who have always criticised me still criticise me. There are certain journalists from 1983 to 1990 who could not fill in an application for a passport without mentioning my name."

But does the condemnation, when it comes, affect your confidence or courage to write about difficult or controversial subjects?

"I don't personally find it a dilemma; I simply make the record and examine the reception it might receive. I can't really answer for the creation of the records, they almost lead me, which sounds terribly arty-farty and terribly surreal, but they lead me. The consequences are just something that I have to face."

Before Morrissey's performance, I introduced him to the warm and friendly Cathy McGowan, and left them together, reminiscing about Fury, Dusty, Cilla, The Beatles, the Stones and all the other great artists she'd met on *Ready, Steady, Go!*

Then, when it came time to record his track – sandwiched between Tom Jones' performing 'Never Going To Turn You Loose' and an Amnesty message of support from Kylie – I fetched Morrissey from the dressing room and waited with him just off the studio floor while his band took their positions in front of the Amnesty audience.

While his rockabilly band waited impatiently in their drapes and the crowd noise increased, Morrissey stood quietly, thoughtfully, looking down at his shoes like a nervous child waiting outside the headmaster's office. Then Cathy MacGowan announced him and the studio lights followed his slow self-conscious walk through the audience and onto the set.

Suddenly, in the spotlight, he seemed transformed, comfortable, overflowing with confidence, as if he'd suddenly become a different person. And perhaps more than any other artist on parade, he'd worked out his performance in advance, probably because it wasn't naturally easy for him.

I know it was only a television show but without doubt he proved that night that he was one of the best showmen in the business. It's never been enough for him to simply stand and sing the song, it's all about performance and, perhaps, like Kenneth Williams, it's the environment in which he comes alive. And it was funny, too, particularly when he looked over at James and complained in song that *he* should have been successful instead of them.

Once he'd left the stage, clutching a bouquet of flowers, to the sound of rapturous applause, I grabbed both Morrissey and Tim Booth and took them to the photographic area where they posed together with the Amnesty International symbol; Morrissey caressing the barbed wire around the burning candle.

Afterwards Morrissey seemed pleased with the performance, delighted to have met Cathy McGowan and to have poked fun at James' chart success, even surprised that worthwhile television events existed beyond *Top Of The Pops*. Until the BBC launched *Later With Jools Holland*, he'd seem reluctant to perform on British television again.

Maybe that was my fault. When the programme was transmitted on ITV, to his and James' great disappointment, 'Sit Down' was axed from the running order for time reasons. It wasn't my decision but I got the blame from Morrissey – after all, his main reason for appearing had disappeared – and from James.*

To add further insult and irritation to Morrissey, when the video of Amnesty International's Big 30 birthday party was released, the production company got the title of his song wrong, listing it as 'I Hate It When My Friends Become Successful'. Morrissey, in a message relayed by Jo Slee, was not amused.

Morrissey had ended 1991 on a high note, albeit pitched between a yodel and a Charles Penrose-style belly laugh, at the close of his 'We Hate It When Our Friends Become Successful' performance. It would make the Top 20 in May 1992 and would soon be followed into the charts by a positive hymn to another socially challenged body, the overweight, in 'You're The One For Me, Fatty'.

These were advance tasters of his third solo studio album, *Your Arsenal*, which would prove to be a controversial release in one of the most difficult years of his career.

Musically, with its Fifties rockabilly meets glam rock production, *Your Arsenal* was heavily influenced by the presence of Boz Boorer in Morrissey's band. Boorer had rockabilly pedigree with The Polecats and, like Morrissey, was an extremely knowledgeable and passionate fan of both David Bowie

* Tim Booth and his partner Martine, James' manager at the time, later accepted my apology when I bumped into them the following year in an antique shop on Manchester's Stockport Road, but Boz Boorer was still complaining about James' omission when I met him in 1997 while producing Granada Television's *T. Rex: Dandy In The Underworld* documentary for Channel 4. In fact, Boorer still seemed grumpy about it backstage on the *Ringleaders Of The Tormentors* tour in 2006.

and Marc Bolan. Bowie's guitarist Mick Ronson had been brought in to produce *Your Arsenal* but only after Morrissey had failed to secure Tony Visconti, who'd overseen the early, successful, Seventies Bowie and Bolan albums, and who would later produce Morrissey's *Ringleader Of The Tormentors* 2006 release. Significantly, Visconti in the late Eighties had produced The Polecats' 'Marie Celeste', and the band had covered both Bowie's 'John I'm Only Dancing' and Bolan's 'Jeepster'.

Apart from Ronson's Northern and Thin White Duke credentials, another intriguing connection was the Spider From Mars' long friendship with Ian Hunter, the Mott The Hoople frontman. As a teenager Morrissey had been a huge Bowie, Bolan *and* Mott fan, and he surely respected the fact that Hunter had played in one of Billy Fury's backing bands.

But politically, with the release of *Your Arsenal* in July 1992, Morrissey found himself plunged deep into the heart of the racism debate, exploring the fine line between negative nationalism and positive patriotism. On the album's most controversial tracks, 'We'll Let You Know' followed by 'The National Front Disco', he writes from the perspective of two very different but affected (or disaffected) groups: an angry English football hooligan and the parents of a boy who'd been drawn into extreme right wing politics and violence.

Rather than making racist statements, in these songs Morrissey questions the Right-wing myth that the England they dream of ever existed. David, the boy who goes to the National Front Disco, cries out for an English-only England, while our aggressive 'football fan' friend, in a song part-inspired by Bill Buford's *Among The Thugs*, claims to be one of the last of the true Brits. But far from being a celebration of extreme Right-wing politics, Morrissey – of Irish rather than English parentage – tries to understand the frustration which fires their badly directed patriotism while at the same time criticising their senseless violence; perhaps a reflection on the hostility he had experienced as a teenage outsider.

Even those of us who were, by now, well aware of his fascination with those violent groups of tormentors from his youth – the tattooed boys, the skinheads and suedeheads, the Seventies football hooligans – found it unsettling that he'd decided to venture into that territory again. But this brave quest for controversy – this commitment to follow Wilde's maxim that "however distasteful to the public . . . the vitality and progress of art depend in a large measure on the continual extension of the subject-matter" – now seemed to be part of his nature. 'Trouble' loved him and 'safety' certainly wasn't his middle name.

There had been clues to Morrissey's state of mind around the time *Your Arsenal* was released. Having found his young rockabilly rebels, it seemed as if he now felt that his last album, *Kill Uncle*, had been too soft or too safe. "I needed to rebuild the gang spirit," he stated. "I wanted it to sound less lonely than previous records, and it is. It's possibly the noisiest record I've ever been involved with."

Inevitably this decision to embrace the gang mentality, coupled with his renewed interest in aggressive, malcontented youth movements – he was reportedly rubbing shoulders with the Left-wing socialist skinhead Mensi of the Angelic Upstarts at the time – would cause Morrissey problems. Having cancelled his appearance at Glastonbury in June, he suddenly decided to join the London Finsbury Park bill on the weekend of August 8 and 9, 1992 as part of Madness' comeback festival.

If he did this out of loyalty to his old ex-Madness producers, Clive Langer and Alan Winstanley, or simply because Madness' singer Suggs had guested on 'Piccadilly Palare', then the gesture would be disastrously lost. The 'Madstock' affair would haunt him for years to come and, for many journalists and newspapers – especially *NME* who ran the headlines "Flying The Flag Or Flirting With Disaster?" and "Caucasian Rut" – his performance would raise serious questions, or reinforce growing doubts, about some of his political viewpoints.

Later, I believe, Morrissey accepted that his provocative actions at Madstock – singing 'Glamorous Glue' while spontaneously wrapping himself in a discarded Union Jack with projected images of skinhead girls behind him – had been open to misinterpretation, particularly given that some of headline band Madness' hard-core fans had been accused of having Right-wing connections.* (Re-watching the footage, it seems as if elements within the crowd only turned hostile when Morrissey, declared in the closing lines of 'Glamorous Glue', that London was dead.)

Whatever the reasons for Morrissey's gestures – whether it was a display of nationalism or patriotism or an awkward attempt to reclaim the Union Jack from the National Front – sections of the audience at Madstock that evening felt so hostile towards Morrissey that they launched a variety of missiles in his direction. Some present felt that Morrissey over-reacted and, uncharitably, Suggs would be quoted as saying, "A fag paper blew on stage last night and nearly took one of his ears off."

In the view of Vince Power, the Madstock promoter: "He (Morrissey)

---

* See Gavin Watson's *Skins*.

184

was complaining on one hand that there's some skinheads that he didn't want there but I just don't understand why the skinhead backdrop was there. The British flag was wrapped around him but then he complained that the National Front were in the audience. In a way, he got the audience he deserved."

I'm *not* an apologist for Morrissey and without doubt the Madstock debacle of August 8, 1991 caused friction between Morrissey and myself. It will sound like a Ronald Reagan-style excuse but, thankfully, I wasn't there for the actual event. Instead I turned up the next day, looking an absolute prat in my 'You're The One For Me, Fatty' T-shirt, to be greeted with news that Morrissey had fled the scene and cancelled his second performance. Subjected to abuse from journalistic colleagues outraged by Morrissey's flag-waving the day before, it wasn't hard to appreciate the damage he had done to his reputation. (His record company, EMI, blamed "the abysmal behaviour of a small group of loathsome yobbos".)

Afterwards I felt he should have been instantly less equivocal and more apologetic about his attitude towards nationalism and patriotism, that he should have explained his intentions clearly and directly in the media. Dr Johnson once stated that "patriotism is the last refuge of the scoundrel" so, if Morrissey really was trying to reclaim the flag from the fascists then he needed to clarify this, while at the same time apologising if he had in any way been misunderstood.

Sadly Morrissey's view, concentrating on the *NME*-led campaign against him ("they had a board meeting and decided Morrissey must go", was his verdict later), was that he'd done nothing wrong and had little to apologise for. Although he later seemed to regret the fall-out from Madstock in interviews elsewhere in the world, stubbornly, he would give little ground or make any unequivocal apology in the UK press. But a year later, in the French magazine *Les Inrockuptibles*, he would explain his reasons for writing 'The National Front Disco': "The ones who listen to the entire song, the way I sing it, and my vocal expression, know only too well that I'm no racist and glorifier of xenophobia. The phrase 'England for the English' is in quotes, so those who call the song racist are not listening. The song tells of the sadness and regret that I feel for anyone joining such a movement."

Years later Morrissey would tell the American press that his relationship with England had been "slandered and ridiculed because, in England, you're not allowed to be patriotic in any way . . . In England if you display the Union Jack, it's considered racist and extremist." Although he'd also argue he was just part of the family line of "unshakably English pop artistes" such as The Who, The Kinks or The Jam (who'd reclaimed the Union Jack for the left), the juxtaposition of the flag with a skinhead backdrop inevitably alarmed many music fans.

Gina Morris, in *NME*, expressed her own frustrations with Morrissey the political animal: "He's tearing down sexual prejudices with his mildly homo-erotic videos ('We Hate It When Our Friends Become Successful') or steering away from promoting female perfection, however humorous ('You're The One For Me, Fatty') but then he writes 'The National Front Disco' and we're further back than when we started." With the benefit of hindsight, Stewart Lee commented in January 2008, after watching Morrissey's performance of this controversial song at the Roundhouse in London, "it's uncomfortable refrain reminds us, provocatively, that writing about an unsavoury view is not the same as endorsing it."

Far from being outspokenly hostile towards him, *NME*'s detailed coverage of Madstock on August 22, 1992 rightly questioned his actions. Under the headline "Caucasian Rut", the introductory blurb read: "Once he wore outsize blouses, hearing aids and gladioli. Now Morrissey's *accoutrements* are the Union Jack, skinhead imagery and a series of question-able public pronouncements."

The socially unhelpful pronouncements in question had recently appeared in Q magazine: "I don't want to sound horrible or pessimistic, but I don't really think, for instance, black people or white people will ever really get on or like each other. I don't really think they ever will. The French will never like the English. That tunnel will collapse."

Dele Fadele, one of the few black writers on *NME* at the time, penned a thoughtful and balanced piece on Morrissey at Madstock, pointing out that one of the critical tracks on *Your Arsenal* was "a sad tale of a bootboy who's lost his friends and whose mother has given up on him because he's gone to the National Front Disco." Post-Madstock, Dele warned, "For what it's worth, I don't think Morrissey is a racist. He just likes the trappings and the culture that surround the outsider element. He has some racist friends, and if he carries on this way, he'll have thousands more."

Writing in *Volume*, John Harris regretted that, after Madstock, "no anti-racist statement was issued and the whole furore provided a distasteful finale to an otherwise triumphant phase of Morrissey's career."

I didn't have any direct contact with Morrissey post-Madstock. I think he felt at the time that, in my fumbled attempts to defend his political reputation, I'd prolonged the furore and expressed too many doubts in letters and articles, notably a Manchester *City Life* magazine piece in which I said I didn't believe he was racist but expressed the hope that he would urgently explain his clarify his position.

Despite several conversations with Morrissey's assistant Jo Slee about this, Morrissey remained silent. In my humble opinion, if he was guilty of anything then it was perhaps the sin of pride; stung by the criticism in *NME*, he remained reluctant to either explain the true meaning of his Madstock actions or apologise for daring to be misunderstood. Even in a March 2003 interview with *NME* he would aggressively argue that the blame lay with the audience at Madstock rather than himself, the provocative performer: "I don't get out of bed for the average Madness audience member. I'm not the kind of person who throws something out to the lowest common denominator. I like to assume that somewhere along the line everyone has a basic gist of intelligence."

At least, in an interview with *Q* in 1995 – when, during Brit Pop, flag-waving seemed compulsory – he reflected on the impact of the controversy on his own career: "I didn't invent the Union Jack, you do realise that don't you? I didn't knock it up on a spinning wheel in the front room. I can't account for other people's reactions. Some people adore it; others are embarrassed by it. I don't get it. I don't understand the Fascist implications of it. I think it happened because it was time to get old Mozzer. Nothing more sophisticated than that."

Intriguingly, in the same year, 1995, Morrissey's friend Michael Bracewell wrote a perceptive piece in *The Observer* comparing the embattled singer with Oscar Wilde: "Both are Anglo-Irish artists; both have been feted by the English media, then savaged by them; each has been accused of the worst crime in the orthodoxy of their respective eras: homosexuality for Wilde and fascism for Morrissey."

It's also worth noting that there had been signs of his defensively pro-English, patriotic concerns as far back as 1988, when he wrote, as part of the *Carry On* actor Charles Hawtrey's obituary, that Hawtrey's death tied in with "the slaughter of the British passport and the advance chill of Britain in 1992". This would seem to refer to the Maastricht Treaty (which introduced pan-European cooperation in law enforcement, criminal justice, civil judicial matters, and particularly in asylum and immigration policy) and the decision to open Britain's borders to other citizens from the European Union.

However, his line about the "advance chill of Britain in 1992" seemed an apt prediction for the effect Madstock had on Morrissey's own career in the early Nineties. Also it was the year in which Johnny Rogan's *The Severed Alliance* lifted the lid on the story of the rise and fall of The Smiths, resulting in Morrissey's famous "fatwa" against the author.

Typically, rather than leave the issues raised by Madstock well alone, to be forgotten with the soothing passage of time, his Top 10 comeback single a decade later, 'Irish Blood, English Heart', tackled the taboo subjects of patriotism and nationalism head on.

It was made perfectly clear, in the 2003 Channel 4 documentary *The Importance Of Being Morrissey* – by an impressive cast including Noel Gallagher and other celebrity supporters – that although the artist had always been very pro-British Isles (through his English *and* Irish origins) and a passionate celebrant of the passing England – the England of his black and white social realist films and of early *Coronation Street* – Morrissey is most definitely *not* racist.* Within the programme he offered an insight into how he feels other's see him: "People see me as pushing against the grain . . . the outsider's outsider. For want of a better term, I fall into the rebel category . . . authentically so."

Despite his decision to move to the United States in the late Nineties, as suggested by a song such as 'America Is Not The World' (2003), he's always been fiercely and consistently against the Americanisation of Britain (particularly by meat-processing empires like McDonalds); opposing the unwelcome dominance of American foreign policy and its negative influence on British politics.

"I do feel sad for the people of Iraq having been invaded by Bush and Blair," he said in 2006, "so many people have unnecessarily lost their lives and Bush and Blair don't care . . . The country's a mess and all we see in response to that is Blair's Cheshire Cat grin all over the place. 'Victory!' Great, all these dead Iraqi children and persecuted people, and every day in Iraq there are 40, 50, 60 dead in car bombs, etcetera . . ."

Although the critical hostility from the *NME* would eventually pass with the Nineties and the warm embrace Morrissey received from the paper in the early 2000s – The Smiths were named "Most Influential Artists Of All Time", and the man himself was celebrated as "The Mozzfather", the comeback king with *You Are The Quarry* and *Ringleader Of The Tormentors* – the love-in would end again, abruptly in late 2007

---

* In April 2008, Morrissey gave major financial support to the 30th Anniversary Rock Against Racism concert in London's Victoria Park.

when he questioned British immigration policies and the effect they were having on national identity.

This time the *NME* cover headline read: "Morrissey: Bigmouth Strikes Again – 'The gates of England are flooded. The country's being thrown away.' OH DEAR. NOT AGAIN." In Morrissey's response, via *The Guardian*, he suggested that his comments had been "butchered, re-designed, re-ordered, chopped, snipped and split in order to make me seem racist and unreasonable". As a result, Morrissey's manager at the time, Merck Mercuriadics, took legal action against the paper and its editor Conor McNicholas.

Although I'm against immigration controls, I think it has to be acknowledged that it's an area of British politics that needs to be discussed more openly. As with most issues that Morrissey tackles in lyrics and interviews, it's not an issue that should be avoided simply because it's too difficult or delicate to deal with; all artists, however controversial, should have the freedom – within a liberal democracy – to question the status quo and to always extend the subject matter.

Personally, as a Labour supporter (with reservations), I feel that – because of Britain's historical role, with our past of Empire and exploitation and our ongoing status as a wealthy and influential nation of the Developed World – we should help and embrace all other less fortunate peoples and countries as and when we can. But I'm also aware that many people, like Morrissey, are concerned about the influx of immigrants and, particularly, about failings within the system to prevent illegal and criminal elements from entering Britain.

Arguably if there was one good thing to come out of the December 2007 legal row with *NME* it was Morrissey's vocal support for the Love Music Hate Racism campaign and his unequivocal statement, fifteen years after Madstock, that "I abhor racism and oppression and cruelty of any kind and will not let this pass without being absolutely clear and emphatic with regard to what my position is. Racism is beyond common sense and I believe it has no place in our society."

10.

Into Exile

"I know I'm blacklisted but I take it as an honour. All the great British writers were exiled, though I wouldn't have the gall to put myself in that company."

– Morrissey

I N the autumn, post-Madstock 1992, before he braved British audiences again that December, Morrissey continued to concentrate his efforts on the American market, appearing on *Saturday Night Live* and selling out the Hollywood Bowl for two nights (the record-breaking takings exceeded $800,000). Strangely, the new rockabilly musical direction which had seemed somewhat retro to a British audience, would only increase his following in the USA.

Beyond the controversial but critical success of *Your Arsenal* (and the Top 20 hits 'We Hate It When Our Friends Become Successful' and 'You're The One For Me, Fatty'), by his own prolific standards Morrissey again seemed to be marking time. His T. Rex-tribute single 'Certain People I Know' struggled into the Top 40 but I caught up with him live again at Newcastle City Hall and also at London's Alexandra Palace in December 1992; the latter, in my biased opinion, a far superior and less shambolic performance than the Stone Roses' appearance I'd witnessed two years earlier.

The following year, 1993, would only see the release of another live album, *Beethoven Was Deaf*, on his 34th birthday – its title apparently taken from Warhol-associate Paul Morrissey's bizarre 'art' film about the aurally-challenged composer. But clearly Morrissey seemed to be struggling in terms of the way he was perceived in the UK if not America. As before, his detractors hoped he'd leave the country for good, or better still, leave the music business altogether. Those of us who found the music world a very dull place without him, and who frankly believed he was misunderstood rather than misanthropic or unpardonably patriotic, secretly hoped that his next release would be less controversial and, above all, of the highest quality.

Sadly, the end of 1993 was a desperate time for me personally. After two decades struggling against rheumatoid arthritis, my mum died suddenly on December 9 aged 67. In sympathy, an advance cassette of 'Interlude' was sent to me from Parlophone. Beautifully produced by Boz Boorer, and featuring a Morrissey duet with Siouxsie Sioux, 'Interlude' helped me through the dark days of Christmas.

A cover of the original B-side to Timi Yuro's 'Hurt' – one of Morrissey's most soulful vocal performances and arguably his best cover version along with 'Cosmic Dancer' – the key lines in this moving song, of hope and survival in the face of fortitude, were: "Let's hold fast to the dream, that tastes and sparkles like wine."

Later, Morrissey corresponded with me about my mother's death. He asked to see *The Guardian* obituary and expressed his own concerns about the mortality of loved ones. He referred to Jimmy Clitheroe's tragic suicide within hours of his own mother's death. Another of Morrissey's early friends, Billy Mackenzie of The Associates – one of the purest voices in British pop and a possible inspiration for The Smiths' single 'William, It Was Really Nothing' – also took his own life in 1997 soon after his mother's death. More significantly, perhaps, in terms of Morrissey's art, Oscar Wilde's mother died while he was in prison in early 1896. Heartbroken Oscar, who was refused permission to visit the dying Lady Wilde, outlived her by only five years.

Despite the magnificent quality of 'Interlude', only undermined by a falling out between Morrissey and Siouxsie, it still wouldn't make Morrissey's finest solo album of the Nineties. *Vauxhall & I* arrived in the spring of 1994 to universal acclaim, reaching number one in the album charts and proving, both artistically and commercially, that Morrissey could survive as an important figure in mainstream pop music well beyond the Eighties.

Listening back, it's still one of the finest and most underrated albums in British popular music. If Morrissey remotely felt that he needed to raise his game, after the reputation-damaging debacle of Madstock 1992, then *Vauxhall & I* surpassed all expectations. Reunited with Steve Lillywhite – who'd produced The Smiths' 'Ask' and would later work on *Southpaw Grammar* and *Maladjusted* – it contains some of Morrissey's greatest solo songs.

Above all else, it opens with the emotional, amusing and uplifting 'Now

191

My Heart Is Full', which pays respect to Graham Greene's British gangland classic *Brighton Rock* while also celebrating the lost pin-up of British cinema Patric Doonan ("raised to wait").

Doonan – brother of Tony Doonan, who'd played the blackmailer Wood in a 1960 film of Oscar Wilde's life – was a suicide-bound Fifties actor who'd first caught Morrissey's eye in *The Blue Lamp* alongside Dirk Bogarde. In a fax Morrissey once told me that he'd tried to use clips of *The Blue Lamp* in one of his promotional videos, 'Hold On To Your Friends', but had received a negative response from the dying Bogarde. Morrissey tried to visit Bogarde to plead his case but, confronted by the near-dead actor and writer, he simply fled the scene. Sir Dirk stood his ground, telling Morrissey that he couldn't break his own rules.*

Arguably the greatest Morrissey solo track – a show-stopping moment to rival the anthemic majesty of The Smiths' 'There Is A Light That Never Goes Out' or 'Last Night I Dreamt That Somebody Loved Me' – 'Now My Heart Is Full' features one of his best vocal performances and some of his finest poetry.

Elsewhere on this perfect album there's 'The Lazy Sunbathers' – a Wildly satirical shot at sleepy hedonists who were blissfully unaware of, or unconcerned by, the problems facing the real world – and 'Billy Budd', another role played on film by Morrissey's pin-up Terence Stamp and perhaps also references to the 'unconventional' sexuality of both American author Herman Melville and Benjamin Britten, the English composer who based an opera on Melville's story. (Melville had published a collection of poems titled *John Marr And Other Sailors* in 1888.)

Other memorable *Vauxhall . . .* tracks include 'Why Don't You Find Out For Yourself',† almost an aggressive warning to his detractors without in any way being apologetic; his stalking single 'The More You Ignore Me The Closer I Get' (which reached number eight in the UK charts); plus a nod to either Elvis Presley's film career (or a pre-Smiths Johnny Marr summer job) with 'Speedway'.

I also talked with Morrissey's former personal assistant Jo Slee around this time, following her split from Morrissey. Jo was bitterly upset about the song 'Lifeguard Sleeping, Girl Drowning', which she interpreted as

---

* Morrissey also revealed that he'd located the Chelsea house where Doonan gassed himself and had even asked the owners if they knew anything about the actor.
† At the London Roundhouse in January 2008, Morrissey introduced the track with the words, "Here's a song that no one likes . . . just for you."

being about how Morrissey ignored her pleas for help while she was being frozen out by his new business manager Nigel Thomas.*

Vauxhall & I – titled in appreciation of Bruce Robinson's cult 1987 British film *Withnail & I*, recognising Morrissey's fondness for the camp character Uncle Monty, and perhaps even celebrating the drag-queen scene of London's Vauxhall Tavern – also extended Morrissey's special interest in 'outcast' male sexuality.

His love of Robinson's film seemed to stem from the two actors fear of Uncle Monty, one of the great humorous, gay characters in modern cinema. Typical Monty quotes included "I can never touch meat until it's cooked. As a youth I used to weep in butcher's shops." And: "I mean to have you, boy, even if it must be burglary," perhaps a comedic inspiration for Morrissey's strange 1998 compilation *My Early Burglary Years*. Monty was played by Richard Griffiths, who'd also star as the teacher Hector in *The History Boys* by Morrissey's Camden neighbour Alan Bennett. Griffiths' Hector has been suggested as one source for Morrissey's 2003 track 'The First Of The Gang To Die'. (Despite the Los Angeles setting, the song could also be about the death of the writer Hector Munro, aka Saki, a contemporary of Oscar Wilde's, who was shot by a German sniper in France on November 13, 1916.)

Although one of the singles from *Vauxhall & I* recognised the vital need to 'Hold On To Your Friends', by early 1995 several of Morrissey's old friends and close associates were taking legal action against him. Having been successfully sued by former Smiths' guitarist Craig Gannon and *Viva Hate* collaborator Stephen Street, Morrissey now found himself involved in an ongoing bitter court battle with The Smiths' rhythm section – drummer Mike Joyce and bassist Andy Rourke – although, bizarrely, this would eventually lead to a non-musical courtroom reunion with Johnny Marr.

As someone who'd interviewed Morrissey several times before these court cases, and who understood first hand his absolute determination to protect the creative reputation of The Smiths, I don't think it's possible to over-estimate the disastrous effect the whole legal process would have on him. Certainly, creatively, the mid-to-late Nineties saw him produce his weakest solo work, and one wondered whether he'd ever recover from repeated defeats in the courts. Watching from the sidelines, it began to

* Sadly Thomas, like video director Tim Broad and *Your Arsenal* producer Mick Ronson, would die in 1993.

look as if Morrissey was determined to disobey the judgements of the British legal system and to end the century, in prison or in exile, like Oscar Wilde 100 years before.

Although Morrissey had always viewed Mike Joyce and Andy Rourke as important members of The Smiths, and would frequently acknowledge their aggressive contributions, no one was really in any doubt that the band's critical success was founded on the united creative talents of Morrissey and Johnny Marr. But their mistake, as joint signatories of the contract with Rough Trade, had been to make Joyce and Rourke payments on an irregular basis rather than offering a more equal share in the band's earnings aside from songwriting. Caught up in the whirlwind of success and celebrity during The Smiths' lifetime, it was only when the band fell apart, and the back catalogue started to be exploited worldwide, that Joyce and Rourke began to feel they were seriously out of pocket.

Of course, it all went back to the early days of The Smiths and how the group was set up financially. Early on, Johnny Marr had spoken about "how everybody got paid. Morrissey had a very healthy outlook on how to run a group financially by not spending money on complete bullshit and nonsensical things, and not being extravagant. His motto was, 'What we make we put in our pockets, and pay everybody from our pocket.' "

It would emerge in the High Court that the division of royalties had been far from fair; of the 100 per cent profit made by the band (aside from songwriting), Morrissey got 40 per cent, Johnny Marr got 40 per cent, while Andy Rourke and Mike Joyce received payments that amounted to approximately 10 per cent each, and then only when they asked for it.

I'd spent most of 1994 making programmes for Granada Television and Channel 4 about British R&B bands like The Animals, who'd had major success in the Sixties but had ended that decade in relative poverty; while they'd been partying like proverbial pop stars, it seemed as if most of their money had disappeared mysteriously into offshore bank accounts.

In Morrissey's defence, it seemed that he'd tried to restrict the leakage of cash from the band's inner circle to outside forces. As he'd later complain, "Every day of my life I have letters from lawyers, whether its mine or somebody else's . . . I can't remember a period of my career where there wasn't something going on, somebody who had managed to get legal aid and decided to chase you for every penny you have." But before he became famous, Morrissey must have been well aware of the pitfalls of the music industry; after all, his teenage hero Marc Bolan had suffered more than most from mismanagement and poor investments. However, self-management, as Eric Burdon had once told me, would be impossible. "You can't be out performing every night and be back in the boardroom every morning," Burdon said, "you *have* to trust someone else."*

The Smiths' court fight had been brewing throughout 1995, while Morrissey limbered up and battled back into the lower reaches of the charts with 'Boxers' and 'Dagenham Dave' ahead of the pugilistic solo album *Southpaw Grammar*, released on RCA after his departure from EMI/Parlophone.

Again, the Oscar Wilde references were well to the fore on *Southpaw Grammar*. One hundred years earlier, in March 1895, Oscar Wilde had unsuccessfully sued the Marquis Of Queensberry – father of Lord Alfred Douglas and original sponsor of the "Queensberry Rules" for boxing – for defamatory libel after the Marquis had accused Wilde in public of "posing as a somdomite" (sic). On May 22, 1895 (nb. May 22 is Morrissey's birthday), Wilde's second trial began; he was convicted of gross indecency on May 25 and sentenced to two years' hard labour.

The strain began to tell on Morrissey during the mid-Nineties. Despite another successful concert tour in early 1995, against the backdrop of Britpop led by Oasis and Blur, there was an ageist critical backlash against *Southpaw Grammar* in the music press. *NME* referred to the Princely veteran as "The Morrissey Formerly Known As Artist" – plus the troubled Outsiders tour that autumn with Morrissey supporting the rusty, post-Tin Machine David Bowie.

Morrissey had been a Bowie fan since the early Seventies. They had already duetted live together in Los Angeles on Marc Bolan's 'Cosmic Dancer' in 1991 and Bowie had covered the Morrissey/Mark Nevin track 'I Know It's Going To Happen Someday' (on his *Black Tie White Noise* album). But their flimsy relationship collapsed that November with Morrissey's withdrawal from the tour through an "undiagnosed illness". (In 2003, when asked if he was still a Bowie fan, Morrissey replied, "he was a fascinating artist in 1970, 1971, 1972 . . . but not now".) The reviews for the Outsiders tour had been universally lukewarm, even bordering on poor, but Morrissey's main worry was the looming High Court case.

He struggled to complete another album, which would be called *Maladjusted* (nb. the *Oxford Dictionary* definition of the word is "unable to

---

* The Animals' story ended badly, with their manager and details of overseas bank accounts, lost in a plane crash over Spain. Even in 1994, Burdon refused to believe that Mike Jeffreys, who also managed Jimi Hendrix, was really dead.

adapt to or cope with the demands of a social environment"); released almost two years after *Southpaw Grammar*, it would be his longest absence from the album charts since 1989. But this would be the least of his worries. In 1996, his court defeat at the hands of Mike Joyce proved to be a devastating personal low-point in his extraordinary career.

Pending an appeal, Morrissey feared he and his estranged collaborator Johnny Marr would have to pay Joyce over £1 million plus costs. More damaging for Morrissey's reputation were his courtroom attempts to justify the failure to pay Joyce and Rourke the additional royalties due to them; it was suggested that he regarded them as replaceable as "lawnmower parts". Concluding and finding against Morrissey – who'd unsuccessfully tried to use his Wilde-like wit under interrogation – presiding Judge Weeks famously branded Morrissey as "devious, truculent and unreliable".

Humiliated by this experience, 1996 saw Morrissey at his lowest ebb creatively and personally. Although he seemed to have found stable, long-term songwriting partners in Boz Boorer and Alain Whyte, he'd nevertheless spend the next decade (the ten difficult years after Parlophone's *Vauxhall & I*) falling out with record companies and managers.

"I've gone through managers like people go through Shredded Wheat," he told Michael Bracewell in 1995. "Nobody looks after you, which is why most groups end up disbanding and most artists end up dead or on heroin."

As if to confirm this chaos, *Southpaw Grammar* came out on RCA/Victor, Elvis' home; *Maladjusted* appeared on Island; a 1998 collection of *Rare Tracks* would be issued in Japan on Mercury. It wouldn't be until his arrival at Sanctuary in 2002/03 that he'd feel secure and at home again, in a position to regain his crown once more.

By early 1997 I hadn't talked directly to Morrissey for almost five years. I'd religiously, faithfully, attended every UK tour, and still gestured at him from the cheap seats (he'd frown and arch one eyebrow in return), but I'd almost begun to accept my friends' verdict that he was a spent force and that *Vauxhall & I* had been the solo peak.

Since the court verdict, rumours abounded that he had gone into exile; living in Ireland most of the time, Los Angeles the rest; like some convict on the run, avoiding paying his debts pending a High Court appeal. In the States it seemed his following was growing, particularly among the rockabilly-loving Hispanic community and, over there perhaps, he seemed to have temporarily escaped Mike Joyce's pursuit of royalties.

Generally it's been accepted that Morrissey only escaped to Los Angeles in the late Nineties but, examine his touring schedules between 1996 and 2000, and its clear that he deserted the UK soon after the November 1996 court case. Out of almost 200 performances worldwide between Xmas 1995 and September 2002, Morrissey played only 15 on the British mainland. Given his oft-expressed devotion to England, this enforced departure, this desperate exile, clearly illustrated the depth of his disillusion with Britain and British justice in particular. Let's not forget that he'd once declared, "I could never live anywhere else . . . I absolutely adore England, I really do." (My life had changed too. In early 1997 I married my girlfriend Bridget. Morrissey's considered response had been, "Marriage?! Yikes!")

Our paths crossed again, unexpectedly, in Manchester in March 1997. I was in Waterstones bookshop on Deansgate, skiving from my job as a television producer at Granada, thumbing my way through the poetry section on the first floor. Picking up a copy of Brian Patten's *The Irrelevant Song*, I shuffled downstairs towards the main till.

I saw Morrissey first and, playfully, walked up and poked him in the ribs. His long-term friend Linder (Sterling of Ludus, the photographer, musician and artist) was standing close by and she grimaced at me as if I was some sort of stalker. As Morrissey turned, his double-take face mixed shock with uncertainty. Just for a moment he looked like Frankie Howerd's Dad.

"Welcome back," I say, then crassly, "We've missed you." He nods and half-smiles in his embarrassed, typically shy way, as if he needed a prompt before deciding whether to stuff me in the Friend or Foe pigeonhole. Thankfully, the awkward silence is broken by a young shop assistant, who clearly has little idea who Morrissey is, and tries to hurry up our purchasing. I hand over my crumpled money.

"What are you . . . buying?" Morrissey asks nosily.

"Brian Patten. Liverpool poet. Wrote a good one called *Notes To The Hurrying Man*. And you?"

He doesn't reply, just raises one eyebrow in a comically disdainful way, then turns away towards Linder. She looks at him nervously as if to say, 'Shall we go?' So I just shout "all the best" and scuttle over towards the biography section, assuming he'll flee before anyone else can doorstep him.

Seconds later – disappointed but not surprised by what's happened, particularly after my post-Madstock criticisms – I find myself flicking through a biography of Saint-Exupery, the French aviator and writer, and still avoiding going back to work.

When I look up Morrissey is hovering nearby, as if we're shaping up for some strange book-throwing duel between two shy middle-aged men.

"You look . . . older," he says charmingly, in what someone at *NME* once weirdly described as "a soft gazelle voice".

"I am," I mutter. "How's things?"

"Oh you know . . ." He stares down at the Saint-Exupery book.

"Weird," I say, "I've just picked up this. Serendipity eh? Reminds me of you and that 'Suedehead' video. James Dean. *The Little Prince*."

"What . . . are you . . . doing now?"

I try to sound upbeat and confident. "Oh still living here, still working at Granada . . . we're making some programmes about British girl singers. Right up your street if you're interested?"

Clumsily I hand him my Granada business card. He takes it reluctantly then looks at me as if I've gone mad. It'd be too obvious and predictable for him to appear. If he went on *Mastermind*, British Girl Singers 1958–67 would probably be his specialist subject. Plus he doesn't do much television; hardly any detailed interviews over the years. When he does, he often comes across as uncomfortable and unnatural. He's a performer, not a pundit.

He frowns again. "Have you read any . . . Housman? You really should read *A Shropshire Lad*."*

He looks again at my business card. "Have you got something . . . to write with?"

I give him a chewed pen. He stares at it in disgust, scrawls his mother's address and fax number on the back of the card, then hands the card and pen back to me.

"I have a fax machine. It's more useful than a telephone because you don't have to speak."

I look at his spidery handwriting. "So, should I fax you and tell you when we're filming?"

"Oh, I don't know . . ."

"How's recording going? Will it be . . . another . . . winner?" (No idea why I said this, I think it was the punch-line from some chat show anecdote about Somerset Maughan.)

With a well-practised derisory expression combining a frown and a

---

* Apart from Housman's "unconventional sexuality" I later discover this also ties in with Morrissey's passion for Diana Dors; as the condemned murderess Mary Hilton in *Yield To The Night* she recites lines from *Loveliest Of Trees*.

smile, Morrissey turns on his heels and heads towards the exit with Linder. No wave, no goodbye, nothing. Oh well.

I purchase both the Saint-Exupery biography and *A Shropshire Lad* and head back towards Quay Street and the red-lettered Granada landmark. Deep down, I'm certain Morrissey won't be appearing on television in our series about British female singers of the Sixties. But, nothing ventured . . .

Remarkably, the initial fruit of our first faxual intercourse (involving a complex exchange of messages quoting Blondie lyrics) and indeed of that meeting in Waterstones, was Morrissey's surprising agreement to be interviewed for the Granada/Channel Four series *The Brit Girls*; his first major UK television interview since 1987.

April 5 1997: It looks bad for both of us – me, a screaming heterosexual; he, an internationally famous homo sapiens – when the Ranger catches us, apparently cavorting in the grounds of Tatton Park near Manchester.

Morrissey is seated, legs akimbo, in the doorway of his silver sports car. Meanwhile I'm crouched before him like some errant knight, awaiting investiture, flagellation or worse. To compound our crime, in the eyes of the Cheshire park police, I'm caught red-handed, fiddling with an unauthorised camera.

Standing up to protest our innocence – like Booboo and Yogi snared in Jellystone by the angry but appropriately named Ranger Smith – I blurt out my hopelessly self-incriminating confession: "But we couldn't find anywhere else to do it."

Shaking his head and producing a soiled rule book from deep within his uniform, the ageing Tatton Park jobsworth starts to sternly lay down the law regarding filming on private property without a permit.

But then, in the middle of bye law four sub-section three, he looks up and gradually clocks Morrissey, who's preparing to face the British gallows again. The ranger half-smiles and utters the almost-Victorian phrase: "Ah yes, I do believe I recognise the gentleman. Isn't he . . . that entertainer?"

Minutes later, having promised we'll never ever do it again, Morrissey and I are speeding away from the Cheshire park, past the Tudor Old Hall, the Mere and the Mansion, thanking our lucky stars we've not been handed over to The Filth.

We'd met an hour earlier outside a drinking hole near Morrissey's mother's home. As I'd pulled up in the car park, thankfully quiet for a

Saturday lunchtime, Morrissey was dressed in a dapper blazer polishing the bonnet of his silver sports car. It looked like a scene straight out of the Sixties, perhaps from *What The Butler Saw* or, more likely, *The Sandie Supplement.*

At first I wondered whether it was some reference to James Dean and his ill-fated Spyder. Years later, I'd stumble across a similar still image of Billy Fury cleaning a sports car.

We shake hands awkwardly again, as if we're both still unsure how to start these meetings. He seems even more nervous, shy and wary than when we first met at the Cadogan Hotel almost a decade before. Perhaps it's understandable given the mauling he's received since the early Nineties at the hands of *NME* and other sections of the British press.

Ahead of the proposed interview, which I'm not entirely sure will happen at this stage of our rendezvous, Morrissey suggests we go for a drive. Partly to ease the awkwardness but mainly to buy him time to decide whether he really wants to go through with all this. After all, he hasn't done much television since The Smiths' *South Bank Show, Top Of The Pops,* and a brief appearance on an animal rights episode of *World In Action.* It's painfully clear from the outset that I'm no cameraman, so maybe this will all be a waste of his time.

He takes off his blazer and slides into the driving seat. He's wearing an antique American rockabilly shirt, expensive apparently, one of the few signs – I suggest – that he's become a tax exile. He winces again when I ask if he'd bought it from Affleck's Palace in Manchester or from Flip in Shoreditch.

I try to make small talk, to break the ice, but instead find myself asking about the forthcoming album, to be released five months later. He doesn't give away much as he starts the engine, but seems shocked that I know the names of some of the tracks. "You really shouldn't," he says unhappily. He seems particularly disappointed when I ask about 'Roy's Keen' but reluctantly admits that the Manchester United and Ireland international footballer lives close to his mother.

Emerging from the pub car park we drift briefly into the dangerous territory of the 1996 court case in which Smiths drummer Mike Joyce was awarded £1 million in unpaid royalties. I'm worried Morrissey will crash the car and the James Dean tribute will be complete, but he won't be drawn, refusing to even mention his antagonist's name. All he does say, bitterly, is "the judge hated me". There's a beaten, pessimistic or totally realistic tone to his voice.

Later in the afternoon, putting the 'Tatton Park Incident' and the dark cloud of the court case behind us, we're cruising through Hale and Altrincham, like Hinge & Bracket on a day off, while Morrissey starts to play myriad singles by Sixties female singers, demanding I "Name That Tune in one".

In truth I'm hopeless at it. Although I'm at Granada producing what will become the troubled but critically acclaimed 1997 Channel Four series *The Brit Girls*, my knowledge of the area doesn't extend much beyond the well-known hits of Dusty Springfield, Cilla Black, Lulu and, above all, Sandie Shaw.

But here's Morrissey, in his element, celebrating Diana Dors' appropriately big and brassy 1964 single 'So Little Time': "Gonna take his face in my hands, kiss him 'til he understands, that we . . . have so . . . little time."

As Cheshire suburbia flashes by through the windows of the sports car, it feels like we're travelling back into the greatest era of three minute pop music. He plays 'Shoes' by Reperata & The Delrons then follows it with The Toys' 'Attack' and even Big Dee Irwin's 'Swinging On A Star'. He tells me the labels they were released on *and* their UK chart positions, enthusing warmly about Little Eva's "amazing" supporting vocals on the Irwin single.

Disillusioned by my relative ignorance of his specialist subject – I'm pretty hot on Wilde, T, Rex, *Coronation Street* and *Carry On* but woefully weak on obscure Sixties singles – Morrissey tries to go more mainstream with morsels of Buffy Sainte Marie and Nancy Sinatra, followed by Francoise Hardy's 'All Over The World' and Sandie Shaw's flopped cover of Harry Nilsson's 'Together'.

By the time we stop the car and try again to restart the interview, my head's already full of swirling girlie groups with nostalgic names like The Pearls and The Paper Dolls.

Next, we troop into a nearby public house in the hope of finding a quiet room where we can talk more about female singers and the great impact their music has had on his own career. I order a pint of bitter.

Morrissey opts for the non-alcoholic Kaliber. Although he's initially comfortable in back-room pub surroundings, we're interrupted once more, this time by a gang of semi-sozzled Manchester United fans in the main bar who spot him and start dancing like pillocks while crooning, 'Heaven Knows I'm Miserable Now'.

"This isn't really my sort of place," he soon admits nervously, so we slope off back towards the car park like a couple of nomads. So finally, I'm forced to interview him right there right then, on the forecourt, car doors open wide, birds twittering in the background, the sound of the Cheshire suburbs all around us. Morrissey's seated comfortably in the sporting leather of the passenger seat. I'm crouching before him once more, camera and questions at the ready.

When did this obsession with Sixties female singers start?

"With the first single I ever bought, Marianne Faithfull's 'Come And Stay With Me', which I bought in Manchester in a shop called Paul Marsh, which was on the Alexandra Road in Moss Side. It was 1965 and I still love it . . . it's a great record. I memorised the words and I would sing them very loudly. I thought she was incredible, I'm sure she still is, but then she was great. And when you consider how old she was at the time . . . even better."

Wasn't it a bit raunchy? You once described her as "a right goer".

"I was only six, I really didn't know what the words meant, I didn't know what she was singing about, certain lines I couldn't fathom at all. It was just something that was grabbing me in. It was the sound of her voice, the feel, the emotiveness and the freedom, and from that moment I just fell in love with pop music. I never stopped playing pop records."

Why were the girl singers so important to you growing up? And why were they more important than the 'boy bands' of the time?

"The boy bands, as you put it, weren't terribly interesting to me. I loved groups like The Foundations and The Equals, The Love Affair and even Amen Corner, but the female singers seemed to be giving everything away and hiding nothing. Billy Fury was an exception but for the most part male voices were more restrained. Female singers seemed to be risking and that's what made them more dramatic and interesting to me. It seemed better to open your heart and throw it away.

"There was just something about female youth in the early Sixties. It was obviously a new type of female. They just walked in off the streets and . . . barked. It was no longer the flowery dresses and Kathy Kirbys, the heavy lips and the Alma Cogans . . . it was cheap and nasty, with cheap and nasty sentiments, you know, 'I'll Stop At Nothing'. Great songs, cacophonous brass . . . just street music. It was very British."

Was it mainly about image, or the sound of their voices, or just what they were saying?

"Female singers were allowed to be very expressive and dramatic. I think, for example, that in the Fifties and Sixties most people didn't think lesbianism existed, or that it hadn't been invented, whereas male singers couldn't sing in a sexually open way about their heart and how they really felt. Also, most female singers sang songs that were written by men. There were very few female songwriters. Carole King was probably one of the first."

How much of it was dictated by the sexual politics and prejudices of the time?

"Men were very repressed, they were playing it safe, they weren't walking the tightrope, they couldn't sing those songs themselves. Whereas singers like Timi Yuro were throwing themselves off a cliff and saying to hell with it. Singers like Shirley Bassey and Judy Garland had such a passionate dramatic audience, because these women were really holding their own heads under water. And rightly so in some cases . . . If only I could have been there.

"The female voice was the slap across the face, pushing you over. That was great. 'He hit me and it felt like a kiss.' Would Cliff Richard ever have sung that? If he had . . . phew! 'Loneliness Remembers What Happiness Forgets'. Very true. Would Anthony Newley have sung that?"

How important were Bacharach & David to the Sixties girl singers?

"Immensely, for Cilla Black and Dionne Warwick especially . . . very important."

Although Marianne Faithfull was your first love, didn't Sandie Shaw become your favourite?

"Sandie, I think, was probably the best of the lot. Her discography was better, longer than the others. There was something about her voice, something very . . . I was going to say cheap but it was close to cheap. Just something very noisy and natural about it.

"I liked her because she was very of the street *and* off the street, very unpretentious, and she was quite raucous and tough almost. All the records were produced by Ken Woodman and they were all slightly hard on the ears and heavily orchestrated. Very brassy. I liked that because it sounded like she'd just walked in off the street and began to sing and then just strolled home and . . . bought some chips. Good old Essex."

What's your favourite Sandie record?

"There are so many. I like one, which you won't know, called 'Keep In Touch'. And 'You've Not Changed', which was a reasonably big hit, that's probably the best one. The simplicity was very touching. Simplicity with a hint of aggression . . . which is always a fantastic mixture.

"And she had great B-sides. 'Stop Before You Start'. She was the best!"

How important were Chris Andrews' songs? (Apart from Sandie's break-through hit, Bacharach & David's '(There's) Always Something There To Remind Me', Andrews wrote most of her songs including 'Message Understood', 'Girl Don't Come', 'Long Live Love' and 'I'll Stop At Nothing'.)

"He's an incredible songwriter and even his solo stuff was very clever; great songs about death and tragedy, all within two minutes and eight seconds . . . which is an achievement."

Significantly, Andrews didn't write her Eurovision Song Contest winner 'Puppet On A String'.

He giggles, relaxing now. "We don't talk about that, not round here. 'Puppet On A String'? Was it really that bad? The answer is yes, it was bad. It was worse that we actually think it was. And she hates it also. But when it won the Eurovision Song Contest it was a tremendous moment. It was a great, runaway victory. And it was Sandie so . . . who cares? Mmm forgiveable."

'Heaven Knows I'm Miserable Now' was inspired by Sandie's last Sixties single wasn't it? ('Heaven Knows I'm Missing Him Now', released 1969, failed to chart.)

"Yes, of course [giggles]. It was an in-joke. But it was so 'in' that nobody really got it. It was a private joke between she and me."

How did you feel when Sandie had a hit with her cover of 'Hand In Glove'?

"It was extremely important but it was so great for me personally that I don't actually remember it happening. It was as if I'd blacked out for a period of time. A tremendous honour. It was just thrilling in a very, very youthful way."

What did you think of her vegetarian 'tribute' song, 'Steven You Don't Eat Meat'?

"I liked it." (He bites his lip to stop himself laughing.) "I thought it was a great song. I think some of the lines were maybe a bit too . . . off the mark, but I liked it. Once again, for Sandie to write and sing a song about me, having spent the last hundred years listening to her, was . . . great." (He raises his eyebrows mischievously.)

Why did the friendship with Sandie end?

"I really really loved Sandie. I really loved her. I played her records for years and years and years and years. I thought she was great. But when we worked together she wasn't the person I'd imagined her to be.

"The friendship ended because Sandie is a very highly strung person.

She's had a very strange life. She had success very quickly in her life. She was very young and . . . suddenly it was gone. I think as a result she's a person that . . ." (he laughs) "such things don't help really. I mean, all Buddhists are neurotic, psychotic . . . you name it they've got it!

"Even though we've had many a fist fight I still think she's great. She'll be remembered for ever."

Let's move on to Cilla Black. [Morrissey gurns.] Why did you once write that you wanted to "Stuff Cilla!"

He turns and rests his head on the car dashboard and laughs out loud and long. "I don't want to stuff Cilla. I actually don't want to touch Cilla at all. Cilla is definitely a memory, she's not a modern reality at all. The person was . . . but is no longer.

"She made some great records and great B-sides but I think she's very dodgy now. But she made some great records, even if she pilfered from Dionne Warwick, records like 'Alfie' were excellent. She was raucous. How anyone would let someone sing like that, with such a cacophonous dustbin lid voice. Then, of course, there were songs like 'Liverpool Lullaby', which you'd cross continents to avoid.

"It's very strange but if you listen to her very first record she doesn't actually have a Liverpudlian accent. But if you hear her now on television she obviously is so broadly, so overblown and theatrically Liverpudlian that it arouses some suspicion somewhat. In her early records she would say "care" instead of "cur" and "hair" instead of "hur" so how she's come to acquire a Liverpudlian accent having been away from the place for 35 years is extraordinary."

Why did you cover 'Work Is A Four Letter Word'?

"I thought it was an amusing song. I think I was the only member of The Smiths who actually did. I thought it was quite funny and very throwaway, and a bit of a tease really. I wasn't attempting to produce a great piece of Gothic Art, it was just a taunting little number. I even got the words wrong, accidentally. All to the better, all to the better . . . I rest my case."*

Did 'Work Is A Four Letter Word' finish The Smiths?

"Yes, it did really. It was very instrumental in breaking up The Smiths

---

* One implication – first suggested by Smiths' producer Stephen Street, when I'd interviewed him back in 1988 – is that Morrissey chose the song as a dig against the other members of the band, who he felt were partying too hard and becoming too nocturnal for his liking.

but what care I?" [He pauses, choosing his words carefully.] "Cilla Black, unbeknown to herself, actually broke The Smiths up." [He laughs, bitterly, almost desperately, and then repeats himself.] "Cilla Black actually broke The Smiths up . . . which is . . . pretty much to her credit." [He laughs again, then shakes his head sadly.] "I really don't know . . . I really don't know." [He frowns, temporarily lost in memories.]

What about the film *Work Is A Four Letter Word*?

"I thought the film was dreadful, absolutely dreadful, un-watchable. Thank God she didn't make another!"

Let's talk Lulu . . . I recall that when you agreed to perform at the Amnesty International 30th Birthday Party you asked me to get Lulu to introduce you? [He giggles again.] You're obviously a massive fan.

"Yes I am, I am. I can point to her errors but that's just the kind of person I am. I think she's also the most well-balanced of that glut of female singers of that time. She's a very nice person, a very natural and open person, which doesn't help in this business. There's no showbizness or flamboyancy about her, and she made some great records!

" 'Dreary Days And Dreary Nights' is obviously a floor filler . . . in my house. You will giggle but 'I'm A Tiger' I thought was an expertly crafted piece of genius gibberish. And 'To Sir With Love', which was a B-side in this country . . .

"You think they're really disposable but if you really listen they are wittily crafted pieces of work. 'Boom Bang-A-Bang'? These are records that we might not even be bothered to burn but there is a cleverness, there is a craft. Maybe it's only people like me who sees it but . . . who cares."

Will you be covering 'The Boat That I Row'?

"I have done. I've done a video. I actually sat in a boat but it didn't cross any ocean." [He giggles.] "No, 'The Boat That I Row' I think is very interesting because, once again, it's nothing to do with a boat as I'm sure that you've guessed. She's more or less saying to the world 'you're not going to change me, this is me, just take me as I am, and if you don't like me then it's up to you'. There's always more to these things than meets the eye."

You forgot to mention 'Shout'?

"I thought 'Shout' was awful. She has dropped a few clangers I'm afraid. She wasn't consistently great. There were a few booboos. But she certainly has her place . . . It's third shelf down."

Tell me about Dusty Springfield. You don't often talk about her. Was she as important to you?

"Oh Dusty was incredibly important. I keep saying 'was' as if these people no longer exist but in their heyday . . . Dusty singing 'The Corrupt Ones' in 1966 or 1967 was thin ice, and there was Dusty skating on it. I think she became known for the bluesy aspect of her singing and became famous in America for that, more so than for the early British singles. She made many great records but I think she seemed to be older than everyone else, more sensible and more liked by the older generation, which wasn't necessarily off-putting but . . . could be."

We've covered Dusty, Sandie, Marianne, Lulu and Cilla . . .

"They were the elite, they were the royalty . . . they were all trying to outdo each other."

Do you admire the longevity of their careers?

"No I hate them for that. Next question!"

Well, why do you think they've survived as performers for so long?

"It's harder for female singers because, supposedly, the theory is that female audiences dream to music so they prefer male performers. Whereas a male audience doesn't dream to music so they don't prefer female singers. So it's supposed to be harder for female performers to last longer.

"I do admire them. Sandie Shaw made so many great records and it's just incredible in this world if one person makes one great record."

It seems, listening to the songs you played while we were driving around and in terms of reference points in your songs, that you're equally interested in less-successful and more obscure female singers. Tell me about some of them. Let's start with Diana Dors?

"Diana Dors made the best record of the Sixties. 'So Little Time' in 1964 on the Fontana label, which sank with a trace. I don't know why but maybe people couldn't accept her as a singer because she was known for other things.

"She was incredibly sexual. Not so much a girl singer, more womanly. She made an album that's very rare called *The Swinging Dors*, which is not really very good. She didn't have a great voice but it's a great single, a great record. Written as I recall by Les Reed and well worth hunting . . . and shooting."

What about Twinkle?

"Twinkle was trouble and that's why she was so interesting. Her major hit 'Terry' was a death disc and was banned by the BBC. She wasn't allowed on *Ready, Steady, Go!* because the song was too morbid. So obviously I bought 12 of them. It reached number four. Great tune, great words. Very unusual to have a teenager singing about death and she also wrote most of her own stuff.

"So Twinkle was amusing and interesting and don't-blink-or-you'll miss her. Sometimes little spurts of career can be more important than careers that go on for hundreds of years."

Why do songs about death appeal to you?

"Because they're more interesting than songs about living and being happy. The Shangri-Las had 10 Top 10 hits in America and six of them were about death. Songs like 'Dressed In Black'. Tragedy, drama, it's all there rolled into this little piece of black plastic. Long live the Death Disc!"

Wasn't your mum shocked at the time?

"Yes she was and continues to be so. But she couldn't stop me. At the age of six I would crawl under the kitchen table and cry until she bought me something. I loved pop music so much."

Why did The Smiths cover Twinkle's 'Golden Lights'?

"Because it reminded me of the Gene Pitney backstage "I'm lonely" type drama. I thought it was very dramatic. I remember Sandie telling me once that she wanted to become famous so that she could have boyfriends and so people would like her. But when she became famous she could never get boyfriends and people wouldn't come near her. They thought she was untouchable.

"So 'Golden Lights' was just a slight interesting twisty insight into the perils of fame and change and all the great things that happen to you when you are no longer anonymous. Just look at . . . Dirk Bogarde . . . and spot the difference."

How do you decide what to cover?

"It's difficult for me because I love so many different styles. I love Cajun music, I love trashy British pop, and then I love Seventies music, Generation X, Siouxsie & The Banshees. So it's very hard to know what to cover."

Tell me why you covered Timi Yuro's 'Interlude'?*

"It was a very obscure song. It was a B-side (of Yuro's finest song 'Hurt' in 1961, later covered by Elvis Presley) and I thought she sang it really beautifully."

What did you make of other, less commercially successful Sixties singers, like Helen Shapiro ?

* Morrissey duetted on the 1994 single with Siouxsie Sioux.

"Helen Shapiro was younger than most. She was 14 or 15 when she had those stomping great hits. 'Tell Me What He Said' was a great record. 'Don't Treat Me Like A Child', that's quite revolutionary. No, it's not my theme tune, not really at the age of 37, but that's what all teenagers were saying at that time, at the end of the Fifties. Nineteen Sixty One – 'Don't Treat Me Like A Child'!

Millie Small?

"Incredible. 'My Boy Lollipop' was about one minute 10 seconds long. Fantastic record. Incredibly energetic and spicy and . . . pert. People don't sing like that any more apart from me. She also had a single called 'Sweet William', 1964. Millie Small. No relation to Biggie Small of course."

What about some of the Brit Girls who didn't really make it in chart terms? Names like Beryl Marsden spring to mind . . .

"She's my mother actually, did I mention that?" [He giggles.] "Beryl was Sandie before Sandie was Sandie. She was the forgotten one. Filed under forgotten. More so even than Timi Yuro or Rita Pavone."

Rita who?

"Rita Pavone! Don't tell me you've never heard of Rita Pavone! She made the best record in the history of . . . abattoirs. It was called 'Heart', it was on RCA and I think it got to number 12 or 26. Incredible, absolutely incredible, almost as good as . . . Tommy Steele."

In the car you played a track by The Paper Dolls?

"The Paper Dolls were very interesting. They made great records, only one of which was a hit, called 'Something Here In My Heart (Keeps A-Tellin' Me Know)'. They were from Manchester, they were on the Pye label and they were great for, god bless them, a year. Then it was back to Woolworths. A great year . . . for Woolworths.

"One of them, Suzy Mathis, ended up as a DJ on Piccadilly Radio. Yes, The Paper Dolls. Definitely worth . . . digging into your archives. I bet you can find a thigh length boot worn by The Paper Dolls. What you'll do with it I really don't know."

At the end of the interview in deepest Cheshire – before shaking hands and waving Morrissey off in his sports car, back towards his mum's in Bowden – I put it to him that most things Morrissey seemed to be somehow linked, in terms of his sources from pop music to film to television, and that, perhaps as he'd once scrawled on a Smiths' run-out groove, "talent borrows genius steals"?

He giggles and nods his head. "Yes, everything's linked, everybody takes from the artists they love. Eventually you develop your own individuality but at first you really do sap your sources dry. Everything's linked, everything's traceable. Everything leads back to . . . Dorothy Squires."*

Meeting Morrissey, that April of 1997, I hadn't heard any of the tracks on the forthcoming *Maladjusted* album but I had heard some of the titles, much to his concern. So I knew about the first single 'Alma Matters' (another nod to James Dean's film career, perhaps also based on Elvis' single 'Steadfast Loyal And True' in response to his legal dressing-down as "devious, truculent and unreliable") and 'Roy's Keen', about a George Formby-style window cleaner and also a too-obvious tribute to the famous Manchester United and Ireland footballer.

When *Maladjusted* did appear in August 1997 it was inevitably mauled by the music press, and Morrissey was written off yet again as a spent force in pop music. It's not that the album was bad just that, after the failure of *Southpaw Grammar* to live up to *Vauxhall & I*, everyone apart from blindly committed fans seemed to be demanding a radical change of direction.

Perhaps the album suffered from his ongoing obsession with defeating Mike Joyce, an ambition that would elude him but remain a subject of great importance to his history; the strain of the case, with hindsight, undoubtedly affected his artistry and his bitter outbursts against the British legal system would become a lyrical feature on subsequent albums from *Maladjusted* through to *You Are The Quarry*.

As a clear example of Morrissey's state of mind at the time, 'Sorrow Will Come In The End' was viewed by Island Records as such a thinly veiled attack on the legal system and Mike Joyce that it was excluded from the UK version of *Maladjusted* in fear of further courtroom drama; it's one of the most menacing and threatening retaliations imaginable. Regardless of his court victory, Mike Joyce must've struggled to sleep with these words spinning in his head.

As usual, with *Maladjusted* Morrissey had refused to deliver what was expected in terms of radio-friendly pop music. Aside from the beautiful 'Trouble Loves Me' and the unsettling title track – complete with vocal sample from king of the Cockneys, Anthony Newley – it's difficult to warm to *Maladjusted* and, as Alan Jackson noted in *The Times*, there's a short supply of "the tune that can be whistled". Also, there was the spine-chilling return – 13 years on from 'Suffer Little Children' – to the subject

---

* The glamorous Welsh diva was bankrupted by legal costs and eventually banned from litigation and the High Court.

of child murders, perhaps even paedophilia, in 'Ambitious Outsiders', which rattled the cages of the tabloid press while proving, once again, that few artists in pop music would dare be as lyrically challenging as Morrissey.

A few days after *Maladjusted*'s release, a cassette arrived from Morrissey of the Diana Dors track 'So Little Time' (marked "Diana Doorknob"). But, apart from seeing him performing live at Battersea Power Station on December 10 that year – one of only two British performances – and then catching him again in London on the Oye Esteban (*Hello Steven*) tour in November 1999, I wouldn't meet Morrissey again in the 20th century.

11.

Return Of The Mozzfather

"I don't think longevity is a particularly good thing. Some artists are extremely powerful within a short space. But I don't see the point with artists just staying around and applauding themselves for the fact that they're still standing and this is their hundredth single."

— Morrissey 1991

AT the dawn of the 21st century Morrissey was beginning to look like history. He hadn't released a new album for over two years (after *Maladjusted* had been critically savaged), he had no record company deal, there were rumours of deep depression and, worst of all, the court case with Smiths' drummer Mike Joyce had ended in utter calamity.

On November 5, 1998, the Court Of Appeal finally ruled in favour of Joyce (and, by inference, Andy Rourke) confirming Judge Weeks original decision that the rhythm section should have been paid substantially more than 10 per cent of all royalties (excluding songwriting) during their five years with band. As a result, Morrissey and Johnny Marr would now have to pay over £1 million plus costs to Joyce. (Rourke had already settled for £83,000 back in 1989.)

At first, it appeared, as if Morrissey was refusing to pay up, preferring to stay in solitary exile in Los Angeles where he'd purchased the house off Sunset Boulevard that Clark Gable had once built for Carole Lombard. But then Mike Joyce's lawyers threatened to put charges on all UK properties owned by Morrissey's family in order to leverage money from the singer. Although Morrissey would drag out the process of paying Joyce for as long as possible, in the summer of 2003 he would assure me he'd paid up and that the messy, ugly, legally divisive, tragic demise of The Smiths had finally been played out.

During these 'lost' years – from *Maladjusted* (1997) through to the critically acclaimed comeback album *You Are The Quarry* (2004) – various opportunistic old record companies inevitably sought to cash in on this

Morrissey vacuum by releasing stop-gap compilations. There was *Suedehead – The Best Of Morrissey* on EMI, *Rare Tracks* on Mercury, *My Early Burglary Years* and *The Best Of . . .* on Reprise in the States, followed by two *CD Singles* compilations again on EMI, charting Morrissey's solo work from '88–91' then '91–95' ("smelling faintly of fish and marketing" was Stuart Maconie's verdict in *Q*). But the overall tone was of backward looking, end-of-century nostalgia. Almost as if Morrissey had died.

I'd tried to keep in touch by fax during the intervening years, often trying to tempt him to get involved in television projects I vainly hoped would be close to his heart (particularly around the centenary of Oscar Wilde's death). But the brevity of his responses reflected the disillusion and anger he felt towards the British legal system after his defeat in the High Court. Mike Joyce was "pure evil" and "has destroyed The Smiths" was his bitter verdict in 1998. In 2003 he was still angry: "There was a terrible miscarriage of justice . . . so it's been really shocking. I wish the very, very worst for Joyce for the rest of his life."

He also blamed the British music press for "the across-the-board rejection of me in the mid-Nineties" and complained at his music being branded miserable whereas, in his opinion, celebrated bands such as Coldplay and Radiohead escaped similar criticisms though "both of those bands sound very unhappy with not a sign of a witty lyric".

Back in 1988, after *Viva Hate* and his split with post-Smiths' songwriting partner Stephen Street, he'd first told me he'd "all but retired". Following the critical mauling he'd received for *Maladjusted* and his subsequent failure to sign a new record deal, those of us who really liked him as a person and an artist were, frankly, glad that he was simply keeping on. There had even been rumours of a suicide attempt in the mid-Nineties and, as I'd talked to him about depression in interviews before, it wasn't hard to understand and empathise with his state of mind following the defeat in the British courts. (His great friend Linder Sterling later talked of "periods of very bad depression . . . debilitating periods when life had absolutely no point".)

There was absolutely no indication of anything approaching a comeback. Although he played some thirty gigs in the spring of 2000, most of them were in the USA followed by a series of performances in Latin America. Even in the early summer of 2002, when he again announced he'd tour America, the prospect of a first British visit since December 1999 looked remote.

Then, suddenly in September 2002, Morrissey returned to play two nights at the Royal Albert Hall in London. Given his downbeat mood in previous communications, I attended both nights hardly knowing what to expect. Would it be a little more than a cash-raising end-of-the-pier-style trip down memory lane made up of old Smiths songs plus a few pre-*Southpaw Grammar* highlights? Was this the final "thank you and good-night" curtain for the famous international playboy? Or would there be new compositions and a fresh spring in the battered old boxer's step?

Coincidentally, I bumped into Johnny Rogan (author of *The Severed Alliance*) outside the RAH before the first gig and we went for a beer. Rogan was much-hated by Morrissey around the time of *The Severed Alliance* (Morrissey wished Rogan would "die in an M3 pile-up") but his affection for The Smiths and obsession with Morrissey's career remained undimmed. It's worth noting that in the High Court, when Morrissey's character was being assassinated by Justice Weeks, Rogan attended the whole trial as an independent observer.

The second night I went along with my great friend Alan Jackson of *The Times*, who'd been a Smiths' fan at *NME* in the Eighties but had seriously doubted some of Morrissey's post-*Vauxhall & I* solo work. Even Alan was astonished at the emotional response this middle-aged Mancunian again received from the packed Kensington congregation.

In truth, both gigs were extraordinary occasions, triumphant shows, as good as anything I've seen at the Royal Albert Hall over the years (every-thing from Abdullah Ibrahim to Santana to The Smiths in 1984 through to Elvis Costello) and, most uplifting of all, featured some really strong spiky yet commercial songs such as 'I Like You', 'The First Of The Gang To Die', 'Mexico', 'The World Is Full Of Crashing Bores' and a preview of the powerful next single 'Irish Blood, English Heart', which outlined his passionately protective views on modern Britain while also attacking the apathy-inducing two-party political system.

These memorable evenings proved, as the post-Smiths Wolverhampton gig had done some 14 years earlier, that there was still a place for Morrissey in people's hearts. More than ever before, he seemed to appreciate this warmth and, between songs, he spoke emotionally from the stage to his audience. Apart from paying tribute to the actress Katrin Cartlidge – she'd appeared in the films *Naked*, *Breaking The Waves*, *Career Girls* and *Clarie Dolan*, but had died tragically aged 41 several days earlier – he also thanked his closest friend Linder and noted that both his parents were present in the Royal Albert Hall.

Against his own predictions in the rare track 'Now I Am A Was' (which stole Orson Welles' quote: "I started at the top and then worked my way down") this would be the beginning of a new era for Morrissey, in which nostalgia for his old classics – 'There Is A Light That Never Goes Out' provided a moving climax to both Royal Albert Hall gigs – combined with slavering enthusiasm, in the audience and in the press, for his new creations. Importantly, the concerts seemed to present a re-energised, more forward looking Morrissey, resigned to losing the court battle with Joyce and finally ready to move on.

More significantly, at least for my personal relationship with Morrissey, the Royal Albert Hall concerts were being filmed by Chrysalis for inclusion in a forthcoming Channel 4 documentary.

It transpired that an old BBC colleague of mine, Ricky Kelehar (who'd worked on music programmes such as *Sixties Soul Top Ten* for Chrysalis and C4) had, together with Tina Flintoff, persuaded Morrissey to participate in a profile. Despite my initial attempt to persuade the elusive pop star otherwise, Ricky was already assembling the programme called *The Importance Of Being Morrissey* for transmission in the summer of 2003. In terms of UK television it would be the first authorised and personal look at Morrissey's career since *The South Bank Show* back in 1987.

I can remember when I first became aware there was a problem with the documentary. I'd gone into Channel 4 to pitch programme ideas for Granada and overheard some legal suit in the lift muttering about how "that bastard Morrissey" was now threatening to sue Chrysalis over a "rough cut" VHS he'd been sent.

Maybe I was wrong to get involved initially but as I knew Ricky and I genuinely wanted to see some sort of documentary transmitted on British television, I sent through an inquisitive fax to Morrissey's mum's home in May 2003.

Morrissey telephoned, from Los Angeles, later the same day. To put it mildly, he was fuming like an old kettle. He claimed "I burst into tears when I saw it."

Responding to the rough edit he'd been sent, he accused the programme makers of "bringing it down to *Sun* level", of being obsessed with celibacy and Mike Joyce and the old unfounded allegations of racism, and he expressed his bitter disappointment that, despite the "incredible access" he'd given them – "they filmed everywhere . . . my home, Greece, Paris, Australia, Blackburn!" – they had been "incredibly nasty" in their selection of edited material. Television, he complained, was obsessed "with revelation and reinforcing stereotypes".

He admitted he'd only gone with Chrysalis because they'd previously made a documentary with Julie Goodyear (Bet Lynch from *Coronation Street*) but claimed he hadn't signed anything legal. He referred to Ricky Kelehar as "the hound with the camera".

With Morrissey's encouragement, I endeavoured to bridge the looming crisis between him and Chrysalis. He urged me to go visit Ricky and view the film at Chrysalis' HQ in London, and to give my independent verdict on the programme: "What's your expert opinion?" he wrote, "Britain can take it." I did this and, surprisingly, reported that the rough-cut version I viewed was flawed but seemed, by and large, a positive even upbeat account of his life.

True, there was a messy section about the flag-waving nationalist Madstock controversy of 1992 – significantly reduced in the transmitted programme – but this was countered with strong affectionate words from Noel Gallagher in particular, who ridiculed anyone who thought Morrissey might be racist. "If he was," Noel observed, "the fucking *News Of The World* would have uncovered it first . . . Forget the fucking *NME!*" Morrissey himself stated, "Why on earth would I be racist? What would I be trying to achieve?"

Importantly, it was beautifully shot, the supporting cast were fantastic (particularly Bono, J.K. Rowling, Linder Sterling and Alan Bennett) and the freshly filmed coverage of Morrissey enjoying life in the 21st century was excellent too. Morrissey riding a Vespa as if in *La Dolce Vita*; having his hair cut in Mayfair (as Oscar Wilde had done); pulling *Carry On* faces in a Los Angeles burlesque club; exchanging hugs with Hollywood royalty in the form of Nancy Sinatra; and appreciating the warm Californian devotion of his growing Latino audience – Los Angeles' incomers who clearly appreciate his lyrical expression of what it means to be an outsider.

Even though Morrissey did consider legal action against Chrysalis, arguably, as he'd granted them the access over a period of time, I suspect he would have lost yet another court case. Nevertheless, when it was transmitted, the documentary was well received. It also kick-started our correspondence again and, throughout 2003, as he signed to Sanctuary and even launched his own record label, Attack, we communicated on a fairly regular basis. (When I'd asked Morrissey, back in 1990, if he'd considered setting up a record label he'd replied, "I think people who do those kind of things they're, oh God, terrible bearded types. I'm too glamorous to do anything like that.")

As I was still working at Granada Television, and would later do a very brief stint on his beloved *Coronation Street* in 2005, much of our contact centred on great television programmes and films of the Sixties and Seventies. Morrissey seemed to remember everything he'd seen on the small screen growing up in Manchester.

I was astonished by his knowledge and recall of productions that Granada had screened up to forty years earlier. Even more mature archivists couldn't remember programmes such as the Irish actor Michael MacLiammoir's remarkable one man show *The Importance Of Being Oscar* from the early Sixties or the original 1976 version of Jack Rosenthal's *Ready When You Are Mr McGill.**

Apart from classic episodes of *Coronation Street* featuring his heroine Pat Phoenix that he desperately wanted to get his hands on, he also wrote fondly about other obsessions such as Jimmy Clitheroe, Diana Dors in *Queenie's Castle*, the American drag artist Charles Pierce on the *Russell Harty Show* and particularly *Bronco Bullfrog*, the gritty 1969 East End drama about skinheads and suedeheads.

After some digging and a few subversive tape transfers I informed Morrissey that some of his desired programmes still existed in the bowels of Granada's bonded warehouse. His typical, faxed response read: "Mr Swindley. How do you cope with the Granada archive? I'd wall myself up in there day and night. I came across a 1961 film of Shelagh Delaney recently and, of course, to me it's like Bloomsbury . . . I don't think you could ever realise how happy you've made me. I will not leave the house for 48 hours. I will not eat." (Leonard Swindley, one of the original *Coronation Street* characters, had been played by Arthur Lowe. In other correspondence I'd be addressed as further Corrie stars such as "Len Fairclough", "Les Battersby", even "Granny Hopkins".)

So it was that, on July 2, 2003, at a pre-arranged time and armed with a few classic Seventies episodes of *Coronation Street* and a copy of *Mr McGill*, plus assorted clips of Diana Dors and Jimmy Clitheroe, I stumbled into The Grapes pub off Quay Street in Manchester, a spit from the Free Trade Hall.

I knew it was owned by Liz Dawn, aka Vera Duckworth, of *Coronation Street*, but I was taken aback to see her meeting and greeting visitors like the Queen Mum "Hello love," she said. (In the real world, the soap opera world, she would, of course, have said "Hello chuck.")

---

* Rosenthal was a key writer on *Coronation Street* through the Sixties and also wrote *Spend Spend Spend* about Vivian Nicholson.

Stranger still, in one corner, Kangol cap in hand (once the choice headgear for serious rappers such as LL Cool J and Run DMC), sat an equally renowned Mancunian legend – Steven Patrick Morrissey; cradling a glass of Guinness, scanning the property guide to Alderley Edge, Cheshire, and looking for all the world like a Victorian Irishman.

"Are you . . . h-a-p-p-y?" he asked, as I sat down opposite him, almost 20 years on from the first time I'd set eyes on him, onstage at the Venue in London in 1983. The pale thin student pin-up with the ridiculous quiff had long gone and, physically and mentally, he'd grown into a more rounded, stronger but still questioning and warm personality.

The eyebrows seemed bushier, the working-class face perhaps more chiselled granite than before, and the hairline distinguished, vaguely greying, yet still somehow rockabilly. While I'd aged and shrivelled into some sort of middle-aged Weetabix-style skinhead, Morrissey now seemed to be turning into a cross between Anthony Newley and Frankie Howerd. (When he moved to Italy to record *Ringleader Of The Tormentors* in 2005 he'd begin cultivate his current Sicilian-godfather-meets-Pasolini image.)

Of course I'd seen him in performance at the Royal Albert Hall a few months earlier but here, in the pub, smack in the middle of his hometown of Manchester, he seemed totally relaxed again, as if the mid-to-late Nineties had never happened.

Our conversation took in everything from football and Ireland – he has a home over there – to mortality, his back problems (the end of his promising five-a-side football career) and the bitter finale of the Mike Joyce court cases: "It's resolved, I've paid him," he assured me, although later he feared that Joyce might want more. I expressed disappointment that the proposed duet with Michael Stipe had never happened but thanked him, sincerely, for the remarkable 'Interlude' with Siouxsie, even though I was aware there had been friction between them. He took the compliment awkwardly and revealed she had been "professional, nice" but "she'd only do a video if she could throw stones at me in it". He reflected that Siouxsie & The Banshees had been dangerous on the first few albums but that The Creatures had become like The Cure, selling out into "soft goth".

The Channel 4 television documentary, *The Importance Of Being Morrissey*, had been broadcast three weeks earlier to positive reviews. He'd ubiquitously appeared again on the covers of major music and listings magazines, and I reminded him there'd also been an unflattering photo of him on the front of Manchester's *City Life*. He grimaced:

"Trust you. I looked 88!" But I congratulated him on this latest come-back, assured him he'd emerged well from the television portrait of the artist, and expressed the opinion that it revealed him to be enjoying Los Angeles. "It wasn't really my real life in the documentary, it was an illusion."

He was enthusiastic about his new record deal and particularly about the launch of his Attack label; his old Smiths/Raymonde friend James Maker's band Noko 440 would be one of his first releases ('Born That Way') alongside the New York Dolls, Jobriath and Nancy Sinatra. Inevitably I talked about my long-dead brother's original Attack Seventies reggae singles (Linval Thompson, Jah Woosh, Ken Parker, etc) and also reminded him he'd played me The Toys' 'Attack' at our previous meeting in Cheshire back in 1997.

Morrissey had told me back in 1988 that he thought reggae was vile – he'd withdrawn this view later – so I was pleasantly surprised that he'd picked the name Attack. Soon I'd send him my brother's favourite record on the label, Gregory Isaacs' 'Love Is Overdue'. This is the single he was photographed with, by Hamish Brown (no relation) in Los Angeles, March 2004 to publicise the launch of Attack.

The month before our meeting, June 2003, had seen the release of the DMC Morrissey-selected compilation *Under The Influence*. Apart from raising money for P.E.T.A. and introducing his audience to some of the extraordinary tracks that sustained him as a teenager – The New York Dolls' 'Trash', Ramones' 'Judy Is A Punk', Sparks' 'Arts & Crafts Spectacular' – *Under The Influence* also beautifully explained in the sleeve notes the importance of music to his soul: "In early 1970s Manchester the grinding horrors of daily life are softened by song . . ." (The compilation also featured the rockabilly tracks Nat County's 'Woodpecker Rock' and Charlie Feathers' 'One Hand Loose', the Cajun classic 'Saturday Night Special' by Lesa Cormier And The Sundown Playboys and The Cats' bluebeat 'Swan Lake'.)

As a result, we got to talking about the remarkable journey from his troubled awkward childhood in Stretford and Salford through to his current millionaire rock star existence in Los Angeles. Even though he was still in a state of "chosen aloneness" (as Linder Sterling described it) and he'd expressed the opinion "I don't think human beings are meant to live together", he certainly seemed a more optimistic man from the Morrissey I'd met in the late Eighties.

LB: Do you think you've changed much over the years?

Morrissey: "People equate success with softness. People believe that once you've had a degree of success you've been given everything you've striven for and therefore you back off, you're consumed by luxurious things. I've been successful but I've never been isolated within that success to the degree where I've never been affected for the good or for the bad by success. I am still quite critically, unbudgeably the same person."

And you're still going strong.

(He laughs.) "Well . . . I don't want to walk onstage with a hair transplant, with shoes on the wrong foot. I find pop senility totally appalling to witness and obviously there're so many strong examples of it now. I don't want to haul the carcass across the studio floor and reach for the bath chair as I put down a vocal."

Although I'm more Scottish than Morrissey is Irish, I expressed surprise that he'd become increasingly interested in his Celtic background as he grew older. Clearly the forthcoming single 'Irish Blood English Heart' confirmed this and, in several recent interviews, he'd even used the Irish expression "jaysus" and expressed admiration for the Dublin singer-songwriter Damien Dempsey.

There had been little mention of Ireland in Morrissey's early lyrics, apart from his celebration of the great Wilde, but I reminded him that when he'd interviewed Pat Phoenix back in 1985, she'd said, "All of us who are half-Irish . . . who have the basic Irish . . . are born with the Celtic twilight in us. That moody Celt, the obvious Celt, stays with us and we never change, whatever our loyalties to the place in which we live."

This inevitably took us on to a discussion of *Coronation Street*. Pat Phoenix had quit after 20 years (she'd first appeared as Elsie Tanner in 1960) and, according to Morrissey, *Coronation Street* "choked and died" when she left.

He'd complained about this once before, to Andy Spinoza in the Manchester magazine *City Life*: "The script is beyond public credulity. It's like Postman Pat. Somebody loses an envelope, somebody breaks an umbrella and suddenly the credits roll and there's sad music. And you're expected to be there next week and be worried about the umbrella. It's terrible, it's like the loss of a limb. It's such an integral part of the way I lived. I saw it the other night by accident and I was terminally ill. I was in intensive care, it was awful. They're just clinging on. They should bury it."

But, regardless of his negative criticisms, he admitted he couldn't stop watching: "The only thing I ever watch on television is *Coronation Street* and mostly unhappily so. Everything else seems to be American or Australian. You can't watch anything home-grown anywhere. I wish occasionally I could tune into something that expresses the British condition.

LB: What's the great appeal of the *Street*?

Morrissey: "I think the most appealing thing is I can tune into an environment where a number of characters are enormously happy with their lot in life. They're content to walk from the postbox to the pub without questioning the past, the present and beyond. And that's quite calming.

"The community spirit no longer exists in England but it's powerfully reflected in the soap. The dream for many people is to live a very uncomplicated life, where they cease to constantly question why they're here, where they're going, what value they have.

"People within *Coronation Street* are happy to live in their houses, on their incomes, and they're very happy with the political situation. It's a dream."

Another memorable aspect of his interview with Phoenix, I suggested, was her mention of suicidal tendencies. She'd told Morrissey, "You're always very sad when you're young. I've known this since my first very weak attempt at suicide. But now, I could fall down tomorrow and break my neck, but that's OK. That's all part of it."

He'd spoken sensitively and movingly about suicide many times over the years, memorably after the passing of Kurt Cobain in 1994: "I felt sad and I felt envious. I admire people who self-destruct. They're refusing to continue with unhappiness which shows tremendous self-will. So many people I admire took their own lives . . . Stevie Smith, Sylvia Plath, James Dean, Marilyn Monroe, Rachel Roberts . . ."

I'd talked death with Morrissey before and, with both of us thundering towards 50, I thought it might be a good time to raise this happy subject again. I'd returned from the West of Scotland the previous day, where, beneath Ben Cruachan in Argyll, I'd helped carry the coffin of my uncle and godfather Hugh MacLarty; a truly gentle man and lover of the Scottish countryside. In the midst of life . . .

Apart from my own tragedies, Morrissey had had to deal with the relatively recent and sudden deaths of several close friends, including Kirsty MacColl in December 2000.

LB: You think about death a lot, don't you?

Morrissey: "Yes, I'm quite obsessed with death. I've gone through periods where I'm intensely envious of people who have died. I have a dramatic, unswayable, unavoidable obsession with death."

Why do you think that is?

"It's just something that's always there, that's never really left me. I can remember being quite obsessed with it at the age of eight or nine. And I often wondered if it was quite a natural inbuilt emotion for people who are destined to . . . take their own lives. That they just recognise it and begin to study it.

"I think if there was a magical, beautiful pill that one could take that would retire you from the world, I think I would take it. And I suppose that's the extremity of the obsessiveness. I think I would get out if it was relatively easy. I'm sorry, Len, but you asked the question."

If you don't die by your own hand, and make it into old age, how ideally would you like to go?

(He laughs deeply, a cocktail of joyful despair.) "The problem with death as with birth is that it's so violent. So . . . probably just propped up on those fluffy pillows in the front room."

Is it best to die at the peak of your career or when you're a spent force?

"Obviously when people die at the peak of their powers they become automatic godheads."

Have you peaked yet?

"I peak . . . every night."

What time and where?

"You'll never know!"

Anything else you want to say?

"Just how . . . tickled I am."

Afterwards, when we left The Grapes and walked back along Deansgate together, Mancunians of all ages smiled and acknowledged him as if they knew him. Not in an aggressive or intrusive way but in an affectionate, welcoming manner, for a prodigal son who'd finally returned to his true home. At the end of Deansgate, we shook hands. He went off alone, towards his car in Kendals car park; while I went shopping for my two daughters.

Even though Morrissey had seemed positive and confident about his own prize-fighting career ahead of his next release – "Yes, this Morrissey album is fantastic, although I predict the same old reviews from precisely the same old faces/names" – he'd been less enthusiastic about the competition in the pop arena. "Sorry I was so grumpy about the state of musical play, but I honestly find it so uncreative and stupid, you'd need to pay me at least £5 million to attend the Q Awards."

But even I, of little faith, doubted whether his debut Sanctuary/Attack release – his first in seven long years – could have anything like the impact of his solo career highlight so far, *Vauxhall & I*. Yet released in May 2004, *You Are The Quarry* was arguably the most mainstream album of Morrissey's career, reaching number two in the UK charts, and launching his biggest hit single 'Irish Blood, English Heart'. *You Are The Quarry* would also be his most successful album in the USA, hitting number 11, and would sell over one million copies worldwide.

Despite the obvious more-commercial quality of *You Are The Quarry*, Morrissey was soon proved right in terms of the "same old reviews by the same old faces". Stuart Maconie perched precariously on the fence at Q by asking "whether *You Are The Quarry* is the glorious prodigal's return that some are trumpeting, or just another episode in one of the rummest and most entertaining soap operas in modern pop?" More hard-hitting and negative, another old *NME* colleague Andy Gill complained in *The Independent* that "not only is he fighting battles that everyone has long ago forgotten, he's fighting them in almost identical terms, lyrically and musically, as he did a decade a go."*

With hindsight, the whole look and feel of the album – Morrissey in aggressive Mafia pose, like Al Pacino on the posters for Scarface – indicated that he meant business. Produced by Jerry Finn (Green Day, blink-182) and sustained by some of Morrissey's cleverest and most commercial songs for a decade – notably the catchy follow-up gun-slinging single 'The First Of The Gang To Die' and the brilliantly titled 'The World Is Full Of Crashing Bores' – *You Are The Quarry* saw the artist escape from the dark shadows of the Nineties and embrace a new audience without, crucially, losing his traditional cult following.

Although he continued to extend the subject matter of popular music, particularly on 'America Is Not The World', 'All The Lazy Dykes' and 'I Have Forgiven Jesus', many of the songs were arguably more radio friendly than previous Morrissey releases. Last but certainly not least, the collection ended with a classic, self-deprecating sideswipe at those who'd

---

* As the pre-show theme, Morrissey's choice of Big Hard Excellent Fish's 'Imperfect List' certainly continued to fight old battles. This Pete Wylie-inspired Scouse track railed against Thatcher, AIDS, loneliness, the Royal Family, judges, Hillsborough, *The Sun* and . . . Bonnie Langford.

written him off, or crossed swords with him in the Nineties, in 'You Know I Couldn't Last'.

The return of the Mozzfather – as he'd be christened by *NME*, who'd almost posthumously declared his Smiths the Greatest Artists Of All Time back in 2002 – seemed like the musical equivalent of Muhammad Ali's defeat of George Foreman in the Rumble In The Jungle 30 years earlier. The battered journeyman – perceived by many to be creatively broken and exiled like Wilde at the turn of the century – made an astonishing comeback at 45. The great showman had returned against all the odds – his name spelt out in huge neon lights across the stage like Elvis' 1968 comeback special – and his triumphant, emotional live performances of Smiths' classics such as 'How Soon Is Now?' and 'Last Night I Dreamt That Somebody Loved Me' alongside solo highlights like 'Munich Air Disaster 1958' and his cover of Patti Smith's 'Redondo Beach', were captured on *Live At Earls Court*.

That year I caught him performing in Manchester, Newcastle and, most memorably, as part of the London Meltdown Festival in June 2004. He'd curated the event, typically promoting some of his favourite acts past and present: the Killers, Damien Dempsey, Ludus, the Ordinary Boys, the New York Dolls, Gene, Sparks and even Alan Bennett. Many of the artists he encouraged, including the Libertines (who he'd championed from the beginning but who'd had to withdraw from Meltdown) would also appear on his *NME* CD compilation *Songs To Save Your Life*.

Reunited with *NME*, 12 years after Madstock, Morrissey explained that the outbreak of peace was possible because "the old nasty old guard have been and gone . . . They obviously outlived their usefulness and were destroyed in a nearby field . . . It isn't the smelly old *NME* any more." It almost felt as if his relationship with the paper had come full circle; he was being hailed again in 2004 with the same language and level of acclaim he'd first received back in 1984. But how long could it last?

By the time I saw him again, that December, at Glasgow SECC, Morrissey was still on exhilarating all-conquering form on the final leg of his 75 date Pan-American and European tour, culminating in Dublin just before Xmas.

If you analysed his solo career then you'd conclude that, following his previous comebacks (*Viva Hate*, 1988) and highpoints (*Vauxhall & I*, 1994) inevitably there would be bad times just around the corner. Despite the constant and prolific quality of his lyrical poetry and soul-stirring live performances, the struggle to form a lasting song-writing partnership had certainly weakened his creativity in the years immediately post–1988. Similarly, the dirty-laundry-in-public court case with Mike Joyce obviously took its toll in the mid-to-late Nineties.

So following the worldwide success of *You Are The Quarry*, frankly it would have seemed predictable had Morrissey's next collection of songs coincided with another downturn in fortunes. But, whereas he'd prolific-ally followed up both *Viva Hate* and *Vauxhall & I* with significantly less successful albums barely a year later, now he seemed determined not to make the same mistake again.

After almost a decade exiled largely in Los Angeles, Morrissey relocated in Rome in 2005 and started work on a new album with long-term collaborators Boz Boorer and Alain Whyte, who had started writing with him after the uncharacteristically-safe 1991 release *Kill Uncle*. Although Whyte had also been working with his own band Red Lightning, he'd write the majority of the tunes on Morrissey's eighth solo album. In contrast Boorer, who'd scored many of the best of the artist's solo tracks – 'Now My Heart Is Full', 'The More You Ignore Me, The Closer I Get', 'Jack The Ripper' plus 'Come Back To Camden' and 'The World Is Full Of Crashing Bores' from *You Are The Quarry* – seemed to lose out in the songwriting stakes to relative-newcomers, Mexican guitarist Jesse Tobias and keyboard player Michael Farrell.

Rather than illustrating a breakdown in relations between the artist and his closest associate Boorer, the division of labour within the band merely indicated the wealth of talent Morrissey now had available. Although Boorer's compositions did not appear on *Ringleader Of The Tormentors*, I'd argue that he composed some of the most brilliant tracks of Morrissey's solo career, notably 'Christian Dior' and 'Noise Is The Best Revenge'.

Ahead of the album's release, positive sounds had been made from the studio in Rome by Morrissey's latest producer, Tony Visconti of Bowie and Bolan fame. Six months before the release Visconti had revealed, "I am two thirds of the way through one of the best albums I've ever worked on, with not only Morrissey at his best, but the plot has twists and turns which somehow involve film composer Ennio Morricone and an Italian children's choir."

When it appeared in April 2006, *Ringleader Of The Tormentors* fared even better in the UK than its successful predecessor *You Are The Quarry*, reaching number one in the album charts. In the States it climbed to 27.

Apart from the eclectic sounds on the album – a Middle-Eastern feel to 'I Will See You In Far Off Places' in addition to the Italian influences and

Tony Visconti's stylish post-Glam production – as with *You Are The Quarry* there was, once again, a clear focus on the need for provocative yet commercial singles (a quality seriously lacking on *Southpaw Grammar* in particular).

'You Have Killed Me', complete with Sixties Eurovision Song Concert parody on the video, instantly established Morrissey in terms of time and place. In love with his new home Rome, he celebrated the bisexual or asexual murdered film director Pier Paolo Pasolini and some of his associates, particularly the passionate actress Anna Magnani. The single name-checked Pasolini's controversial 1961 work about prostitution, *Accatone* (aka *The Procurer*) but, with reference to another *Ringleader* . . . track 'Life Is A Pigsty', it's also worth noting that the Italian director made a 1969 film called *Porcile* (English title – *Pigsty*). Perhaps even more significantly there's a famous photograph of Patti Smith, taken by her lover Robert Mapplethorpe, with the words "Pasolini est vie" scrawled in lipstick beside her. (Pasolini's image would be the backdrop for the Tormentors tour in Spring 2006.)

Alongside three strong follow-up singles – 'The Youngest Was The Most Loved' (with its attack on the concept of "normality"), 'In The Future When All's Well' and 'I Just Want To See The Boy Happy' – 'Dear God Please Help Me' contained some of Morrissey's most sexually explicit lyrics, revealing the teasing tormentor at his provocative best. Inevitably, it would be interpreted by most reviewers as a lurid confession, an overdue admission even, that Morrissey's membership of the celibate club had finally expired. However, it's my firm belief that the artist invariably writes in character and that these were either references to one of the Italian director's many sexual encounters or, more likely, based on the guilt-ridden experiences of an earlier famous visitor to Rome.

In contrast to the slightly half-hearted critical reception for Morrissey's comeback with *You Are The Quarry*, many writers went overboard with praise for *Ringleader Of The Tormentors*. Paul Morley decided it was "the Morrissey masterpiece" in *The Observer*, while *NME* announced it was "his boldest, most adventurous and intensely personal collection to date". Naturally, his "explosive kegs" gained most attention and, once again, there was intense speculation about the truth behind his sex life. At last, some relieved commentators convinced themselves, it seemed that decades of the artist's sexual frustration had finally been laid to rest somewhere in Rome 2005.

I caught up with Morrissey several times on the *Ringleader Of The*

Tormentors tour in the Spring of 2006; first in Glasgow, then at London Alexandra Palace (where we briefly met and shook hands again at the after-show party), at Nottingham Ice Arena and at his Manchester Opera House performance. But, in my humble opinion, Morrissey's finest concert of the year took place in his home town just before Xmas. Apart from being an extraordinarily emotional return for Morrissey himself – he'd played GMex with The Smiths 20 years before – it was also a truly memorable night for ageing Smiths' fans, for fresh disciples of his solo career and for the city of Manchester itself.

In the seasonal spirit of nostalgia, I dusted down my rusty critical quill and, for the first time in over a decade, adventured back into the old railway station and onto the sweaty Tom Tiddler's Ground of music journalism.

A Dickensian smog shrouds the city centre and the increasingly familiar ghost of Manchester's Christmas' past shuffles onto the stage. "Well, they look friendly," he growls, as if still haunted by years spent in the pop wilderness.

Twenty years ago, in 1986, when he last stood on this very platform under-neath these tarted-up railway arches, his Smiths were at their creative peak with The Queen Is Dead *and looked set to conquer America. As if to remind himself (rather than his audience) of those heady Eighties days, Morrissey launches into 'Panic' and its infamous attack on cloth-eared radio DJs.*

Alas and alack, within a year of the original GMex event, The Smiths had ceased to exist and this extraordinary frontman and lyricist would have to struggle valiantly to build a solo career, to be heard on the radio and, once again, to tattoo his name on the neck of popular culture.

Apart from the universally acclaimed solo album Vauxhall & I *back in 1994, critically and commercially it seemed he'd never fully regain past glories. For most of the Nineteen-Nineties he was caught up in acrimonious legal battles with former members of The Smiths and, at the dawn of the new Millennium – without a record deal and exiled to Los Angeles – he seemed to have all but disappeared from public view.*

Yet here he stands, at the summit of 2006, branded "the Gay Elvis" by Rufus Wainwright and voted the number two British Living Icon in the BBC Culture Show poll, behind Sir David Attenborough but ahead of Sir Paul McCartney. (If there's a knighthood in the post it would be the perfect Queen Is Dead *anniversary present.)*

Watching him make a celebrated return to this city, on the streets he ran, soaking up the warmth of the cross-generation fan-base that now hang on his every word, tribute should be paid to guitarist Boz Boorer and bassist Gary

Day, the Ronnie and Reggie to Morrissey's Charlie (or is he Violet?). Or, physically at least, perhaps they're Fletcher and Godber to the Mozzfather's quietly menacing Grout. (Boorer, the old rockabilly Polecat, has played an influential and constant role alongside his master since the early Nineties; it's a good ten years more than Morrissey spent with his most famous collaborator, Smiths' guitarist Johnny Marr.)*

As ever with Morrissey, the selection of songs is deliberately unusual and unpredictable; not for him a Take-That-style greatest hits package. Yes there's the usual smattering of Smiths' singles – 'William, It Was Really Nothing', 'Girlfriend In A Coma' – plus infectiously aggressive, more recent material, such as 'You Have Killed Me' and 'The First Of The Gang To Die'.

But the obvious showstoppers, his Rodgers & Hammerstein moments, are absent. No 'There Is A Light That Never Goes Out', no 'Last Night I Dreamt That Somebody Loved Me', no 'Now My Heart Is Full'. But the emotions still flow on a yearning Christmas version of 'Please Please Please Let Me Get What I Want', in the audience-participation of 'Disappointed' and in his beautifully melancholic 'I'll Never Be Anybody's Hero Now', with its exquisite echoes of Wilde's Requiescat.

Overall, there's a strong sense of nostalgic music hall and even burlesque to the proceedings, plus a whiff of Seventies Eurovision and a pinch of Sinatra-style showman. Now thundering towards his fifties, against all the odds, Steven Patrick Morrissey looks destined to become a very troublesome inmate of the Dinosaur Senior Rock & Roll Hall Of Fame.

Different, deliberately difficult to predict, and hell-bent on irritating the pants off the rest of the music industry, he continues to make his own life a work of art. On tonight's evidence, 21st century popular music would be a very, very dull place without him.

Following Xmas 2006 in Manchester, Morrissey returned to the States and spent 2007 touring from April to November, increasing his congregation and consolidating his following, particularly in New York and California. Most significantly, as if to confirm his resurrected transatlantic popularity, he sold out the Los Angeles Palladium for ten nights in succession, New York's Hammerstein Ballroom for five nights and San Francisco's Fillmore for four.

The success of this adventure prompted him to book six nights at

---

* In 2006 Morrissey declared, "I'd rather eat my own testicles than reform The Smiths. And that's saying something for a vegetarian."

London's revamped Roundhouse in Camden Town in January 2008, partly to promote a new *Greatest Hits* collection – more accurately, his greatest hits on Sanctuary – but also because some of the heroes of his youth – Patti Smith, Blondie and The Ramones – had performed at the original Roundhouse in the Seventies. More importantly, the venue had staged Andy Warhol's play *Pork* (featuring the punk transsexual Wayne/Jayne County – who'd been part of the New York Dolls' scene – and Jaime De Carlo, one of David Bowie's close associates) and also Lindsay Kemp's celebrated mimes based on the outcast lives of Lorca, Genet and Oscar Wilde. (Kemp had close connections with David Bowie, appearing onstage in the 'Ziggy Stardust' days and also in the Mick Rock promo for 'John, I'm Only Dancing'. He also worked with Derek Jarman, who made The Smiths' films for *The Queen Is Dead*. Kemp, like Morrissey, had relocated to Rome.)

Despite suffering from a cold, which would reduce Morrissey's Round-house residency, the sell-out theatres and critical reactions to his perform-ances again confirmed the man's ongoing, extraordinary appeal 25 years on. Naturally he's thicker set than in the early days of The Smiths; the hair is greyer and the eyebrows even more unruly. But, onstage, with his unstoppable rockabilly rebels (Boz Boorer's still there alongside Mexican guitarist Jesse Tobias) in front of a backdrop image of Richard Burton, possibly from *Who's Afraid Of Virginia Woolf?*, the "gay Elvis" remains a unique and, thankfully, unsettling presence in popular culture.

Watching him from the floor of the Camden Roundhouse, and again at the Doncaster Dome (as he crooned through his singles 'That's How People Grow Up' and the excellent 'All You Need Is Me'), it seems clear that the momentum of the Tormentors tour will continue through to the release of his next major work in autumn 2008 provisionally titled *Years Of Refusal*.

It will be his ninth solo studio album – his *twentieth* in 20 years if you include compilations and live albums – and should feature some strong new songs including 'Something Is Squeezing My Skull', 'Mama Lay Softly On The Riverbed' (very Virginia Woolf!) and 'I'm Throwing My Arms Around Paris'. Perhaps the latter is a signpost to Morrissey's next home on his current tour in exile? He's nearly 50 now so let's hope, like Wilde, it's not the final stop on his European travels.

Appropriately, I'm reminded again of *The Importance Of Being Earnest* when Jack says, of his supposedly dead brother Ernest: "He seems to have expressed a desire to be buried in Paris." Mr Chasuble replies: "In Paris! I fear that hardly points to any very serious state of mind at the last."

12.

Wilde Man In His Head

"Yes, everything's linked, everybody takes from the artists they love. Eventually you develop your own individuality but at first you really do sap your sources dry. Everything's linked, everything's traceable. Everything leads back to . . . Dorothy Squires."

– Morrissey, Bowden, 1997

IT would be utterly brilliant if everything Morrissey had ever written could be traced solely back to Dorothy Squires, the famous Welsh diva and big band singer who recorded on the Parlophone, Pye and Columbia labels from the Forties through to the late Seventies. Famously impersonated by drag artist Danny La Rue, Squires was a glamorous figure in British entertainment and was once married to *The Saint* and 007 actor Roger Moore.

But, aside from his obsession with British female singers, why would Morrissey have singled Squires out? Could it be that, like Morrissey, she had serious brushes with the law lords? Squires' real tragedy was that she became addictively litigious, spent much of her fortune on legal fees and was eventually banned from the High Court. By the time she died of lung cancer in 1998, she'd lost almost everything through bankruptcy proceedings.

Back in 1997, in Bowden, when Morrissey told me that everything led back to Dorothy, it crossed my mind that Morrissey himself might be heading this way in his legal conflict with Mike Joyce? Perhaps by mentioning Dorothy Squires he was giving me a teasing indication of the lengths he was prepared to go to in his ultimately futile and potentially ruinous battle to defeat the Smiths' drummer? Already at that point, the High Court decision of December 1996 had left Morrissey and Johnny Marr with a £300,000 legal bill plus back royalty payments in the region of £1 million due to Joyce.

Or was there much more to this? If everything about Morrissey's art really was linked then how? If not directly to Dorothy Squires then who or what were many of Morrissey's sources really connected to?

Initially I wondered if it was to do with the fact that, back in 1973, Squires was arrested following the infamous President Records BBC chart-rigging scandal and, as a result, shared a cell with Janie Jones, the London madam celebrated by The Clash? More significant, I believe, was the location of their incarceration.

London's Bow Street Magistrates Court – which closed for business in July 2006 after 250 years meting out justice – had been the scene of many of the most famous criminal cases in British history and also saw the launch of the capital's police force; an early magistrate, the novelist Henry Fielding, started the Bow Street Runners back in 1749.

Morrissey has been fascinated with crime, perhaps scarred by crime, since childhood when Moors Murderers Myra Hindley and Ian Brady roamed the streets of Manchester, torturing, sexually abusing and murdering their young victims. Later serial-offending subjects for songs would range from Victorian villains Jack The Ripper and Spring-Heeled Jim to the Krays and Richardsons. But since his own uncomfortable legal experiences began in the late Eighties and early Nineties – conflicts with Craig Gannon, Stephen Street, Andy Rourke and Joyce – perhaps he became more interested in the workings of the British judiciary and Bow Street in particular.

Although, to my knowledge, Morrissey has never personally overnighted in the establishment, the role call of diverse guests who've appeared there at Her Majesty's pleasure makes for heady reading. Interestingly those famous Stretford lasses, the suffragettes Emmeline Pankhurst and her daughter Christabel, were both tried there, as were sinister figures such as wife murderer Dr Crippen and Nazi propagandist William 'Lord Haw Haw' Joyce, both later executed.

More Morrissey heroes and villains had also loomed large and menacing in the dock at Bow Street during the Sixties. Reggie and Ronnie Kray, celebrated in 'The Last Of The Famous International Playboys', were tried there; as were The Richardsons, the Krays' rival gang from south of the river; their boss, Charlie Richardson, was pictured on the inner sleeve of *Southpaw Grammar*. Morrissey would later celebrate their East End haunts in promotional films like 'We Hate It When Our Friends Become Successful' and by being photographed at locations such as Valance Road, Repton Boxing Club, West Ham Boys' Club and The Grave Maurice pub. Among the women who knew the Krays were *Carry On* starlet Barbara Windsor, East End singer Queenie Watts and the British Marilyn, Diana Dors.

While D. H. Lawrence's *The Rainbow* was declared obscene by a Bow Street magistrate in 1915, more significantly for Morrissey, one of his favourite novels, Radclyffe Hall's *The Well Of Loneliness* was banned there in 1928 for subject matter expressing lesbian tendencies. Other notable books banned at Bow Street would include *Lady Chatterley's Lover* and Hubert Selby Jnr's *Last Exit To Brooklyn* – one of the key sources for *The Queen Is Dead*.

It might be wild guesswork on my part but perhaps even the fiddling image of Morrissey on the cover of *Ringleader Of The Tormentors* owes something to another celebrity tried by the Bow Street magistrates. Giacomo Casanova, the infamous libertine, violinist and man of letters, appeared before Henry Fielding's half-brother John, The Blind Beak Of Bow Street, charged with abusing a prostitute while staying in London.

Could it also be significant that in *Oliver Twist* – another favourite book of Morrissey's – Charles Dickens' Artful Dodger goes on trial at Bow Street? The voice of young Anthony Newley, another Morrissey icon, playing the Dodger in the David Lean film version of *Oliver Twist* (1947), can be heard calling out "Don't leave us in the dark" at the close of 'Billy Budd' on *Vauxhall & I*. Much later in his solo career, on 'Noise Is The Best Revenge', Morrissey sang of his lost-hope in British justice.

But putting aside the significant presence of all these defendants, and struggling to unweave the threads and sources behind Morrissey's lyrics and much of his subject matter, clearly one guest of Bow Street rises above all others. Forget, if you can, Dot Squires. Of all the characters dragged before the Bow Street Magistrates, historically and physically, one stands head and shoulders in the dock above everyone else . . . Oscar Wilde.

This may not seem particularly revelatory given Morrissey's open tribute to Wilde in *The Queen Is Dead* track 'Cemetry Gates', not to mention his early career tradition of being photographed surrounded by flowers (cost-cutting gladioli rather than lavish Wildean lilies) or scattered amongst editions of Wilde's literary works. 'Cemetry Gates' also dealt head on with the subject of plagiarism, a crime Morrissey was accused of.

It's worth remembering that Oscar himself was also accused of plagiarism and embraced the charge, stating "the true artist is known by the use he makes of what he annexes, and he annexes everything". After the publication of his first collection of poems, the copy Wilde offered to his Oxford

College was rejected on the grounds that the verses were "for the most part not by their putative father at all, but by a number of better-known and more deservedly reputed authors" such as Shakespeare, Sidney, Donne, Byron and Swinburne. The Victorian actors Charles Brookfield and Sir Charles Hawtrey Snr.* even wrote a travesty of Wilde's *Lady Windermere's Fan*, portraying him as The Poet Of The Lily and accusing him of stealing Shakespeare, Ibsen and Sheridan.

Early on Morrissey preached the Wilde maxim that "talent borrows, genius steals" (it's even scratched on the run-out groove of 'Bigmouth Strikes Again'). The "everybody's clever nowadays" sound bite at the close of the wonderful 'Rubber Ring' is lifted from Wilde's theatrical masterpiece *The Importance Of Being Earnest*. Also Morrissey's solo track 'Glamorous Glue' echoes the line from *The Picture Of Dorian Gray*, "I am too much in love".

Add to that his declaration in *NME* that "C33" is the greatest person who's ever lived and there can be no question over the identity of the artist who has inspired Morrissey more than any other. C33 was Wilde's prison number during the two years he served hard labour for "the grave offence" from 1895 to 1897, and because of the scandal, early published versions of *The Ballad Of Reading Gaol* carried the pseudonym (or perhaps *nombre de plume*) C33 rather than the shameful, unspoken name Oscar Wilde.

But, to my inquisitive mind, Morrissey's devotion, obsession, admiration for Oscar Wilde goes much much deeper than this, beyond the realms previously imagined by journalists and biographers. I'd even argue that it's absolutely central and crucial to Morrissey's story. After all, three of my interviews with Morrissey have centred on locations painfully close to Wilde's life story. Firstly, the Cadogan Hotel, where Wilde was arrested before being carted off to Bow Street; secondly, Oscar's last resting place in Paris' Pere Lachaise Cemetery; and thirdly, at Hook End Studios, just outside Reading, a few miles from the famous old gaol on the banks of the River Kennet. Inevitably, many of our discussions and communications have touched on Wilde and his special place in Morrissey's world.

With most artists you tend to find that a wide number of influences colour their palette, a roll call of musical pioneers and creative forces who, for various reasons have inspired particular lyrics or, at most, a significant song. Although Morrissey's always name-checked plenty of other iconic,

---

* "Father" of *Carry On* star Charles Hawtrey, see Morrissey's People appendix.

"outcast" and "outsider" figures – using them as cover stars on The Smiths' albums and singles, or stealing choice lines from key books and films to elevate his wordplay (Shelagh Delaney, Elizabeth Smart) – Oscar Wilde's life and art has had far more impact on Morrissey's creative canon than anyone else. In fact, I can't think of any other figure in 20th or 21st century popular culture who's been *so* inspired by one singular, extraordinary individual. Wilde's influence seems to have infiltrated or inculcated Morrissey's whole creative life.

Richard Ellmann writes, in the introduction to his extraordinary biography of Wilde, "from as early as 1881 . . . to the middle of 1895 . . . literary London was put out of countenance by this outrageous Irishman . . . who declared he was a socialist and hinted he was a homosexual, while patently mocking wise saws on all subjects."

I'm not suggesting that Morrissey is an equal or comparable talent to Oscar Wilde – he'd mock as ridiculous the very suggestion – and, of course, it's false to chart The Smiths' greatness from as early 1981, or to equate Morrissey's first High Court defeat in 1995 with the tragic fall from grace and public humiliation of Oscar Wilde in 1885. But in terms of his own life, the trajectory of his own creative career, Morrissey has been well aware of the parallel history between his own existence and Wilde's life exactly a century earlier. In truth, Morrissey has sought to follow Wilde's example by seeking to make his life a work of art.

As he explained to Michael Bracewell in 1995 in *The Observer*: "There is something unstoppable about the Wilde story, and my own: the story probably has been told, but it's a very unusual story."

The story of Oscar Wilde's influence on Morrissey began at an early age when he was first exposed to Wilde's genius through his mother's influence. Beyond the wit, the plays and the poetry of Wilde, the artist's ambition to be famous or even infamous struck a chord with Morrissey. When he decided he would be called "Morrissey" rather than "Steven Morrissey" he was certainly following in the footsteps of Oscar: "I started as Oscar Fingal O'Flahertie Wills Wilde. All but two of the five names have already been thrown overboard. Soon I shall discard another and be known simply as 'The Wilde' or 'The Oscar'." (In prison, of course, he lost his name altogether and became simply the inhuman C33.)

Other crucial youthful connections included the fact that Morrissey's beloved New York Dolls famously had a residency at the Oscar Wilde Rooms in the Mercer Arts Center in New York. Also, when Morrissey attended the Sex Pistols now-legendary performances at Manchester's

Free Trade Hall in June 1976, he would have known that Oscar Wilde lectured there on his "Personal Impressions Of America" on October 8, 1883.

The early Smiths songs were clearly riddled with Wildean influences. Maybe it's a total coincidence but, in his letters, Oscar Wilde often describes the love of his life, Lord Alfred Douglas, as "very charming". Also, a travel companion on Wilde's on his 1877 trip to Rome, George Macmillan, described Wilde as "aesthetic to the last degree, passionately fond of secondary colours, low tones, Morris papers, and capable of talking a good deal of nonsense thereupon, but for all that a very sensible, well informed and charming man." More obviously, on tour in America in 1882, when confronted by Harvard students who'd imitated his aesthetic dress-sense, Wilde initially cried out "save me from my disciples" but later in the same lecture, said, "these charming young men might be inclined to follow in our footsteps".

Another track on *The Smiths*, 'The Hand That Rocks The Cradle', may well have been inspired by Wilde's prediction of his own tragedy: "I was made for destruction. My cradle was rocked by the Fates." Likewise, the lyrics of 'Miserable Lie' clearly echo a line in *De Profundis*: "by his sweetness and goodness to her through the brief years of his flower-like life". More striking still, the title of The Smiths' third single, 'What Difference Does It Make?' stands out in a letter from Lord Alfred Douglas on July 15 1896. Accused by Robert Ross, a long time and loyal friend of Oscar's, of having sponged off the imprisoned Wilde for years, Douglas replied: "What difference does it make? Everything that I had and was going to have in the future was and always will be his." (Douglas failed to stay true to this promise; although he inherited a considerable fortune on his father's death, little of it went to help the dying Wilde.)

So much of Wilde shines through in the making of Morrissey, perhaps even the playwright's verdict on England: "This dull land . . . with its short summer, its dreary rain and fogs, its mining district and factories . . ." And, although many of his fans make pilgrimages to various iron bridges in the Manchester area, I wonder if Morrissey could have been writing, in 'Still Ill', about Le Pont Des Arts in Paris – the first iron bridge – near where Wilde spent his last tragic days.*

---

* Once on Le Pont Des Arts, Wilde approached a man he feared was about to drown himself. "Hey, my poor man, are you desperate?" asked Wilde. "No, sir," the man replied, "I'm a hairdresser."

Given the speculation concerning the title of 'William, It Was Really Nothing' in previous books about The Smiths, I'd like to propose an alternative theory about the source. Some write confidently of Morrissey's friendship with Billy Mackenzie of The Associates, who later replied with 'Steven, You Were Really Something'; others settle on the character of William Fisher in Keith Waterhouse's *Billy Liar*. But, as the run-out groove on the single is etched with the words "The Impotence Of Ernest", I'd make a case for Oscar's brother William. Willie Wilde was, by all accounts an expert at doing nothing, except marrying for money. "He was of no use to me, either by day or by night," wrote his wealthy American wife.

The Wilde brothers had a difficult relationship. Bitter about Oscar's success, and known to entertain the Lotus Club in New York with mocking impressions of his younger brother's voice and his poetry, Willie once 'anonymously' contributed a negative review of *Lady Windermere's Fan* to the *Daily Telegraph*: "The author peoples his play with male and female editions of himself . . . The play is a bad one but it will succeed." Their friendship deteriorated further when William pawned Oscar's clothes while he was in prison, and was then later accused of having taken money from their dying mother. They would not meet at her funeral and were not reconciled before William's death in 1899.

It's even crossed my mind that although Morrissey's onstage habit of wearing a hearing aid is often attributed to his affection for Fifties American crooner Johnnie Ray, the original Nabob Of Sob and Prince Of Wails, it's interesting to note that Wilde's father, the physician Sir William Wilde, was a leading ear surgeon and that Oscar himself suffered from deafness, caused by syphilis.

Wilde is certainly *the* major influence and inspiration throughout Morrissey's poetry with The Smiths. It's not about plagiarism, more that Wilde's wit and style seems to flow easily with the ink from Morrissey's pen. In 'The Headmaster Ritual', there are definite echoes of Oscar's views on schoolteachers: "the man who is so occupied in trying to educate others . . . he never had any time to educate himself". Mrs Cheveley says in *An Ideal Husband*, "I have forgotten my schooldays. I have a vague impression they were detestable." While Lady Bracknell, in *The Importance Of Being Earnest*, argues that, "Fortunately, in England, at any rate, education produces no effect whatsoever. If it did, it would prove a serious danger to the upper classes, and probably lead to acts of violence in Grosvenor Square."

Which leads on to the crucial issue of the choice of subject matter in

236

Morrissey songs; this remarkable ability to turn any topic, the more edgy or sensitive the better, into a three minute pop song. As Wilde once noted "any attempt to extend the subject matter of art is extremely distateful to the public; and yet the vitality and progress of art depend in a large measure on the continual extension of the subject-matter". Clearly Morrissey embraced this gospel and, as he explained in 1988, "I think I became interested in introducing a new language into pop using certain words that I feel would be totally revolutionary . . . I'm still quite proud that words like 'shoplifter', 'coma', 'bigmouth', even 'suedehead' are available in pop music."

He expanded on this philosophy in November 1992, when he was interviewed in Paris by Adrian Deevoy: "Within the exciting world of pop music, the reality is that we are restricted. Whether you choose to write about wheelchair bound people, 'November Spawned A Monster', or the subject of racism, 'National Front Disco', the context of the song is often overlooked. People look at the title and shudder and say, 'Whatever is in that song shouldn't exist because the subject, to millions of people, is so awful."

Death and suicide, as cheerful examples, are subjects that Oscar Wilde often confronted in his plays, poetry and epigrams, even though he once declared, "One should live as if there were no death. One should die as if one had never lived."

Having spoken to Morrissey on several occasions about his own attitudes towards death, particularly in relation to "death discs" such as Twinkle's 'Terry', I'd always detected the influence of Wilde on some of his more terminal lyrics such as 'Death At One's Elbow'. While a beautiful track like 'Asleep' tackles the subject of suicide like no other poetry in popular music, it seems to owe something in mood to Wilde's line that "sometimes I think that the artistic life is a long and lovely suicide, and am not sorry that it is so."

Similarly – recalling how at the end of his own life, Wilde dramatically announced "the Morgue yawns for me" – I believe there are definite echoes of this sensibility in The Smiths' most-moving funereal song 'I Know It's Over'.

Elsewhere in The Smiths' canon of Wildean songs – beyond the obvious 'Cemetry Gates', 'Oscillate Wildly'* and 'Paint A Vulgar Picture' (from

---

* On 'Oscillate Wildly' Andy Rourke plays cello, possibly in tribute to Oscar's famous cello coat of 1877.

The Picture Of Dorian Gray), there's 'Unhappy Birthday' on *Strangeways, Here We Come*, probably informed by the experience of a visitor to Wilde's house on October 16, 1891 who was greeted by the author wearing black. Oscar explained: "Today happens to be my birthday and I am mourning . . . the flight of one year of my youth into nothingness."

When we met to discuss the creation of *Viva Hate* in early "Nineteen Eighty Hate", Morrissey clearly wanted to reflect the provocative climate that existed in the Victorian Britain of Oscar Wilde exactly 100 years before.

The Smiths had released their veiled attack on Thatcherite anti-homosexual legislation with 'Shoplifters Of The World Unite' in 1987 while, a century earlier, the Labouchere Amendment to the Criminal Law Amendment Act first enabled courts to prosecute homosexual men for "gross indecency" with a maximum sentence of two years' hard labour. The most famous victim of the new legislation was the sensualist Oscar Wilde.

Also, as Professor William Fishman's social history *East End 1888* details, it was an era of Victorian values that many Eighties Thatcherite conservatives looked back at with misplaced fondness. In truth the late 1880s were in fact a very troubled period when poverty, crime and social unrest were at their height, particularly in East London. Aside from the British establishment's growing fear of anarchy, particularly among the Dickensian poor, it was also the year in which Jack The Ripper murdered at least five prostitutes in the Whitechapel area of London.

The East London of the Ripper crimes would increasingly fascinate Morrissey, perhaps because, among those seriously suspected of being the original Ripper were Wilde's friends, the painter Walter Sickert (part of the Camden Town Group of post-Impressionist artists) and The Prince Of Wales. The Prince became a lover of the actress Lillie Langtry and also attended Wilde's séances in Chelsea.

The Wilde connections are strengthened further if you take into consideration ill-founded public rumours concerning other "outsider" suspects of the time. These even included the famous inmate of nearby Whitechapel Hospital, John Merrick (aka The Elephant Man), Lewis Carroll, Dr Barnado, Randolph Churchill and, more ridiculously, the caped-figure of Oscar Wilde himself.

Certainly the 1886 publication of Robert Louis Stevenson's *Strange Case Of Dr Jekyll And Mr Hyde* had combined with the Ripper case to influence Wilde's murderous novel *The Picture Of Dorian Gray*. The decadent Dorian visits the drug dens of Limehouse and, although Oscar himself once stated that "a gentleman never goes East of Temple Bar", this wouldn't prevent his self-destructive involvement with rent boys from the East End.

Having persuaded EMI Records to re-activate the HMV label purely for his solo career, Morrissey would later reflect directly on these troubled times with his own track 'Jack The Ripper' (released in 1992), partly also a tribute to Joe Meek who produced Screaming Lord Sutch And The Savages' 'Jack The Ripper', released in 1963 on the original HMV label.

Back in February 1988, when Morrissey appeared for the first time as a solo artist on the cover of *NME*, his provocatively naked pose seemed to parody Wilde's favourite painting, *San Sebastian* by Guido Reni. (He'd repeat the pose, complete with arrows, for *Uncut* in May 2006.)

During Wilde's ignominious, tragic last days as a social pariah in exile, he went by the name Sebastian Melmoth, a name derived from Saint Sebastian (often regarded the patron saint of gay men, and referenced in both Patti Smith's 'Boy Cried Wolf' and Thomas Mann's *Death In Venice*) and also from the gothic novel *Melmoth The Wanderer*, written by one of Wilde's mother's ancestors, the Reverend Charles Maturin. The fact that Oscar's post-prison luggage bore the initials "S.M." had not been lost on the impressionable young Steven Morrissey.

Elsewhere on *Viva Hate*, there's 'Alsatian Cousin', inspired by lines from Alan Bennett's *Forty Years On* but also surely connected to Wilde's death in the Hotel D'Alsace in Paris in 1900. Similarly, although 'Late Night Maudlin Street' steals its title from Bill Naughton's short story *Late Night On Watling Street*, it's worth noting that in George Du Maurier's carica-tures in *Punch* magazine in the late 19th century, Oscar Wilde was lampooned as the poet Maudle. Meanwhile, 'Hairdresser On Fire', one of the tracks on the 'Suedehead' single, tackled a subject very close to Wilde's heart: "When I travel to new countries I always look at hairstyles . . . for me nothing counts but hairstyles . . . but to be a hairdresser, one must be a physiognomist too."

This Wilde influence would continue to play a part in the strange subject matter for Morrissey's early 1990 HMV singles. 'Ouija Board, Ouija Board' might have seemed an unusual topic for a pop song but Oscar had been fascinated by ouija boards and fortune-telling until the palmist Cheiro read his hands and announced, "The left hand is the hand of a king, but the right that of a king who will send himself into exile." Cheiro rightly predicted that Wilde's ruin would arrive at around his 40th year. (Morrissey's exile status would be confirmed, at 40, in 1999.)

Although 'Piccadilly Palare', released in October 1990, was about male prostitution and referenced the gay slang used by Kenneth Williams and Kenneth Horne in BBC Radio's *Round The Horne* programme (and in Neil Bartlett's *Who Was That Man?*), it also tied in with Oscar Wilde's recollection of shopping with his wife at Swan & Edgars in Piccadilly Circus and first seeing the painted boys, the "Rough Trade", on the pavement waiting for business. "Something clutched at my heart like ice," he wrote. His sexuality would be questioned in the Oxford magazine *The Ephemeral* in May 1893: "Ossian Savage, a man of coarse habit of body and of coarser habits of mind, was enjoying the cool summer morning in his own way in Piccadilly."

Then there's the title *Kill Uncle*, which apart from linking with the Sixties film, *Let's Kill Uncle*, is also the theme of Wilde's largely forgotten play *The Duchess Of Padua*, centring on a plot to assassinate a treacherous uncle as in *Richard III* and *Hamlet*, while 'My Love Life' would seem to have definite echoes of Lord Alfred Douglas' most famous poem, *The Two Loves*: "I know you love one person, so why can't you love two."

Similarly Morrissey's *Your Arsenal* singles, 'We Hate It When Our Friends Become Successful' and 'You're The One For Me, Fatty' both, in my opinion, have strong Wilde connections. "Anyone can sympathise with the sufferings of a friend, but it requires a very fine nature . . . to sympathise with a friend's success," Oscar wrote in *The Soul Of Man Under Socialism*. Biographers always note that Wilde's weight increased rapidly with his success and that he was depicted in caricatures by Whistler, Max Beerbohm and Alfred Bryan, and in the painting by Henri de Toulouse-Lautrec, as large and fat in contrast with the diminutive, small-featured Lord Alfred Douglas

In the early Nineties, again like Wilde a century before, Morrissey seemed to spend much of his time in Paris, being photographed outside Parisien sex shops, even recording *Beethoven Was Deaf* at The Zenith. But it might have been expected that, by the time of his solo masterpiece *Vauxhall & I* in 1994 – one of Douglas' memoirs is titled *Oscar Wilde & Me* – Morrissey the plagiarist would have exhausted his greatest obsession.

The most obvious influence is clear in the title of 'The Lazy Sunbathers' which annexes directly from Wilde's *The Decay Of Lying*, which Morrissey once declared was his favourite Wilde work. In this essay, divided into a conversation between Oscar's sons, Wilde invents a club called The Tired Hedonists.

There's even a tenuous connection in the wonderful 'Now My Heart Is

Full', which clearly refers to Graham Greene's classic English novel, *Brighton Rock*. Just before Oscar's death in Paris in 1900, Greene's father and another travelling teacher encountered the broken Wilde in a café, were charmed by his conversation – "the only currency he had", Greene observed – but noted that he left them to pay for his coffee. Greene's father later told his son, "Think how lonely he must have been to have expended so much time and wit on a couple of schoolmasters on holiday."

Released in the summer of 1995, the timing and titles of the 'Boxers' single and *Southpaw Grammar* again definitely reflected Morrissey's ongoing awareness of events exactly a century earlier.

In 1895, Oscar Wilde met his nemesis in the shape of John Sholto Douglas, ninth Marquess of Queensberry, a man who'd changed the nature of boxing by getting England and America to agree to the Queensberry Rules; the adoption of weight differences so that boxers would be evenly matched. (A "southpaw" is the term for the unconventional stance of a left-handed boxer.)

Calamitously, for Wilde, his love affair with Lord Alfred Douglas caused great friction with Bosie's father. It was Queensberry who would bring Wilde down, accusing him of being a "somdomite" (sic) thereby forcing Wilde to take legal action to try and clear his own name. When Wilde's action failed and the court accepted Queensberry's allegation, Wilde was open to public prosecution for "the grave offence".

A hunter and a pioneering cyclist – famously pictured in *The Cycling World Illustrated* of 1896 – Queensberry was ferociously hostile to homosexual relationships, particularly following the death in 1894 of his eldest son Drumlanrig in a shooting accident that supposedly covered up suicide because of Drumlanrig's relationship with Lord Roseberry. Queensberry had responded with an attack on "The Snob Queers", which almost sounds like a Morrissey song-title to match 'All The Lazy Dykes' and 'The Slum Mums'.

Wilde's great opposition to hunting as expressed in his play *A Woman Of No Importance* – "The English gentleman galloping after the fox . . . the unspeakable in full pursuit of the inedible" – merely added to the conflict. (Morrissey would use a similar line in relation to the British monarchy's love of blood sports.) In addition, Wilde referred to Lord Alfred Douglas' family as "the mad, bad line from which you came". Perhaps the troubled Queensberrys inspired '(I'm) The Last Of The Family Line' or even 'The Queen Is Dead'.

When I met Morrissey in Cheshire in the spring of 1997 I was already well aware of the parallels between his life and Oscar Wilde's. At the time Morrissey was living in Los Angeles and still reeling from his defeat in the High Court case by Mike Joyce. Owing well over a million pounds to The Smiths' drummer and refusing to pay the debt, he'd accepted exile as the only realistic way out. But despite the legal defeat and the disappointing critical response to *Southpaw Grammar* at least Morrissey was well and wealthy and living in relative luxury.

In dramatic contrast, exactly a century earlier, Oscar Wilde left prison and England for the last time on the May 19, 1897. He told a waiting reporter that he "coveted neither notoriety or oblivion". Without doubt, Wilde had been broken by his prison experiences. He'd served two years' hard labour which meant the dreaded treadmill – six hours daily, an ascent of 6,000 feet a day, 20 minutes on with five minutes rest.

The parallel paths in terms of these two lives, 100 years apart, ended at the dawn of the 20th century, with Wilde dying at only 46 on November 30, 1900. In contrast, although Morrissey remained reclusive in 2000, it soon became clear he wouldn't given up on Wilde's ghost just yet.

Any suggestion that Morrissey had finally exhausted his central source of inspiration would be shot down in 2003 when he signed to Sanctuary Records and relaunched his own career on the Attack label with *You Are The Quarry*. Chapter 18 of Richard Ellmann's *Oscar Wilde* is appropriately titled "Doom Deferred". It begins: "The quarry was about to fall."*

There's another strong political link between Wilde's life and Morrissey's 21st century work. From an early age, Oscar's nationalism must have naturally appealed to the youthful Irish Mancunian and, as Morrissey's career has developed, the importance of his Celtic roots have come more to the fore.

Ellmann wrote, of Wilde's successful lectures in America, that "he rediscovered himself as an Irishman", due to the embrace of Irish and other settlers in the States. Perhaps the same could be said of Morrissey following his self-imposed exile in Los Angeles. After all, his heroine Pat Phoenix had once told him, "All of us who are half-Irish . . . are born with the Celtic twilight in us."

Apart from 'Irish Blood, English Heart', his first single from *You Are The Quarry*, Morrissey told me in the summer of 2003 that he'd been spending an increasing amount of time in the West of Ireland. Maybe it's worth

---

* Queensberry had sent Wilde a message saying, "I will not prevent your flight, but if you take my son with you, I will shoot you like a dog."

noting that Oscar spent his holidays at Moytura House near Cong, with views of Lough Corrib, and at Illaunroe, near Galway.

If Irish birth, parentage and upbringing played a huge part in the development of both Wilde's character and the power of his personality, then clearly the outlook of Wilde's formidable mother has also influenced Morrissey's increasingly Irish worldview. Lady Wilde (Jane Francesca Elgee) styled herself into the nationalist poet Speranza, writer of inflammatory verses such as 'The Young Patriot Leader'. One of her poems for the Dublin-based anti-British magazine *The Nation* began "A Rush, a charge from North, South, East and West and the land is ours" clearly inspiring The Smiths' *Strangeways, Here We Come* track 'A Rush And A Push And The Land Is Ours'. Once, when asked about Home Rule for Ireland, Oscar responded, "My own idea is that Ireland should rule England." (Similarly, when accused of patriotism, he mused "What is patriotism but the love of the food one ate as a child?")

Further Wilde references can perhaps be traced in *You Are The Quarry* songs such as 'Come Back To Camden' and 'I Have Forgiven Jesus'. Although the former is clearly a tribute to Camden, London where Morrissey shared tea that tasted like the Thames, it could easily be connected with Wilde's famous visit to the American poet Walt Whitman in Camden, New Jersey. Whitman was openly homosexual and Wilde would later admit "the kiss of Walt Whitman is still on my lips".

Similarly, 'I Have Forgiven Jesus' might be inspired by Wilde's discovery in prison of Christ, which even prompted him to forgive those mad bad Queensberrys: "And the end of it all is that I have got to forgive you. I must do so. I don't write this letter to put bitterness into your heart, but to pluck it out of mine. For my own sake I must forgive you."

More Wildean still, with reference to the closing track on *You Are The Quarry*, are the lyrical attacks on critics – "The whispering may hurt you, but the printed word might kill you" – coupled with Andre Gide's recollection of Wilde's prediction of his own catastrophe: "Oh, of course, of course! I knew that there would be a catastrophe, that way or another . . . It had to end that way. Just imagine: it wasn't possible to go any further, and it couldn't last." ('You Know I Couldn't Last')

Long-dead Oscar continued to influence Morrissey's second album of the 21st century, the internationally acclaimed *Ringleader Of The Tormentors*. Recorded in Rome, it featured a fiddling Morrissey on the cover – perhaps a nod to the lustful violinist Casanova or a comic reference to Nero and his burning Rome? Inevitably it brings to mind Wilde's famous quote that "the spectator is to be receptive . . . he is the violin on which the master is to play".

Certainly 'I'll Never Be Anybody's Hero Now', one of Morrissey's finest songs in recent years, reminds me of Wilde's earliest poem *Resquiescat*, movingly written when his nine-year-old sister Isolda died. Morrissey once quoted the line "all my life's buried here, heap earth upon it . . ." to me and his own lyrics echo these words. Perhaps, overall, it's Morrissey's most magically Wilde-like song, reflecting on Oscar's desperate last days, snubbed by old friends, staring enviously into the grand houses he once graced when the world would listen. At the end he was like a ghost even though he wasn't dead yet.

According to Ellmann, "The dramatis personae of his earlier life returned as phantoms of his later life, some pretending not to see him, making him feel he was the phantom, from whom they fled. He was reliving his life as if it had all been a failure, not a success."

Despite this, Wilde tried to be optimistic and even wrote, after leaving prison but before his final illness: "The two years of silence kept my soul in bonds. It will all come back, I feel sure, and then all will be well." Could these words have inspired 'In The Future When All's Well'?

The most controversial and publicised track on *Ringleader Of The Tormentors* is the graphic (and for Morrissey) almost sexually explicit song 'Dear God, Please Help Me', in which the subject walks through Rome, struggling with his desires and apparently losing out to the temptations of the flesh. Wilde travelled to Rome several times during his life, although unlike Morrissey he was a Protestant not a Catholic. Nevertheless, on Easter Day 1900, months before his death, Oscar received the Pope's Blessing among the pilgrims.

On an earlier Roman tour – to the great disappointment of Oxford friends who were trying to persuade him to convert to Roman Catholicism – Oscar visited the Protestant Cemetery outside Rome and prostrated himself on the grave of John Keats, who'd died half a century earlier. Wilde later proclaimed Keats "that godlike boy, the real Adonis our age . . . in my heaven he walks eternally with Shakespeare and the Greeks", and the visit inspired his poem *The Grave Of Keats*: "The youngest of the martyrs here is lain, Fair as Sebastian, and as early slain." In Rome for *Mojo*, in spring 2006, Morrissey was photographed leaning on Keats' tomb.

Last but not least, of the Wildean *Ringleader . . .* tracks, there's Morrissey's most Oscar-inspired title, 'To Me You Are A Work Of Art'. It's a theme that crops up throughout Wilde's plays, epigrams and particularly the novel, *The Picture Of Dorian Gray*, in which Dorian makes a pact with the devil to preserve himself as a work of art.

Elsewhere Wilde declares "The secret of life is art" and "To become a work of art is the object of living". Once he told Ernest Raynaud, on the Boulevard des Capucines, "My ambitions do not stop with composing poems . . . I want to make of my life itself a work of art." Even in prison, discovering religion, he wrote of Christ, "His entire life is the most wonderful of poems. He is just like a work of art himself."

Many years ago, when I asked Morrissey if Wilde was still an important influence on his own life, he replied, "Oh yes, and it grows even stronger." So understandably Oscar continues to be a dominant force in Morrissey's writing well into the first decade of the 21st century.*

Other Morrissey/Wilde connections would include the 2008 track 'I'm Throwing My Arms Around Paris' (the city which tolerated the scandalised Wilde and where he's buried), 'The Father Who Must Be Killed' and the single 'Kill The Father' by Kirsteen Young on Morrissey's Attack label (inspired by Wilde's line "remember, in literature you must always kill your father") and Morrissey's affection for John Betjeman who – apart from writing *The Arrest Of Oscar Wilde At The Cadogan Hotel, Slough* (which inspired 'Every Day Is Like Sunday') and *A Child Ill* (selected by Morrissey for his 2004 *NME* compilation) – was also a friend of Lord Alfred Douglas and the Sitwells.

Even Morrissey songs that openly purport to be about someone else seem to be about Wilde. The most obvious example would be 'Christian Dior', a remarkable song, written with Boz Boorer, that appeared as a minor almost-throwaway track on the 'In The Future When All's Well' CD. While celebrating the art of the single-minded fashion designer, the key line, about Dior's wasted life, seems to have been lifted, consciously or subconsciously, from Wilde's romantic liason with Lillie Langtry. She told him, in 1879, "you have wasted your life", hurting Wilde's feelings but thereby inspiring the lovesick young poet and playwright to dramatically conquer London with the force of his personality.

Typically, in the last verse of 'Christian Dior', Morrissey (or Wilde)

---

* There's an unreleased Morrissey track titled 'No Room For Oscar', which might also refer to the New York Dolls' famous seventies residency at the Oscar Wilde Rooms in New York.

seems to reflect on his failure. But it's actually a statement about priorities in life, an explanation how controlling one's desires can free an artist to "discipline" their days and, ultimately, become works of art.

In my opinion, more than any performer in late 20th/early 21st century pop culture, Morrissey has aspired to this great goal. Even those who do not like him or his creations should, at least, acknowledge the dedication and discipline, the single-mindedness and the sacrifices, that have enabled him to survive and flourish as one of the most original and extraordinary artists of our time.

The Moz launches his Attack label, 2004. The single he holds aloft – Gregory Isaac's 'Love Is Overdue' on the original reggae label – belonged to the author's brother Don Brown, who died in May 1982 aged 21. (HAMISH BROWN/GETTY IMAGES)

April 2004, California: The "*Quarry*" men aka The Chuckle Brothers (left to right)
Dean Butterworth (drums), Mikey Farrell (keyboards), Alain Whyte (guitars), "Fury", Gary Day (bass)
Boz Boorer (guitars and Ronnie Kray impression). (KEVIN ESTRADA/RETNA)

The spirit of Speranza - Morrissey's 21st Century comeback launched with
the 'Irish Blood, English Heart' video shoot, April 2004. (His most successful single,
it reached number 3 in the UK charts.) (KEVIN ESTRADA/RETNA)

ime for heroes: Patron Saint of Indie bands, e Mozzfather embraces Libertine Carl Barat, backstage at Glastonbury, June 2004.
(ANDY WILLSHER)

Understated reaction from a sober-shirted songwriter on receiving a Silver Clef Award – the awards ceremony raises funds for the Nordoff-Robbins Music Therapy foundation – from… (JM ENTERNATIONAL/REDFERNS)

…, in his own words, "the most perfect pop group", the New York Dolls: David Johansen, Arthur Kane and Sylvain Sylvain. (Sadly, "Killer" Kane died within a month after this event, which took place on June 18 2004, Mayfair, London.) (JON FURNISS/WIREIMAGE.COM)

Nancy In London, for Morrissey's Meltdown
Festival, summer 2004. Ms Sinatra, a neighbour
in Hollywood, probably inspired 'The Last
Of The Famous International Playboys' and
also covered 'Let Me Kiss You'.
(BRIAN RASIC/REX FEATURES)

Linder "Ludus" Sterling - musician,
photographer, artist, legend of the Mancunia
post-punk scene and close friend of Morrisse
for over 30 years – performing at Meltdown
(BRIAN RASIC/REX FEATURES)

The Bard of Reading Festival, August, 2004, celebrating the success of *You Are The Quarry*
in the UK and USA album charts (number two and eleven respectively). (REX FEATURES)

The living sign? An incensed 'Pope of Mope' with his charming nuns, Devore, California, Halloween 2004. (KELLY A SWIFT/RETNA)

Visconti, the great 'director' of *Ringleader Of The Tormentors,* Rome, 2006. Morrissey said of the producer's work with T. Rex, David Bowie, Sparks and himself: "Tony understands the code of music brilliantly…the Visconti style is timeless and lionized and is therefore forevermore". (EBET ROBERTS/REDFERNS)

The First of the Gang to Die, on stage
at the Heineken Jammin' Festival, Imola,
Italy, 2006. (LFI)

Shot in Texas, March 2006.
Morrissey interviewed at the South By Wes
Festival in Austin. (The famous Oscar Wilde
Collection is held in the city university's Har
Ransom Humanities Research Center.)
(EBET ROBERTS/REDFERNS)

"What Kind Of Fool Am I?' Nearly Newley,
Later With Jools Holland, May 2006.
(ANDRE CSILLAG/REX FEATURES)

Twenty five years after the birth of The Smiths
Morrissey arrives at *Letterman* to perform
'That's How People Grow Up' in June 2007
(HENRY LAMB/BEI/REX FEATURES)

'The Outsider's Outsider' discusses his growing Latino following with Beto Cuevos on LATV, December 2007. (NEWSCOM)

'All You Need Is Me' – re-treading the tracks of Patti Smith, Blondie and the Ramones, the old contender in typical knock-out pose during his Camden Roundhouse residency January 2008. (HAYLEY MADDEN/REDFERNS)

"That godlike boy, the real Adonis of our age". The grave Morrissey follows in Oscar Wilde's footsteps in pilgrimage to Keats' grave in the Protestant Cemetery outside Rome.
(Wilde had prostrated himself before the grave in 1876 describing it as "the holiest place in Rome". He also wrote a sonnet called *The Grave Of Keats*.) (ANDY FALLON/CAMERA PRESS LONDON)

MORRISSEY'S PEOPLE:
Icons, Influences And A Walk On The Wilde Side

Allen, Richard – *nom de plume* of Canadian writer James Moffat whose controversial, unpleasant teenage trash or "youthsploitation" 'novels' – from *Skinhead* in 1970 through to *Mod Rule* in 1980 – reflected (in a stereotypically offensive and tawdry way) various discontented, violent youth cultures of the Seventies. One Allen volume was the source of the title for Morrissey's debut single 'Suedehead'; other works included *Boot Boys, Knuckle Girls, Skinhead Escapes, Glam, Punk Rock, Teeny Bopper Idol* and *Terrace Terrors*.

Angeli, Pier – Sardinian-born actress turned Hollywood starlet in *Flame And The Flesh* and *The Silver Chalice*. Celebrated in Morrissey's pre-Smiths recollection of also-ran screen stars, *Exit Smiling* (Babylon Books). Prevented from marrying James Dean by her disapproving mother (because Dean wasn't a Catholic). Also starred, alongside Paul Newman – who replaced the newly dead Dean – and Sal Mineo, as the wife of boxer Rocky Graziano in *Somebody Up There Likes Me*. She took her own life in 1971 having written, "I have loved one person in my whole life and that was James Dean." One possible inspiration for the suicidal subject matter of Morrissey's 'Angel, Angel, Down We Go Together', although the title clearly comes from the weird 1969 psychedelic film called *Angel, Angel Down We Go*, featuring lesbian protest singer Holly Near who'd appeared in *Slaughterhouse Five* and had written 'It Could Have Been Me' – shades of Morrissey's 'We Hate It When Our Friends Become Successful' – and 'We Are A Gentle, Angry People'.

Angers, Avril – Smiths cover star of 'I Started Something I Couldn't Finish'. Briefly played Nora Dawson in *Coronation Street* but more memorably appeared in *The Family Way*, a Northern film about newly-weds with problems 'in the bedroom', alongside Murray Head, Hayley Mills and John Mills. Mills' father-of-the-bride Ezra Fitton is stubbornly against education and literature: "All this reading books he does, it's not natural." Written by Bill Naughton and produced/directed by the Boulting Brothers. Avril Angers also appeared in the early BBC sketch show *How Do You View?* (with Diana Dors), *The Green Man* with Alistair Sim, *All Aboard* with Arthur Lowe, *Be My Guest* (with David Hemmings, Steve Marriott and the Nashville Teens), not forgetting *The Best House In London* (1969), a daft comedy about an unhistorical, government-backed, Victorian brothel frequented by Wilde, Lord Alfred Douglas, Dickens, etc, also featuring Hemmings and Queenie Watts. Angers featured in the clumsy but gay 1969 comedy drama *Staircase*, in which Rex Harrison and Richard Burton played two West End hairdressers who live together but whose relationship is threatened by the demands of one of their mothers. She also appears in *There's A Girl In My Soup* (with Peter Sellers, Goldie Hawn and Diana Dors) and *Confessions Of A Driving Instructor* alongside Anthony Booth (Mr Pat Phoenix).

Bankhead, Tallulah – hard-drinking, drug-taking, chain-smoking, brilliantly bitchy Hollywood actress, who rarely wore underwear and often liked to converse in the nude, previously lived in Morrissey's Los Angeles home. (Other past residents included P.G. Wodehouse, Joan Crawford, F. Scott Fitzgerald, Clark Gable, Carole Lombard and designer William Haines.) Bankhead's life had been an inspiration for the screen-play of *All About Eve* (1950) so she despised Bette Davis for being awarded the film role ahead of her: "Don't think I don't know who's been spreading gossip about me . . . After all the nice things I've said about that hag. When I get hold of her, I'll tear out every hair of her moustache!" Openly bisexual she once quipped, "I've tried several varieties of sex, all of which I hate. The conventional position makes me claustrophobic; the others give me a stiff neck and/or lockjaw." Appeared in the creepy 1965 Hammer film *Fanatic* (with Yootha Joyce) as mad religious vegetarian mother-in-law Mrs Trefoile, whose son Stephen has died in a car accident. (The American title was *Die! Die! My Darling.*)

Bardot, Brigitte – French actress and later militant Animal Rights activist, Bardot was one possible source for The Smiths' 'Jeanne' after her character in the 1976 film *Don Juan (Or If Don Juan Were A Woman)*. Paris-born, she also appeared in Jean-Luc Godard's *Contempt* (with Jack Palance), *Doctor At Sea* (with Dirk Bogarde and Joan Sims), *The Truth* plus *And God Created Woman*. Archive of Bardot's pop career, including

'Harley Davidson', 'Bubble Gum' and 'Contact', has been screened before Morrissey's 21st century concerts. Also acted alongside Smiths' cover stars Alain Delon (*Famous Love Affairs, Spirits Of The Dead*) and Jean Marais (*School Of Love, Royal Affairs In Versailles*). Politically controversial, her 2003 book *A Scream In The Silence* was criticised by gay rights campaigners, resulting in her response: "Apart from my husband – who maybe will cross over one day as well – I am entirely surrounded by homos. For years, they have been my support, my friends, my adopted children, my confidants". Like Morrissey, Brigitte Bardot has been accused of harbouring right-wing views on immigration. However, in Bardot's extreme case, this has led to several convictions; most recently in June 2004, on charges of "inciting racial hatred" resulting from comments about the "underground and dangerous infiltration of Islam". The film director Jean Cocteau once said of her influence on modern France, "Her beauty and talent are undeniable, but she possesses some other, unknown quality, which attracts idolaters in an age deprived of gods." The Brigitte Bardot Foundation for the Welfare and Protection of Animals was founded in 1986.

Barrie, Amanda – played *Coronation Street*'s Alma Baldwin (nee Sedgewick) for two decades and starred as Cleopatra in the British comedy classic *Carry On Cleo*. Most likely inspiration for Morrissey's 1997 single 'Alma Matters' (along with Alma Cogan and James Dean). Started out as a nightclub dancer working with Danny La Rue and Barbara Windsor, followed by diverse theatre work including Oscar Wilde's *Lord Arthur Saville's Crime*, before moving into films such as *Doctor In Distress* (with Dirk Bogarde), *A Pair Of Briefs* (with Joan Sims) and, importantly in terms of further Morrissey connections, *I Gotta Horse* with Billy Fury in 1965. (She sings 'You've Got To Look Right For The Part' with Fury and Jon Pertwee on the soundtrack.) Her 2003 autobiography, *It's Not A Rehearsal*, talked frankly about her bisexuality and detailed her love affair with Billy Fury. "Billy was incredibly charismatic and good-looking, a truly beautiful creature." Fury proposed to Barrie but she rejected him: "I wouldn't have dreamed of marrying Billy without telling him about the side of me that was attracted to women . . . He was like a child in many ways and I felt I couldn't burden him with my worries."

Bartlett, Neil – theatre director and author of the influential *Who Was That Man? (A Present For Mr Oscar Wilde)*, an inspiration for 'Piccadilly

Palare'. Morrissey invited him to stage *An Evening With Oscar Wilde* at the Meltdown Festival in London, 2004.

Bastedo, Alexandra – beautiful cover star of The Smiths' *Rank*, Bastedo appeared in TV series *The Champions* as global intelligence agent Sharron McCready. Also played the lead in *I Hate My Body* (1974) – the tagline read: "The brain of a man . . . the body of a woman . . . the sexual horror story of our time!" – and as a lesbian-seductress in *Blood Castle* aka *The Blood Splattered Bride*. Bastedo appeared in *Doctor In Clover* and took the role of "England" in the 1963 teen thriller *13 Frightened Girls*.

Beaton, Cecil – great British photographer and costume designer (credits include the 1947 film version of Wilde's *An Ideal Husband*), who took the famous portrait of Edith Sitwell that adorned the cover of her Penguin classic *English Eccentrics* – used by Morrissey as the backdrop for his *Kill Uncle* tour – and the photo of Truman Capote that appears on the cover of 'The Boy With The Thorn In His Side'. Famously bisexual, Beaton's photographic subjects included W.H. Auden, the Duke and Duchess Of Windsor, Princess Margaret, T.S. Eliot, Nancy Mitford, Jean Cocteau and Noel Coward.

Bennett, Alan – Leeds born playwright and close neighbour of Morrissey when the latter lived in London's Camden Town. Bennett spoke positively about his friendship with Morrissey in the Channel 4 documentary *The Importance Of Being Morrissey*. The Smiths' 'I Started Something I Couldn't Finish' would feature a line inspired by Bennett's 1968 play *Forty Years On* (set in a public school called Albion House): "One generation treading on the toes of the next – that's what tradition means." Also, the title of Morrissey's track 'Alsatian Cousin' on *Viva Hate* seems to have been drawn from the same play: "I was distantly related to the Woolf family through some Alsatian cousins." The son of a butcher, Bennett's distinctly English, observational writing often deals with similar subject matter to Morrissey; chiefly, failures in personal relationships, sexual difficulties and general disappointments in life. His television credits have included *All Day On The Sands*, *Breaking Up*, *Objects Of Affection*, *Talking Heads* (particularly the episode 'A Cream Cracker Under The Settee') and *An Englishman Abroad*. His most-acclaimed works have been *Prick Up Your Ears* (about Joe Orton), *The Madness Of King George* and *The History Boys* (his central character, Hector, is thought to have given his name to the antagonist in Morrissey's 'The First Of The Gang To Die'). It's worth noting that Bennett's 1990 TV series, *Poetry In Motion*, looked at many of the poets who reflected on England's decline in the 20th century, including Auden's 'September 1, 1939' (see 'There Is A Light That Never Goes Out'), MacNiece's 'Prayer Before Birth' and Larkin's 'Going, Going'. Bennett first wrote about his homosexuality in *Untold Stories* (2005), having previously declared himself celibate. (He'd told *The Observer*, in answer to interrogation about his sexual preferences, that it was like asking a man dying of thirst to choose between Perrier and Malvern.) In *The Uncommon Reader*, Bennett's imagined Queen finally discovers books and starts to read voraciously, which results in her questioning the world she moves in. At a state banquet she asks the French President, "I've been longing to ask you about Jean Genet . . . homosexual and jailbird, was he nevertheless as bad as he was painted?" One of Morrissey's Meltdown events in 2004 was *An Audience With Alan Bennett* at London's Queen Elizabeth Hall. Morrissey's affection for the distinctly Northern dramatic world of Alan Bennett began as a teenager. In 2005, having struck up a neighbourly friendship back in the Nineties with the Leeds-born playwright, Morrissey explained: "I was the dull, fat kid in spectacles sitting in a Manchester council house who caught the first transmission of his plays in 1978–79 and I was thunderstruck because it was the first time I'd seen what I pitifully considered to be my sense of humour on screen . . . He's so terribly funny that when he writes a line full of biting sadness it cuts through all the more. I also like the fact that he doesn't seem to envy or even much care for other writers." When asked if Bennett's work defined a particular type of Northerness, Morrissey replied: "Yes, it's largely the sodden gloom of the North – the walled-in, lack-of-choice North that, really, he loves. The family is a battleground and every character trembles on the edge of confession. Sex is on everybody's mind, but nobody says anything."

Betjeman, John – very English poet laureate and friend of W.H. Auden, his "Come friendly bombs . . ." poem 'Slough' was a clear inspiration for Morrissey's 'Everyday Is Like Sunday' and he also wrote 'The Arrest Of Oscar Wilde At The Cadogan Hotel'. According to A.N. Wilson's biography *Betjeman* (2006), the poet first became obsessed with Wilde's tragic story as a teenager at Marlborough School and "Betjeman's hatred of the society which sent Oscar Wilde to prison was lifelong". He even corresponded, and later became friends with, Lord Alfred Douglas. Bosie's famous verse *Two Loves* is referenced in Betjeman's autobiographical *Summoned By Bells* and Betjeman was once photographed in Brighton with Douglas and Nancy Mitford. Also, according to Wilson, illustrating Betjeman's penchant for "collecting out-of-the-way friends", he ignored disapproval by remaining in contact with the "social pariahs" and British fascists Oswald Mosley and his wife Diana (Mitford). Wilson argues that Betjeman had "a natural sympathy with those who were in disgrace". An unlikely fan of *Coronation Street*, Betjeman once likened the series to Dickens' *Pickwick Papers*: "At 7.30 p.m. on Mondays and Wednesdays, I am in heaven." (Along with Russell Harty, Michael Parkinson and play-wright Willis Hall, Betjeman formed the British League of Hilda Ogden.) Morrissey paid further tribute to the poet by selecting Betjeman reading *A Child Ill* as the closing track on his 2004 *NME* compilation *Songs To Save You Life*. A BBC tribute on the centenary of his birth in 2006 concluded that "Depression was for him what daffodils were for Wordsworth."

Bindon, John – "Biffo" played the violent gangster on *and* off the screen. Associate of The Krays and The Richardsons, he was cast by Ken Loach alongside Terence Stamp in *Poor Cow*. Also appeared in *Get Carter*, *Performance* and *No Sex Please We're British*. A close friend of Princess Margaret and an occasional security man for Led Zeppelin, he was charged with the nightclub murder of Johnny Darke in 1978 but he was acquitted and subsequently fell into decline. Died of AIDS aged 50 in 1993.

Black, Cilla – Liverpudlian singer who helped split The Smiths when Morrissey, to the dismay of Marr, wanted to cover her 1967 film theme 'Work Is A Four Letter Word'. Whereas Morrissey had once declared, "I worship every belch of Cilla Black," Marr stated bluntly, "I didn't form a group to perform Cilla Black songs."

Bogarde, Dirk – encouraged by Noel Coward, Bogarde's film career started as an uncredited extra with George Formby in *Come On George* in 1939, but he first began to make his name as a Rank-signed actor along-side Diana Dors in *Dancing With Crime* and as the cad William Latch in *Esther Waters*. His first key role came in a film loved by Morrissey, *The Blue Lamp*, with Bogarde playing the cop-killer Tom Riley alongside his accomplice Spud (see Patric Doonan). Once branded the "British Rock Hudson", Bogarde became a British star through his matinee idol performances in comedies such as *Doctor At Sea,* with Brigitte Bardot, but showed his true colours in more challenging, professionally brave early Sixties films such as *The Servant* and particularly *Victim* (1961). In the latter he played married lawyer Melville Farr, who was being blackmailed over his true and, at the time, illegal sexuality; it was arguably the first British film to question the legal persecution of homosexuals. Bogarde also appeared in *Modesty Blaise* alongside Terence Stamp, in John Schlesinger's *Darling*, in Luchino Visconti's *The Damned* and – in his own opinion – reached his artistic peak "and end of my career" with his moving portrayal of Gustave Von Aschenbach in Visconti's film of Thomas Mann's novel *Death In Venice*. The dying composer becomes infatuated with a beautiful young boy, Tadzio, described by Mann as the "Sebastian-figure", the idyllic form of Apollonian beauty. Apart from his leading role in Rainer Werner Fassbinder's take on Nabokov's *Despair* (1978), Bogarde's final major role was that of the dying father in Bertrand Tavernier's moving but tragic *Daddy Nostalgie* in 1990, perhaps an inspiration for Morrissey's track 'Don't Make Fun Of Daddy's Voice'. He died of a heart attack in 1999. After his death his authorised biographer John Coldstream revealed that Bogarde had failed in Hollywood because he'd refused to enter into an arranged marriage to disguise his true sexuality. Bogarde was also an outspoken critic of celebrity and described Cannes Film Festival as "my idea of hell. You see all the people you thought were dead and all the people who deserve to be dead. After a while, you start to think you might be dead too." In response to questions about adulation from his female fans, he replied, "Cinema is just a form of masturbation, sexual relief for disappointed people. Women write and say, 'I let my husband do it because I think it's you lying on top of me.'"

Bolan, Marc – Morrissey pin-up. An early, more-folky Bolan track, Tyrannosaurus Rex's 'Great Horse', was chosen by Morrissey for his *Under The Influence* compilation. Steven Patrick's first adventure to a pop concert was to see the electric T. Rex at Manchester's Bellevue in 1972. Like Morrissey, Bolan was a great fan of Elvis Presley; tragically the T. Rex frontman would die within a month of Presley in 1977. Bolan's sound clearly inspired Smiths' tracks such as 'Panic', not to mention Morrissey's solo single 'Certain People I Know'. (Sleeve designs for Morrissey's solo singles in 1992 copied the style of Bolan's hits, replacing the red-on-blue word "TREX" with "MOZ".) It's also interesting to note that Gloria Jones, the mother of Rolan Bolan, was introduced to

Marc by Jobriath. See also, Bolan's producer Tony Visconti. (Early in his career, when playing with the Simon Napier-Bell managed band John's Children, Bolan's 'Desdemona' was banned by the BBC because of the lyric "lift up your skirt and fly". John's Children's 1967 album *Orgasm* was also censored.)

Bowie, David – Morrissey was a fan of the pre-*Aladdin Sane* Bowie in the early Seventies, and died his hair gold ('I Know Very Well How I Got My Name') in tribute to Ziggy Stardust. Bowie had celebrated one of his (and Morrissey's) heroes on the track 'Andy Warhol' from *Hunky Dory* and The Smiths' 'Sheila Take A Bow', with its reference to burning homework, steals from the same album's 'Kooks'. As a solo artist, Morrissey duetted with Bowie on T. Rex's 'Cosmic Dancer', then supported Bowie on their troubled Outsiders tour in 1995. Bowie had even covered Morrissey's 'I Know It's Gonna Happen Someday' (from *Your Arsenal*, producer Mick Ronson) on his *Black Tie, White Noise* album. They fell out soon afterwards. Morrissey said of Bowie, in 2003, "He was a fascinating artist in 1970, 1971, 1972 . . . but not now." Morrissey's cover of 'Drive-In Saturday', recorded in New York in 2000, appeared on the B-side of his 2008 single 'All You Need Is Me'.

Bradford, Richard – cover star of The Smiths' 'Panic', Bradford appeared as the cool-looking former spy turned jobbing detective McGill in ATV's late Sixties series *Man In A Suitcase* (1967). According to Sergio Angelini, writing for *BFI Screenonline*, every episode ended unhappily with McGill "always alone . . . often beaten and frequently unpaid".

Campbell, Colin – an alternative Smiths' cover star for 'Ask', Campbell became famous for his bisexual role in one of Morrissey's favourite films, *The Leather Boys* (images from the film were also used behind Morrissey in the 'Girlfriend In A Coma' promo) alongside Rita Tushingham.

Capote, Truman – cover star of 'The Boy With The Thorn In His Side', the image of Capote was taken by Cecil Beaton. Inspiration for the character Dill in his friend Harper Lee's *To Kill A Mockingbird*, Capote became the controversial and successful writer of *In Cold Blood*, *Other Voices Other Rooms* and *Breakfast At Tiffanys*. ('Moon River' was the theme tune to the 1961 film starring Audrey Hepburn as Holly Golightly, although the character, bisexual in Capote's original, had been written for his close friend Marilyn Monroe. Monroe's agent advised her against playing a call-girl.) Openly courageously gay, Capote was worshipped by the young Andy Warhol; in 1952, Warhol's first art show, at New York's Hugo Gallery, was titled *Fifteen Drawings Based On The Writings Of Truman Capote*. Other Capote works included *Music For Chameleons*, which featured interviews with, or literary portraits of, his celebrity friends, including Monroe, originally published in Warhol's *Interview* magazine.

Cartlidge, Katrin – former *Brookside* actress who grew into an emotionally powerful film star in *Breaking The Waves* and *Naked*. Also made memorable appearances in *Before The Rain, Claire Dolan, No Man's Land* and, as a Ripper victim, in *From Hell* with Johnny Depp. She died, aged only 41, from pneumonia in September 2002. Days later, Morrissey mourned her passing from the stage of the Royal Albert Hall. (Morrissey appeared in the Brookside spin-off *South*. He described his acting as "compulsive non-viewing, essential kettle-on time".)

Clitheroe, Jimmy – four foot three inch entertainer who lived all his adult life with his mother; and who took his own life on the morning of his mother's funeral. Beloved by the youthful Morrissey, the diminutive Lancastrian Clitheroe spent his life playing a 12-year-old schoolboy on radio as *The Clitheroe Kid*. Classic episodes included *How Tickled Am I?, A Far Far Better School I Go To, Funny Thing Happened At The Fair, Any More For The Beach?, Beware Of The Neighbour* and *Stop The Wedding I Want To Get Off*. Clitheroe also appeared with music hall star Frank Randle in the 1949 feature films *Somewhere In Politics* and *School For Randle* (filmed in Manchester by John E. Blakeley, who also helped launch Formby's movie career). His comedic genius disguised a desperately sad and lonely private life. Once admitted, "The time I come to life is when I set foot on stage". Morrissey may have seen Jimmy Clitheroe's 'mystery' appearance on the BBC's *Looks Familiar*, in December 1972, six months before his suicide aged 51; on the programme, panellists including Diana Dors and Victor Spinetti, failed to spot it was Clitheroe. This incident could have inspired the *Viva Hate* track 'Little Man, What Now?' (although the title is taken from Hans Fallada's German Depression novel about the struggle for love amidst working class poverty, made into a 1934 Hollywood film by director Frank Borzage).

Cochran, Steve – Morrissey's parents named him after the tough guy American actor who appeared in gangster films such as *White Heat* with James Cagney and *I, Mobster*, and also starred with "teen queen" Mamie Van Doren* (she's celebrated in *Exit Smiling*) as a rapist-chasing cop in the misogynistic *The Beat Generation* (1959). Like James Dean, Cochran appeared in television plays such as the *Studio One* series (1953–55), *Schlitz Playhouse Of Stars* and *Robert Montgomery Presents*. Died in mysterious circumstances on board his yacht en route to Guatemala in 1965. Once said of his thespian talent, "With this puss of mine, I could play the corpse and be accused of overacting."

Cocteau, Jean – French film-director, writer, actor, painter and lover of his *Orpheus* and *Beauty And The Beast* star Jean Marais. Morrissey's poem *Poppy Cocteau*, an everyday tale of losing one's trousers in Liverpool to a couple of merchant seamen, appeared on the back of a free 'London' flexidisc in 1988. Roberto Rosellini's 1948 film *L'Amore*, partly based on Cocteau's play *La Voce Umana*, starred Anna Magnani.

Cogan, Alma – possible subject of 'Alma Matters', East Londoner Cogan died young aged only 34. A major British star in the Fifties and Sixties – as a Big Band singer, on television and as an old-fashioned female vocalist – she's best remembered for her number one 'Dreamboat', the EP *She Loves To Sing*, 'Bell Bottom Blues', 'Couldn't Resist Her With Her Pocket Transistor', 'Sorry Sorry Sorry', 'Last Night On The Back Porch', her version of 'Lucky Lips' and 'All Alone'. Although, according to her sister and biographer Sandra Caron, she had an affair with John Lennon (when she worked alongside The Beatles), the great loves of Cogan's life were the gay composer Lionel Bart and the Beatles' manager Brian Epstein. Her last television appearance before her death, from ovarian cancer in 1966, was presented by Kenneth Williams. Gordon Burns' 1991 novel, *Alma Cogan*, suggested that Moors Murders Myra Hindley and Ian Brady killed one of their victims while Alma was being played on the radio. Known as "The Girl With A Laugh In Her Voice", she appeared (uncredited) in the Dirk Bogarde film *For Better For Worse* (1954) and on the pop TV show *Oh Boy!* (with Billy Fury) on St Valentine's Day 1959.

---

* Van Doren's 1957 film *Untamed Youth* was condemned by the Catholic Legion of Decency.

Conn, Billy – cover star of 'Boxers', Conn was the Irish–American World Lightweight Champion "The Pittsburg Kid", who failed to take Joe Louis' Heavyweight crown in May 1941. After the fight Conn commented, "I lost my head and a million bucks." (Morrisssey released the 'Boxers' single around the time of his court case versus Mike Joyce.) In Brando's "I coulda been a contender" speech in *On The Waterfront*, his brother Charlie replies, "You coulda been another Billy Conn.")

Conrad, Jess – singer and actor, close friend of Diana Dors, his 1961 Decca single 'This Pullover' was featured on Kenny Everett's 1978 compilation album *The World's Worst Record Show* and seems to have influenced Morrissey's 'Our Frank'. He performed 'Why Am I Living?' in the 1958 film *Rag Doll*, appeared in *The Cockleshell Heroes* with Patric Doonan and Anthony Newley, and was one of the bad lads arrested for stabbing a night-watchman in 1962's working-class crime drama *The Boys*. Conrad also appears in *The Great Rock & Roll Swindle*.

County, Wayne/Jayne – transsexual performer, who appeared in Derek Jarman's *Jubilee* as Lounge Lizard, made his dramatic debut in Jackie Curtis' *Femme Fatale* with Patti Smith, and also starred in Andy Warhol's *Pork* (at London's Roundhouse). County, whose controversial band The Electric Chairs recorded the famous single 'Fuck Off' in 1977, features in *The Blank Generation* alongside Blondie, Patti Smith, Johnny Thunders, Richard Hell and other New York Morrissey favourites from the punk era. His 1995 memoir is titled *Man Enough To Be A Woman*.

Courtneidge, Cicely – sings 'Take Me Back To Dear Old Blighty (from *The L-Shaped Room*, with Pat Phoenix, Anthony Booth, Tom Bell and Emlyn Williams) at the start of *The Queen Is Dead*. Also a regular in 1969's *On The Buses* (as Mum), a Thirties film star alongside Max Miller and Jack Hulbert, and also featured in Ray Cooney's 1973 sex farce *Not Now Darling* (with Joan Sims, Barbara Windsor and the wrestler Jackie Pallo).

Curtis, Jackie – part of the Warhol set, and celebrated in *"Jackie is just speeding away, thought she was James Dean for a day"* (Lou Reed's 'Walk On The Wild Side'). Curtis was a 'transgendered' singer, film star, poet and playwright – real name John Holder Jnr – who appeared in Paul Morrissey's *Women In Revolt* (1971) with Candy Darling and Holly Woodlawn, and in *Flesh* (1969) with Joe Dallesandro and Darling. Curtis

257

was involved with the genderbender San Francisco hippy band The Cockettes and also worked with The New York Dolls in May 1972. Died of a heroine overdose in 1985.

Dallesandro, Joe – cover star of The Smiths' debut album, in a still image from Andy Warhol and Paul Morrissey's *Flesh*, Dallesandro also appeared in *Trash* and *Heat* by Warhol/Morrissey. Well-endowed porn star, aka Little Joe, is also mentioned in Lou Reed's 'Walk On The Wild Side': *"Little Joe never once gave it away, every body had to pay and pay . . ."*

Darling, Candy – Transexual actor, famous for his/her ability to impersonate Hollywood divas such as Marilyn Monroe and Liz Taylor – and featured on the cover of The Smiths' 'Sheila Take A Bow'. Another iconic figure from Warhol's Factory stable. Darling was also name-checked on Lou Reed's 'Walk On The Wild Side' – *"Candy came from out on the island, in the back room she was every body's darling . . ."* – and Reed also wrote 'Candy Says' about her. Died from leukaemia aged 27 in March 1974.

Davalos, Richard – cast alongside James Dean in Elia Kazan's *East Of Eden* (1955). Davalos' face appears on the cover of The Smiths *Strangeways, Here We Come* and he's also the cover star on two compilation albums. The mute screen tests of Dean and Davalos were shown before Morrissey's solo concerts in 2006. He was celebrated in Morrissey's pre-Smiths book *Exit Smiling*, but with the conclusion "seems doomed to virtual obscurity. Sad".

Davis, Bette – Hollywood diva, starred in *The Man Who Came To Dinner* (1942) from which Morrissey took his early nom de plume Sheridan Whiteside. In the film, one of Whiteside's famous lines is "Is there a man in the world who suffers as I do from the gross inadequacies of the human race?" The track 'Whatever Happened To Baby Jane', from the film of the same name – sung by Davis and Debbie Burton with Bobby Heller & His Orchestra – was played before Morrissey shows in 2002.

Dawson, Les – Lancastrian comedian, television presenter, piano player and pantomime dame, famous for his double act with Roy Barraclough of *Coronation Street*. Morrissey took the title of his 1993 video collection from Dawson's book *Malady Lingers On And Other Great Groaners*. Dawson had borrowed it from the 1935 musical, *The Melody Lingers On*. Born in

Collyhurst, Manchester in 1931, Dawson died of a heart attack in Whalley Range on June 10, 1993. Morrissey's *Malady* video was released a month later.

Dean, James – eternal youth icon, key Morrissey pin-up and bespectacled, motorbiking Smiths cover star ('Bigmouth Strikes Again'). Dean's most famous for his portrayal of youthful outsiders struggling to come to terms with post-war America in *East Of Eden, Rebel Without A Cause* and *Giant*. Branded "America's rebel" by Ronald Reagan, Dean died in a car crash in 1955 aged only 24. Morrissey's first book was *James Dean Is Not Dead* (published 1983). The world-ending lines from *Rebel Without A Cause*, uttered by Sal Mineo as Plato, are referenced in 'Stretch Out And Wait'. The video for Morrissey's first solo single, 'Suedehead', was filmed in Dean's hometown of Fairmount, Indiana, re-enacting the 1955 "Moody New Star" *Life* magazine portraits by Dennis Stock, and paying a visit to Dean's last resting place (resulting in the ridiculous and inaccurate *Daily Mirror* headline: "Weird – Morrissey Sits On James Dean's Grave"). In the promo film, Morrissey carries a copy of Dean's favourite book, *The Little Prince* by Antoine De Saint-Exupery. Other Dean connections include the 'Maladjusted' single 'Alma Matters', in part a pun on Alma Mater (Latin for school or college) and also the original title of the 1953 film *Trouble Along The Way* in which Dean was an extra. Dick Davalos, cover star of *Strangeways, Here We Come* and The Smiths' *Best Of . . .* compilations acted with Dean in *East Of Eden*. Although bi-sexual, he once claimed the love of his life was Italian actress Pier Angeli. At the time of his death, he was contracted to play opposite her in *Somebody Up There Likes Me* (about the boxer Rocky Graziano), and also to star as Billy The Kid in *The Left Handed Gun* and as Brick in *Cat On A Hot Tin Roof*. (All three roles went to Paul Newman instead.) Morrissey, in several interviews, has expressed his belief that Dean took his own life. In terms of Oscar Wilde connections, Dean was a great admirer of Wilde's work and echoed Oscar when he declared: "There was no God, there was only art, only the composer, the creator of the symphony." James Dean clearly had an obsession with death. According to his friend John Gilmore, "Jimmy's talk of death, dying and dismemberment wasn't as exciting or interesting to me as it was to him. It was never morose, though, and at times tended to become almost ecstatic . . . the image of his mother's coffin was indelibly etched in his mind – the idea of dwelling in caskets in general obsessed him." Like Wilde, Dean was also very interested in spiritualism and the occult. He even visited a hotel where Wilde's friend French actress Sarah Bernardt had slept and lay on the same bed to be closer to her. (Dean also believed the ghost of his dead mother came to him; Mildred Dean had died when he was only nine and her death had led his father to send Jimmy away to be raised by relatives. He never had a close relationship with his father.) Furthermore, James Dean made his Broadway debut as the Arab boy who seduces a British male tourist in *The Immoralist* by Oscar Wilde's friend Andre Gide and, months before his death, appeared in *The Life Of Emile Zola*, another Wilde acquaintance (although whereas Gide had campaigned for Wilde's early release from prison, Zola refused).

Delaney, Shelagh – Salford-born playwright who was a major influence on Morrissey in his early lyrical years. Cover star of 'Girlfriend In A Coma' and *Louder Than Bombs*, Morrissey plagiarised Delaney's *A Taste Of Honey* to great effect, notably on 'Reel Around The Fountain' and 'This Night Has Opened My Eyes'. Morrissey said in 1986: "I've never made any secret of the fact that at least 50 per cent of my reason for writing can be blamed on Shelagh Delaney." Delaney also worked with the radical East London theatre director Joan Littlewood. Other screenplays, mainly about the writer's own bitter-sweet relationship with Manchester and the North, included the Albert Finney-directed *Charlie Bubbles* (1967) – starring Albert Finney and Billie Whitelaw, alongside Liza Minelli, Yootha Joyce and Alan Lake (one of Diana Dors' husbands) – and *The White Bus* (1967), with Arthur Lowe.

Delon, Alain – actor and director, the French James Dean, cover star of *The Queen Is Dead* from the 1964 film *L'Insoumis (The Unvanquished)*. Also starred with Marianne Faithfull in the famously racy *The Girl On A Motorcycle* (1968). See also Nice.

Doonan, Patric – British film and stage actor, celebrated by Morrissey in 'Now My Heart Is Full' (*Vauxhall & I*), Doonan took his own life aged only 32. He appeared with Anthony Newley in the war film *The Cockleshell Heroes* and the spy thriller *Highly Dangerous*, and also with the unlikely combination of Sid James and Gene Kelly in *Seagulls Over Sorrento* (1954). In terms of further Morrissey icons, he featured with Joan Sims in *What Every Woman Wants*, starred in *Wheel Of Fate* as one of two brothers fighting for the affection of nightclub singer Lucky Price (Sandra Dorne from *The Weak And The Wicked* and *Hindle Wakes*) plus the 'Speedway' drama *Once A Jolly Swagman* with Dirk Bogarde (1949). In the same year he was in *All Over The Town* – a possible inspiration for the opening lines of 'Sister I'm A Poet' – followed by a memorable performance as a juvenile delinquent Spud alongside Dirk Bogarde's cop-killer Tom Riley in *The Blue Lamp*. (Doonan's character Spud dies in a car crash.) Morrissey told me, in 2003, that he'd once tried to license excerpts from *The Blue Lamp* to use in the promo video for 'Hold On To Your Friends' but Dirk Bogarde – who didn't die until 1999 – had refused permission. Other Doonan film performances came in *The Man In The White Suit* and *The Gentle Gunman* – about IRA bombers in London during World War Two, and again starring Bogarde (this time with John Mills). Doonan's father George had starred with Frank Randle in *Somewhere In Civvies* (1943), while his brother Tony played the blackmailer Wood in Gregory Ratoff's film of the life of *Oscar Wilde* (1960), appeared with Pier Angeli in *The Angry Silence* and as a cop hunting a misogynist strangler in *Cover Girl Killer*.

Dors, Diana – British sex-bomb, often likened to Marilyn Monroe but already an established star in Britain before Marilyn mania hit Hollywood. Celebrated by Morrissey in his film stars book *Exit Smiling*, and again on his *Under The Influence* compilation with her brassy early Sixties track 'So Little Time' (from her album *Swinging Dors*: "Very sexual, very heaving, sort of string-drenched and very beautiful. You want to nestle in her bosom," was his verdict). Born Diana Mary Fluck, Dors became a Rank starlet, appearing alongside Frank Randle in *It's A Grand Life* (filmed in Rusholme, Manchester by John E. Blakely) and Dirk Bogarde in *Dancing With Crime*. She first played the juvenile delinquent in *Good Time Girl*, then later in *A Boy A Girl And A Bike* (1949) with Anthony Newley. She'd met Newley on David Lean's *Oliver Twist* (1948) and they became life-long friends. Morrissey regards her best film as *Yield To The Night* (aka *Blonde Sinner*), J. Lee Thompson's 1956 anti-capital punishment drama, based on the Ruth Ellis case, in which Dors' passion-crime murderess faces the gallows reciting A.E. Housman's *A Shropshire Lad*. (Dors knew Ellis, the last woman to be hanged in Britain, as they'd appeared together in the 1951 romp *Lady Godiva Rides Again*, which was censored in the USA.) A much-desired glamour model, Dors later appeared in erotic movies – notably the Jack-The-Ripper sex 'comedy' *Victorian Fantasies* (aka *What The Swedish Butler Saw*), *The Groove Room* and *The David Galaxy Affair* (with her husband Alan Lake) – in the low-rent Seventies

TV series *Queenie's Castle* (written by Keith Waterhouse), its offspring *All Our Saturdays* and in the film *There's A Girl In My Soup*. By this time she had transformed herself from a sex bomb into a mostly cheerful, over-weight, salt-of-the-earth, brassy blonde, mother-hen character. She once famously flew celebrity hairdresser Raymond "Teasy-Weasy" Bessone (arguably the first camp star to appear on British television in the Fifties) to the States to give her a cut and blow dry (cost £2,500). She knew the Krays and drank in The Grave Maurice pub in the East End of London (Morrissey stands outside this pub on the covers of *Under The Influence* and the 1994 single 'Sunny'). She died in May 1984, after filming Nell Dunn's *Steaming*. Alan Lake, who'd also played a minor role in *Charlie Bubbles*, took his own life later that year. (NB. Diana Dors, like Oscar Wilde, is immortalised on the cover of The Beatles' *Sgt. Pepper's Lonely Hearts Club Band*.)

Douglas, Lord Alfred – see Chapter Twelve: Wilde Man In His Head.

Elliot, George – real-name Mary Ann Evans, she wrote *Middlemarch* in the 1870s. It's the source for the opening lines of The Smiths' 'How Soon Is Now?'

Fagin, Michael – hapless Palace burglar who broke into the Queen's bedroom in 1982 and was celebrated in the title track of *The Queen Is Dead*.

Faithfull, Marianne – Morrissey once described her as "a right goer". Marianne's 1965 single 'Come And Stay With Me' was the first record that he bought. She also played Lord Alfred Douglas in the post-Redlands promo film for The Rolling Stones 'We Love You', which satirised the 1895 trial of Oscar Wilde for gross indecency. (Jagger played Wilde with Keith Richards as the Marquess Of Queensberry.) The early Smiths are rumoured to have released a version of Marianne's early hit 'Summer Nights' and, according to one source (Nick Kent, *The Face*) possibly covered her 1965 debut album track 'The Sha La La Song'. See also Delon, Alain.

Fellini, Federico – Italian film director who celebrated Roman life with *La Dolce Vita* (1960) – Nico appeared in it and Pasolini contributed to it – and *Roma* (1972), an autobiographical reminiscence of the young direc-tor's arrival in the city under Mussolini's rule. Along with Roger Vadim and Louis Malle, Fellini directed segments of *Histoires Extraordinares* (1968), adaptations of Edgar Allan Poe short stories starring Brigitte Bardot, Alain Delon and Terence Stamp. (Stamp plays the decadent English movie star Toby Dammit.) Early in his career, as a writer, Fellini worked on Rossellini's anti-Nazi film *Rome, Open City*, which featured Anna Magnani (celebrated in Morrissey's 'You Have Killed Me'). Locations from Fellini's *La Dolce Vita* were echoed in Morrissey's publicity shoots for his Rome-recorded 2006 album *Ringleader Of The Tormentors*.

Finney, Albert – Mancunian actor (he actually attended Salford Lads Club as a kid and The Smiths were photographed outside the Salford shopfront "Albert Finney"), he played hard-living Northern rebel Arthur Seaton in one of Morrissey's favourite films, *Saturday Night And Sunday Morning* (also featuring Rachel Roberts). He also starred in *Charlie Bubbles* with Billie Whitelaw. Finney started out in *The Entertainer* with Laurence Olivier, Alan Bates and George Doonan – father of Patric and Tony Doonan – and also played a psycho in Emlyn Williams' 1964 screenplay *Night Must Fall*. In 1994 Finney starred in *A Man Of No Importance*, about a sexually repressed Dublin bus driver who's fascinated with the life and works of Oscar Wilde.

Formby, George – Lancashire toreador, film star, comedian and ukelele exponent. Banned by the BBC in 1937 because some of his lyrics were too risqué (e.g. 'With My Little Stick Of Blackpool Rock' and 'She's Got Two Of Everything'), Formby also wrote Morrissey-style songs like 'I'm Too Shy', 'Have You Ever Heard This One, Have You?', 'They Laughed When I Started To Play', the motorbike classic 'Riding In The TT Races' and 'Mother, What'll I Do Now'. Morrissey was photographed with Formby's banjo at his grave in 1986. Dirk Bogarde made his film debut as an extra in *Come On George* (1939) and Formby's Forties films, such as *Bell Bottom George*, also featured a young Charles Hawtrey. In addition to writing a song called 'Sunbathers In The Park', during the Second World War Formby also accused other performers of being "lazy sunbathers" instead of doing more to entertain the troops.

Fury, Billy – England's Elvis, the cover star of The Smiths' 'Last Night I Dreamt That Somebody Loved Me' and the British performer who had most impact on Morrissey's stage style : "Billy Fury is virtually the same as James Dean. He was entirely doomed too, and I find that quite affectionate." Discovered by the pop svengali Larry Parnes, who Ron Wycherley met backstage at a Marty Wilde concert in 1958; Parnes gave him the name Billy Fury. In his early days Fury was banned because of his overtly sexual stage act, but he hit big in the early to mid Sixties with singles such as 'Colette', 'Halfway To Paradise', 'Jealousy', 'I'll Never Find Another You' and 'Last Night Was Made For Love'. Several Fury tracks probably inspired Morrissey songs, for example 'Let Me Know' ('We'll Let You Know'), 'She Cried' ('He Cried'), 'Phone Call' ('The Loop'), 'It's You I Need' ('All You Need Is Me'), and perhaps even 'Love Love Love' ('Found Found Found'). Other important connections include his meeting with Elvis Presley on the set of *Girls, Girls, Girls*, and his work with The Tornados and Joe Meek. Ill-health, following major heart surgery in December 1971, retired him to his Welsh farm where he pursued his interest in animal welfare. He died in January 1983 having recorded his last single 'Forget Him'. (See Barrie, Amanda.)

Genet, Jean – juvenile delinquent and career criminal who became one of the great French writers of the 20th century. Celebrated in Bowie's 'The Jean Jeanie'; written when he was hanging with actress Cyrinda Foxe, who appeared in Warhol's 1977 film *Bad* and who later became the girlfriend of David Johansen of the New York Dolls. The young Genet was imprisoned for vagrancy in a penal colony, kicked out of the French Legion (he was caught engaged in an indecent act) and began writing, in the 1940s, explicitly about homosexuality and criminality, resulting in his work being banned outside France. Playwright (*The Maids*, *The Blacks* . . .), novelist (*Funeral Rites*, *The Thief's Journal* . . .), and political activist, Genet's life is best read in his own memoir *The Prisoner Of Love* and in Edmund White's 1993 biography. Genet died in a Parisien hotel in April 1986, months before the release of *The Queen Is Dead*.

Gordon, Ruth – Oscar winning actress (*Rosemary's Baby*) and writer celebrated in Morrissey's book *Exit Smiling*. Gordon starred as Maude in the death-loving, life-affirming *Harold And Maude* (1971). The pro-animal rights Maude declared, "I used to break into pet shops to liberate canaries. But I decided that was an idea way before its time. Zoos are full, prisons are overflowing . . . oh my, how the world still dearly loves a cage." According to Morrissey, Gordon wrote screenplays which "were very sensitive to women . . . at a time when men controlled all areas of film".

With her husband Garson Kanin, she also wrote the Spencer Tracy and Katherine Hepburn film vehicles *Adam's Rib* and *Pat And Mike*.

Greene, Graham – author of the 1938 novel *Brighton Rock*, source of the smalltown gangsters Dallow, Spicer, Pinkie and Cubitt who appear in Morrissey's 1994 track 'Now My Heart Is Full'. A very Catholic novelist whose major themes included redemption and damnation. Near the end of Oscar Wilde's life, the dying playwright drank coffee with Greene's father in Paris. (The American title for the film *Brighton Rock* was *Young Scarface*.)

Hall, Radclyffe – 1880–1943, she wrote the pioneering lesbian classic *The Well Of Loneliness*; published in 1928 it was judged to be obscene and initially banned in the UK.

Hanratty, James – convicted of the A6 murder at Dead Man's Hill in 1961 and hanged in Bedford Prison in April 1962. His conviction, for the murder of Michael Gregsten, was disputed for 40 years until DNA evidence proved his guilt "beyond doubt" at the Court Of Appeal in 2002. A Morrissey track titled 'Hanratty', recorded around the time of *Maladjusted* in 1997, remains unreleased. (NB. The last official execution in the United Kingdom took place at Strangeways Prison, Manchester on August 13, 1964, when 24-year-old Gwynne Owen Evans was hanged.)

Hawtrey, Charles ('Jnr') – Played an important part in the success of the *Carry On* films and rewarded with a Morrissey obituary in *NME* in 1988 which claimed he was "60 per cent of *Carry On* appeal" and "the last death wheeze of the real England". Born George Hartree, he stole his stage name from Sir Charles Henry Hawtrey, the Victorian/Edwardian actor and director who famously celebrated the downfall of Oscar Wilde. Destined for fame in the *Carry On* films, Hawtrey first appeared with Will Hay in Thirties and Forties comedies such as *Good Morning Boys* and *The Goose Steps Out*, and with George Formby and Jimmy Clitheroe in *Much Too Shy*. Also played a Teddy boy in *As Long As They're Happy* (1955), featuring Diana Dors and Joan Sims, and appeared in *The Army Game* with another *Carry On* regular Bernard Bresslaw (who recorded the 1958 single 'Mad Passionate Love' – echoed by Morrissey's own 1992 B-side 'Pashernate Love'). Hawtrey is also seen at the pub piano accompanying Jane Hilton singing 'I Don't Want To Set The World On Fire' in *Passport To Pimlico*. Star of 23 *Carry Ons* between 1958 and 1972,

Hawtrey was name-checked by The Beatles on 'The Two Of Us' (*Let It Be*), is rumoured to have rejected the chance to cover 'Hand In Glove' with The Smiths but was destined to posthumously be the cover star of *The Very Best Of The Smiths* compilation (2001). He also utters the line "stop me if you've heard this one before" as Seneca in *Carry On Cleo*. Morrissey's obituary for the comedian, whose personal life had been affected by alcohol and arthritis, concluded, "by never giving press interviews, and by all accounts being unfriendly and friendless, Hawtrey's mystique surpasses Garbo. I personally loved him."

Head, Murray – Smiths' cover star for 'Stop Me If You Think You've Heard This One Before', Head appeared alongside Avril Angers in Bill Naughton's *The Family Way* (1966) and as bisexual Bob Elkin in John Schlesinger's *Sunday Bloody Sunday* (1971), with Peter Finch (who played the lead in *The Trials Of Oscar Wilde* and *Sunday Bloody Sunday*) and Glenda Jackson.

Housman, A E – verses from his poetic collection *A Shropshire Lad* are recited by Diana Dors' murderess in the dying moments of *Yield To The Night*, and there are also Housman references in Alan Bennett's *The History Boys* (*A Shropshire Lad* is quoted by Hector). Was at Oxford at the same time as Wilde but there are doubts whether they actually met, although Tom Stoppard's *The Invention Of Love* imagines that they did. Morrissey recommended I buy *A Shropshire Lad* when we met in Waterstones in Manchester in 1997. (*A Shropshire Lad* was published a century earlier.) Some of the poems refer to Housman's unrequited love for Moses Jackson and his grief at the death of Moses' brother Adalbert in 1892. Housman's later poems were protests against the persecution of gay men like Oscar Wilde; Housman sent an autographed copy of *A Shropshire Lad* to Wilde in prison (Wilde knew Housman's brother Laurence). Gilbert Adair wrote of Housman, in *The Independent On Sunday* in 1999: "He was also the kind of homosexual this country has always preferred: stoically buttoned-up and consumed by guilt".

Howerd, Frankie – British comedy actor and *Carry On* star who also appeared in the bawdy Roman comedy *Up Pompeii*. (In one episode he turns to the camera and quips, "Now I know how Joan of Arc felt.") Howerd also appeared in *An Alligator Named Daisy* (with Diana Dors), and *The Great St Trinian's Train Robbery*.

Hunter, Ian – associate of Bowie, and leader of Mott The Hoople (one of Morrissey's favourite bands of the early Seventies). Hunter had been a backing musician for Billy Fury in the Sixties and, post-Mott, worked closely with Mick Ronson (producer of Morrissey's *Your Arsenal*) until Ronson's death in 1993. (Hunter's solo albums include *The Artful Dodger* and *Rant*.)

Jack The Ripper – In the final chapter of Alan Moore and Eddie Campbell's graphic novel *From Hell* – inspiration for the 2001 movie with Johnny Depp and Katrin Cartlidge – the ghost of Jack observes Ian Brady and Myra Hindley watching the black and white film *Jack The Ripper*. *Coronation Street* and Smiths' cover star Pat Phoenix played a prostitute in this 1959 version. Morrissey celebrates the dark side of the East London life in songs as diverse as 'Jack The Ripper', 'The Last Of The Famous International Playboys' (which name-checks those later infamous East London villains the Krays), and 'Spring Heeled Jim' (based on another mysterious Victorian villain also known as Spring Heeled Jack).

Jarman, Derek – influential artist/director and AIDS campaigner, he made the only authorised 'promotional films' for The Smiths during the band's creative life. His 1986 works 'The Queen Is Dead', 'Panic', 'There Is A Light That Never Goes Out' and 'Ask' perfectly captured the spirit of The Smiths at their peak. Morrissey had been drawn to Jarman's art through the punk-era feature films *Sebastiane* and particularly *Jubilee*, which featured Wayne County, Adam Ant, Lindsay Kemp and Siouxsie Sioux. Other memorable works by Jarman – who died of an AIDS-related illness in 1994 – include *The Last Of England*, *Caravaggio, The Garden* and his short films, *Sloane Square: A Room Of One's Own* and *Every Woman For Herself And All For Art*. He'd also shot early footage of The Sex Pistols in 1976, made videos for Marianne Faithfull's *Broken English* album, worked with the Pet Shop Boys (1991) and filmed the documentary of Suede's *The Next Life* in 1993.

Jobriath – self-styled "True Fairy Of Rock & Roll", marketed as America's answer to David Bowie, this openly gay glam rocker, while working on *Hair* in Los Angeles, first introduced Gloria Jones to Marc Bolan. Despite the financial backing of Elektra Records and a British audience that included the young Steven Patrick Morrissey, Jobriath was clearly too flambuoyant for his time. Died in 1983 of AIDS-related illnesses, having become a recluse in New York's Chelsea Hotel. When Morrissey launched his Attack label (through Sanctuary) in 2004, he lovingly put together the Jobriath compilation *Lonely Planet Boy* (named after The New York Dolls' song), including 'Street Corner Love', 'Movie Star' and 'Morning Star Ship' (which also appears on Morrissey's *NME* compilation *Songs To Save Your Life*). On the inner sleeve of *Morrissey: Live At Earls Court* (2004), his band are pictured in Jobriath T-shirts. Jobriath's famous 1973 appearance on *Midnight Special* was screened before Morrissey concerts in 2006.

Jones, Christopher – Sixties pin-up, heralded as the "new James Dean" in *Wild In The Streets* (1968) – he played LSD-loving rock star Max Frost who gets elected President Of The USA – Jones also appeared in *Ryan's Daughter* and is mentioned by Morrissey in *Exit Smiling*. Tennessee-born Jones was obsessed with Dean and also with Elvis Presley and once remarked "Dean had a sophisticated subtlety about him and, although people have always compared me with him, at the time I would have preferred to be thought of as more flashy like Elvis. After seeing *Love Me Tender* (1956) and *East Of Eden* (1955) at around the same time I realised how brilliant James Dean was. I've always been torn between the two role models though." Jones even became close friends with Dean's family, the Winslows, and stayed at their Indiana home. His monosyllabic performance as shell-shocked Major Doryan in *Ryan's Daughter* disappointed director David Lean, resulting in Jones' voice being over-dubbed by Julian Holloway (who'd played Major Shorthouse in *Carry On . . . Up The Khyber*). Christopher Jones' career stalled following a nervous breakdown after the murder of his friend Sharon Tate by the Manson Family in August 1969.

Joyce, Yootha – Smiths cover star of 'Ask'. Started out working with Joan Littlewood's Theatre Workshop in East London and appeared in the locally shot 1962 film *Sparrers Can't Sing*. Written by actor Stephen Lewis – he was Blakey in on *On The Buses* alongside Yootha's Jessie – and filmed in nearby Vallance Road, *Sparrers . . .* featured Barbara Windsor, Queenie Watts and Victor Spinetti, not forgetting a cameo role by the Kray Twins. Yootha Joyce went on to achieve fame in television sitcoms as the desperate-to-be-upwardly mobile Mildred Roper in *Man About The House* and *George & Mildred*. She died of liver failure in 1980. Of her final television appearance, singing on the Max Bygraves show, Kenneth

Williams wrote in his *Diaries* (January 14, 1981): "It had an extraordinary poignancy and she looked as if she was crying."

Keitel, Harvey – a still image of the American actor, taken from the early 1967 Martin Scorsese film *Who's That Knocking At My Door?* (aka *I Call First*), was used as a backdrop on Morrissey's 1991 tour. Scorsese's early work deals with sexuality and Catholic guilt.

Kemp, Lindsay – inspirational dancer and mime artist, close to David Bowie, who choreographed the Ziggy Stardust performances at London's Rainbow Theatre in 1972 and also appeared in the promo video for 'John, I'm Only Dancing'. According to Michael Bracewell's *England Is Mine* (1997), "Kemp's hugely influential interpretations of Wilde, Lorca and Genet – all three of which, as the hymning of homosexual outsiderdom as the last act of Glam aesthetics and the tense pause before the storm of punk, were staged as mimes at the Roundhouse, in Camden Town, in the mid 1970s." This is one reason why Morrissey pitched his January 2008 residency at the North London venue (it had also been the scene of the first UK dates by The Ramones and Blondie.) Kemp also appeared in the Derek Jarman films *Sebastiane* (1976) and *Jubilee* (1977), and re-emerged as a pantomime dame in Todd Haynes' 1998 Wilde-influenced glam tribute movie *Velvet Goldmine* (the soundtrack featured a Teenage Fanclub cover of the Dolls' 'Personality Crisis'). Like Morrissey, Lindsay Kemp lives in Rome.

The Krays – East End Sixties icons, photographed by David Bailey (like Morrissey), twin brothers Ronnie and Reggie were born in Vallance Road, Bethnal Green and drank in The Grave Maurice public house, near Whitechapel Hospital, where Morrissey is pictured on the cover of both his *Under The Influence* compilation and his 'Sunny' single. The Krays are mentioned in his 1989 single 'Last Of The Famous International Play Boys', although Morrissey later quipped that "The last of the international playboys are Bowie, Bolan, Devoto and me." Ganglords and nightclub owners, who had connections with the West Ham and Repton Boys Clubs, the Krays' celebrity friends included Diana Dors, Judy Garland and Frank Sinatra, and they also appeared in the 1962 film *Sparrers Can't Sing* (see Yootha Joyce). Battled the Richardson Gang in Mr Smiths nightclub, Catford (see Richardson, Charles) and urban myth has it that the Krays tried to take over Manchester's nightlife but were sent packing by their Northern equivalents The Quality Street Gang. Sentenced to life imprisonment in 1968 for the murders of George Cornell and Jack 'The Hat' McVitie, Ronnie died in Broadmoor Hospital in 1995 while Reggie died in a Norwich hotel in 2000. Ronnie Kray was the inspiration for the homosexual gangster Harry Starks in Jake Arnott's 1999 debut novel *The Long Firm*. (Morrissey was interviewed by Arnott for London's *Time Out* magazine.)

La Rue, Danny – Dublin-born female impersonator who dislikes the phrase "drag artist", preferring instead "comic in a frock" ('Vicar In A Tutu'?). Pioneer of British cross-dressing, he stepped out of vaudeville and onto television in the Fifties and Sixties. Key diva impressions included Elizabeth Taylor, Zsa Zsa Gabor and Dorothy Squires.

Langtry, Lillie – great Victorian and Edwardian actress, friend and lover of Oscar Wilde and the woman who told Wilde, in 1879, that he had wasted his life ('Christian Dior'). Some believe Wilde fathered Langtry's illegitimate daughter Jeanne – one possible source for The Smiths' track – although other biographers suggest Jeanne was the daughter of Prince Louis of Battenburg (or another Langtry lover, Arthur Jones). When in London, between 1892 and 1897, Lillie stayed at the Cadogan Hotel, scene of Oscar Wilde's arrest.

Mackenzie, Billy – contemporary of Morrissey's, although his band The Associates peaked creatively with *Sulk* in 1982. Mackenzie had one of the truly great voices in modern pop (his covers of 'God Bless The Child' live at Ronnie Scott's and of Bowie's 'Boys Keep Swinging' and 'Wild Is The Wind' provide the evidence you need). Morrissey and Mackenzie were friends in the early Eighties and Mackenzie is often rumoured to be the subject of 'William, It Was Really Nothing', based on the notion that Mackenzie had written the song 'Stephen, You're Really Something' in response (Mackenzie didn't write the track). Tragically, Mackenzie took his own life following the death of his mother in 1997.

Mansfield, Jayne – busty blonde Hollywood star of the late Fifties and early Sixties who, in Morrissey's opinion in *Exit Smiling*, "overshadows Monroe in the comic-erotic stakes". Appeared in *The Girl Can't Help It*, *Too Hot To Handle* (with Barbara Windsor), *Will Success Spoil Rock Hunter?* and *Kiss Them For Me* (which became the title of Siouxsie & The

Banshees' 1991 hit). Arrested for indecent exposure on stage in 1963, Mansfield was brighter and wittier than her curvaceous image presented: "I've got the strangest build, it's big in the hips, small in the waist and I've got these enormous . . . shoulders". Died aged 34 in a car crash in 1967.

Marais, Jean – cover star of 'This Charming Man' in a narcissistic, autosexual image from Cocteau's *Orphee*. French director Jean Cocteau was Marais' mentor and lover.

Meek, Joe – pioneering record producer. An unconventional outsider described as an "indoor boy" by his brothers in the BBC Arena documentary *The Strange Story Of Joe Meek*. Worked for Philips and Pye record labels, then set up on his own recording studio above a leather shop on the Holloway Road, North London. Produced hit records by artists such as The Tornados ('Telstar'), Heinz, The Honeycombs ('Have I The Right'), John Leyton ('Johnny Remember Me'), Screaming Lord Sutch ('Jack The Ripper'), Jess Conrad, and The Crying Shames ('Please Stay'). Interested in the occult, Meek used a ouija board and recorded in a graveyard to get the sound of the supernatural. Homosexual at a time in England, pre-1967, when it was still a crime, he fell in love with Heinz who rejected him with the words: "If there's something you can't have then you want it even more." (The Tornados' B-side 'Do You Come Here Often?' ventures into the gay underworld of "The Dilly" 25 years ahead of Morrissey's 'Piccadilly Palare'.) In 1963, after Meek was fined £15 for "persistently importuning for an immoral purpose", his career went into decline and his brothers later claimed he was being blackmailed. In February 1967, using a shotgun he'd taken from Heinz, Joe Meek shot his landlady and then himself. He was 37.

Mineo, Sal – Morrissey pin-up who acted alongside James Dean, appearing as Plato in *Rebel Without A Cause* and as Angel in *Giant*. Plato speaks the 'Stretch Out And Wait' lines about the world ending in *Rebel* and Morrissey commemorated the film's tragic ending by being photographed at the crime scene, the Griffith Observatory in the mid–Nineties. Mineo once said of James Dean, "We were never lovers, but we could have . . . like that." Also claimed Dean had kick-started the whole youth movement. In the late Sixties Mineo courted controversy by producing and directing John Herbert's play *Fortune And Men's Eyes*, about a young man's experiences of homosexuality and sexual slavery in an American prison. Mineo was stabbed to death aged 37 in February 1976. In *Exit Smiling*, Morrissey writes. "His death was described as a 'homosexual murder', which doesn't make sense. His closest friends were underworld Mafia-types. He died penniless."

Moors Murderers (Ian Brady & Myra Hindley) – their hideous crimes were lyrically addressed by Morrissey on The Smiths' controversial but sensitive early track 'Suffer Little Children'. The track echoes Hindley's confession, "Whatever Ian has done, I have done." Speaking of his reasons for writing the song, Morrissey explained: "I happened to live on the streets where, close by, some of the victims had been picked up. Within that community, news of the crimes totally dominated all attempts at conversation for quite a few years. It was like the worst thing that had ever happened, and I was very, very aware of everything that occurred. Aware as a child who could have been a victim. You see it was all so ungraspably evil. I remember it at times like I was living in a soap opera."

Morrissey, Paul – (see Warhol, Andy) Morrissey's namesake played a crucial role in Sixties and Seventies films made by the Warhol Factory, directing *Chelsea Girls*, *Flesh*, *Trash*, *Heat*, *Lonesome Cowboys* and *Women In Revolt* (starring various Smiths' cover stars such as Joe Dallesandro and Candy Darling). Paul Morrissey also made the strange 1983 film *Beethoven's Nephew*, probable source of the title of Steven Patrick Morrissey's 1993 live album *Beethoven Was Deaf* and even directed Kenneth Williams in the Peter Cook/Dudley Moore movie vehicle *The Hound Of The Baskervilles* in 1978 from the novel written, of course, by Oscar Wilde's friend Sir Arthur Conan Doyle. (Paul Morrissey's *Trash* also inspired The New York Dolls' 1973 track.)

Moss, Jennifer – another Morrissey TV favourite, she played wayward Lucille Hewitt in *Coronation Street* from the early episodes in 1960 through to 1974. Moss left the street after almost 1,000 episodes due to alcoholism brought on by the death of her father and her estrangement from her mother. Her personal life was distinctly tragic, involving four marriages, two daughters (one disabled, both taken into care) and an infant son who died. Later in life she faced court appearances for breaking and entering and shoplifting (*The Guardian*, Obituary, October 2006). Early in her career Moss recorded a single produced by Joe Meek called 'Hobbies'

(1963) and also took a break from *Coronation Street* to appear in *Live It Up* (with David Hemmings) miming a Meek composition titled 'Please Let It Happen To Me'.

Bill Naughton – Irish-born, Lancashire-raised, he wrote the short story *Late Night On Watling Street*, an inspiration for Morrissey's 1988 reflection on his Seventies childhood 'Late Night, Maudlin Street'. Naughton also penned the screenplays *Alfie, The Family Way* and the 1970 "kitchen sink drama"-style film *Spring And Port Wine* (starring James Mason as the tough patriarch of Bolton family the Cromptons).

New York Dolls – "the most perfect pop group," in Morrissey's biased opinion. Led by guitarists Sylvain Sylvain and Johnny Thunders and fronted by David Johansen, with Billy Murcia (drums) and Arthur Kane (bass), the Dolls were a major influence on the teenage Morrissey, who soon became UK President of their fan club and documented their story in a 1981 fanzine-style book. The opening line read: "The New York Dolls were the first real sign that the Sixties were over. Their unmatched vulgarity dichotomised feelings of extravagant devotion and vile detestation." Very *Viva Hate*. Also from Morrissey's biography of the Dolls, published by Babylon Books: "Theirs was a sinister sense of transvestism. 'High camp' for Roxy Music, 'poovery' for Marc Bolan, and even less for 'lovable norms' Slade and Sweet – such terms would never be accurate if aimed at The Dolls. The Dolls were just a little *too* real." The New York Dolls' early advertising slogan was "Too fast to live, too young to die . . . Let It Rock!" Famously played a residency in New York at Mercer Arts Center's Oscar Wilde Rooms every Tuesday between June and October 1972 before visiting the UK for the first time. (With The Pink Fairies, they supported The Faces at Wembley's Empire Pool on October 29.) Morrissey had tickets for their Manchester Hard Rock gig on November 9 but drummer Billy Murcia died in London on November 7 and the tour was cancelled. (Morrissey still has the unclipped ticket.) Murcia was replaced by Jerry Nolan (who'd played with Wayne County's Queen Elizabeth). Reviewing the punk pioneers 1973 debut album for *NME*, Nick Kent wrote: "Listen to 'Bad Girl', 'Jet Boy' and 'Frankenstein' and you're hearing musical street fights, a bastardised brand of hell-cat cacophony teetering on pure anarchy . . ." Morrissey favourites Mott The Hoople often supported the Dolls' in the States. Heroine-addicts Thunders and Nolan died relatively young in the early Nineties, having quit the Dolls to form The Heartbreakers. Morrissey covered 'Trash' on *Live In Dallas* from his 1991 tour and 'Human Being' on his 'You Have Killed Me' CD single (2006). (He once said that 'November Spawned A Monster' was "my version of the New York Dolls' 'Frankenstein'.") They're also celebrated on his *Under The Influence* compilation. After a phone call from Morrissey to David Johansen, the surviving Dolls reformed for the first time in almost 30 years for the Meltdown Festival on June 16, 2004, then supported Morrissey on tour. Morrissey also appeared in *New York Doll*, Greg Whiteley's documentary portrait of alcoholic-turned-Mormon-turned-librarian Arthur Kane, just prior to the bassist's sudden death from leukemia, aged 55.

Newley, Anthony – another Morrissey favourite, Newley's voice as the Artful Dodger (taken from David Lean's 1948 *Oliver Twist*) is sampled at the end of 'Billy Budd' on *Vauxhall & I*. And there's more Newley, this time from *The Cockleshell Heroes* (1955) – Patric Doonan's last film before his suicide – uttering the line "On this glorious occasion of the splendid defeat" on *Maladjusted*. Anthony Newley was a friend and lover of Diana Dors; they were both in *Oliver Twist, Vote For Hugget* and *A Boy A Girl And A Bike*. Obscure film work includes *How To Murder A Rich Uncle* (1957) and the X-rated film *Hieronymus Merkin*. Morrissey also valued his cult 1960 TV series *The Strange World Of Gurney Slade* and his musicals, co-written with Leslie Bricusse, such as *Stop The World I Want To Get Off* and *The Roar Of The Greasepaint – The Smell Of The Crowd*. Morrissey's also a great admirer of Newley's crooning career and 'Piccadilly Palare' and 'All You Need Is Me' may have been inspired by Newley's 'Piccadilly Lily' and 'I'm All I Need'. In May 1998, Anthony Newley presented Morrissey with an Ivor Novello award for his Outstanding Contribution To British Music.

Nicholson, Vivian – Northern girl made good thanks to a 1961 football pools windfall. Rags-to-riches-back-to-rags story was dramatised by Jack Rosenthal in 1977's *Spend Spend Spend*. She also recorded a single called 'Spend Spend Spend' and later, when the money had gone, she became a stripper and a Jehovah's Witness. Featured on the covers of The Smiths' 'Heaven Knows I'm Miserable Now' and 'Barbarism Begins At Home' and also appeared with Morrissey on the October 1987 *South Bank Show*. (The opening words to *Spend, Spend, Spend* – voiced by Nicholson herself

– succinctly defined her relationship with her father: "Where we lived, all the fellers were coal-miners. Except me Dad – he was a full-time, fully-paid-up, fully-fledged bastard." More significant for Smiths' scholars, her autobiography contains the sentence: "We walked for miles . . . over the iron bridge and down underneath on the towpath. We were kissing away and touching and getting really sore lips.")

Nico – real name Christa Paffgen, 'Nico' was the model, actress, 'Warhol Superstar' and singer has been described as the German Marilyn Monroe. Her music was celebrated by Morrissey on his *Under The Influence* compilation ('All That Is My Own'); he's clearly a fan of *Chelsea Girls*, *The End*, her seminal LP *The Marble Index* (with John Cale) and also her solo album *Camera Obscura* from 1985 (Morrissey's 'Now My Heart Is Full' from *Vauxhall & I* could well be a response to Nico's 'My Heart Is Empty'.) Aside from her many Andy Warhol/Factory/Velvet Underground connections – she worked with Warhol and Paul Morrissey on *Chelsea Girls*, *The Closet*, *Sunset* and *Imitation Of Christ* – and her close relationships with Lou Reed and Cale, it's worth noting she also appeared in Fellini's *La Dolce Vita* (1960) and 1963's *Strip-Tease* (aka *Sweet Skin*) with Serge Gainsbourg (who wrote and produced her title track). Apart from the fact that she had a son with Smiths' cover star Alain Delon – he denied he was the father – and recorded her first single 'I'm Not Sayin'' for Immediate Records (B-side 'The Last Mile'), Bob Dylan also gave her his early classic 'I'll Keep It With Mine' in early 1965. Nico's one of the artists regularly featured in the warm-up music before Morrissey concerts. In the Eighties, Nico lived in Salford, Greater Manchester and became close to the Mancunian punk poet John Cooper-Clarke. Having kicked a heroin habit, she died tragically of head injuries following a bicycle accident in Ibiza in 1988.

Nomi, Klaus – operatic-sounding German singer and experimental artist, his 'Death' appears on *Under The Influence* and tracks such 'Wayward Sisters' and 'After The Fall' have been used in Morrissey's pre-show music. Nomi moved to New York in the early Seventies, worked with Bowie and became part of the Warhol scene. He died of an AIDS-related illness in 1983. Of 'Death' Morrissey said, "An incredible voice, particularly on this track. The poignancy is overwhelming: 'Remember me, forget my fate.'"

Novello, Ivor – Romantic renaissance man: actor, playwright, song-writer and composer of musical comedies, Novello dominated the English stage in the Twenties, Thirties and Forties, rivalled only by Noel Coward. Wrote 'Keep The Home Fires Burning', acted in Hitchcock films such as *The Vortex, Downhill* and *The Lodger: A Story Of The London Fog*, co-wrote the Hollywood screenplays *Mata Hari* and *Tarzan The Ape Man*, plus scores of hit British musicals including as *Gay's The Word* (written for, and played by, Cecily Courtneidge). Openly homosexual, Novello was imprisoned by a homophobic judge during World War Two – on a charge of evading gasoline restrictions – and died in 1951 aged 58. In *The Lodger* (1927), Hitchcock's first film, Novello played a serial killer based on Jack The Ripper.

Orton, Joe – Leicester-born playwright who shook the British establishment in the Sixties with his satirical, sexually charged black comedies and his unconventional private life. Considered (but never used) as a Smiths' cover star by Morrissey, his early play *The Boy Hairdresser* could have inspired the solo track 'Hairdresser On Fire'. With his boyfriend Kenneth Halliwell, Joe Orton first achieved notoriety when he was prosecuted in 1962 for defacing a copy of Betjeman's poems and other library books. They were both gaoled for six months. After the success of *Entertaining Mr Sloane* and *Loot*, Orton followed up with *Crimes Of Passion, Funeral Games, The Seven Deadly Sins* (an attack on Christian charity) and *Up Against It*, a screenplay for The Beatles which was rejected by manager Brian Epstein as being 'unsuitable for his boys'. Orton became a close friend of the actor Kenneth Williams, who documents the playwright's colourful, promiscuous but tragic life with Halliwell in his diaries. *What The Butler Saw* was performed following Orton's death in August '67; he was bludgeoned to death by the jealous Halliwell who then took a fatal overdose. (The incident may well have inspired the "fame fatal fame" lines in 'Frankly Mr Shankly'.) The screenplay for the 1987 bio-pic *Prick Up Your Ears*, based on John Lahr's biography of Orton, was written by Alan Bennett. (Originally an Orton title, "ears" is, of course, an anagram.)

Palance, Jack – Palance (*Shane, Requiem For A Heavyweight*) starred in the 1953 Jack The Ripper-based *Man In The Attic* and in *The Silver Chalice* with Pier Angeli. Palance appeared in a film called *Panic In The Streets* (inspiring the opening lyrics of 'Panic'), plus worked with Diana Dors on *Craze*, and with Brigitte Bardot on Godard's *Contempt*. It may be significant, in terms of Morrissey's 21st century label, that he also starred in Robert Aldrich's *Attack*. Palance died in 2006.

Pasolini, Pier Paolo – politically radical, sexually unconventional Italian writer and film director celebrated in Morrissey's 2006 single 'You Have Killed Me' and used as a backdrop to the *Ringleader Of The Tormentors* tour (probably an image taken during the filming of Pasolini's celebrated *The Gospel Of St Matthew*). One of the reasons why Morrissey has re–located to Rome in the 21st century could be connected with his affection for Pasolini's amoral/amorous, sexually charged works including *Accatone*, *La Dolce Vita* (he contributed to the screenplay) and *Porcile* (Pigsty). There's also a famous photograph of Patti Smith, taken by Robert Mapplethorpe, in which the words "Pasolini est vie" are graffiti'd on the wall behind her. Controversial works as a director include versions of *120 Days Of Sodom*, *Decameron*, *Arabian Nights* and *The Canterbury Tales*. As a writer he was responsible for *La Giornata Balorda* (aka *Pick-up In Rome*) and the tragic Sophia Loren film *La Donna Del Fiume, Woman Of The River*: perhaps an inspiration, along with Virginia Woolf's suicide, for Morrissey's 2008 previewed track 'Mama Lay Softly On The River Bed'. Anna Magnani, also mentioned in Morrissey's 'You Have Killed Me', starred in Pasolini's 1962 film *Mama Roma*, and Terence Stamp played the bisexual character The Visitor in his 1968 film *Teorema*. (NB. In *Accatone*, Pasolini's artistic attack on heterosexual men who exploit women, the lead character Vittorio Cataldi declares, "Either the world kills me or I kill it".)

Pat Phoenix – Manchester-born, but of Irish stock, much-loved by Morrissey and once branded "the working man's Raquel Welch", Phoenix played *Coronation Street*'s formidable, unforgettable female lead Elsie Tanner for almost 25 years. Prime Minister James Callaghan famously described her as "the sexiest thing on television". She also worked with Joan Littlewood, first appeared as an uncredited prostitute in *Jack The Ripper* (1959) and then starred in 1962's *The L-Shaped Room* – tagline: "Sex is not a forbidden word!" – with Cicely Courtneidge, Anthony Booth, Emlyn Williams and Tom Bell. Cover star of The Smiths' 'Shakespeare's Sister', she was interviewed by Morrissey for *Blitz* magazine in 1985, where she celebrated female passion in the form of Anna Magnani. Born Patricia Pilkington, she was a huge fan of James Dean and even worked under the name Patricia Dean early in her acting career. A week before her death from lung cancer, she married her third

277

husband and old friend the actor Anthony Booth. Morrissey attended Phoenix's funeral in September 1986.

Presley, Elvis – Cover star of The Smiths' 'Shoplifters Of The World Unite', Presley's image was also used as a backdrop on the 1992 tour and appeared on the prison walls in the 'Last Of The Famous International Playboys' video. Live (as on *Rank*) The Smiths' 'Rusholme Ruffians' often started with a version of Presley's '(Marie's The Name) His Latest Flame'. (The Smiths also covered Elvis' 'A Fool Such As I' but it was never released.) Morrissey's first solo single after his 1996 court defeat, 'Alma Matters', may also be a Presley reference; *"Dear Alma Mater"* is a line from Elvis' *King Creole* track 'Steadfast Loyal & True' and seems to be Morrissey's response to Judge Weeks' damning verdict that he was "devious, truculent and unreliable". Presley, like Morrissey, was a huge fan of James Dean. The stage for Morrissey's early 21st century performances was lit in the red-neon style of Elvis' *1968 Comeback Special*. ('Shoplifters . . .' cover star Elvis had performed the track 'Shoppin' Around' in his 1960 film *GI Blues*.)

Ray, Johnnie – The Nabob of Sob, The Prince of Wails . . . epithets that have been applied to Morrissey during his career but were invented for influential Fifties crooner-on-the-cusp-of-rock & roll – the writhing, theatrical "Cry Guy", Johnnie Ray. In his early years with The Smiths, Morrissey wore a hearing aid in tribute to the aurally challenged Ray, who'd suffered from deafness since a Boy Scout accident as a teenager. Ray's most famous songs were 'The Little White Cloud That Cried' and 'Cry', which coupled with the fact that he wept onstage, may have inspired Morrissey's *Maladjusted* track 'He Cried' (1997). Johnnie Ray's career was cut-short by intense speculation, in American tabloids such as *Confidential* and *Hush-Hush*, about his true sexuality. His intimations of bisexuality weren't helped by the 1954 divorce from his wife Marilyn Morrison; she claimed she'd been aware of Ray's unconventional sexuality before they married but believed she could "straighten it out". Ray was arrested for indecency in 1959 and, although he was acquitted, his career was effectively over by the early Sixties. Memorable Ray moments include 'I Want To Be Loved', 'Song Of The Dreamer', 'You Don't Owe Me A Thing', 'A Sinner Am I' and '(Here I Am) Brokenhearted'. There are also shades of Morrissey in some of Ray's self-deprecating responses to questions about his audience appeal: "People come to see what I'm like. I make them feel . . . I exhaust them . . . I destroy them." He died of liver failure in 1990.

Reed, Lou – his 1972 album *Transformer* (produced by David Bowie and Mick Ronson) had a huge impact on the teenage Morrissey, particularly the single 'Walk On The Wild Side' (which namechecks future Smiths' cover stars Joe Dallesandro and Candy Darling). A member of The Velvet Underground, a close associate of Andy Warhol, Nico and Paul Morrissey, Lou Reed is one of the few 20th century lyricists who (like Morrissey) has extended the subject matter of popular music. Topics tackled in his songs include depression, suicide ('The Bed' on *Berlin*, a forebear of The Smiths' 'Asleep'), homosexuality, prostitution and child welfare ('The Kids', which perhaps inspired Morrissey's 'The Slum Mums'), domestic violence, drug addiction ('I'm Waiting For The Man', 'Heroin') and, of course, sexual deviancy and transexuality. As a teenager, Reed received ECT (electro-convulsive therapy) to curb his homosexual tendencies, a mentally scarring treatment he wrote about on his 1974 song 'Kill Your Sons'. (Significantly, one of the first singles released on the Attack label, by Morrissey protégé Kristeen Young, was titled 'Kill The Father'. Morrissey himself followed this with 2006's 'The Father Who Must Be Killed'.)

Reisz, Karel – "New Wave" Czech-born director, exiled in Britain, who led the influential Free Cinema documentary movement in the Fifties (included Tony Richardson, who Reisz worked with on the jazz film *Momma Don't Allow*). Made *We Are The Lambeth Boys* (1958) – source of samples for 1994's 'Spring-Heeled Jim' – and produced *This Sporting Life* (directed by Lindsay Anderson), but more famously in terms of Morrissey connections, he directed both *Night Must Fall*, an Emlyn Williams' screenplay which starred Albert Finney as a sex-mad working class psychopath and, of course, *Saturday Night And Sunday Morning* (1960), with Finney, Rachel Roberts and Hylda Baker.

Richardson, Charles – photographed on the inner sleeve of *Your Arsenal* (1992), at a point in Morrissey's career when he'd hooked up with his young rockabilly band and was relishing being part of a gang again. Richardson was the leader of the notorious South London gang, which included Mad Frankie Frazer, and feuded with the Krays. Infamous for bribing the police, torturing victims and investing in "long firms" (fraudulent companies), one of the Richardson Gang's most violent clashes with the Krays took place in March 1966 at a nightclub called Mr Smiths in Catford – owned by two Manchester-based businessmen Dougie Flood and Bill Benny – and eventually led to the murder of Richardson Gang member George Cornell by Ronnie Kray. (Cornell had called Ronnie a "fat poof".) Charlie Richardson was arrested on World Cup Final day in 1966 and sentenced to 25 years in prison. He was released in July 1984. Richardson's image also acted as a backdrop to Morrissey's 1992 tour, along with Krays' associate Diana Dors. (Rumour has it that Morrissey turned down the chance to play Richardson in a biographical British gangster movie. If this was *Charlie* [2004] then the lead role eventually was taken by Luke Goss of Bros!)

Richardson, Tony – Yorkshire-born "New Wave" director who wrote the screenplay to *A Taste Of Honey* with Shelagh Delaney and produced and directed the film. Also directed *The Loneliness Of The Long Distance Runner, Tom Jones* and *The Entertainer*, and was the producer of *Saturday Night And Sunday Morning* and the controversial 1960 television drama, *A Subject Of Scandal And Concern*, written by John Osborne. It starred Richard Burton as the atheist George Holyoake, the last man to be imprisoned for blasphemy in Victorian England, with Rachel Roberts as his wife. (Holyoake House in Manchester is named after him.) Richardson also Executive Produced *The Girl With Green Eyes*, starring Peter Finch and Rita Tushingham. Tony Richardson died in 1991.

Riley, Harold – photographer and friend of famous Salford painter L. S. Lowry, Riley's portraits of Inner City Manchester in the late Fifties/early Sixties document the landscape of Morrissey's childhood, particularly Weaste "Cemetery Gates", a series called "Strangeways" and other images of Pendleton, Hanky Park, Seedley, Chimney Pot Park, the real Coronation Street and Brindle Heath. Other documentary photographers admired by Morrissey include Sefton Samuels (famous images include George Best, Lowry and Pat Phoenix plus photographs entitled Boy Meets Girl, the pugilists of Smack and Fun Fair) and Roger Mayne, whose portrait Girl Jiving graced the cover of Morrissey & Siouxsie's 'Interlude'.

Roberts, Rachel – Welsh actress, memorably starred in Sixties 'kitchen sink' classics directed by Lindsay Anderson *This Sporting Life* (with Richard Harris) and Karel Reisz' *Saturday Night And Sunday Morning*, opposite Albert Finney. Also played a key role in the women's prison drama

The Weak And The Wicked alongside Diana Dors (directed by J. Lee Thompson). Later appeared in *Picnic At Hanging Rock* and, on television, in Alan Bennett's *The Old Crowd*. *No Bells On Sunday: The Rachel Roberts Journals* were published after her suicide in California in November 1980.

Ronson, Mick – Co-producer of Lou Reed's *Transformer* (he arranged 'Walk On The Wild Side' and played piano on 'Perfect Day') and David Bowie's right hand man/lead guitarist in the Spiders From Mars. Made his debut with Bowie and bassist Tony Visconti in The Hype at the Roundhouse in Camden Town, 1970. A key figure in the British Glam scene, the Hull-born guitarist became a close friend and musical ally of Mott The Hoople's Ian Hunter and had solo success with his *Slaughter On 10th Avenue* album in 1974. Curiously, in view of his glam CV, he played in the band that backed Bob Dylan on his Rolling Thunder Review in 1975/6. Mick Ronson produced Morrissey's 1992 glam–meets-rockabilly album *Your Arsenal*. He died of liver cancer aged 46 in 1993.

Sainte-Marie, Buffy – Cree Indian-born folk singer who campaigned for the cause of Native Americans in songs such as 'Universal Soldier', 'My Country Tis Of Thy People You're Dying' and 'Now That The Buffalo's Gone'. Morrissey was a teenage fan and her 'Better To Find Out For Yourself' seems to have sparked his *Vauxhall & I* track 'Why Don't You Find Out For Yourself'. Also, his *Your Arsenal* song 'You're Gonna Need Someone On Your Side' may have been inspired by Buffy's 1964 album track 'You're Gonna Need Somebody On Your Bond' (from *It's My Way*). Her 1969 album features a track called 'Suffer The Little Children' and, interestingly, 'Guess Who I Saw In Paris'. In late March 2008 Morrissey announced he'd appear at a Montreal celebration of Sainte-Marie's 50th year making music, stating "I first bought a Buffy Sainte-Marie record when I was 12, and her music has always remained with me. In the 1960s, as a political activist, Buffy's lyrics were fearless, and I'm very grateful for all the risks that she took."

Schlesinger, John – Morrissey's LA house had previously been occupied by Schlesinger and his life-partner Michael Childrers (before that it had been owned by Carole Lombard). British-born Schlesinger directed many of Morrissey's favourite Sixties films including *Billy Liar*, *A Kind Of Loving*, *Darling* (with Dirk Bogarde, Laurence Harvey and Julie Christie) and *Far From The Madding Crowd*, starring Terence Stamp, Christie and Alan Bates. He also directed the Alan Bennett screenplays *An Englishman Abroad* (1983, with Alan Bates) and *A Question Of Attribution* (1992, starring Edward Fox) about the gay Soviet spies Guy Burgess and Sir Anthony Blunt respectively. Apart from its relatively daring subject matter, about a young woman who uses sex to get where she wants, *Darling* also featured Roland Curram as the openly, happily gay photographer Malcolm. In Schlesinger's *Sunday Bloody Sunday* (1971) Smiths' cover star Murray Head plays the bisexual bed-hopper Bob Elkin. Alan Bates was set to play the homosexual doctor Daniel Hirsch but the role went to Peter Finch instead when Bates' work on *The Go Between* over-ran. Late Schlesinger successes included *Midnight Cowboy, The Day Of The Locust* and *Marathon Man*. He died, following a stroke, in 2000.

Selby Jnr, Hubert – American author of a volume of thematic short stories called *Last Exit To Brooklyn*, source of The Smiths' album title *The Queen Is Dead* (named after one of the collection). Morrissey planned that the album's release should come exactly 20 years after the book was banned under the Obscene Publications Act in 1966. Justice Rigers decreed that women should be protected from reading about "homosexuality, prostitution, drug-taking and sexual perversion" and *Last Exit To Brooklyn* remained banned in Britain until 1968.

Sex Pistols – managed by Malcolm McLaren, who'd been involved with The New York Dolls. Morrissey attended the famous Pistols' concert at Manchester's Lesser Free Trade Hall in June 1976. Like Morrissey, although somewhat less sensitively, the Pistols (with Great Train Robber Ronnie Biggs on vocals) tackled the subject of the Moors Murders on their 1978 single 'No One Is Innocent': *"God save Myra Hindley, god save Ian Brady, even though he's horrible and she ain't what you'd call a lady"*.

Shaw, Sandie – barefoot Dagenham diva, former Ford worker Sandra Goodrich, was transformed into a teenage star with Bacharach & David's '(There's) Always Something There To Remind Me' in 1964. Possibly the most important of the Brit Girl singers, thanks to the youthful, vulnerable nature of songs written by Chris Andrews. Favourite pin-up of the youthful Morrissey who wrote to her in August 1983: "The Sandie Shaw legend cannot be over yet – there is more to be done." The Smiths' 'Heaven Knows I'm Miserable Now' was a comical steal from the title of her 1969 single 'Heaven Knows I'm Missing Him Now' plus Morrissey's solo album *Viva Hate* seemed an alternative take on Sandie's 'Long Live Love'. Morrissey and the singer became friends in the Eighties and Shaw's 1984 version of 'Hand In Glove' reached number 27 in the UK charts. He also, memorably, duetted with her on 'Jeanne' and on an unreleased version of her 1964 hit 'Girl Don't Come'. Later Shaw paid tribute to Morrissey with 'Steven (You Don't Eat Meat)' and covered The Smiths' 'I Don't Owe You Anything'. A committed Buddhist and vegetarian, further Sandie tracks that have informed Morrissey's work include 'I'd Be Far Better Off Without You', 'Tomorrow' , 'London' and 'Hide All Emotion' (1966). Albums such as *Love Me, Please Love Me* (1967) and the EPs *Run With Sandie* and *Sandie Shaw In Italian* have also been influential. A Pye Records star, she's often remembered for her 1967 *Eurovision Song Contest* victory with 'Puppet On A String' of which she once said: "It is a song which has been the source of much grief, hilarity, circumspection and, I have to admit it, financial reward for many years." Morrissey and Shaw later fell out but she remains, in my opinion as the producer of Channel 4's 1997 series *The Brit Girls*, a great woman.

Sims, Joan – first lady of *Carry On*, aka Queen Of Puddings and star of Morrissey's 1989 'Ouija Board, Ouija Board' video (she'd attended 'real-life' séances with Charles Hawtrey and his mother). Sims started out in films such as *The Square Ring* (a 1953 boxing drama), *The Belles Of St Trinian's* (1954), *Doctor At Sea* (with Dirk Bogarde and Brigitte Bardot), *The Sea Shall Not Have Them* (again with Bogarde), *Passport To Shame* (with Diana Dors), before boarding the *Carry On* bandwagon for 24 films between 1959 and 1978. Also appeared as Gran in *Til Death Us Do Part, Love Among The Ruins* (1975) with Katherine Hepburn and Laurence Olivier, *Not Now Darling* (also featuring Cicely Courtneidge), *A Pair Of Briefs* (with Amanda Barrie) and *Please Turn Over* (with Hawtrey). She's rumoured to have turned down a marriage proposal from Kenneth Williams, although stated in her autobiography *High Spirits*, "I don't think I've ever had anybody say 'Will you marry me?' Not even someone tight as a tick at a party." She died in 2001 aged 71.

Sinatra, Nancy – daughter of Frank, neighbour of Morrissey's during the Los Angeles years and featured in Channel 4's 2003 documentary *The Importance Of Being Morrissey*. Her 1966 B-side 'The Last Of The Secret Agents' (from the *James Bond*-based comedy film of the same name) inspired his 'The Last Of The Famous International Playboys' single, Nancy covered Morrissey's 'Let Me Kiss You' and appeared at London's Royal Festival Hall as part of Morrissey's Meltdown Festival in 2004. She also appeared in the controversial 1966 Hells Angels film *The Wild Angels* (pre-*Easy Rider*, starring Peter Fonda as biker leader "Heavenly Blues" and with Bruce Dern as "The Loser") and the 1968 Elvis Presley film *Speedway*, inspiration for Morrissey's *Vauxhall & I* track of the same name. Her 1976 Private Stock single 'Kinky Love' was banned by American radio.

Sitwell, Edith – Scarborough-born, posh English poet whose portrait by Cecil Beaton – taken from the cover of the Penguin edition of her weirdly brilliant observational book *English Eccentrics* (1933) – was used by Morrissey on his *Kill Uncle* tour. Friend of Lord Alfred Douglas in his post-Wilde days and author of *The Outcasts* (1962), she once declared "I am in mourning for the world."

Smart, Elizabeth – Canadian poet whose 1945 masterpiece, *By Grand Central Station I Sat Down And Wept*, provided inspiration and lines for Morrissey's Smiths' lyrics such as 'Reel Around The Fountain', 'Shakespeare's Sister' and 'London'. Also the album title *Louder Than Bombs* comes from Smart's "louder than bombs or screams or the inside ticking of remorse". Died 1986 and buried in South Elmham, Suffolk, her grave's marked "Non Omnis Moriar" ("Not all of me shall die"). A 1991 documentary about her life was titled *On The Side Of The Angels*.

Smith, Patti – primary source of The Smiths' name. Performance poet, feminist, painter, political activist and punk pioneer, she is a crucial figure in the history of Morrissey and The Smiths. Her 1975 album *Horses*, produced by John Cale of The Velvet Underground, had a huge impact on both Morrissey and Johnny Marr. Marr later recalled seeing Morrissey earlier at a Patti Smith concert. When Steven Morrissey began advertising in the music press for like-minded spirits to form a band he stipulated applicants should be "Patti Smith/New York Dolls" fans. There were even shades of "Hang The DJ" in an early 1976 Morrissey letter to *NME* when he attacked the paper for ignoring Manchester's Buzzcocks, concluding that "in these dark days when Patti Smith, Loudon Wainwright or even The New York Dolls fail to make any impact on Radio One DJs, common sense is therefore not so common." After a strict religious childhood in New Jersey, Patti Smith moved to New York in 1967, became close friends with controversial photographer Robert Mapplethorpe (they lived together in the Chelsea Hotel and Mapplethorpe became a staff photographer on Andy Warhol's *Interview* magazine), spent time as a performance artist in Paris, and appeared with Wayne County (aka Jayne County) in Warhol "Superstar" Jackie Curtis' 1969 play *Femme Fatale* and Tony Ingrassia's *Island*. (A friend of Bowie's, Ingrassia contributed to *Ziggy Stardust* and also directed Warhol's *Pork* in 1971.) From 1975 onwards, the Patti Smith Group's art-punk tracks such as 'Hey Joe'/'Piss Factory', 'Because The Night', 'Frederick', 'Gloria' and 'Land Of 1000 Dances' had a growing impact on the teenage Morrissey, especially 'Rock N Roll Nigger' which celebrated being "outside of society". The Smiths' 'The Hand That Rocks The Cradle' (1984) was clearly influenced by 'Kimberley' on *Horses* while, as a solo artist in 2005, Morrissey released a cover of Patti Smith's song about suicide 'Redondo Beach' in the States. Patti's religiously hostile tracks 'Easter' and 'Privilege (Set Me Free)' (1978) could almost have been written by Morrissey a decade later and his 2004 track, 'I Have Forgiven Jesus' (from *You Are The Quarry*) seems to be a response to Smith's opening lines on her famous cover of Van Morrison's 'Gloria': "Jesus died for somebody's sins, but not mine . . ." Further connections include the fact that another track by The Smiths, 'Is It Really So Strange', was inspired by 'Ain't It Strange' from *Radio Ethiopia*, and Sandie Shaw, encouraged by Morrissey and Marr, covered Patti Smith's 'Frederick' in 1986. More recently, Morrissey's passion for Pasolini on 'You Have Killed Me' echoed the fact that Patti's *Easter* was inspired by the Italian director's controversial 1964 film *The Gospel According To St Matthew* (at the time, many critics challenged Pasolini's right to make the film on the grounds that he was a Marxist, a homosexual and an atheist). Billed as "punk rock's poet laureate" – following a late 20th century comeback encouraged by fan and friend Michael Stipe – in 2005 Patti Smith succeeded Morrissey as the curator of the London Meltdown Festival. Her chosen artists included Johnny Marr's band and The Healers.

Smith, Stevie – Hull-born poet and novelist, who often artistically contemplated death, depression and suicide. Her most famous poem *Not Waving But Drowning* clearly inspired Morrissey's 'Lifeguard Sleeping Girl Drowning'. Other verses, such as *Deeply Morbid, My Heart Was Full, I Forgive You* and *November* may also have been influential. Her novels include *The Holiday* and *Novel On Yellow Paper* (aka *Work It Out For*

Yourself) and she also published a sketchbook titled *Some Are More Human Than Others*.

Sparks – the teenage Morrissey embraced the Tony Visconti-produced Sparks and later poetically wrote, in his 2003 sleeve notes for *Under The Influence*, that Ron Mael's "lyrical take on sex cries out like prison cell carvings". In their early days, like the New York Dolls, the Mael brothers were also produced by Todd Rundgren. The title of Morrissey's 2006 track 'In The Future When All's Well' was probably inspired by Sparks' 'In The Future' (from *Indiscreet*.)

Springfield, Dusty – Dusty's track 'Sunny', from her 1967 album *Where Am I Going?*, probably inspired Morrissey's 1995 single 'Sunny', while his *Viva Hate* track 'I Don't Mind If You Forget Me' might have been a response to Dusty's 'Don't Forget About Me'. A Roman Catholic, like Morrissey, Mary Isabel Catherine Bernadette O'Brien was one of the greatest female vocalists of the 20th century. A supporter of animal rights, she was also bravely open (for the time) about her sexuality: "I know I'm perfectly as capable of being swayed by a girl as by a boy," she told London's *Evening Standard* in 1970. She went even further in the *Los Angeles Free Press* in 1973: "People say I'm gay, gay, gay, gay, gay, gay, gay, gay . . . I'm not anything . . . People are people . . . I go from men to women, I don't give a shit. The catchphrase is: I can't love a man. Now, that's my hang up. To love, to go to bed, fantastic, but to love a man is my prime ambition . . . They frighten me."

Stamp, Terence – cover star of 'What Difference Does It Make?' (although he initially objected to The Smiths' use of his still from *The Collector*, resulting in Morrissey's enforced appearance on the seven-inch as a grinning 'lookalike'), East End-born Stamp was one of the great British male pin-ups of the Sixties and dated iconic figures such as Julie Christie, Jean Shrimpton and Brigitte Bardot. Morrissey celebrated his performances in a series of films from *Term Of Trial* in 1962 through to Pasolini's *Teorema* in 1968. (Morrissey had also tried but failed to use a still of Stamp with Laurence Olivier from *Term Of Trial* on the cover of The Smiths' 'The Headmaster Ritual' single.) In *Billy Budd* (1963), which inspired Morrissey's track on *Vauxhall & I*, Stamp played the angelic sailor who was victimised by a sadistic master-at-arms (Robert Ryan). Lines from the film version of John Fowles' *The Collector* (1965) – starring Stamp as butterfly collector

Freddie Clegg – appeared in The Smiths' 'Reel Around The Fountain' and Stamp also appeared, alongside another Morrissey favourite Dirk Bogarde, in 1966's secret agent romp *Modesty Blaise*. His two, very different, 1967 films, *Far From The Madding Crowd* (directed by John Schlesinger) and *Poor Cow* (directed by Ken Loach) – about a single mum attracted to criminals – confirmed Stamp's versatility and film star status. In Pasolini's *Teorema* he plays a bisexual seducer who infiltrates a wealthy family. More recently, he played a transsexual in *The Adventures Of Priscilla, Queen Of The Desert* and the gangster Wilson in *The Limey* (using scenes from *Poor Cow* to illustrate Wilson's past). In the early Nineties, Morrissey sometimes went under the anonym Terrace Stomp.

Sterling, Linder – close friend and, briefly, former flatmate of Morrissey during the Seventies. Punk Renaissance woman and the leader of art-pop/agit-prop act Ludus. Vegetarian and radical feminist behind *The Secret Public** fanzine, ex-partner of Mancunian punk protagonist Howard Devoto and visual artist responsible for the striking cover of the Buzzcocks' 'Orgasm Addict' and Magazine's *Real Life*. An inspirational figure in Morrissey's development. He selected Ludus' 'Breaking The Rules' for his *Under The Influence* compilation stating that Linder "has an enormously sexual voice . . . I find these lyrics remarkable, suggesting that all forms of love are wonderful, whether it's three women together, four men together – why can it not be so?" Sterling has documented Morrissey's career as a photographer, notably on the covers of *Your Arsenal* and in the collection *Morrissey Shot*, sang backing vocals on 'Driving Your Girlfriend Home' and also contributed to both the 1987 *South Bank Show* and the 2003 documentary *The Importance Of Being Morrissey*. Ludus reformed to play *Morrissey's Meltdown* in 2004.

Tushingham, Rita – Liverpool-born character actress who played the vulnerable, teenage outsider in several of Morrissey's favourite Sixties films, notably *A Taste Of Honey* (see Delaney, Sheila) and *The Leather Boys* with Colin Campbell. She appeared as Cat opposite Mike Sarne in the

---

* In *Linder: Works 1976–2006*, *The Secret Public*'s co-founder Jon Savage recalled that the fanzine was published in 1978 during "the death rattle of first-wave Punk . . . *The Secret Public* attempted to dive further into the sea of possibility heralded by Patti Smith". Apart from Linder, Jon Savage and Howard Devoto, Richard Boon and the Buzzcocks, Rough Trade's Geoff Travis was also among those involved, five years before signing The Smiths.

Bethnal Green-based crime melodrama *A Place To Go* (1963) and starred with Peter Finch in the film version of Edna O'Brien's cross-generation love story *The Girl With Green Eyes*. Tushingham's unhappy, silent role as the wife in *The Trap* (1966, with Oliver Reed) could have inspired Morrissey's 'Mute Witness' on *Kill Uncle*. She also stars as Nancy, the Northern girl who gets off the train at Euston and heads for the YWCA, in the "Swinging London" sexual revolution comedy *The Knack . . . And How To Get It* (1965). Further memorable film performances included Merchant-Ivory's *The Guru* and Richard Lester's *The Bed Sitting Room* (both 1969). The latter – starring Tushingham alongside Peter Cook, Dudley Moore and Arthur Lowe – is a bizarre comedy about England, post-nuclear holocaust, in which patriotic survivors crown Mrs Ethel Shroake (Dandy Nicholls) as their Queen.

Twinkle – real name Lynn Ripley, the blonde teenager who briefly crashed to fame in 1964 with the death disc 'Terry' (banned by the BBC). The Smiths' covered her song 'Golden Lights' on the B-side of 'Ask'. Other influential Twinkle Sixties songs included 'Unhappy Boy', 'So Sad' and 'Poor Old Johnny'.

Visconti, Tony – producer of key Bowie and Bolan albums in the early Seventies. Also worked with Boz Boorer's rockabilly band The Polecats (who covered 'John, I'm Only Dancing' and 'Jeepster'). Morrissey tried to book Visconti to produce *Your Arsenal* (ahead of Ronson) but secured him for 2006's *Ringleader Of The Tormentors*.

Warhol, Andy – important American Pop Artist, controversial film-maker and "scene-creator", Warhol's Factory (essentially the diverse cast of characters who worked with him and director Paul Morrissey) had a huge impact on the New York music scene in the late Sixties and early Seventies – The Velvet Underground, Lou Reed, Nico, David Bowie, The New York Dolls, Patti Smith . . . – and, inevitably, on Steven Patrick Morrissey's own creative development. Candy Darling and Joe Dallesandro, who both appeared in Warhol/Morrissey films celebrating life in the gay underworld, became Smiths' cover stars. More obscure films, such as *Hedy The Shoplifter*, *Sleep*, the Wildean *Salome & Delilah* and *Suicide* (with Dennis Hopper) may also have influenced some of Morrissey's choice of subject matter; certainly Bowie's 'Andy Warhol' from *Hunky Dory* and Lou Reed's 'Andy's Chest' (about the attempt on the artist's life by Valerie

Solanas) on *Transformer* made an impact on him. The "fifteen minutes" line, from The Smiths' 'Reel Around The Fountain', is a reference to Warhol's famous quote about disposable celebrity. Also, Morrissey's decision to play the Roundhouse in early 2008 was partly inspired by the fact that Warhol's *Pork* was staged there in the early Seventies.

Waterhouse, Keith – wrote *Billy Liar*, probable source for 'Frankly Mr Shankly' (although Billy's "bloody awful poetry" writing funeral director boss is called Shadrack) and definite source for the title *Strangeways, Here We Come* (based on the throwaway delinquent line "Borstal here we come".) Waterhouse also wrote the screenplays for other important Northern films such as *Whistle Down The Wind* and *A Kind Of Loving* (both with Alan Bates) plus *West 11* (1963) and also the TV series *Queenie's Castle*, which both starred Diana Dors. In the latter, Dors played no-nonsense matriarch Queenie Shepherd, lover of light ale and matriarchal ruler of Buckingham Flats, a Leeds tower block.

Watts, Queenie – East End character actress and blues singer who appeared in Joan Littlewood's *Sparrers Can't Sing* (with Barbara Windsor, Yootha Joyce and the Krays), *Poor Cow* (with Terence Stamp and John Bindon), *Alfie*, *Up Pompeii*, *Dad's Army*, *The Best House In London* and *George And Mildred*. Her later work included appearances in the saucy comedies *Come Play With Me* (1977) with porn-star Mary Millington and *Confessions From The David Galaxy Affair* (1979), featuring Diana Dors and her husband Alan Lake, Anthony Booth and Millington again. The ATV variety series *Stars And Garters* (1963–66) – featuring Watts alongside Kathy Kirby, Vince Hill and Salford-born Clinton Ford, hosted by Ray Martine, Jill Browne and Willie Rushton – was filmed at her pub, The Ironbridge Tavern on Barking Road, East London.

White Edmund – considered influential in early interviews with Morrissey. Gay writer, famous for *A Boy's Own Story* and *The Beautiful Room Is Empty*, White has written extensively about the Paris of Wilde and Genet, and his 1998 work *The Last Symphony* (about the deaths of hedonists in the Seventies) could well have inspired Morrissey's fine 2004 track 'The Never Played Symphonies'.

Whitelaw, Billie – great English actress who also became a Smiths cover star on the re-released 'William, It Was Really Nothing'. The image is from *Charlie Bubbles*, a Manchester-based detective film starring and directed by Albert Finney. The screenplay was written by Shelagh Delaney, and the cast also included Yootha Joyce, Liza Minelli and Alan Lake. Whitelaw also appeared in Morrissey's 'Everyday Is Like Sunday' video.

Wilde, Oscar – the major influence on Morrissey's artistic life; see Chapter Twelve. Tom Stoppard, comparing Oscar Wilde's life with his Oxford contemporary A.E. Housman (*A Shropshire Lad*) wrote in *The Observer* 1998, wrote that Wilde "sacrifices himself to self-fulfilment . . . When Housman died he got the memorial service from Trinity and a leading editorial in *The Times*, yet he was the one who failed in life emotionally, if not intellectually. Though Wilde crashed in flames, and ended as a disgraced, pathetic, maladjusted, poverty-stricken wreck, he had the successful life." (NB. Few of Wilde's contemporaries criticised his harsh punishment, but W.T. Stead, in *The Review Of Reviews*, June 1895, pointed to Victorian hypocrisy: "If Oscar Wilde, instead of indulging in dirty tricks of indecent familiarity with boys and men, had ruined the lives of half a dozen innocent simpletons of girls, or had broken up the home of his friend by corrupting his friend's wife, no one could have laid a finger upon him. The male is sacrosanct: the female is fair game.")

Williams, Emlyn – great Welsh actor and playwright who appeared in *The L-Shaped Room* (with Pat Phoenix, Tom Bell, Anthony Booth and Cicely Courtneidge), and also wrote the 1967 account of the Moors Murders, *Beyond Belief* (another possible source for the name "The Smiths" after the killers' in-laws and neighbours.). His Broadway successes, as a writer and later performer of a celebrated one-man show about Charles Dickens, encouraged actresses such as Bette Davis and Katharine Hepburn to star in his work. Other Morrissey connections include the fact that, at the time of James Dean's death, the actor's intended next project was the lead role in Williams' play *The Corn Is Green*. Emlyn Williams was also mentor to young, fellow Welshman Richard Burton – Burton's image was the backdrop to Morrissey's early 2008 concerts – who made his stage debut in Williams' play *Druid's Rest*.

Williams, Kenneth – celebrated by Morrissey in a fine obituary, *NME*, April 1988: "I loved his bomb-shelter Britishness, his touch-me-not wit, his be-ironed figure, stylishly non-sexual; his facial features were as funny as anything he ever said . . . The passion absent in his celibate existence appeared to the brim, and past the brim, in his work . . . Another irreplaceable strip of Britishness falls away." A great comedic actor and raconteur, the star of 26 *Carry On* films, and also celebrated for his radio work with Tony Hancock and Kenneth Horne. The son of a hairdresser, Williams adored his mum Louisa but hated his dad Charles Williams. After serving in the Army's Combined Services Entertainment with Stanley Baxter and Peter Nichols, he got his theatre breaks as Algernon Moncrief in Oscar Wilde's *The Importance Of Being Earnest* (1948) and, on television, with Orson Welles in *Moby Dick Rehearsed* (1955) and as the Dauphin in George Bernard Shaw's *St Joan* (1958). On radio he spent five years on *Hancock's Half Hour* (alongside eventual *Carry On* colleagues Sid James and Hattie Jacques) before joining Kenneth Horne in *Beyond Our Ken* (1958–63) and *Round The Horne* (1964–69); Williams played Sandy as part of the camp couple Julian and Sandy who spoke in risque double entendres and used the underground gay slang polari (an inspiration for Morrissey's 'Piccadilly Palare'). NB: *The Bona World Of Julian And Sandy*, BBC Audio 1996, features the "Bona Guest House Bogmouth". Apart from the *Carry On* films – which Williams grew to hate: "It lacks verbal wit, it lacks comic situation, it lacks any credible characters . . . it is a *Carry On*" – his other movie appearances were in *Land Of Fury* (aka *The Seekers*), *Innocents In Paris*, *Make Mine Mink* (with Billie Whitelaw and Terry-Thomas), *The Beggar's Opera* with Laurence Olivier, *Twice Round The Daffodils* and *His And Hers* (both with Joan Sims). Publicly celibate, *The Kenneth Williams Diaries* (published 1993) revealed his struggle to deal with his homosexuality, particularly during the Sixties when it was still a criminal offence in England. The *Diaries* refer to unconsummated or barely-consummated relationships by using the phrase "tradiola" or "traditional matters". A close friend of the playwright Joe Orton, who wrote the *Loot* character Truscott for him, and Ken Halliwell, Williams also writes in his *Diaries* about working with the Factory director Paul Morrissey (on *Hounds Of The Baskervilles*), and his friendships with Joan Sims, Rachel Roberts, Maggie Smith and John Gielgud. When he pre-deceased his mother, who lived next door, on April 15, 1988 aged 62, many believed his death was caused by an accidental overdose of barbiturates rather than suicide. However the last words in his Diaries are, "Oh . . . what's the bloody point?"

Wood, Victoria – Lancastrian-born comedienne whose fairground sliceof-life song 'Fourteen Again' inspired The Smiths' 'Rusholme Ruffians': "I want to be fourteen again, tattoo myself with a fountain pen . . . free rides on the waltzer of the fairground men, for a promise of a snog the last night of the fair."

Woolf, Virginia – The Smiths' single 'Shakespeare's Sister' took its title from two lectures Woolf gave to the Cambridge womens' colleges, Girton and Newnham, on the subject Women And Fiction in October 1928. Later she re-worked the speeches into *A Room Of One's Own*. Woolf argued that women had been artistically repressed throughout history – she invented Shakespeare's sister Judith as an example of a creatively frustrated Elizabethan woman driven to suicide – but told her audience, "She lives in you and me, and in many other women who are not here tonight, for they are washing up the dishes and putting the children to bed." This important feminist tract encouraged women in education to value their growing freedoms and to find the courage "to write exactly what we think" so that "the dead poet who was Shakespeare's sister will put on the body which she has so often laid down". There are also echoes of Morrissey's 2006 *Ringleader Of The Tormentors* track 'At Last I Am Born' in Woolf's closing words: "Drawing her life from the lives of the unknown who were her forerunners . . . she will be born." The image of a drinking Richard Burton, used as the backdrop to Morrissey's January 2008 London Roundhouse concerts, was taken from the film of Edward Albee's *Who's Afraid Of Virginia Woolf*. It's also worth noting that one of Alan Bennett's early television plays was titled *Me – I'm Afraid Of Virginia Woolf* (1978).

Youens, Bernard – in January 2008 at the Camden Roundhouse Morrissey introduced himself as "Stanley Ogden from Sidcup". *Coronation Street*'s lorry driver turned window cleaner Stan Ogden, played by "Bunny" Youens for 20 years, was the long-suffering, hen-pecked husband of Rovers Return cleaner Hilda. In June '64, his first words in the Rovers were "a pint of mild and twenty fags, missus". He also appeared in the made-in-Manchester 1948 film by John E Blakeley, *Cup-Tie Honeymoon* (with Pat Phoenix).

Yuro, Timi – having once described her as his "favourite singer", Morrissey joined Siouxsie Sioux to cover Yuro's version of 'Interlude', George Delarue's title track for a 1968 film about the illicit love story between a married composer and a magazine reporter. Yuro's 'Interlude' appeared on the B-side of her American Top Five single 'Hurt', later covered by another great Yuro fan... Elvis Presley. Her other US Top 40 hits were 'What's A Matter Baby (Is It Hurting You)?', 'The Love Of A Boy' and 'Make The World Go Away', plus her cover of Willie Nelson's 'Permanently Lonely'. She died in 2004 of throat cancer aged 63. Morrissey once listed the Yuro track 'Insult To Injury' as one of his 'Singles To Be Cremated With' (*NME*, 1989).

SING YOUR LIFE

An Essential Smiths/Morrissey Compilation Celebrating 25 Years Of An Extraordinary Career

Part One:

All You Need Is Me

A naked laughing man disturbs your sleep but will you miss his soft voice when he's gone? Blame the destructive forces on this planet rather than the singer of pain. (2008)

Well I Wonder

The final stand of a rain-soaked, half-alive, unrequited lover, possibly waiting in vain at a Withington bus stop. (1985)

Irish Blood, English Heart

In praise of unshackled freedom and unashamed patriotism, while attacking the antiquated British party political system. (2004)

The Hand That Rocks The Cradle

Jolson's 'Sonny Boy' turned into the poetry of patriarchal protection that, at the same time, explores every child's worst nightmare: ghosts, storms, bogeymen, bloody cleavers. (1984)

Everyday Is Like Sunday

With a nod to John Betjeman, Armageddon and memories of cheap-as-chips, out-of-season holidays in England's run-down coastal towns. (1988)

Accept Yourself

Plans falling through, dreams that don't come true, and the difficulties of learning to love yourself . . . in a pair of awkward shoes. (1983)

Jack The Ripper

Following in the bloody footsteps of HMV predecessor Screaming Lord Sutch; in a dark cloak touring London's East End, Morrissey encourages his subject (or victim) to crash into his arms. (1993)

Stretch Out And Wait

A cool debate about deferred sexual gratification in a tower block, complete with James Dean/Sal Mineo, *Rebel Without A Cause* references. (1985)

Subway Train/Munich Air Disaster 1958

Live At Earls Court, this combines the New York Dolls with the tragic deaths of the Busby Babes a year before Morrissey's birth; a strangely, moving tribute to Manchester United's lost golden boys. (2005)

Cemetry Gates

Perhaps in remembrance of Harold Riley's photograph of Salford's Weaste Cemetery, or a reference to *On The Buses*? Definitely a defence of plagiarism which openly celebrates the "talent borrows, genius steals" philosophy of Oscar Wilde. (1986)

You Have Killed Me

Pier Paolo Pasolini (and his pimp Accatone) put on a Roman pedestal alongside Anna Magnani and Luchino Visconti. (2006)

This Night Has Opened My Eyes

A Taste Of Honey track that deals with loss of innocence, unwanted pregnancy and even desperate thoughts of infanticide. Melancholy and haunting. (1984)

Boxers

Punchy single, released to mark the centenary of Oscar Wilde's bout with the Marquess of Queensberry, father of Lord Alfred Douglas and original sponsor of the pugilistic Queensberry Rules. (1895, or rather 1995)

This Charming Man

The Smiths at their most distinctive, breath-taking, original best, sampling *Sleuth* (Olivier and Caine) on *the* perfect single illustrating the "magical chemistry" between Morrissey and Marr. (1983)

Work Is A Four Letter Word

The Cilla-spawned track that killed The Smiths, exacerbating the growing rift between M and M. A love song that praised the work ethic yet suggested a relationship that was going nowhere. (1987)

November Spawned A Monster

A Day In The Death Of Joe Egg meets *A Taste Of Honey* in a rare pop song about hypocritical and negative attitudes towards disability. Morrissey holds the mop and bucket while Mary Margaret O'Hara gives birth. (1990)

Back To The Old House

The sad nostalgia of a bicycle boy, for a previous life and a missed opportunity to declare his love. (1984)

I Won't Share You

The Smiths' last gasp on *Strangeways . . .* in which our hero ponders on the transience of life, sickness and cruelty, not to mention the debilitating effect of mineral water. (1987)

Trouble Loves Me

Barrel-scraping, flesh-rampaging, Morrissey stars as the ultimate magnet for mayhem and mischief. An absolute classic. (1997)

Last Night I Dreamt That Somebody Loved Me

The show-stopping sound of loveless, lonely Fury, emerging beautifully from a madding crowd. (1987)

Part Two:

I'll Never Be Anybody's Hero Now

True love is dead with ghostly echoes of Wilde's childhood grief and painful last days. (2006)

Rubber Ring

One of The Smiths' greatest moments, typically buried as an extra track on the 12″ of 'The Boy With The Thorn In His Side'. A life-saving, life-affirming song, railing against passing time and sickening crimes. Genius. (1985)

First Of The Gang To Die

Pistol-packing, gullet-piercing *Quarry* single with some of the greatest opening lines in the history of the pop single. Los Angeles meets Troy, perhaps even the First World War (if the Hector in question is Saki). (2004)

Heaven Knows I'm Miserable Now

Orwellian times, against the deepening Northern misery of the Miners' Strike, Morrissey invades the charts with his unhappiest and funniest re-modelling of Sandie Shaw's 'Heaven Knows I'm Missing Him Now'. (1984)

Redondo Beach

Suicidal subject matter, courtesy of key influence Patti Smith; an American seaside-town tale of mistaken identity. Waving, for once, not drowning. (2005)

The Boy With The Thorn In His Side

On *Top Of The Pops*, clutching his ribs, like an asthmatic schoolboy with stitch, Morrissey wonders whether those who still refuse to believe in The Smiths will ever see the light. (1985)

The Lazy Sunbathers

Shades of Wilde's *Tired Hedonists* mingle with echoes of George Formby's war-time criticism of unpatriotic entertainers. Collapsing religions, suffering children – it's a long way from 'Agadoo'. (1994)

I Want The One I Can't Have

Frustrated love, fascination with crime, a reworked portrait of James Dean (once described as "a tough kid who sometimes sleeps on nails"), mixed in with an extract of Edith Sitwell's *English Eccentrics* – "Health, health, the blessing of the Rich, the Riches of the Poor". Plus one of Morrissey's finest hooklines rhyming mentality with biology. (1985)

Now My Heart Is Full

Brighton Rock, family frictions, the deathly Doonan, loafers, all-night chemists, lovers and poets; a work of uplifting, joyful genius and a message to all his few friends, good and true. (1994)

Panic

The radio world wouldn't listen so Morrissey decided it was time to throttle DJs. The Smiths' fiery revolution launched in Carlisle, Dundee, Humberside, perhaps even Wordsworthian Grasmere. (1986)

We Hate It When Our Friends Become Successful

More wise, Wilde words, wittily transformed into a laugh-along pop single. A funny, competitive attack on the Madchester successes of some of his Northern contemporaries, such as James. (1992)

Please Please Please, Let Me Get What I Want

Almost optimistic, suggesting that, against all the odds, good times were just around the corner. Another B-side of bitter-sweet brilliance; less than two minutes long, Morrissey once described it as "a very brief punch in the face". (1984)

Last Of The Famous International Playboys

Shades of Nancy Sinatra's 'Last Of The Secret Agents', twisted into a boy's own fantasy about criminal recognition from the infamous Krays. (1989)

Margaret On The Guillotine

Thatcher gets the chop, two years before she was officially dumped as Tory leader. Ding dong, the witch is dead. (1988)

You Know I Couldn't Last

Laughing loud and long in the face of those who doubted his powers of longevity; 22 years after the launch of The Smiths, the long-staying, long-playing Mozzer proves he's in the marathon, not the sprint. (2004)

Stop Me If You Think You've Heard This One Before

Nicely revived by Mark Ronson in 2007 (the original single was stifled at birth by Hungerford); a playful attack on critics who complained all Smiths' songs sounded the same. Battered and bruised, painfully injured by the crossbar of his beloved bike, our hero's love survives (almost intact) despite a Friday night visit to Casualty. (1987)

Girl Afraid

Like a lyrical scene from a Sixties kitchen sink drama (see *The Leather*

Boys), exploring doubts about the true intentions of two lovers, brooding in separate rooms, within a relationship going nowhere. (1984)

Come Back To Camden

A romantic celebration of Morrissey's London life; the incessant chatter of taxi drivers, popping in for a cuppa of Thames-tasting tea with neighbours like Alan Bennett. Perhaps it's also a celebration of Wilde's visit to Whitman in Camden New Jersey? Either way, one of his finest love songs. (2004)

How Soon Is Now?

Johnny Marr's most awesome creation, The Smiths' greatness in a nutshell. Unique, shy and alone, which a smidgeon of George Eliot: "To be born the son of a Middlemarch manufacturer, and inevitable heir to nothing in particular . . ." 'Stairway To Heaven' of the Eighties according to Sire boss Seymour Stein, but thrown away by Rough Trade as both a B-side and a minor album track before finally gracing the A-side of a single. (1985)

Interlude

Sweet and sad and sparkling like wine; emotional, almost optimistic, dream-holding spin on Timi Yuro's B-side, accompanied by Siouxsie Sioux. (1994)

Part Three:

There Is A Light That Never Goes Out

The Smiths' moving hymn to human unity; together forever in a double-decker bus crash or under the wheels of a ten-ton truck. Echoes the "affirming flame" of Auden's poem *September 1 1939*. Morrissey once admitted that certain lines in the song were too personal: "It's like someone hitting me with a hammer." (1986)

Friday Mourning

Dressed in black, with shades of The Smiths' 'Unloveable', Morrissey's on his way again, possibly to another world, a better world, leaving behind those who judged him a loser. (2005)

Hand In Glove

The 'Kiss My Shades', male–buttock–flaunting single that launched The Smiths; an original celebration of different love, of pride despite the rags, and expressing hope for the Good Life to come. (1983)

Moon River

A journey round the bend, without his Huckleberry friend; the mooning crooning Morrissey improves on Gracie Field's cover of the theme from Capote's *Breakfast At Tiffanys*. (1994)

Some Girls Are Bigger Than Others

Best heard live at The Smiths' last UK concert, Brixton Academy, December 1986 (later released on the 12″ B-side of 'I Started Something I Couldn't Finish'). A very British B-Movie-style tribute to the diversity of the feminine form, apparently with particular reference to *Carry On Cleo*, starring Amanda Barrie (Alma from *Coronation Street*). (1987)

Hairdresser On Fire

Morrissey's struggle to get *hold* of a hairdresser in the Sloane Square area of West London. Busy scissors, hot air and psychological salvation. Something for the weekend? (1988)

Meat Is Murder

The powerful agit-pop track that urged a generation of "Thatcher's children" on the road towards militant vegetarianism; a chilling, uncompromising defence of animal rights backed by moving music and extraordinary sound effects. (1985)

Why Don't You Find Out For Yourself

Introduced at London's Roundhouse in January 2008 with the words "here's a song that no one likes . . . just for you". Expresses Caesar-like fears of being stabbed in the back and also worries about someone pinching all the money. The ides of March. (1994)

Shoplifters Of The World Unite

United in crime, a comically anarchic call-to-arms for those who'd been prosecuted or persecuted for 'lifting without permission. A crash of alabaster and a six month prison sentence. (Supporting merchandise included the young Elvis image on an easily-concealed plastic bag.) (1987)

Christian Dior

Uses the fashion designer's non-frivolous, disciplined lifestyle as a model for the singer's focused approach to art and music. Details temptations of the flesh to be avoided, including Neapolitan street boys and fertile women. (2006)

Sweet And Tender Hooligan

The Smiths' defined; hard as heroes, soft as butter. Rarely played live, so best to make do with the live version from Morrissey's Xmas comeback at Wolverhampton, performed by the ruffians without Marr. (1988)

Sing Your Life

The perfect response to those who said he couldn't and shouldn't sing. Even claims he and his ilk originated the very notion of singing out of tune; ably supported by another operatic tenor, Suggs of Madness. (1991)

Suedehead

Six months after The Smiths' death, with the band's critical enemies still dancing on their burial ground, Morrissey crashes into the Top Ten with a synthesised single (almost a dance track) plus a video of himself at James Dean's grave. What can it mean? (1988)

The Queen Is Dead

This time it's 'er Majesty who tells our hero he cannot hold a tune. Unites Dear Old Blighty with Buckingham Palace and a cross-dressing Prince Charles, in an MC5-meets-Ramones rocker that, frankly, scuppered all hopes of a Royal Variety Performance. (1986)

Yes, I Am Blind

Echoes of Louis MacNiece's *Prayer Before Birth*. When Morrissey was once asked, in a newspaper questionnaire, when he was happiest he replied "May 21 1959" (yes, the day before he entered this world). Typically, the all-seeing singer dwells on the bad things in life, blinkered to the good, and questions whether the Lamb of God is really up there. (1990)

Sister I'm A Poet

The opening lyrics seem to echo the 1949 Patric Doonan film, *All Over The Town,* but maybe it's simply about Citroen vans and criminal romance. Best heard either live at Wolverhampton or, in the studio, on *My Early Burglary Years.* (1988)

Asleep

The most sensitive, understanding song about suicide ever written; almost an optimistic lullaby for those who no longer want to be part of this word. Lyrically *and* musically it's truly extraordinary. (1985)

Disappointed

Cheers as our hero announces he's finally hanging up his boots, followed by groans when he changes his mind. Ill winds, too much to drink, the inevitably of growing up and feeling . . . down. (1990)

I Know It's Over

Ode on Intimations of Mortality. A year before The Smiths' demise, the poet imagines how it'll all end – for the benefit of his mum. Burial on land or at sea? He knew it wouldn't last. (1986)

The Never-Played Symphonies

Last-gasp Morrissey on his deathbed, propped up on the pillows in the front room, reviewing his life; balancing the ditches against the riches and regretting missed opportunities in love. Typically, he manages to be funereal and funny as the light fades. (2004)

FURTHER READING

Antonia, Nina. *Too Much Too Soon: The New York Dolls* (Omnibus, 1998)

Auden, W. H. *Collected Poems* (Faber & Faber, 1991)

Bartlett, Neil. *Who Was That Man? A Present for Mr Oscar Wilde* (Penguin, 1988)

Bennett, Alan. *Poetry In Motion* (Channel Four, 1990)

————— *The History Boys* (Faber & Faber, 2004)

————— *Untold Stories* (Faber & Faber, 2006)

————— *Writing Home* (Faber & Faber, 2006)

Betjeman, John. *The Best Of Betjeman* (Penguin, 1978)

Bockris, Victor & Malanga, Gerard. *Uptight: The Velvet Underground Story* (Omnibus Press, 1983)

Bracewell, Michael. *England Is Mine: Pop Life In Albion From Wilde To Goldie* (Harper Collins, 1997)

Buford, Bill. *Among The Thugs* (Arrow, 1992)

Capote, Truman. *The Complete Stories* (Penguin, 2005)

Coldstream, John. *Dirk Bogarde: The Official Biography* (Phoenix, 2005)

Dalton, David. *James Dean: The Mutant King* (A Capella, 2001)

Delaney, Shelagh. *A Taste Of Honey* (Methuen, 1959)

————— *The Lion In Love* (Methuen, 1961)

Eliot, George. *Middlemarch* (Wordsworth, 1993)

Ellmann, Richard. *Oscar Wilde* (Hamish Hamilton, 1987)

Fowles, John. *The Collector* (Vintage, 2004)

Goddard, Simon. *The Smiths: Songs That Saved Your Life* (Reynolds & Hearn, 2002)

Greene, Graham. *Brighton Rock* (Vintage, 2007)

————— *England Made Me* (Vintage, 2006)

Hibbin, Sally & Nina. *What A Carry On* (Hamlyn, 1988)

Holland, Merlin. *The Wilde Album* (Fourth Estate, 1997)

Houseman, A. E. *A Shropshire Lad* (Silent Books, 1995)

Hyde, H. Montgomery. *Famous Trials 7: Oscar Wilde* (Penguin Crime, 1962)

————— *Lord Alfred Douglas: A Biography* (Methuen. 1984)

Lahr, John. *The Orton Diaries* (Methuen, 1986)

Lewis, Roger. *Charles Hawtrey 1914–1988: The Man Who Was Private Widdle* (Faber & Faber, 2001)

McKenna, Neil. *The Secret Life of Oscar Wilde* (Arrow, 2004)

Morley, Sheridan. *Dirk Bogarde: Rank Outsider* (Bloomsbury, 1996)

Morrissey. *Exit Smiling* (Babylon Books, 1986)

——— *James Dean Is Not Dead* (Babylon, 1983)

Murray, Douglas. *Bosie: A Biography Of Lord Alfred Douglas* (Miramax, 2002)

Nichols, Peter. *A Day In The Death Of Joe Egg* (Faber & Faber, 1967)

Nicholson, Vivian. *Spend Spend Spend* (Jonathan Cape, 1977)

Orton, Joe. *The Complete Plays* (Eyre Methuen, 1976)

Paytress, Mark. Bolan, *The Rise And Fall Of A 20th Century Superstar* (Omnibus, 2006)

Reid, Pat. *Morrissey* (Absolute Press, 2004)

Riley,Harold. *Photographs 1946–2007* (The Riley Archive, 2007)

Roberts, Rachel. *No Bells On Sunday* (Pavilion, 1984)

Robinson, Bruce. *Withnail & I, Original Screenplay* (Bloomsbury, 1989)

Rogan, Johnny. *Morrissey & Marr: The Severed Alliance* (Omnibus, 1992)

——— *The Smiths: Visual Documentary* (Omnibus, 1994)

——— *Morrissey: The Albums* (Calidore, 2006)

Russell, Willy. *The Wrong Boy* (Doubleday, 2000)

Schmidgall, Gary. *The Stranger Wilde: Interpreting Oscar* (Dutton, 1994)

Selby, Hubert, Jnr. *Last Exit To Brooklyn* (Bloomsbury, 2000)

Simpson, Mark. *Saint Morrissey* (SAF, 2003)

Sitwell, Edith. *English Eccentrics* (Penguin, 1933)

Smart, Elizabeth. *By Grand Central Station I Sat Down And Wept* (Flamingo, 1992)

Smith, Patti. *Patti Smith Complete* (Bloomsbury, 2000)

Truffaut, Francois. *The Films Of My Life* (Simon & Schuster, 1978)

Various. *Short Stories Of Our Time* (Harrap & Co., 1963)

Visconti, Tony. *Bowie Bolan And The Brooklyn Boy* (Harper Collins, 2007)

Waterhouse, Keith. *Billy Liar* (Penguin, 1973)

Watson, Stephen. *Factory Made: Warhol & The Sixties* (Pantheon, 2003)

White, Edmund. *Genet: A Biography* (Alfred A Knopf, 1993)

Wilde, Oscar. *De Profundis & Other Writings* (Penguin, 1973)

——— *The Decay Of Lying* (Kessinger, 2007)

——— *The Importance Of Being Earnest* (Heinemann, 1962)

——— *The Picture Of Dorian Gray* (Penguin, 1994)

——— *The Soul Of Man Under Socialism* (Journeyman, 1988)

Williams, Emlyn. *Beyond Belief* (World Books, 1968)

Williams, Kenneth. *The Kenneth Williams Diaries* (Harper Collins, 1993)

Wilson, A. N. *Betjeman* (Hutchinson, 2006)

Witts, Richard. *The Velvet Underground* (Equinox, 2006)

Woolf, Virginia. *A Room Of One's Own* (Penguin, 1929)

ACKNOWLEDGEMENTS

To all my friends (I have so many . . .)

In addition to the doughty crew of *NME* (1983–90) and my television colleagues at the BBC and Granada in Manchester, the following people (whether they know it or not) have helped, encouraged, supported, in some cases rescued me, at various points in my life: Graciela Ainsworth, Julia Allen, Sam Anthony, Louise & Roger Baird, John Barratt, Andrew Baybutt, Moya Brennan, James Brown, Colin Bell, Matthew Bennie, Mike Blackah, Deretta Branche, Will Bryant, Murray Chalmers, Julia & Alan Cheek, John Clarke, Stuart Cosgrove, Susan Cross, Rajan Datar, Ges D'Souza, Lynn Evans, Doug & Fiona Faircloth, Sarah Hunt & Simon Fanthorpe, Wayne Foskett, Alan Gilsenan, Jim Gray & Helen Andrew, Stuart Greig, Vicky Gunn, Margaret & Peter Harper, Mary Hodgkinson, Andy Holland, Barney Hoskyns, Jo Isotta, Mike Jempson, Danny Kelly, Steve Lamacq, Alan Lewis, Nigel & Charlotte Malik, Richard Makinson, Eugene Manzi, Brian Martin, Annie MacAulay, John McCready, Mark & Sarah McGreevy, the MacLartys, James Millar, Jorge Morales, Andrew Morgan, Dave Morley, Carl Morris, Sarah Myland, Julie-Ann Ollerenshaw, John Piper, Bill Prince, Ian Pye, Paul Quinn, Rose Rouse, Werner Schussler, Jo Slee, Graham K. Smith, Neil Spencer, Tony Stewart, David Swift, Michelle Turner, Simon Vyvyan, Vivienne Walt, Bob Watkins, Angela Williams and Karen Williams.

With sincere thanks (for his knowledge, expertise and patience) to my editor and publisher Chris Charlesworth, my picture editor Sarah Bacon, Johnny Rogan (for advice and indexing), and also to my encouraging agent Mark 'Stan' Stanton of Jenny Brown Associates in Edinburgh.

With respect to the many musicians, over the past 25 years, who have helped create the soundtrack for Morrissey's poetry, particularly Stephen Street, Boz Boorer and Johnny Marr.

A special mention for my closest family and pals . . . to my oldest, most long-suffering friends Richie 'Just Magic' Farrell, Tim 'King Of Stoddy' Jarvis and Nigel 'Toon Army' Welch; to my in-laws Brian, Janet & Rachel Boseley (for their vital support during the writing of this Casaubon-style epic); to Alan Jackson for his warmth, encouragement, and wise counsel over the past two decades; to Andrew Martin, golf-partner, bar-room philosopher, fellow Smiths' and Morrissey traveller; and with love to my Dad Drew, my sister Kathleen and my lovely nieces Isla and Maeve.

When I got married in 1997, my wedding speech hailed my friends but failed to mention my bride. I would like to set the record straight now. Everlasting thanks to Bridget for so much love and support and, above all, for two wonderful daughters: Grace and Flora. Now my heart is full.

INDEX

Singles releases are in roman type. Albums, poems, books, films and plays are in italics.

Index